Harvard Historical Studies, 150

Published under the auspices
of the Department of History
from the income of the
Paul Revere Frothingham Bequest
Robert Louis Stroock Fund
Henry Warren Torrey Fund

To Exercise Our Talents

The Democratization of Writing in Britain

Christopher Hilliard

HARVARD UNIVERSITY PRESS
CAMBRIDGE, MASSACHUSETTS
LONDON, ENGLAND

2006

Printed in the United States of America

Library of Congress Cataloging-in-Publication Data

Hilliard, Christopher.

To exercise our talents : the democratization of writing in Britain / Christopher Hilliard.

p. cm.—(Harvard historical studies ; v. 150)

Includes bibliographical references and index.

ISBN 0-674-02177-0 (alk. paper)

1. English literature—20th century—History and criticism. 2. Literature and society—Great Britain—History—20th century. 3. Authorship—Social aspects—Great Britain—History—20th century. 4. Democratization—Great Britain—History—20th century. 5. Social classes—Great Britain—History—20th century. 6. Working class—Great Britain—History—20th century. 7. Working class writings, English—History and criticism. 8. Middle class—Great Britain—History—20th century. 9. Working class in literature. 10. Middle class in literature. I. Title. II. Series.

PR478.S57H55 2006 820.9′0091—dc22 2005052771

FOR SARAH

Contents

To Exercise Our Talents

Introduction

Literary History from Below

Flora Thompson was an unlikely candidate for literary success. Born into a poor rural family in 1876, she left school at fourteen and went to work in country post offices. While her children were young, she began writing—poems, articles about wildlife, formulaic short stories for popular magazines. In the 1920s she started a corresponding society for would-be writers. She did not tell her neighbors about the writing she did under pseudonyms, and her husband disapproved; through the correspondence circle she found a community of students and colleagues, people with whom to share the pleasures and disappointments of being a writer.[1] She was sixty-five when she published the first volume of her trilogy *Lark Rise to Candleford*. The requiem for a vanished rural England made her famous after such a long apprenticeship.

Aspiring writers like the apprentice Flora Thompson and her correspondents were not from the privileged backgrounds that had long characterized British authors. To focus on them is to pursue literary history from below. Examining this large but virtually unstudied domain of creative activity can tell us a great deal about literature and its institutions, and about culture more generally: the feasibility of writing as a career or as an interest is bound up with many other problems of cultural life. The most famous meditation on these questions is Virginia Woolf's *A Room of One's Own* (1929). Woolf argued that constraints on women's knowledge of the world outside the home inhibited their capacity to evoke human experience. And women usually lacked the independence, symbolized by an annual income of five hundred pounds and a room of their own, that enabled artists to concentrate on their work. Woolf returned to the theme of literary creation and social privilege in a 1940 essay, "The Leaning Tower." This time she placed class rather than gender in the foreground. Turning her fire on the left-wing intelligentsia of the 1930s, she argued that however much they wanted to transcend the boundaries of class, they could not renounce the benefits of their bourgeois upbringing. "Their education could not be thrown away; as for their capital—did Dickens, did Tolstoy ever throw away their capital?" Losing that capital, that source of five hundred pounds a year, was death for a writer.[2]

"The Leaning Tower" was published in *Folios of New Writing,* a journal connected with the young, left-leaning literati Woolf was criticizing. The journal's editor, John Lehmann, solicited a response to Woolf's essay from the miner and author B. L. Coombes. Coombes redefined "a writer's capital": rather than economic security, it was "all his experiences; his environment; his knowledge of human life and how people live and aspire, love and desire, hate and die." The chief source of this "capital" for a working-class writer was "living amongst the people of our kind." It might be creative death for a middle-class writer to work in a factory or a mine, but it "is just as surely the creative end of a working class writer if he leaves his own sphere; he has grown into it and labour is part of his being." Writing's relation to these two types of "capital" echoes through the lives of many aspirant writers. The problem of financial independence and the intellectual opportunities that go with it looms large for would-be authors from middle-class women to working-class men like Coombes, who spoke explicitly of needing "a room of my own to write in." And the relationship between writing and personal experience, what Coombes considered to be a writer's capital, was central to the meanings that literary creativity held for ordinary writers.[3]

Readers of literary biographies will be familiar with the social advantages that usually preceded a successful writing career in Britain in the first half of the twentieth century. Rentier incomes, access to London flats and country cottages, and valuable family, school, and university contacts are stock features of the biographies of prominent authors. Such opportunities provided time and freedom to write, and access to the levers of publishing—to say nothing of a rich artistic patrimony. A bourgeois young man, observes the literary historian Valentine Cunningham, enjoyed "relatively easy acquisition of literacy and bookishness," a "glut of school and college magazines eager to receive his veriest juvenilia," and "publishing and editing elders ready to give the youthies' early poems and first novels an avuncular leg-up into the big publishing world." Well-off and well-connected young men of modest literary talent, such as Woolf's nephew Julian Bell, had huge advantages over clerks and typists who wanted to become authors.[4]

Surveys of "the sociology of authorship" are fraught with problems of sampling and classification, but it is not certain that the best of them, Richard Altick's, could be improved on greatly: some of the more important "class" variables do not lend themselves to quantification.[5] These works nevertheless make it clear that the most common profile for a published British author of the early twentieth century was that of a man from a professional or merchant family who had been educated at a public school and then Oxford or Cambridge. This profile represents a small section of the bourgeoisie: in interwar Britain, most middle-class men and the overwhelming majority of middle-class women did not have a university education. The highly educated were not the only ones who became writers, of course, and freelance writing in Fleet Street was a well-trodden career path for energetic people without elite backgrounds (the novelist Arnold Bennett is a good example). It was, however, not a route hospitable to women.[6]

The aspirants I discuss in this book come from less usual backgrounds and have less usual career trajectories. They fall into three social categories: the working class, the lower middle class, and those large sections of the middle class without higher education. How does a historian connect with these mute inglorious Miltons? Publishers do not archive the "slush pile" formed by the unsolicited manuscripts that flow into their offices. And even if they did, such an archive would not reveal much about the writers who never sent a book manuscript to a publisher, or who were less interested in publishing than in writing for themselves and their friends and acquaintances. Aspiring writers do leave intermittent paper trails through publishers' archives, the records of the BBC and the Arts Council, and the correspondence files of established authors whom they approached as fans or supplicants. But my principal way of gaining access to their world has been to examine three major movements and moments that drew ordinary people into imaginative writing.

The first of these is the amateur writers' "movement" (as some called it) associated with writing magazines, textbooks, correspondence schools, and writers' clubs. Its constituency was predominantly middle class and oriented toward publication in commercial magazines and newspapers; after the Second World War, many writers' club members wrote for radio as well. This development of writing into an organized and even collective enterprise is itself historically significant, and the records of this movement furnish a rich body of material on ordinary people turned authors.

Second, I examine working-class literary activity of the interwar period. Working-class writing has a long pedigree in Britain, but the 1930s were especially important in that tradition, as established publishers and left-wing intellectuals encouraged manual workers' literary efforts. My third focal point is popular literary activities and initiatives during the Second World War. All three of these strands may be called "popular writing." The phrase has been used to refer to the working-class literary projects of the twentieth century,[7] and it was also the title of a magazine launched in the late 1920s for amateur writers: there was "popular writing" as well as "popular mechanics."

The amateur writers' movement, the campaign to recruit worker-writers, and wartime popular writing were all part of "the democratization of culture"—what Karl Mannheim, in the essay translated under that title, called the broadening of "the strata actively participating in cultural life, either as creators or as recipients." My approach differs from D. L. LeMahieu's in *A Culture for Democracy*, the key book on this subject in Britain and one to which my work is indebted. LeMahieu's primary concern is with the way "cultivated intellectuals" responded to twentieth-century mass communication—some regarding it as a threat to art and culture, others seeing opportunities in it. My focus, in contrast, is on people who were at once members of the less "cultivated" populace *and* intellectuals or producers of cultural goods. I locate the democratization of culture in their acts of production, rather than in the nature of what they produced. At the end of his book, LeMahieu takes J. B. Priestley as an emblem of a "common culture" emerging in the 1930s. It is a claim open to the rejoinder that (in Ross McKibbin's words) "the majority of the population probably never read him." Both the assertion and the criticism imply that a democratic cultural life is to be defined by a widely shared corpus of texts and ideas. Few actual societies would satisfy this test. Instead, I would suggest that if anything makes the place of literature and the arts in a society "democratic," it is a shared sense of entitlement to participate in cultural activities.[8]

The campaign to find working-class authors in the 1930s is the best known of the democratizing efforts I discuss. The collaboration between assorted anti-fascists during the Popular Front period of the 1930s dramatically recast the relationship between politics and the arts, and created opportunities for working-class writing. I chart the ways working people negotiated the literary scene that the Popular Front created, and also their involvement with other publishers, both mainstream and underground. Using editorial correspondence and other manuscript sources more than published material, I also consider what literary activity meant to working-class authors. They did not see themselves as straightforward documentarists or pamphleteers as some scholars have assumed they did. Even as they assumed their capacity to speak from working-class experience, they conceived of themselves as artists, and they sometimes referred to the desire to write as if it were a mystical ailment. I extend my account of the 1930s worker-writer campaign by looking beyond 1939, chiefly to *Seven,* a wartime "magazine of people's writing." *Seven* absorbed some of the working-class contributors to earlier left-wing journals, and also encouraged "ordinary" people of the middle class to write about their lives and experiences: it combined Popular Front energies with wartime populism and the interests of aspiring writers. A comparable mix of concerns and ambitions colored other wartime literary initiatives, from barracks writers' groups to the handwritten "magazines" produced by prisoners of war.

Campaigns to recruit plebeian authors abated after the Second World War. The predominantly middle- and lower-middle-class "writers' circles" that spread throughout Britain from the 1920s onward were more consistent vehicles of cultural democratization. In *English Journey* (1934), J. B. Priestley observed that the things in Britain that were the most "democratic" tended to be the most modern and commercialized. The emergence of writing as an organized hobby certainly occurred in tandem with the development of commercial culture. The writers' circles grew out of the constituency of the how-to-write manuals and correspondence courses that sprang up from the end of the nineteenth century, when changes in reading and publishing opened up new opportunities for freelance writers. Many writing club members sought publication in commercial outlets, though the financial rewards of writing were not the only ones that counted, as we shall see. Amateur writers' groups were "democratic" in several senses. They encouraged an egalitarian view that almost anyone could write creditably if willing to work at it. These clubs pulled in men from the middle class, and, significantly, attracted a similar or larger number of women. Like other associational forms that took shape in the interwar period, the writers' circles created a "depoliticized" but implicitly conservative kind of middle-class sociability, and one in which both women and men could congregate.[9]

In *A Room of One's Own,* Woolf's character Mary Carmichael widens the horizons of fiction by describing a friendship between two women who have careers: "Chloe liked Olivia. They shared a laboratory together." In some respects Mary Carmichael, an "unknown girl writing her first novel in a bed-sitting-room," would have fitted in well at a writers' circle meeting. She gives some thought to whether a character's eyes will be blue or brown; she clips her sentences lest her style be thought flowery and "feminine."[10] But the women in writers' circles were less likely than Mary Carmichael to push back the gendered frontiers of fiction. Many of them wrote for socially conservative outlets. A majority of writers' group members contributed to the organs of popular print culture that symbolized a culture for democracy for contemporary jeremiahs. While press barons and London-based companies and marketing strategies justifiably shape our thinking about these modern popular cultural institutions, a good deal of their huge volume of "copy" came from outside the metropolitan neighborhoods of Grub Street and Fleet Street, from freelance writers in the provinces. The democratization of writing, and of "culture" more generally, was played out in provincial cities and towns (and London suburbs) at least as much as it was in the metropolis. Studying amateur writers helps us make sense of mass communication and commercial culture in a way that studying only cultural *products* such as magazines or radio programs cannot, because it shows us how the kinds of people who made up the *audience* of the culture industry worked through the challenges posed by creative activity and "mass culture" as they turned themselves into *producers* of texts for the popular market.

As they became writers, both middle- and working-class people adopted and reworked the discourses of popular and canonical literature. In his acclaimed book *The Intellectual Life of the British Working Classes,* Jonathan Rose argues that working-class autodidacts clung to traditionalist values and repudiated modernism as a bourgeois conceit.[11] I take a different position, seeing 1930s working-class authors as more eclectic in their literary judgments. The social groups most in tune with conservative poetics were those parts of the middle and lower middle classes without a university education—the constituency of the writers' circles. The theory of literature dominant in the writers' circles set great store on the sincerity with which an author gave voice to experience and observation. Form was of secondary importance, a mere vehicle for the more personal essence of a fiction or even a poem; "modernist" authors who declined to treat formal questions in this way were regarded as unpleasantly cerebral. Denunciations of modernism in the press of the period can strike subsequent observers as unaccountably strident, but what was at stake was not just taste but a theory of art and creativity.[12]

This theory owed much to English romanticism: writers' guidebooks sometimes echoed Wordsworth almost to the verge of quotation. Meredith Veldman argues convincingly that the common denominator of the otherwise disparate phenomena of fantasy fiction, the New Left, and the Green and antinuclear movements is the continuing vitality of romantic ideas in postwar Britain. Veldman is chiefly concerned with the romanticism of Carlyle, Ruskin, and Morris—a tradition that distrusted industry and commercialism and celebrated nature, craft, community, and personal authenticity. It was a heritage that could be appropriated by figures as different as the socialist E. P. Thompson and the pro-Franco J. R. R. Tolkien. The branch of nineteenth-century romanticism pertinent to this book issued from Wordsworth's statements on poetry in *Lyrical Ballads.* Late nineteenth- and early twentieth-century anthologies and surveys of English literature popularized a selective version of this romantic discourse about the nature of art and its relation to the artist and to what is being represented. As the intellectual historian Stefan Collini points out, this interpretation, the idea that (English) literature was a product of robust life, rather than an exquisite, formal (French) concoction, resonated with notions of British identity that enjoyed a wide currency in the early twentieth century.[13] This romantic tradition shaped popular understandings of the relation between authorial sincerity and the written text; it also helped cast poetry as an outlet for strong emotion. This value of poetry was especially clear during the Second World War, when many people in the armed forces took up the writing of poetry. Believing poetry to be "the spontaneous overflow of powerful feelings," they were practicing, as writers, precepts commonly applied to the *reading* of poetry.

That romanticism underpinned a vernacular theory of literature and experience well into the twentieth century complicates any sweeping judgments about "modern" consciousness. It also has implications for how we think about popular intellectual history. Seldom was any tension suggested between the demands of the market and the dictates of the romanticism of "sincere" writing. Even some unashamed literary mercenaries considered sincerity compulsory, believing the buying public could always detect humbug or irony. Sincere writing's compatibility with profitable writing testifies to the extent to which the British middle classes were culturally as well as economically reconciled to the market as a distributor of value. Middle-class aspirants who suggested that the reason they were unsuccessful was that the market was a racket were often laughed at. Middlebrow culture in Britain did not have to reconcile fashion and consumption with the "genteel" tradition of self-improvement as did its American counterpart, represented most prominently by the Book-of-the-Month Club.[14] Anxieties about commercialism's effects on literature and culture generally were the preserve of intellectuals such as F. R. and Q. D. Leavis and some on the 1930s left. Moreover, American influences and models—the literary advice business had started in the United States—were adopted without a backlash, and often imperceptibly. At the popular level, British intellectual life could be remarkably absorptive.

From the 1950s, the culture of popular writing that had taken shape in the interwar period began to come apart. The reformulation of mainstream literary culture from the late 1940s made the boundaries between "literary" and "popular" writing more porous, and the far-reaching changes of the 1960s and 1970s altered the place of this older style of writers' group in British life. While some old-fashioned writers' circles survived, others fell by the wayside, and a profusion of new types of writing group appeared. These new groups were much more "permissive" in their literary styles and less impressed by social and commercial orthodoxy. In the 1970s feminist writing workshops and a new working-class writing movement emerged, both of which drew on the technical innovations of the underground press of the 1960s as well as on new kinds of cultural politics. Postwar developments in education, which included the entrenchment of creative writing in school curricula, made literary activity an even more common part of people's lives. The new climate was more pluralist and more confusing—a stimulating prospect for some, and no doubt a discomfiting one for those who had valued the combination of creative activity and decorum that the writers' circles had provided. The transformation of popular writing from the 1960s—the end of the stories told in this book—is not suited either to an unqualified celebration of the forward march of cultural egalitarianism or to the declinist nostalgia often applied to pre-1960s Britain.

Chapter 1

Middlemen, Markets, and Literary Advice

❧ It was "the age of the middleman," the publisher William Heinemann declared in 1893. And the middleman, he said, was "generally a parasite."[1] Unsympathetic readers might think of publishers themselves as "middlemen," but the parasites who bothered Heinemann were literary agents. Agents were one species in the genus of intermediaries—the others were publishers' readers and the Society of Authors—that emerged in the world of writing and publishing in the late nineteenth century. The dramatic expansion and increased complexity of book and magazine publishing at that time created new opportunities—and, at least as important, the appearance of opportunities—for novice writers. It also helped turn the literary agent and the authors' professional society into fixtures of the publishing scene. Their advent opened up a mediating space between authors and publishers, which in turn made possible a battery of literary advice services. These services promoted the idea that the "secrets" of writing could be learned by novices. These developments laid the foundations for the aspiring writers' movement that began in the 1920s.

For its first three decades, the primary goal of the Society of Authors was the reform of domestic copyright law and the establishment of an international copyright system that would put an end to American piracy of British books and articles. Of more significance for the history of popular writing are the society's efforts to defend authors against the depredations of other actors in the literary marketplace. Walter Besant, the society's founder, and his long-serving successor as secretary, G. Herbert Thring, enthusiastically hunted literary frauds and exploitative publishers. Purists regarded the Society of Authors as excessively commercial, but Besant did not see himself as an apostle of the commercialization of literature, a kindred spirit to Jasper Milvain in George Gissing's novel *New Grub Street*. Rather, as Peter Keating observes, Besant aimed to improve the lot of the upright author by teaching the writer "how to sell his manuscript sensibly, not by urging him (as Milvain does) to write differently."[2]

Thus the society sought to make authors more aware of their rights and to make publishing more transparent and consistent. It offered bespoke advice as well. Members were encouraged to use the society's own lawyers, and could write to the secretary for free advice. In this respect the society was verging on territory beginning to be claimed by another player in the space between writers and publishing, the literary agent.[3] The first agent is generally agreed to have been A. P. Watt, who set up shop in London's Paternoster Row in 1875 or 1876. Watt offered for a fee the sorts of services that had previously been performed informally and gratis by relatives and friends of successful authors, such as John Forster for Charles Dickens. Watt had worked as an assistant to his brother-in-law, the publisher Alexander Strahan, and the contacts he had made and the credibility he had earned must have opened some doors for him, though many publishers refused to deal with such an intermediary. Lacking a clear precedent for what to charge for his services, "he began by charging a lawyer's fee for letter-writing, telegraphic expenses and the like." When he found that his clients did not always pay him, he instituted two practices that would become standard in the industry: he would take ten percent of the author's earnings, and he would arrange for the publisher to pay him, the agent, who would keep his share and send the remaining ninety percent of the payment to the author.[4]

Between 1875 and 1894 nineteen people were listed in the *Post Office Directory* as literary agents. But there were never more than six at a time: not until 1896, when J. B. Pinker opened for business, would Watt have a durable competitor. Even then, twenty years after Watt began, literary agency was not firmly established, as the story of Curtis Brown shows. An American, Brown arrived in London in 1898 as a correspondent for the *New York Press.* When he interviewed Pearl Theresa Craigie, who wrote under the pen name John Oliver Hobbes, she asked him to keep an eye out for an opening for a serialization of her new novel. Craigie had heard that there was such a thing as a literary agency, understood that the fee was ten percent, and told Brown she would pay him that amount if he found a berth for her work. The next day, as Brown told it, he ran into the editor of the *Pall Mall Gazette,* who, unprompted, professed himself in need of "a smart society serial." Brown matched author and editor. After this "pure fluke" and a few more incidents in which Brown's contacts and knowledge of the periodical market positioned him to act as a "middleman," he set up formally as an agent. His firm prospered and by the 1920s was the largest London agency. For the first third of the twentieth century, a number of publishers remained suspicious of agents, and the Society of Authors remained ambivalent, losing no opportunity to go after an apparently crooked agent. But when, in 1903, Arnold Bennett declared the "agent question" resolved, he was substantially right.[5]

Aspirant writers were not a major part of the constituency of the agencies or the Society of Authors. The latter required prospective members to have published a book. Nor did agents have much truck with beginners. Curtis Brown commented in 1906: "Unless an author's work gives decided promise, he is of little interest to . . . the first-class agent. No agent, except one who takes 'retainers,' can afford to spend much time over him." Why, then, was the advent of these middlemen significant for would-be writers? The answer lies in the message their appearance sent to the public. Developments in authorship and publishing were widely publicized in newspapers and magazines, and the 1890s and 1900s witnessed a succession of light books of interviews with writers, a collection called *Homes and Haunts of Famous Authors,* and at least nine novels or "confessions" about the writing life. Even publishers' readers, another relative novelty, lodged themselves in the public mind: Arthur Waugh recalled receiving hundreds of applications in the 1890s from people in need of work who had heard of publishers' readers and fancied that they would be up to the job.[6] The emergence of professional literary advisors held out the lure of demystifying authorship and publishing. Their existence implied that there were ways into writing, procedures for becoming a successful writer. And from there it was a short step to thinking that those procedures could be learned by novices.

Agents and the Society of Authors became lasting presences in part because of contingencies such as the copyright battle, but also as a result of the "rapid expansion and diversification of the literary market." A larger, more complex market made interpreters and intermediaries useful, and it appeared to promise opportunities for new writers. One of the reasons for the expansion of the print market was the achievement of near-universal literacy. In retrospect, the 1870 Elementary Education Act was not quite a watershed, and for contemporaries the definitive arrival of a universally literate public was a moveable feast. Commentators were announcing the advent of "the New Reading Public," an "ever-increasing company drawn from what we commonly call the lower middle class and the working class," as late as 1922. But the general increase in print matter catering to a mass audience is unmistakable. The average number of novels for adults published annually in Britain from 1875 to 1885 was 429. In 1886 the number soared to 755, beginning a novel boom that would continue until just before the First World War. In 1894—when 1,315 new novels were published—the commercial circulating libraries demanded that publishers abandon the Victorian institution of the three-volume novel so that libraries could keep pace with the production of fiction. The abolition of the three-decker meant a reorganization of the novel and the fall of some publishers and rise of others.[7]

The periodical press, too, expanded and diversified. Again, this was a result of both changes in literacy and changes within the industry. The invention of illustrated letterpress miscellanies like the *Strand,* the *Pall Mall Magazine,* and *Pearson's Magazine* owed more to American-influenced technological and commercial innovations than to social trends, but the spread of literacy was a crucial factor in the proliferation of cheaper periodicals. In the interwar years the number of periodicals published held steady, though toward the end of this period some titles disappeared as sales suffered from "competition from other leisure activities." However, particular sectors of the market expanded, especially the story papers of the 1920s aimed at young working-class women. The periodical market, not book publishing, was the prime target of aspirant writers. The magazine market was voracious, whereas rising costs made it less likely for new novelists to be published after the First World War than before it. So much fiction was being published in periodicals that a good proportion of it must have come from people outside Grub Street and Fleet Street. In the early 1930s, even someone as securely established as the popular novelist Compton Mackenzie thought so many "brilliant amateurs" were emerging that they threatened professional writers.[8]

As Billie Melman, Cynthia L. White, and Raymond Williams have shown, the amount of fiction in a periodical in the inter-war period tended to be in inverse proportion to the social and economic status of its readership. Magazines aimed at working-class readers carried a lot of fiction. Magazines for working-class men featured stories with sporting settings, big-game hunting and other imperial or exotic adventures, and crime and violence. Some papers for women also published crime fiction. The Dundee-based firm of D. C. Thomson maintained two discrete lines of women's papers—romance magazines such as the *People's Friend,* and "blood-and-thunder" papers such as *Red Letter,* which carried tales of crime, domestic violence, and forbidden love. Working-class periodicals published both short stories and what were called "novelettes" or "novels" of ten to twenty thousand words. Serials were also common in magazines for women as well as for girls and boys. From the late nineteenth century, serial fiction became more and more the province of periodicals aimed at the working class.[9]

In magazines for middle-class readers, fiction was most likely to be in the form of the short story. The late nineteenth-century boom in magazines and newspapers had created a new demand for self-contained short fiction rather than serials, both as "filler" and as an attraction in itself. The short story became established as a genre in its own right rather than a miscellaneous category of narratives that simply were not very long. Drawing on the work of Edgar Allan Poe, the American critic Brander Matthews defined the genre as depending on a "unity of impression." His definition, set out in *The Philosophy of the Short-Story* (1901), became "widely accepted" in Britain as in America. Echoes of Matthews, and Poe, can be detected not only in "literary" short stories but also in prescriptions of economy and singleness of effect or impression for very short newspaper and magazine stories decades later. For middle- and lower-middle-class people, as for working-class aspirants, short fiction's lesser demands on the time and concentration of a writer with a day job made it more feasible than the novel.[10] It was the standard genre of the aspirant writer for much of the twentieth century.

One of the most coveted successes for a short story writer was an acceptance by the *Strand*, published from 1891 to 1950 by George Newnes. The *Strand* was the most famous general-interest magazine that catered to, and shaped, a taste that for want of a better label may be called "middlebrow." As the *Strand*'s penultimate editor remarked, "the middle classes of England never cast a clearer image of themselves in print than they did in *The Strand Magazine*"; the periodical confirmed "their preference for mental as well as physical comfort." It was there that Sherlock Holmes made his debut and his exit; P. G. Wodehouse was one of the magazine's drawcards in the 1930s; and the *Strand* made the name of W. W. Jacobs, a chronicler of the Gentile East End much admired by aspiring writers and their instructors. The short stories the magazine published are typical of the fictions aspirant writers sought to write and were encouraged to work on. Stories involving crime were valued; political or social questions scarcely found their way into the *Strand*'s articles, let alone its fiction. Contributors were expected to leave out extraneous material and strive for something like Matthews's "unity of impression." It was especially desirable for stories to end with a "twist," after the fashion of O. Henry and Guy de Maupassant. The *Strand* published old O. Henry stories, and an early editor was a fan of Maupassant.[11]

Those authors' wryness and penchant for surprises can be discerned in some of the *Strand*'s stories. W. W. Jacobs's "The Interruption" concerns a man who has killed his wife and is being blackmailed by his cook. The man concocts a scheme to make it look as if the cook is poisoning him and so must have killed his wife as well, but he gets very sick and must, in his addled state, have made the mistake of drinking the medicine to which he had added poison to in order to frame her. The tale combines the phantasm of the "perfect crime" with the irony of the crime's rebounding. The perfect crime is at the heart of Sapper's "The Idol's Eye," which also features other commonplaces of crime or supernatural stories written after Poe or Maupassant. A group of men are talking in a drawing room of the house they are staying in for the night. In the first sentence a skeptic declares that he doesn't believe in curses. Baiting him, another man dares him to hold a Tibetan "idol's eye" for the night. The skeptic dies in the night, apparently of natural causes. Later the hitherto unobtrusive narrator discovers that the man with the idol must have murdered the skeptic. He confronts the suspect, who confesses, or rather explains: he is an expert on poisons, and to the police it will look as if the other guests are implicated, making it a perfect crime.[12]

Newspapers too published short stories, usually more compact ones than those in the *Strand*. Like Sapper's story, Louise Heilgers's "The House with the Crimson Creeper" begins with a character questioning the supernatural: "'Well, it doesn't *look* haunted,' said Carden." The character of the tale can be gauged from that opening one-sentence paragraph and its closing one-sentence paragraph: "Carden himself was dead." Heilgers was a successful writer who was best known for her vignettes, sentimental but not maudlin sketches of unglamorous lives, which were written with obvious patterning that makes them very different from the "slice of life" story associated with Katherine Mansfield and others. Heilgers's stories were published in the *Sketch,* the *Daily Sketch,* the *Sunday Herald,* the *Sunday Chronicle,* the *Novel Magazine,* and the *Royal Magazine.* At the end of the First World War she would set herself up as a correspondence school instructor in writing.[13]

The twin prospects of a panorama of new opportunities and the chance to learn the secrets necessary to grasp them formed the basis for a literary advice industry. Its first goods were guidebooks. The *Writers' and Artists' Year Book,* the earliest incarnation of which dates from 1897, gave advice about what was often called "the business side of writing," listed publishers and periodicals, and specified the kinds of writing they sought. Other books targeted amateurs and those thinking about "the literary life." Some of these early works were by noted writers, such as Arnold Bennett's *How to Become an Author* (1903). Others were by less successful figures, such as the jobbing novelist Percy Russell, who would not be the last unsuccessful writer to sell advice to those who had not yet failed. Literary guidebooks multiplied in the twentieth century, issued by publishers ranging from shoestring concerns to major houses. It is a testimony to the public demand for the genre that even with paper rationing in the 1940s, generalist publishers continued to pour out new titles.[14]

In the early twentieth century guidebooks were joined by other commercial dispensers of advice: writers' magazines more analogous to the hobby press than to literary reviews; correspondence schools; and manuscript criticism and placement-advice services or "bureaus." All three came into their own in the interwar period, though correspondence schools and advice bureaus opened their doors, or rather, their post office boxes, before that. Of the three sorts of business, an advisory bureau was the easiest to set up: its minimum outlay was a postal address, stationery and stamps, some reference books, and a classified ad. A dearth of source material makes it hard to gauge how many bureaus went beyond those minimum requirements, or to tell how qualified the people offering these services were. Many of those who touted their services in flyers sent to writers' circles or in classified advertisements in writers' magazines remained obscure figures. It is quite possible that there was not much behind a marble name like the Institute of Self-Expression (which was based in Bradford). When John Gray set up the more modestly titled Gray's Literary Service, he was a member of the lumpen-literati, living in a bedsitting room in Finchley. When he started his typing and advice service, he went off the dole, but running a literary bureau was a precarious existence and at one point he was reduced to meals of stale bread soaked in milk. After some of the "amateurs" he helped had successes, he gave up the bureau and concentrated on writing short stories of his own to sell. To encourage him, a friend bought Gray a copy of Cecil Hunt's *Short Stories and How to Write Them*. In the 1930s and 1940s Hunt became one of the captains of the literary advice industry, running a correspondence school and speaking to writers' circles around the country. But as struggling young freelances in about 1920, Hunt and a friend, with an anonymous advertisement, set themselves up as manuscript critics and advisors on the market. They had numerous customers; people "pour[ed] out" their aspirations to them. Embarrassingly, one of their clients was a friend who lived nearby.[15]

Most advice bureaus provided criticism of manuscripts, especially those returned by editors, and advice about appropriate publications to send them to. In the interwar period and just after the Second World War, the standard fee for criticism of an unpublished manuscript was 2s. 6d. for the first thousand words of the story, with the rate often dropping for every subsequent thousand.[16] Other services supplied authors with plots to get them started. Some entrepreneurs combined prepackaged plots with general formulas for generating plots. Mack's Plot Service, established in 1931, offered the following: "Ordinary Plots—2s. 6d. each; Extra Strong Plots—5s. each; Plots for 10,000 word (long complete) stories—10s. each . . . MACK'S PLOT FORMULA—30s . . . . Indispensable to the busy writer. Will construct a saleable plot in fifteen minutes."[17] A few consultants built up a repertoire of services. G. J. Matson, who dealt mostly with nonfiction articles, began supplementing his freelance journalism by doing manuscript criticism for a fee. In 1934 he began the *Writer's Monthly,* a rambling but thoughtful diary addressed to the aspirant. In it he told of writers and editors he had seen that month and passed on tips from them, recorded his own acceptances and explained what lessons could be learned from them, and noted new openings and markets. The *Writer's Monthly* lapsed after two years, but Matson went on to publish other periodicals, *Free-lance Writer and Photographer* and *Market Notes.* He also published writing textbooks written by himself and others, along with the *Writers' and Photographers' Reference Guide.*

Writing "schools," which provided correspondence courses with prepared lessons and exercises, stood outside the traditional channels of education. Few of those in charge of such schools and other services had university degrees, and adult education organizations largely left imaginative writing to commercial instructors. Britain had much less of a tradition of formal schooling in written expression than the United States. Creative writing was a part of American schoolchildren's curricula well before it became orthodox in Britain in the 1960s; journalism was taught in American colleges from the 1890s, but not until 1919 in Britain; and the idea that creative or even expository writing could be formally taught in a university setting was not accepted in Britain for much of the twentieth century.[18] In the interwar period and later, the Workers' Educational Association and the University of Oxford's extramural program were concerned with teaching their students how to appreciate and assess a work of literature or history, not with preparing them to go out and make their own. Possibly the only adult education institution to offer formal instruction in writing was the London County Council's City Literary Institute, which emphasized the arts and served a predominantly middle-class student body. In 1939–1940 Kennedy Williamson, the editor of the *Writer,* lectured there for two hours twice a week on "the Art of Writing."[19]

The early correspondence schools of writing bore signs of the heritage of self-improvement schemes with which correspondence courses had been associated. Courses in the short story appeared alongside courses in "Mental Training" and "Mental Culture" at what would become the longest-running such school, which was founded in 1909 by T. P. O'Connor as the London Correspondence College.[20] W. J. Ennever, who took over from O'Connor, remained involved in the Pelman Institute, which taught an eponymous system of "memory training" by correspondence.[21] Despite Ennever's links with Pelmanism, the courses on mental training were allowed to lapse after O'Connor gave up the college, and the school focused on the teaching of writing. Ennever remained the majority shareholder, though he moved to the United States on Pelman business.[22]

Ennever went west to promote the British system of Pelmanism to Americans, but the Pelman Institute's correspondence education was itself modeled on American practice. Correspondence courses were an American invention that quickly became popular in Britain. The United States was also the capital of writing instruction, both by correspondence and through textbooks and magazines. A magazine called the *Writer* was published in Boston nearly thirty-five years before the London magazine of that name was launched. British writers were conscious of

American models, and one textbook author and correspondence school principal regularly pointed out that Britain lagged behind the United States in the systematic teaching of writing.[23] For the most part, though, American ideas about writing circulated unobtrusively in Britain, seldom raising fears—or hopes—of cultural colonization in amateur writers and their teachers. Moreover, British authors quickly built up a substantial corpus of texts on writing and a canon of ideas that made it unnecessary to draw directly on American precedents. The way British aspirants and their would-be teachers appropriated American practices is symptomatic of the British reception of American (and European) cultural goods generally. British readers and writers warmed to O. Henry and Maupassant without any nativist compunctions, despite the former's unmistakable Americanness and the latter's obvious Frenchness. The scholarly literature positing a ruralist, nostalgic culture of "Englishness" can foster the mistaken impression that, with the exception of working-class enthusiasm for Hollywood, British culture in the first half of the twentieth century was inward-looking and unreceptive to foreign cultural goods. To embrace this misconception is to miss a fascinating aspect of interwar British culture: the fact that "no other major state was culturally so open."[24]

When Ennever moved to America, he left the running of the London Correspondence College to the new minority shareholder, the novelist Max Pemberton.[25] It was renamed the London School of Journalism, and under Pemberton it prospered and became the least distrusted institution of its kind.[26] After graduating from Cambridge with no profession in mind, Pemberton did some freelance journalism in the 1880s. This experience convinced him that there was a living to be had in catering to "the reading tastes of the masses." He secured the editorship of the boys' paper *Chums,* then *Cassell's Magazine,* a competitor of the

Strand, and then moved into writing unabashedly derivative novels—initially imitations of Robert Louis Stevenson and Rider Haggard. His work sold but did not give him the security he wanted. Like many later writers, Pemberton sought to capitalize on his measure of literary success by going into the literary advice business.[27]

To this end he sought the help of the press magnate Lord Northcliffe. The two men were old friends, and were on "Max" and "Alf" terms, though Pemberton sometimes, like others around the great man, called Northcliffe "Chief." Pemberton had played sidekick to the rising Alfred Harmsworth and became a long-term client of his. From the correspondence that remains it is not clear whether Northcliffe lent Pemberton the money he asked for as he moved into the writing-school business, but he at least handled the negotiations with Ennever and his deputy Neil MacLaren that were needed to set Pemberton up at the college. Pemberton was installed with a one-third stake in it and a salary of £1000 a year, a figure that testifies to the commercial viability of instruction in writing (an annual income of £250 was often cited as the threshold of the middle class, and a doctor or solicitor earning £1000 would have been doing substantially better than the average for their professions). Northcliffe drew the line at being identified in the college's promotional material as its sovereign patron, though he was happy to be one of a number of people designated as patrons. The college's letterhead accordingly listed him as just one member of a pantheon of patrons. After he died, the letterhead was changed to read: "Founded under the direct patronage of the late Viscount NORTHCLIFFE."[28]

Students of the London School of Journalism received their lessons in printed installments. The bulk of these lessons dealt with the craft of writing, but they also touched on "the business side of writing," including copyright law and the technicalities of correcting page proofs. Kennedy Williamson's 1930s course on poetry, though chiefly concerned with imagery and form, concluded with a discussion of how to market poems. It suggested suitable periodicals (*Poetry Review*, the "leading literary Sunday papers") and repeated the Society of Authors' injunction to avoid vanity publishers. Some courses were written almost exclusively by one person, while others featured guest "lecturers." At the end of each lesson were assigned exercises. The student sent the completed exercises to the school for comment, not necessarily by the person who had written the lessons. The comments were then sent to the student along with the next installment of the course. In the early days these exercises often had only a tenuous pedagogical connection with the lessons. In one of Pemberton's own short story courses, the exercises for the lesson on "atmosphere" required students to copy out a passage of 200–300 words that they considered atmospheric from any novel they had at hand, and then write a 300-word outline for a short story beginning with one of the sample sentences Pemberton supplied. How, we may wonder, was an outline going to test and develop the novice's ability to evoke an atmosphere? In later courses, such as Williamson's on poetry, the exercises were much more closely tied to the aspects of the writer's craft under discussion in the lesson. For instance, after a lesson on rhymed and unrhymed poetry, students were instructed to rewrite in blank verse W. E. Henley's metrical clanger "Invictus," a poem much favored for ceremonial moments both public and private in Britain in the early twentieth century. Sometimes the final "exercise" in a course would be the submission of several finished stories or poems, which would "be criticised . . . and advice given as to their disposal should the directors deem them worthy of publication": in effect, the school was offering the services of a literary bureau at the end of a course.[29]

Other schools combined correspondence education with literary bureau services. The Louise Heilgers Correspondence College, which was in operation around 1920 and seems to have suspended business abruptly in 1923, ran a literary bureau that was generally available, but free to students. Heilgers and her staff also gave advice and criticism in person. The college took pains to stress the value of the feedback and consultation it offered, presumably to discourage people from thinking that borrowing or buying the printed lesson plans from acquaintances would give them the full benefit of the college's instruction. For sixpence a month students, and members of the public whose newsagents stocked it, could buy the *Louise Heilgers Magazine,* which catered to "the needs of the aspirant . . . to the aspiring journalist, to the would-be writer of fiction." It consisted of promotions for the college, competitions, sample short stories, sketches, poems, and articles of advice by Heilgers, D. Kennedy-Bell (apparently its editor), and anonymous members of the college staff. Though the magazine was addressed to aspirants in general, its main function was to bind into a "community of common interest all those who take our courses."[30]

The Louise Heilgers Correspondence College thus offered a more comprehensive array of services than the London School of Journalism. Both, however, sought to tap what Pemberton had sensed was "a very large number of young people each year, who desire to be coached for the profession of journalism." The Heilgers college presented itself as providing training in a rising and profitable profession. It urged prospective students to look on its fees as an investment comparable to those required for professions such as the law. The course in article and story writing consisted of fifteen lessons—to be completed, ideally, in thirty weeks—and cost fifteen guineas. Advice in person cost either a guinea or half a guinea. At the standard minimally acceptable rate of a guinea—a pound plus a shilling, 21 shillings—per thousand words, novice writers would have to sell between ten and fifteen short stories to recoup their investment in the course, and more if they availed themselves of in-person advice.[31]

Heilgers marketed her "profession" to young women especially. In this "era of the emancipation of women," according to an anonymous member of the college staff, writing was an obvious career choice: "Journalism and fiction writing offer great scope for . . . [women's] peculiar qualities, ability and labour." The college's prospectus announced: "In view of the great possibilities this Course opens to women, Louise Heilgers will at times be prepared to advise specially, when asked to do so, on the careers of daughters."[32] Part of the strategy of appealing to young women may have been the presentation of Heilgers herself as a starlet: her books and her articles in the magazine were adorned with glamorous photographs of her, in much the same style as the photos of actresses and other celebrities in profiles in popular magazines.

The Heilgers college, like the London School of Journalism, used the word "journalism" in the expansive sense current at the time, which included all work for newspapers and other "journals." The term "journalism" did not have the exclusively nonfictional connotations it now has until as late as the 1950s.[33] Both the professional and the generic boundaries between fiction and journalism in its more limited sense were blurry. People like Philip Gibbs shuttled back and forth between salaried work on Fleet Street and the writing of novels and other books. Much of the material published in magazines and newspapers fell into a gray area between short stories and articles. A core of factual material could be fleshed out into an "article," a "sketch," or a short story depending on the author's inclinations, a publication's requirements, or the sensitivity of the material. Thus a novice author could be told that her piece "was more a story than an article and would be worth re-writing." In the early 1950s John Braine, still far away from becoming a bestselling novelist, put a lot of effort into a piece based on his attendance of a Communist Party meeting in 1943. It was initially going to be a humorous "article" written in the first person. Braine then decided that "the communist article should be written as a story . . . there's too much risk of a libel action otherwise."[34]

Presumably on the evidence of her own career, Louise Heilgers argued that there could be a fruitful interplay between the writing of nonfiction articles and short stories. Though her college's magazine offered some specimen topical articles, it was mostly devoted to the writing of fiction for the mass market. Heilgers wrote a textbook entitled *How to Write Stories for Money,* and the college's magazine was both defensive about formulaic fiction—"[Charles] Garvice was not a highbrow, but he died a rich man for the simple reason that he had mastered the mystery of telling a story as it should be told"—and insistent that part of the appeal of successful commercial fiction lay in its embodiment of the desirable personal qualities of its author. Hence a purported accolade from a female fan of "a very human and tender sketch" by Heilgers in the *Sunday Chronicle:* "You *real* thing, God bless you."[35]

The Louise Heilgers Correspondence College and the London School of Journalism have left more documentary traces than other writing schools of the period, but there were many others, some of which clearly had better resources than Heilgers's college. Among those that advertised regularly and lavishly were the Regent Institute, the Premier School of Journalism, the Meiklejohn Institute, the Fleet Street School of Writing, and the A.B.C. Writer's Course. Their principals came from journalistic backgrounds: as a university graduate, Max Pemberton was a rarity in this milieu. Hugh Tuite, of the Meiklejohn Institute, had something approximating Heilgers's combination of a background as a staff journalist and experience in fiction and other kinds of writing. He had been on staff of the Amalgamated Press and had edited the *Scottish Weekly Record;* he wrote short stories, several books on bridge, and a writing guide entitled *Profits and the Pen.* Others were working their way up through the newspaper ranks or had migrated from editorships to freelancing.[36]

To pay their way, these schools needed large enrollments and probably relatively cheap labor. "Kobold Knight," a short story writer who started a smaller but durable and well-advertised tuition business in 1927, observed that with advertising costing forty pounds a page, "the number of enrolments in the big schools must, quite obviously, be beyond the *capacity* of any one man to attend to without . . . assistants." "Famous writers may devise and write the course; and may 'direct' it. But salaried assistants like Mr. [Cecil?] Hunt's fifty-shillings-a-weeker will do much of the actual work." Smaller or newer operations needed a distinctive angle. With Kobold Knight, it was personalized tuition in fiction only, both "what are so rudely called 'potboilers'" and stories with more literary ambitions; with Martin Walter, it was his "plot formula." Walter's school, the British Institute of Fiction Writing Science, was active from the 1930s into the 1950s and advertised as much as Kobold Knight did. The cornerstone of its printed lessons was what Walter regarded as a universal grammar of plot. Students were supposed to carry a card summarizing the formula in their pockets or handbags so that they could test the formula against every story they read and use it on the fly to translate an idea or observation into a fully fledged plot. Students paid the course fee and agreed to pay a royalty on the sale of stories written under the formula, so the institute incorporated agency functions as well (or at least the revenue-collecting function).[37]

The last major branch of the writing advice industry was the writer's magazine. There were many such publications—*Writer's Monthly, News Letter,* the *Writer's Own Magazine,* the *Writer's Journal,* the *Writer's Medley, Writing News, Freelance Register, Popular Writing.* The most important of them was the *Writer.* Its significance lies in its durability (it lasted until 1976), the substance and breadth of its information about the world of amateur writers, and its influence on that world—an influence registered in articles contributed to the magazine and in its role as a resource for writers' groups. The magazine grew out of the *Louise Heilgers Magazine,* which lasted only a year under that name. After a transitional period in the early 1920s, the *Writer* reinvented itself as a publication independent of the Louise Heilgers Correspondence College, and in mid-1924 the publishing firm of Hutchinson bought it. In the following years Hutchinson expanded dramatically, its publications ranging from "quality" fiction to its Shilling Novels series, which included Ethel M. Dell and Sydney Horler.[38] Now Hutchinson was becoming a major player in the literary advice market, like A. & C. Black, which published the *Writers' and Artists' Year Book.* As well as the *Writer,* Hutchinson published guidebooks, including Michael Joseph's various guides to "the commercial side of literature." It also owned the A.B.C. Writers' Course, which was run in tandem with the *Writer,* though there are no overt signs of muzzling by Hutchinson in the magazine's advice.

The *Writer* had three editors in the 1920s and 1930s: (Major) Owen Rutter, Philip Harrison, and Kennedy Williamson. Rutter, who edited the magazine for only a few years, was a prolific travel writer and a popular historian of the *Bounty* mutiny. His successor fitted more snugly into the developing niche of the writing advisor. Harrison wrote guidebooks, which Hutchinson published, for "those who write because they want to make money," rather than "those who are striving to become artists and write because they feel a definite impulse to express themselves in literature." Williamson, the editor from 1929 to 1942, undertook more duties and concerned himself with a broader range of constituents. He could write about "the business side," like Harrison, but he was also concerned with those "striving to become artists." His interest in noncommercial writing is evident in his occasional scholarly or parsonical musings: he was, conspicuously, Kennedy Williamson, M.A., in a predominantly degreeless and often anti-academic milieu, and he had published some collections of essays on Christian themes. Williamson's interest in aspiring artists is evident also in the attention he devoted to the not very profitable genre of poetry.[39]

Competitions, lists of suitable markets, advice on what periodical was appropriate for what sort of manuscript, advice on the elements of good writing, ways to find ideas for plots or topical articles, productive times and places to do one's writing, profiles of well-known authors: all were perennial features of the *Writer*. It also ran pieces about matters such as the presentation of manuscripts and whether to write separately to editors before submitting a manuscript. By the mid-1930s ancillary articles were appearing on the particulars of police procedure, the law of succession, trains, ships, gas mains, and so on, so that writers did not get their details wrong or base their plots on false assumptions about the workings of trains, gas, wills, or fingerprinting. These items may have been useful to the magazine's readers, since editors and publishers' readers could be irritated by factual errors and were understandably hostile to stories whose plots turned on mistakes or impossibilities, as when an Allen and Unwin reader eye-rollingly explained the resolution of an "unreal, and extremely crude" novel's plot: "His heart is faithful to Madeline, a pianist, who marries his brother. In the end she obtains what the author calls a 'restitution decree' and marries Eugene."[40]

Articles in the *Writer* were generally written by London-based freelance journalists or figures in the writing-advice industry, but the magazine also printed articles by amateur writers. Some talked about their work habits; others told how they had achieved a measure of success (often under the heading "How I Did It"). The correspondence columns were also open for aspirants to relate stories less conducive to optimism and to discuss problems. The value or worthlessness of particular methods of writing, ways of getting inspiration, and tools like plot-formulas was also open for discussion. Advice pages where the editor responded to queries also brought readers into closer contact with the world of publishing. The ostensible purpose of the *Louise Heilgers Magazine* had been to turn the Heilgers college's alumni into "community of common interest"; as the *Writer*, the magazine went some way toward creating a wider community of aspirant writers.

By that time writing had become a "hobby" with an apparatus of clubs, guidebooks, periodicals, and ancillary services. Literary veterans—and some novices masquerading as such—capitalized on a lesson that intermediaries such as agents and publishers' readers presented to an interested public: the lesson that the literary marketplace had some rules, and that those rules could be learned. Plenty of aspiring writers kept their distance from advisory services, but sufficient numbers were interested to make literary advice profitable. And among those novices who did not buy textbooks or pay for coaching, many nevertheless bought the dream of a writing career that the advice business was selling.

Chapter 2

A Chance to Exercise Our Talents

Patricia Williamson of Flixton in Manchester said in a letter to the *Writer* in October 1923: "It has occurred to me that in the wilds of Manchester there may be other 'Writer Lovers' who, were they known to each other, could meet and discuss literary and journalistic affairs to their mutual benefit . . . In London there are clubs, societies, etc., for the meeting of writers and journalists; in Manchester there appears to be nothing of the kind." The following month the magazine published a letter from a man in Reading, saying: "I have already got several of my literary friends interested, and we propose to hold meetings, at each other's houses, two or three times a month during the winter months." The magazine's editor, Owen Rutter, endorsed the idea of "'Writer Circles' for the discussion of literary and journalistic affairs," to mitigate the loneliness of writers outside London.[1]

Nursing the writers' circle movement in the 1920s was the magazine's most significant work in building up a community of aspiring authors. As the circles spread throughout Britain, they eclipsed, and helped transform, an earlier movement of aspiring writers—"amateur journalists"—who had spurned commercial publication and printed their own periodicals on small presses or written them out by hand. The writers' circles had no such aversion to the market: they provided a peaceable setting in which men and women could pursue their creative ambitions and profitably involve themselves in the culture industry. They were at once self-consciously local and connected to a "standardized" national commercial culture. My account here is based on manuscript and printed sources. Scholars such as Janice A. Radway have worked wonders with interviews of contemporary readers, but I am cautious about their value for a study of *writing* seventy years ago and more.[2] Interviews could provide useful information about how writers' groups worked and how people became involved in writing; but what writing *meant* to a novice in the 1920s is a more elusive kind of knowledge, one repeatedly reformulated in memory.

Soon after Williamson's initial letter, Rutter launched a competition in the *Writer* for the best set of rules for a writers' circle. It elicited a lot of entries, and letters from around the country trickled in appealing to others interested in forming such circles in Edinburgh, Hull, South-East London, Cardiff, Bradford, Chesham Bois, Norwich, and Nottingham. So many of the magazine's subscribers lived in Birmingham that Rutter himself initiated plans for a circle there. By April 1924 Rutter could report that various parts of Britain now had writers' circles "for mutual help." He lent his personal support to the proposal for a London Writer Circle. True, he conceded, London already had "a multiplicity of clubs and literary societies" that could stimulate "the writer who is well founded in his craft." But they were not directly related to the activity of writing, and the would-be author "will want exactly what a WRITER Circle can give him." Rutter, and others without a proprietary interest in doing so, referred to "'Writer' circles" or "*Writer* circles" to indicate what they saw as the institutions' kinship with the magazine. Indeed, the instigator of the London Writer Circle, Colonel Trevor St. P. Molony, declared that its objects "were practically synonymous with those of THE

WRITER." Rutter was elected chairman of the circle, and his assistant editor played a prominent part in its business as well.[3]

The London circle announced in the *Writer* that it "welcome[d] all those who write and are interested in freelance work." Many of its recruits were women, and at least some had sought help from the writing advice industry. Christabel Lowndes-Yates, who was active in the London Writer Circle from the beginning, had been a pupil of Max Pemberton's and belonged to another literary aspirants' club. But the London circle also included people with Fleet Street connections and representatives of the advice business, such as Patrick Braybrooke and the *Writer* staff members. Consequently, as the circle grew, it was well placed to arrange accommodation with appropriate connotations and to tap well-known writers to speak. It met in rooms above Foyle's bookshop in Charing Cross Road for eighteen months, and then in the hall at the Institute of Journalists. Among its guest speakers were G. K. Chesterton and the short story writer Stacy Aumonier, a respected figure for would-be writers of popular fiction in the 1920s.[4]

As Rutter had realized, evenings with speakers such as Chesterton and Aumonier did not sharply differentiate the London Writer Circle from the capital's existing "multiplicity of clubs and literary societies." The circle's claim to novelty was its criticism evenings. Early meetings were dominated by the discussion of manuscripts submitted anonymously by members and read aloud at the start of the meeting by a designated reader. The group soon grew too big for intimate discussion: in two years it had 250 members, and by 1932 the total was 300, with the average attendance at meetings reckoned at 120. As the membership swelled, the circle's scope and organization changed. Most meetings were now devoted to guest speakers, and the bulk of the criticism was relegated to "postal, circulating clubs . . . These now provide criticism for members' MSS., and those selected by each club are later read before the Circle." By 1932 those postal "clubs" had been replaced by meetings of sectors of the circle. "There are also special groups forming, Manuscript Groups & a Short Story & Article Group," John Marsh reported to the writers' circle in his home town of Halifax in the West Riding of Yorkshire, "which usually meet on the alternative Mondays to the General Meeting. Mr Marsh was a member of the Short Story Group which he found particularly useful. The members met & criticised a short story written by one of them, but without knowing the author."[5]

While many of its activities mirrored those of other writers' circles throughout Britain, the metropolitan context of the London circle—its access to Fleet Street, its links with other associations such as the Institute of Journalists—set it apart. In the mid-1930s several writers' circles formed in London suburbs—Raynes Park, Muswell Hill, Thornton Heath, and Wandsworth—but they proved ephemeral; after the war more durable ones were founded in Croydon and "South London." The list in the *Writer* for February 1939 registered 27 circles.[6] The majority were scattered around England, with two enduring ones in Scotland, in the two largest cities. There was none in Wales, despite attempts to establish circles there; Cork had one, but there was none in Northern Ireland. The suburban London circles were formed in new, predominantly lower-middle-class suburbs, the ideal type of which was Raynes Park, a 1930s development.[7] Beyond these observations, the geographical distribution of the circles resists correlation with particular kinds of urban economies, or with the North of England over the South. It is clear, though, that Patricia Williamson's original letter to the *Writer*, which saw writers' circles as suitable for those without access to "literary London," could have supplied a motto for the movement.

What sort of backgrounds did these would-be writers come

from? Even if street addresses were an infallible guide to income and social standing, insufficient records exist to build up such a picture consistently over any one circle's lifetime, let alone to enable comparisons between circles. And while conversation at meetings must have disclosed an abundance of information about members' social positions, the secretaries were not obligingly indiscreet enough to record it for posterity. But some broad generalizations can be made. A majority of members came from the middle and lower-middle classes. Discussions at circles or in the *Writer* about how to find time and energy to write did not mention the difficulty of writing after a day's factory work. Of course, the middle class was heterogeneous, and it underwent dramatic change in the 1930s and 1940s with the emergence of new kinds of work, principally in scientific and technical areas. Employment in the "lower professions" in the public sector, such as teaching and librarianship, also boomed. More and more women entered white-collar work—and were largely confined to its least prestigious reaches. And in the 1920s and 1930s being middle class increasingly meant being suburban.[8]

The suburban London writers' circles catered to this "new" middle class, but on the whole circle members came from both "old" and "new" parts of the middle and lower-middle classes. The secretary of the Bromley circle provided an informal club census in 1941: among the "ordinary folk" who made up the small membership were "several housewives, . . . a bank official, a metal-worker, a sub-post-master, an ex-editor of a technical journal, an accountant, a clerk . . . a school-master," two people in war work, and a spinster (the writer was not the only English person to see spinsterhood as a profession). Recurrent occupations in the writers' circles were "home duties" (the most common for women, married and unmarried), librarianship, clerical work, and teaching. There was the odd clergyman and doctor, representatives of the "old" higher professions. For the most part, however, writers' circle members did not have a university education. In that respect they were like most of the middle class.[9]

Aspects of their behavior distinguish writers' circle members from more privileged sectors of the middle class. They tended to be forthright about the pecuniary returns they sought from writing: the extra guineas that the sale of stories or articles would bring into the household. Like some other hobbies, writing could be regarded as lucrative as well as recreational or "constructive."[10] Many members were willing, in addresses to their circle, discussions at meetings, and even, as the Bradford group's scrapbooks make clear, in interviews with the local press, to disclose how much money they were making from their writing. The original name of the Gloucester Writers' Circle was the Gloucester Profit-Writers' Circle. "If you peep into a meeting of these 'literary gents,'" a local newspaper reported of the Halifax circle in 1931, "you will not hear them discussing the aesthetic side of the business always. They might talk of style, but they also talk of marketing novels, the best agencies, how much money they can earn (or the reverse) by their pens (or typewriters), how to start writing a thriller, catering for juvenile tastes, or tackling historical novels."[11]

Such behavior would have seemed vulgar at the Manchester Literary Club, an established society that had nurtured or patronized working-class authors in the nineteenth century, and where original stories and poetry were still read as overtures before the presentation of apparently more serious papers. The club charged a higher subscription fee and enjoyed impressive quarters, and would-be members had to be proposed by other gentlemen. In this "clubbable" atmosphere, social status was enshrined in a *refusal* to talk about commerce. The club, as its humorous versifier put it in 1906, was a refuge "Where we find life worth living, take small thought of time, / And for coal, corn or cotton we don't give a dime." "The concern with books was not a business to its members," the *Manchester Guardian* paraphrased the group's president as saying in 1927; "it was genuine recreation." Unsurprisingly, the Manchester Literary Club appears to have had had no formal contact with the Manchester Writer Circle.[12]

The background and outlook of writers' circles also meant that they were not natural havens for working-class autodidacts, though they did include a few. Fred Dean of Halifax was a classic representative of the tradition: born in 1867, he spent his life working in textile mills, and counted as his formative influences Primitive Methodism, "Bands of Hope, S[unday] S[school] teaching, Mutual Improvement classes . . . Through W. T. Stead I was introduced to one hundred and fifty poets . . . Carlyle taught me courage, Emerson taught me the inner life." His values seldom found an echo in the circle's market- and practicality-oriented moots and lectures, but he attended faithfully. The draw may have been regular contact with the circle's star, Phyllis Bentley, the most prominent West Riding author (it was unusual for a writer with a national reputation to be an active rather than ceremonial participant in a writers' circle) and also someone who reveled in being generous with her experience and ideas.[13]

While high-minded autodidacts were rare, other working-class people could be found in writers' circles. Jon Lawrence has pointed out that for all the talk of a deep divide between manual and nonmanual workers, a degree of "common culture" bound them together in industrial cities.[14] White-collar and manual workers coexisted in neighborhoods of terraced houses; in the interwar years the clerks migrated to the suburbs, but such neighborhoods could still be found in the 1950s.[15] Not only did respectable clerks have things in common with factory workers: lowlier white-collar workers, such as secretaries, could participate in the same cultural activities as middle-class people. At least they did so in the field of popular writing. Molly Weir, who grew up in a tenement in Glasgow, began writing for publication in newspapers while she worked as a secretary during the day, all the while remaining a member of the family household. Margaret Thomson Davis was also raised in a Glasgow tenement. She worked in retail, and after her son was born she wrote short stories for popular magazines. She went to the first writers' circle summer school in 1949, and the autobiography-cum-guidebook she wrote late in life is a treasury of writers' circle nostrums.[16] Davis's story is an example of the way commercial culture could cut across the cultures of different social classes.

The most striking aspect of the composition of writers' circles was the number of women in them. In the Halifax Authors' Circle, seven of the original twenty members were women, and the proportion edged upward over the next two decades as the number of men declined (six women to eight men in 1935, ten women to eight men in 1945). There seems to have been little friction along gender lines in the Halifax, Leeds, and Croydon circles. At Newcastle, though, the female secretary recorded an occasional barb against the circle's members of "the so-called superior sex, who sit in silent dignity all together." Associations in which men and women mixed were still relatively unusual, and the historian Marcus Collins has emphasized just how much of a change "mixing" was.[17] Most clubs and societies, including hobby associations, were male-dominated; women were numerous or dominant only in church groups and charities, and "even those strongholds of women's associationalism, Women's Institutes . . . had a decidedly 'social service' role." Yet between the wars, especially in new suburbs, "mixed" organizations developed—tennis clubs, for instance. Amateur dramatic and operatic societies, too, involved both men and women. But women tended to join such associations as part of a couple. In contrast, recruits to writers' circles usually did not join with their spouses.[18]

Doubtless one reason married women joined writers' circles without their husbands was the probability that a couple would have a greater difference in aptitude and inclination for writing than they might for something like bridge. But it is also possible that husbands' attitudes to wives' writing were one reason women sought the company of other writers. Aspirants were sensitive about the maddening way "one's friends and relations always refer to one's work as 'little stories'"; an advertisement for the A.B.C. Correspondence Schools shrewdly beckoned: "THOSE SCEPTICAL RELATIVES! . . . What fun it would be to confound them!"[19] Skeptical or hostile husbands could be particularly hurtful. One woman wrote anonymously to the *Writer* to thank the editor for the difference the magazine had made to her. As a young woman she had dabbled in writing, but then she had married a man who "laughed my efforts to scorn until I dried up like an autumn leaf." His comments about the money she was spending on stamps to submit her work to editors finally made her give up. After their children were grown, she went back to her old manuscripts. She showed one to Max Pemberton, who advised her to go on writing. "But either I was too sensitive to ridicule or my creative faculties were still engaged with my family, for my efforts were abortive." After discovering the *Writer,* though, she began writing again: "My inner self is happier than it has been for years."[20]

Eva Hope Wallace, who came from a more secure background—her husband was a doctor, they had servants, and the cost of stamps was probably less troubling—was also sensitive about her writing. Remembering how her brothers had teased her when she wrote in childhood, she kept secret her decision to write a short story in response to a local paper's appeal for material for its women's page. While her children and her husband slept, she slipped into her husband's surgery and wrote. The newspaper accepted her story, and later she wrote a novel in secret. According to her account in the *Writer*, she felt justified in her endeavors when her husband read her a glowing review of the novel.[21]

It is tempting to interpret the experiences of these two women in terms of the opposition sometimes set up, especially in an American context, between masculine "genius" and feminine "scribbling."[22] The temptation should be resisted. While it is easy to find certain kinds of mass-market writing being associated with the feminine in the higher reaches of interwar literary criticism, there is scant evidence that this way of thinking obtained elsewhere in British culture, least of all in the aspirant writers' movement. Slurs about feminine scribbling interlocked with a critique of the commercialization of culture. That critique carried no weight in the aspirant writers' movement: this culture of popular writing was, as we shall see, quite untroubled by the market.

What is at work in these two stories about female writers and their husbands is something subtler than a trivialization of women's writing and a view of "minor" writing as essentially feminine. Men too could feel sensitive about their literary efforts, and they did not necessarily feel they were being effeminate in trying to write. The stories these two women told the *Writer* are less about gendered inscriptions of *writing* than about the gender dynamics of marriage. The woman whose husband's ridicule made her dry up like a leaf added: "He resented not only the time I gave to it, but also the demands that writing made on my inner self. (I think the latter is a commoner form of grievance than one might suppose.)" The domestic expectations placed on a wife made her writing more of a battle than a husband's. When describing their writing habits, male as well as female aspirants referred to struggles to find time and a relatively quiet place to write. But the men's accounts display an implicit sense of entitlement to peace that is absent from the women's. As a single mother wrote: "Men may be married, but while they are working work comes first and the family 'also ran,' however devoted a husband and father the man may be. A woman with a family has to choose either to run the family or write; she can't do both."[23]

Before her marriage, Irene Byers had quite a glamorous career as a freelance journalist, renting office space on or near Fleet Street and specializing in interviews with famous people, including John Gielgud and Sybil Thorndike. Byers also contributed to the Court Page of *The Times*. When she married, around 1930, she gave up this career, and missed it badly. After her children were at school she started inching back toward writing. During the war, before she was evacuated from London, she wrote poems for her children. The idea of a charity concert with local youngsters seized her imagination. "I see a chance to do some writing for once. What a thrill it will be to take up my professional pen again. I have been for too long just a Mum and the verses I wrote in the shelter to distract the children have a new significance." When the concert was held in August 1943, she felt "a little shiver of pride. My work is actually being performed. My own verses were included . . . But when eventually the applause dies down and we return home, Cyril tells me that I must now get used to being plain Mrs Byers again." Irene was asked to write and organize another concert, but "Cyril puts his foot down firmly and says 'enough is enough.'" Her husband was more supportive about the "mother's thoughts in wartime" that she wrote up for the BBC's *Woman's Hour* several months later, helping her with the final draft. Several days after that Irene recorded in her diary, "Cyril returns from a session at the Bank to find me writing children's stories," as if to imply that she had been caught at something she should not have been doing. The following year, when her book of children's poems was accepted for publication, she recorded Cyril's praise in her diary.[24]

Like Eva Hope Wallace, Irene Byers was mindful of her husband's criticism of her work, and appreciative of his praise when he extended it. We cannot know for sure what made Cyril Byers ambivalent about his wife's writing. Did he resent the demands it made on her "inner self"? Was he wounded by the implication that family life and domestic entertainments such as playing the piano and reading novels aloud were not enough stimulation for her? "I may never publish them," Irene said of the stories he found her writing, "but the exercise of working out the plot stimulates me mentally." After the war she went on writing and had many children's books published. She became an active member and secretary of the Croydon Writers' Circle.[25]

The obligations and expectations faced by wives and other women who looked after relatives meant that the claims of the literary advice industry were especially pertinent to them. The advice industry and circle speakers held out the promise that those who could not relocate to Fleet Street could still become published writers by studying at home or with like-minded local enthusiasts. Less able to make the classic artistic move of packing up and heading to London to try their fortune, women had all the more reason to embrace potential surrogates like writers' magazines and writers' circles. Opening the Festival of Britain proceedings in Haworth in 1951, Phyllis Bentley—a single woman who had looked after her widowed mother—pointedly commented: "All of us cannot live in great cities, nor do we want to do so; but all of us should have a chance to exercise our talents . . . All ages, both sexes (very important, this!), many kinds of talent, many types of spiritual aspiration, seem to be catered for [in contemporary Haworth,] give[n] a chance."[26]

"All of us cannot live in great cities, nor do we want to do so":

while there were limits to the localism of the writers' circles' orientation, in organization, at least, they were decidedly provincial. The London group was not a central coordinating body for circles around Britain. If anything served as the hub of circle organization, it was the *Writer*, through its notice-board function and its articles on how to get a group started and make it work. Often, though, the *Writer* was a reference point rather than an institutional presence. At least one thriving group, the Halifax Authors' Circle, was formed without any help from the magazine, and writers' circles inevitably owed a great deal to the determination of those who founded them. They often started as the idea of unknown writers, and came into being through their persistence in cajoling others to join them (as in Bromley, for instance), or through their recruitment of one or two of the local pond's medium-sized fish.[27]

Thus when nineteen-year-old John Marsh founded the Halifax circle, he knew that the town was home to Phyllis Bentley, who "had already published two novels which had been well received," and to Frank King, who had written a romance entitled *Miriam of the Moorlands.* But Marsh "felt that an approach should be made, in the first place, not to these local giants of literature, but to someone nearer my own level . . . Accordingly I wrote to the Minister of the King[s] Cross Wesleyan Church whose cheery articles—'Tonic Talks'—had been appearing in the local newspaper for some time . . . Together Mr Cumberworth and I made out a list of people we thought it wise to invite to a preliminary meeting. I agreed to draft out a letter of invitation, book a room at a local cafe, and, for the time being, act as secretary." Other figures of local cultural life, such as the city or borough librarian, often played important roles in promoting and establishing a circle.[28]

Fledgling circles often drew support, and sometimes a substitute for a quorum, through exchanges with other circles in their region. In the West Riding, the younger circles in Leeds (founded in 1928), Huddersfield (1935), and Bradford (1942) appealed to the Halifax group for advice, visiting speakers, and joint meetings. Farther north, where writers' circles were fewer, the Newcastle circle depended quite heavily on its Glasgow and Edinburgh counterparts. Article two of its provisional guidelines reads: "Monthly competitions would be taken from the 'Writer' or on members suggestions, or suggestions of the Glasgow Circle." The Newcastle and Scottish circles would exchange batches of manuscripts that the receiving club would criticize at a meeting. A digest of the criticisms would then be sent home with the manuscripts. In this way the groups expanded their circles of comparison and criticism, coming somewhat closer to the variety of larger circles (those with more than, say, forty members) such as London and Nottingham and, after 1945, Leeds and Croydon.[29]

Writers' circles were not extravagant operations. Subscriptions in the interwar period ranged from five to thirteen shillings per year, with annual dinners and summer picnics extra. This enabled circles to rent for an evening every week or every two weeks a room in a hall, a hotel, or an office building. Budgets did not stretch to hefty fees for celebrity speakers. In his autobiography the children's writer Geoffrey Trease recalled with some annoyance the travails of lecturing for minimal recompense at Women's Institutes, Book Weeks, and at least one writers' circle (the Nottingham one) in the late 1940s. At least he got some money: most people who spoke at writers' circles did so without payment. Consequently, they fell into three categories: generous celebrities; figures with ties to the literary advice industry or the writers' circle movement, such as Kennedy Williamson or Cecil Hunt; and local people of note in the world of writing and publishing. Thus Phyllis Bentley of Halifax and the novelist Phyllis Hambledon of the Bradford group would speak to other West Riding writers' circles, and all circles would periodically hear addresses by librarians, antiquarians, journalists, newspaper editors, lawyers talking about libel, and locals who had made good in literary and journalistic London and were back home visiting.[30] Members of a circle would also address their fellows. Circle organizers tried to schedule talks that had some relation to "practical" writing matters, such as "markets" (the hobby press, serialized romances, and so on), the opportunities therein, and how to tailor one's style to the predilections of editors in a particular market. Talks on these topics would frequently be given by successful circle members whose niche was the subject under discussion. Especially welcome were addresses by editors—most often local newspaper editors, but also others, such as regional BBC producers, particularly after the Second World War.

The circles' most distinctive and writerly activity was the "workshop" or "manuscript night," where members would criticise one another's work.[31] The London circle, as we have seen, began by having members submit manuscripts anonymously, and not reveal their authorship until after the discussion. Other circles did not attempt this: in small or long-standing circles it would have been almost impossible to preserve anonymity. The only circle records that include a concerted effort to summarize criticisms are those of the Newcastle group. Is this character plausible? Does this material work best in this genre, or pitched at that class of publication? These were criticisms consistent with the mission of being "practical." Circle minutes tend to be uninformative about the tone of the discussion, and we cannot know how personally or trenchantly the criticism was conducted. Ross McKibbin has argued that changes in middle-class sociability in the 1920s and 1930s made conflict and embarrassment less socially acceptable. Conversational taboos on "talking politics" were pervasive. A concomitant taboo on discussing religion apparently helped facilitate socializing between Anglicans and Dissenters, groups that were no longer the social monoliths they had been in the nineteenth century.[32] Writers' circles were generally averse to talking about politics, but the occasional recorded spats in Newcastle and Croydon suggest that the members did not altogether conform to this pattern of middle-class social behavior. It would probably be wrong to expect circle participants, however respectable, to have avoided all conflict: professing creativity and exposing their inventions to others meant that they differed, albeit within limits and perhaps only one evening each week, from the type of person who would do anything for a quiet life.

The other distinctive writers' circle activity was the writing exercise, either impromptu and during a meeting or as a competition or homework. Competitions and homework assignments confronted circle members with some of the problems that textbooks hammered away at, and genres they might not have tried before. A representative competition from the Halifax circle in 1931 gave members three options. The first was to describe a character in 100 words. Failing that, they could write a "description of a stream of consciousness while musing by the fire—or while out walking with the dog." (The expression "stream of consciousness" did not, in Halifax in 1931, imply Joycean experiment, but a meandering first-person narrative. A retrospective narration in front of a fire was a familiar device in the short story.[33]) Finally, competitors could compile "a list of words to be used instead of 'he said' in dialogue." Anxiety about endlessly repeating "said" was widespread, and a number of thesauri of "verbs of speech" were available to help stuck authors.[34]

Impromptu exercises took a number of forms. A designated member might bring several household objects along as a spur to writing, not a textual still-life, but a miniature story involving the items in some way. Topics for "impromptu story-weaving" might be drawn out of a hat, rather like subjects for extemporaneous speeches and debates in public speaking clubs.[35] Sometimes impromptu activities were just games, their diversionary nature manifest in the way members explained them with reference to existing games such as Consequences.[36] In other circumstances they were treated more earnestly as technical exercises.[37] Circle activities were thus suspended between entertainment and self-improvement, a combination also evinced by other recreational pursuits from public speaking to craft hobbies.

The same can be said of amateur drama, an important reference point for an understanding of the writers' circles. "The strength and significance of the amateur dramatic movement in the north, as an instrument of civilisation," Phyllis Bentley wrote, "is not always appreciated in London." In Yorkshire an enormous number of small amateur companies coexisted with major concerns like the Bradford Civic Playhouse, the Huddersfield Thespians, and the Halifax Thespians; and there were said to be more than 300 amateur drama societies in Liverpool alone in 1949.[38] The relationship between writers' circles and amateur drama was close and for some members symbiotic. The Bradford Writers' Circle, which began life as the Bradford Civic Playhouse Writers' Circle, had regular exchanges with the Old Hansonians drama group. Later, while a member of the Bradford Writers' Circle and the Bingley Little Theatre, John Braine would begin writing his novel *Room at the Top*, which evokes in detail the significances of amateur theatricals in a Yorkshire town. As well as personal and institutional connections, writers' groups and amateur theatricals were linked by supply and demand. Small amateur companies could rarely afford to pay the fees for performing well-known or published plays, and those without in-house playwrights sometimes turned to writers' circles.[39]

In the spectrum of provincial cultural life, the writers' circles occupied a position between amateur theatricals on the one hand and philosophical and literary societies on the other. The writers' circles tended to have fewer direct personal relations with literary societies than with amateur theatricals. Some literary societies were heavily masculine and more socially exclusive than the writers' groups (as we have seen in the case of Manchester). Others that did not present such social barriers, such as the Bradford English Society or the Edinburgh Poetry Club, were receptive to modernism to a degree that writers' circle members would probably have regarded as unhealthy.[40] A rare documented exchange between a writers' circle and a literary society is the visit of members of the Hull Writers' Club to the Hull Literary Club in November 1937; the writers read short stories, poems, sketches, and an essay. Some organizers were anxious to keep their circles distinct from literary societies. The Halifax Authors' Circle spent much of one early meeting discussing "how to restrict the membership from getting away from a practical Circle & turning into a literary gathering." Nevertheless, many circle evenings revolved around lectures reminiscent of a literary society—on the state of the novel, the art of the short story, or even "The Political Situation of France To-day," which the Newcastle Writers' Club heard about in 1946.[41]

The writers' circles also shared with literary societies the goal of safeguarding a locale's literary tradition. The preservationist and promotional impulse was perhaps most conspicuous in the North, but it was present too in other regions outside London—or rather, not sufficiently outside the influence of London—such as the West Country.[42] Like literary societies, writers' groups listened to many talks by local antiquarians and students of dialect and discussed ways of writing about local life. Circles thus often talked about regional identity as they talked about writing. One night in Newcastle, for instance, members spontaneously debated whether or not Durham was "a writer's paradise. Some declaimed it, declaring it left them cold, while others are thrilled with every stick and stone of the city which teems with antiquity, history and romance." Writers whose métier was pen-portraits of "Yorkshire characters" and tales and poems in dialect for a local audience could be found in some circles, perpetuating the nineteenth-century tradition of dialect writing. But these members were a minority, and they were consciously fighting a rearguard action. Other circle members were interested in ways of using regional detail in work seeking a wider audience, of converting it into "local color." How much dialect was evocative and how much was too much, and how phonetic one should be in rendering regional accents on the page, were questions that writers' circles—and the *Writer*—never deemed exhausted. Writers also pondered the national appeal of particular regions. "How is it," a member of the Newcastle circle asked, "that we have so many best selling novels of Yorkshire, Cumberland, etc, and none of the North East . . . the rest of the country must be educated to appreciate the N.E."[43]

The use of regional material as local color for the national market points to a crucial difference between the localism of writers' circles and that of, say, the Lancashire Authors' Association or the Manchester Literary Club. The gentlemen of the Manchester Literary Club luxuriated in a sense of local cultural leadership that had less and less foundation, and the local literary traditions defended by preservationist bodies like the Lancashire Authors' Association were under increasing stress. Regional identities and the civic culture of provincial cities were weakening from within (because of the decline of Nonconformity after 1900, for instance), and they were also being worn away by "the concentration of key national cultural institutions in London."[44] The centralization of publishing and the standardizing effects of the London press from the late nineteenth century were critical elements in this process. The pressure exerted by Northcliffe's *Daily Mail* in the provinces "inevitably undermined the variety of provincial attitudes and encouraged a uniformity of standard."[45] Writers' circle members were clearly attached to their regions, but they had nevertheless enlisted in the national commercial culture, courting national markets for periodical fiction and novels.

Much of the advice heard by writers' circles was geared toward publication that paid. Wearying of discussing market information and strategies for getting acceptances from lucrative publications, a Croydon circle member in the 1950s was moved to request "a poetry or non-commercial-writing speaker by way of an evening off occasionally." The point should not be overstated: each circle included people who seemed not terribly interested in publishing, or people who published in respected but not lucrative literary magazines such as *Modern Reading;* the Bradford Writers' Circle had a man whose rule was to write a sonnet a day. That the circles were heavily weighted toward writing for publication but did not exclude those wanting to write for other purposes is reflected in the lists of completed works they regularly posted. (Publicizing "successes," as they were always called, was a routine and important aspect of circle business, and was intimidating as well as encouraging. It echoed a trend in working-class hobbies toward greater competitiveness.)[46]

The "markets" that circle members pursued most energetically were those for short stories, serials, and local articles and fiction. Since their rise in the nineteenth century, provincial newspapers had printed creative work by local amateurs. They continued to do so in their twentieth-century decline, and partly *because* they were in decline: after the First World War, evening papers steadily became the standard for dailies outside London, and since they were put to bed early they contained less news than morning papers, and thus had more room for entertainment and "filler." Much of this filler was locally produced until national syndicates distributing feature material became dominant in the 1960s. At least some of it was written by freelances, a fact attested to by the number of circle members whose light verse, stories, and local "sketches" were regularly published by local newspapers. Anthony Powell, a sharp observer of most zones of British literary culture, provides a glimpse of this sort of freelancing in a minor character in *A Dance to the Music of Time*. Odo Stevens is a young Midlander who, before entering the army in the Second World War, makes money on the side—enough to buy a car—through a "spot of journalism in the local paper—'Spring comes to the Black Country'—'Sunset on Armistice Day'—that sort of thing."[47]

Local newspapers were thus one outlet for the short stories and semifictional "articles" of aspiring authors and freelances. Circle members also submitted their work to national newspapers, magazines—the *Strand* was among the most coveted destinations—and a host of lesser periodicals. Women's magazines and the women's pages of newspapers were attractive markets for men as well as women. Margaret Lees of Halifax and Elizabeth Woan of Newcastle both profited from writing serials for women's papers. Woan wrote for the Thomson-Leng syndicate, the Dundee-based company that produced a number of women's magazines, including the *People's Friend*, which was extraordinarily popular in Scotland; it also produced the leading boys' weeklies. Thomson-Leng's strict editorial formulas frustrated some newcomers but evidently made life easier once one broke in, as Woan did. (After the firm had bought several stories from a contributor, a traveling editor would often go to meet the author to cement the working relationship; successful contributors graduated from afternoon tea to lunch, dinner, and ultimately an invitation to Dundee to be shown around headquarters. By the late 1950s Woan was receiving Christmas gifts from the company.) Some circle members also wrote formula romances in book form. Lilian Chisholm of the Bromley Writer Circle, for example, began writing for Mills & Boon during the Second World War. The formulas of "light" women's fiction tended to be very socially conservative: ironically, women like Chisholm and Woan struck out and established themselves as authors by writing for publications that were leery of such independence and creativity in women. "Magazine fiction," Lees advised in 1955, needed heroines with whom readers could sympathize; "editors did not like heroines to be writers, or artists, or successful business women, as they consider these types to be unsympathetic."[48]

There were also strictly masculine markets. Woan's Newcastle colleague Norman A. Lazenby wrote boys' fiction and adventure and "gangster" stories for serial publication in Britain or for the American pulp market. Pulp fiction paid a fairly poor rate per thousand words but in partial compensation the industry required a high volume of copy. Other circle members, both male and female, tried detective novels more British in their tone. Some attempted the kind of novel usually designated "middlebrow." Others who wrote for profit targeted Britain's immense trade and hobby press and a miscellany of other markets from greeting-card verse to cycling-tour guides to bedtime stories for Hull's independent telephone company. Not until after 1945, as circle records and the BBC archives make clear, did significant numbers of circle members begin to have their work broadcast; when they did, BBC staff had to start addressing writers' circles as part of their strategy for dealing with the flood of unsolicited manuscripts they received.[49]

Their endorsement of writing to the perceived demands of the market helped mark the writers' circles off from other cultural and leisure associations in their towns. It also made them very different from a smaller movement of writers, the "amateur journalism" movement, which was eventually eclipsed by the writers' circles. The movement's central institutional vehicle was the British Amateur Literary Association (BALA), originally called the British Amateur Press Association—a network of publications, newsletters, and manuscript folios rather than a chain of writers' groups.[50] The "amateur journalism" movement—here, too, "journalism" meant much more than news and topical nonfiction—was primarily an American phenomenon. American teenagers, taking advantage of the new, inexpensive printing presses available from the late 1860s, produced their own little magazines of poetry, essays, and topical items. The extent of the movement was extraordinary, and among the famous people who had amateur journalism in their past are Horatio Alger and Thomas Edison. Edison, who in his teens had a job selling fruit, candy, and magazines to railway passengers, bought a small press and ran it on the train while he worked. Amateur journalism was primarily a youth movement: veterans such as the science fiction writer H. P. Lovecraft, though prominent, do not appear to have dominated conferences or the National Amateur Press Association. American amateur journalism, which remained strong as a movement well into the twentieth century, was resolutely "amateur" in the lofty sense of the word. Its adherents insisted on writing and publishing for love rather than money. Judging by the expense entailed by the conferences, and by the family names and subsequent careers of amateur journalists, there were probably several boys from old money for every one who sold candy on trains.[51]

The British Amateur Press Association was founded by two brothers from Manchester, one of whom had returned from an American trip inspired by amateur journalism. It brought together a weak Amateur Printers' and Publishers' Association and the "Amateur's Miscellany," a supplement to the *Boy's Pictorial.*

Thus in Britain too amateur journalism began as a boys' movement, though by the 1920s women were well represented in its ranks (albeit not in its highest office until 1943). British amateur journalism maintained ties with, and received some funding from, its American inspiration, but the two differed substantially.[52]

The central institution of British amateur journalism was not the printed magazine or newssheet but the "pass-round" magazine. These were folios of manuscript material and drawings, selected, laid out, and sometimes typed or retyped by editors who would send them to circulate among their "subscribers." Some pass-rounds were more interactive: contributors would submit a short story with blank comment sheets; each recipient would comment on the stories in the folio, add a story of her own, and pass the magazine on; by the time it got back to the first contributor, he would remove his story and the feedback on it, replace it with a new one he had written, and send the pass-round on its way back round the circuit.[53] Some writers' circles used this mechanism as a way of getting feedback without turning every meeting into a workshop night (or where not enough members were interested in a particular genre to form a subset of the circle dedicated to it).[54] People on a pass-round circuit, and most "amateur journalists" generally, interacted through correspondence and magazines rather than in face-to-face meetings. Only in the early 1920s was a local branch of the BALA founded, in Manchester, where the organization had begun. When promoters of the idea of a Scottish branch hired a hall for a meeting on the matter, not a single member turned up.[55]

This episode, and the many times when no volunteer could be found to take over an office or to succeed the editor of a magazine, prompted charges of apathy among the membership. Throughout the interwar period, the association struggled with a low membership—in 1923 there were 191 members in the British Isles, and the total crept down further—and with difficulties in filling their printed magazines and getting them out on time.[56] There are some indications that its fortunes later revived somewhat, and new amateur magazines appeared. Olive Teugels had edited *Our Own Mag.* and *International Amateur* in the 1930s and forties when she lived in Brighouse and Halifax (she never joined the Halifax Authors' Circle); from 1959 to 1964, after moving to London and becoming a landlady, she edited a duplicated monthly called *Bedsitter.* Aimed at those who "Live in Rooms . . . Let Rooms . . . Own or Manage Houses," *Bedsitter* contained short stories and poems set in seedy digs, practical articles about bedsit life (on decorating, vending machines, and so on), and recipes for meals that could be cooked on a single gas-burner.[57] It was not explicitly identified as a BALA publication, but the BALA advertised in it regularly. As late as 1969, a member of the West Country Writers' Association was casting about for a new editor for his long-running magazine *The Rambler,* a bulky pass-round of prose, poetry, and illustrations, accompanied by an exercise book for criticisms.[58]

Nevertheless, amateur journalism was in a comparatively weak state at a time when writers' circles were blossoming and an array of other magazines, some of them produced on small presses or duplicated, were tapping a viable readership of aspirant writers. One reason may have been the lack of face-to-face interaction, which was one of the appeals of writers' circles to writers who felt isolated. But the existence of the Manchester branch did not make aspirant writers in the area gravitate to it rather than to the Manchester Writer Circle. A more fundamental reason seems to be that, as the twentieth century went on, the idea of amateur journalism became less and less compelling. This is evident not only in the decline of the BALA but also in its qualified embrace of the market at the expense of purist amateurdom. Just what "amateur journalism" meant had become increasingly cloudy. The BALA was not as committed to the amateur principle as its American counterpart was. Indeed, the association dropped the "amateur" from its name and its flagship printed journal in 1931. Presumably the upper-class connotations of the word played some part, though in his explanation of the change Noel James, the editor of the journal, took a different tack. To his father, James wrote, "the amateur was the man who strove under glorious disadvantages and succeeded gloriously. To-day, in the minds of some, 'amateur' stands for dabbler, tinkerer, botcher." Five years earlier, the editor at the time, Lilian Crawford, had commented: "It cannot be denied that there are some in our ranks who have no wish to become professionals. They scribble away quite happily, and like to see their work in MS. magazines, but have no wish to go further." Deliberate amateurs, once the primary constituency for the association, had become a minority to be humored.[59]

Therefore, although the BALA's magazine—successively titled *Literary Amateur, Literary Aspirant,* and *Twelve Pages*—gave space every so often to the opinion that everyone must contribute to what the veteran amateur journalist Arthur du Soir called "the great Library of Humanity," and to the opinion that the association catered not only to those eager to succeed in the professional press but also to "those who merely wish to acquire some degree of proficiency in composition and to indulge in writing essays, articles and verses as a mental exercise and intellectual hobby," it also published material that would not have been out of place in *Writer's Monthly* or the *Writer,* to which it referred favorably several times. It gave advice about writing "saleable stuff" and offered suggestions about "markets." In 1929 the association offered a twenty-six-week correspondence course whose terminal point was supposed to be "a salable short story." It also published notices of members' publishing successes. These reports indicate that amateur journalism's rank and file, as well as those who contributed to the magazine, had drifted away from the movement's prior position on commercial publication. Members who joined after anti-commercial sentiments had dimmed do not seem to have regarded membership of an "amateur" association as incompatible with professional aspirations or institutions supportive thereof. Thus R. M. Lester and Hugh Stephens, leading lights of the London Writer Circle in the 1930s and 1940s, belonged to the BALA; Lester was one of the valiant few who kept trying to establish a stable London branch.[60]

Similar, apparently untroubling, combinations of "amateurism" and professional aspirations could be found outside the BALA. The Quill Club was a "co-operative organisation" for "the unfledged author and literary student," in which the BALA's Noel James was active. One of the Quill Club's poets was Christabel Lowndes-Yates, whom we have already encountered as a pupil of Pemberton's and a member of the London Writer Circle, where by 1924 she was regarded as an expert on markets to which to submit manuscripts. The author of a sonnet about a "sun-wrapt valley" in the Quill Club's 1921 anthology was none other than Enid Blyton, destined to be a commercial success *par excellence*, her books fixtures in an extraordinary number of children's lives. At this time she was an aspiring author submitting poems to noncommercial organs such as *Poetry Review* as well as romantic stories to *Home Weekly* and short stories to *The Bystander*.[61]

There was, then, no longer anything very distinctive about the mission of organized amateur journalism. One of its exponents remarked in 1925: "In these days of Writer Circles . . . etc., we are not alone in our pursuits, we but differ in our methods, our fees are much lower, and we offer all but one item . . . We cannot organise lectures by leading critics or journalists because of the great distances which separate our members, but I have still to be convinced that this is a serious handicap. Personally I have learned little from the many papers I have read and heard read on 'How to be successful with the Pen.'"[62] He clearly underestimated the appeal of those lectures: the promise that the mysteries of how to be successful with the pen could be revealed was alluring enough to sustain an industry. But the fact that amateur journalists were now "not alone in our pursuits" begged the question of what particular good *their* association and magazines served. The standard answer was that writing for amateur magazines, both printed and pass-round, was good training, and that since neither took copyright, one could still submit a story or poem to a commercial publication after getting feedback on the version appearing in the amateur magazine. Writers were even advised to submit to amateur magazines pieces that had been rejected by paying organs, as a means of boosting confidence.[63] The BALA appeared to be an organization of last resort at a time when correspondence schools and guidebooks presented the quasi-professional study of craft and markets as central to a writer's apprenticeship. As the BALA stagnated, the writers' circles grew. Unlike the BALA, they presented themselves as "amateur" only in the sense of not having succeeded *yet*. Even if they were sometimes uncomfortably competitive for some members, writers' circles created a forum for aspirant writers who needed company, either because of continued rejection or because of unsympathetic family or friends. The BALA member who opined that his organization's lack of meetings and lectures was not a serious handicap failed to see just how attractive the prospect of a meeting was for amateur writers: regardless of whether they would hear an interesting speaker, or any speaker, they would be in the company of like-minded optimists and aspirants.

Still, corresponding societies could effectively provide fellowship and criticism. The Peverel Society illustrates the point well. This was the group founded by Flora Thompson that was mentioned briefly at the beginning of this book. Thompson, who left school at fourteen and spent her working life in rural post offices, began to write while bringing up her three children. She entered and won literary essay competitions in the *Ladies' Companion*, and then began sending poems, short stories, and nature articles to it and other magazines. She also took a correspondence course in fiction writing that was graded by a *Daily News* journalist, A. Brodie Frazer. From 1920 Thompson was a frequent contributor to the *Catholic Fireside* (though she was an Anglican), publishing stories and then writing a regular column about the countryside. In 1923 she talked the *Fireside*'s editor into letting her run a literary page that would publish pieces by aspiring writers, submitted under pseudonyms and criticized by Thompson. Men and women—many of the women were nuns—seized the opportunity. At the end of 1925 Thompson brought the "Fireside Reading Circle" to an end and launched the Peverel Society, which combined correspondence-course instruction with the postal organization of amateur journalism and the direct exchanges of a writers' circle.[64]

The society offered members a six-lesson correspondence course in writing and marketing verse. Thompson also organized members, who at one point numbered nearly one hundred, into groups served by portfolios circulating by mail. These portfolios had much in common with amateur journalism and the "circulating clubs" of the early London Writer Circle. The portfolio of a subgroup or "circle" "circulates by post from one member to another until the whole Circle has read, and each member commented in writing upon each of the entries." In addition, each portfolio was accompanied by a "chat book" in which "topics of literary and general interest are discussed, questions asked and answered, valuable information as to markets exchanged." Through Thompson's tuition work and the chat books, the Peverel Society's members established "many interesting literary friendships," as the prospectus put it.[65]

Thompson herself benefited from the friendships and networks the society fostered. Writing was not something she shared with her family and neighbors. She kept her writing secret from the villagers who often served as informants for her countryside articles and later her books. Her husband "did not entirely approve" of her writing, at least in part because he wanted his wife to live privately and modestly. Two of her short stories from the 1920s and 1930s are about middle-aged women with artistic talents, one in writing and the other in painting. Each woman, having subordinated her creative desires to domestic obligations, attempts to realize them anew later in life, only to be denied the opportunity.[66] Her warm and lively correspondence with Peverel Society members clearly gave Thompson a much-needed chance to talk shop and communicate with kindred spirits.

Thompson gave advice and encouragement about writing and publishing, and received some in return. Her letters also performed the writers' circle function of reporting others' "successes," in indiscreet detail. The news became personal as well, and Thompson's letters convey her sense that interactions through portfolios and chat books could be almost like spending time together in person: "Did you meet Myldrede Humble Smith in either of the portfolios? . . . I heard last week that Mary Burdett (was she not once a member of your portfolio?) has just had her first novel accepted." People who "met" in portfolios and through letters became close, and the society evolved into a circle of friends. "I often think about the old times when the Peverel Society was at its zeneth and wonder what has become of the old friends," Thompson told Anna Ball in 1941. She corresponded with Ball and her husband Arthur for well over a decade without meeting them in person. She encouraged Arthur in his unsuccessful struggles to get his novels published, and tried to talk Anna into continuing with her own "delicate" sketches of character and place: "You must not give yourself wholly to furthering Arthur's career, but carry on your own, side by side with his."[67]

Thompson's writing career was in a protracted state of apprenticeship even as she mentored other would-be writers. By the late 1920s she had been a published author for two decades, but with the exception of a short book of nature poems, her output had all been magazine stories and articles. Her ambition was to write a full-length book. Thompson's prewar stories had dealt with a countryside inhabited by farmers, craftsmen, and "gypsies"; she did not start writing in earnest about the rural poor, the work for which she is remembered, until the mid-1930s, when she resurrected a story about a poor mother that she had written while taking the correspondence course some fifteen years earlier. The fairly upscale magazine *The Lady* published it in December 1936. "In the 1930s," according to Thompson's biographer, "it was a small revelation to Flora to discover that there was a market for stories of poverty." She began to work on material based on her childhood in Juniper Hill that she would rework a few years later in *Lark Rise*.[68]

The freelance writing she did before this time is typical of that of writers' circle members. There were historical anecdotes for newspapers and magazines introduced by a reference to an often tenuous contemporary parallel. One of her short stories is a tragic rich-and-poor romance set in Mayfair. The protagonist is one of those types Margaret Lees later pronounced "unsympathetic": a female writer. "All the winter she had supported herself meagrely with her pen, a trifling paragraph placed here and there—a dozen rejected; a guinea now and again for some sugared love-tale—her best work returned to her apparently unread." The heroine meets a rich man, whose yellow satin dressing gown and other accoutrements of metropolitan wealth Thompson surely derived from books and magazines. He takes the writer in and she "[gives] up her body to him." He overcomes his "middle-class prejudice" and resolves to marry her. Then the writer finds that she has won a novel-writing competition, and receives a check for £400. This, she decides, is real money; the money he has given her is a whore's fee. In shame she jumps from her garret window to her death.[69]

It is not clear whether Thompson regarded stories like this as fulfilling, or whether she had really wanted to write something along the lines of *Lark Rise* all along but had settled for commercial fiction. Whatever the case, before the mid-1930s at least, there was not necessarily any incompatibility between the Flora Thompson who wrote fey poetry and the Flora Thompson who wrote magazine fiction and freelance articles—the payment for which was very welcome in the Thompson house, despite her husband's attitude to her writing.[70] The idea of writing for money was not unproblematic for every aspirant, and there was often a belligerently defensive tone to writers' circle speakers' declarations of their interest in writing "saleable fiction," even though they were preaching to the choir. Yet it would be misleading to suggest that the emergence of writers' clubs and a support industry for freelance fiction-writers entailed a confrontation with a highly charged opposition between art and money. In *Fame and Fiction* and *The Truth about an Author*, Arnold Bennett had attacked the mythology of literary art for art's sake, but the myth was not so sacred or monumental as to have deterred Samuel Smiles in *Self-Help* several decades earlier from presenting no less than Shakespeare as a man of "practical qualities" who "prospered in his business, and realized sufficient to enable him to retire upon a competency."[71] The idea of the artist unconcerned with money was both a myth to be repeatedly debunked and an idea never quite as strong as its debunkers feared (or boasted).

The figure of the unsuccessful writer who blamed his or her failure on an unsophisticated public was regularly scorned by relentlessly practical advice-givers. The objects of the frustrations vented in writers' circles or letters to the *Writer* were usually not members of an amorphous public but editors or better-connected freelances.[72] Aspiring writers seldom discussed "the market" as a system, thinking instead almost exclusively in personal terms. Magazines and writers' circle minute books were stuffed with information about "market study," but it was almost always in terms of a particular publication or handful of publications and the proclivities of the editors in question. Even the reading public was often collapsed into the figure of the editor; only rarely was a difference of interests posited between the distant readership and the editorial gatekeeper.[73] Failure was a result of one's own inadequacies or other individuals' decisions or actions. A few players might be bad, but the legitimacy of the game was not compromised.

The accommodation between creativity and the market helps make sense of what, apart from pocket money or a second income if one was really successful, freelance writing gave the people who joined writers' circles. In one sense, it was a form of self-improvement. The writers' circles had clear organizational affinities with mutual improvement societies, and in their mission statements they echoed the vocabulary of classical self-improvement institutions ("to offer mutual assistance . . . to the coming free-lance writer"). But their sort of improvement was about training in a craft, about learning to meet the market's demands. They were, on the whole, more concerned with worldly success than with self-culture, and their idea of worldly success was different from that held by others for whom self-development and self-presentation were (inevitably) intertwined. Their ambitions were different, for example, from those of Leonard Bast, E. M. Forster's icon of lower middle-class cultural aspiration. Socially the writers' circles were at once more ambitious than Bast, since they valued celebrity rather than a socially emollient cultural literacy, and less so: few of their members were writing for periodicals or publishers whose dividends were more in cultural capital than money. The Halifax Authors' Circle had a disproportionate number of members who earned a living from their writing, but only Phyllis Bentley, with her nationally recognized "regional novels," and not Margaret Lees or John Marsh, both of whom at times turned out a thriller or romance novel every month, had the cachet to become a fixture at civic functions and on local committees. Frequent publication did not of itself make one a member of the local Great and Good.[74]

Yet aspirants' acceptance of the market, their general faith in the reading public and in editors' capacity to represent that public, meant that if publication brought little in the way of cultural prestige, it was still a kind of social validation. Saleable writing was creative work that someone else thought valuable. To the women whose husbands were ambivalent about or dismissive of their writing, an offer of publication would have been an acceptance in more than one sense of the word. That the payment for a piece of work might, for some, serve as a public justification for writing rather than a sovereign motive for it is hinted at by some of the pitches correspondence schools made to aspirants, as when the A.B.C. school suggested how satisfying it would be to confound one's "sceptical relatives." For some aspirants, one suspects, the financial rewards were in part a cover for the personal ones, the practical payoffs a justification, conscious or not, for what might otherwise seem "unpractical," possibly embarrassing desires.[75]

There is a parallel with the social research movement Mass-

Observation and the left-leaning magazine *Picture Post.* In the 1970s the Birmingham cultural studies group concluded that the liberal middle and lower-middle classes flocked to Mass-Observation and *Picture Post* because they lived in a society that fostered their cultural and political aspirations without, before this point, providing institutions through which those aspirations could be articulated. In replies to a questionnaire about reasons for joining Mass-Observation, members described themselves as special in some way, but lacking a proper channel or forum for their specialness, and wanting a social order more consonant with their values and goals. While many people recognized the cachet of writing in Britain, it was another thing to enter the elect group of successful authors. Writers' clubs and advisory services offered a seductive path to that goal, but like the Mass-Observers who seized on diary-keeping and eavesdropping as a focus for their imagination or an education in popular psychology, many people must have found writers' circles less than a perfect fit. Those members who aspired to write for "little magazines" rather than the evening papers must have gained little critical stimulation from all the discussions of the periodical market and the craft of light fiction. Yet they clearly derived some support and fellowship from their writers' groups. To style oneself as a writer could seem self-important, something personally reprehensible as well as publicly ridiculous. The writers' circles created a space in which respectable, unostentatious people could pursue creative ambitions, and fashion themselves as creative, special people, without renouncing their normal lives.[76]

The writers' circles were for middle- and lower-middle-class people who believed they were creative but who were not dissatisfied with the cultural mainstream. Others from comparable backgrounds who were not so at home in that mainstream found different avenues for their cultural aspirations: Mass-Observation or the Left Book Club, for instance, or London's bohemia or its provincial counterparts.[77] Those more general social discontents seem largely absent from the writers' circle population—circle members hardly ever talked about politics, and they did not spurn the prevailing system's representatives in the sphere of publishing. And the role of the embattled artist was, if not fully absent from the circles, certainly discouraged in such "practical" organizations. A writers' circle would have been no place for the reader of *A Room of One's Own* who wrote to Virginia Woolf describing herself as "A woman . . . who has *not* 'got there'—who has struggled for years with that desire for expression, & has met with no success;—a short novel, written to please neither publisher, nor public, but merely to express an ideal which burnt to be expressed, & needless to say met with but scanty notice . . ."[78] Such people remained in their garrets or in bohemian cliques, not in the church halls and municipal buildings where writers' circles assembled and where—in the open, at least—there was nothing fundamentally wrong with the ideals of publisher or public.

Chapter 3

Fiction and the Writing Public

Writers like the woman who told Virginia Woolf that she had "struggled for years with that desire for expression, & . . . met with no success" pose serious problems for the historian. Because they did not join writers' groups, they leave little record of their literary activities. Publishers' archives offer a tantalizing glimpse—but only that—into their productions. That glimpse is refracted through the jaded eyes of the readers charged with assessing unsolicited manuscripts. Judging by readers' reports undertaken for Allen and Unwin and Wishart & Co., many people working beyond the influence of the literary advice business wrote "to express an ideal which burnt to be expressed": an intriguing number of utopian political novels arrived unannounced. Topics such as the revitalizing of British Christianity, the resolution of Ireland's troubles, and land nationalization were given fictional treatment by writers who, in the judgment of one reader, did not "know the difference between a novel and a political wish-fantasy." Other submissions, as unsympathetically described in readers' reports, tempt the judgment that they were therapeutic autobiographical fictions and exercises in wish-fulfillment. Flora Thompson was not the only aspiring author to write about gifted writers, artists, and musicians.[1]

Other novels that unknowns sent to Allen and Unwin were attempts at some of the genres of bestselling fiction: family melodramas, crime stories, and medieval romances. The firm's readers remarked on the popularity of governesses as heroines in these manuscripts, a vogue established by Ethel M. Dell's romances. Some authors mimicked Elinor Glyn's novels of luxury and sex. The violent eroticism pioneered by E. M. Hull's *The Sheik* also made its mark in novices' efforts ("there really *is* a bit too much pseudo-Freudian emphasis on bestiality—on rapes & beatings"). Some of these would-be authors appeared to be consciously trying to master the formulas that had proved so successful for Dell, Hull, and Glynn; one reader resorted to the mechanical analogy beloved by intellectuals worried by mass culture, complaining of "machine-made sensationalism." Another reader detected the influence of the literary advice industry in one manuscript: "Responding doubtless to what I may term 'Correspondence School formulas' ('Young aspirant, ALWAYS have a LOVE INTEREST in your novels!') the author has added a subsidiary theme, which certainly helps a little in integrating the whole, but otherwise remains less felicitous and rather perfunctory."[2]

Those "Correspondence School formulas" were one contributor to the conventional wisdom about writing fiction, along with the advice that aspiring writers gave one another and the counsel they received from speakers, textbooks, and articles. As I trace aspirants' understanding of and approaches to popular fiction, my primary reference point is not the novel but the short story, the principal genre of novice writers. The respectability of writers' circles and the advice business means that my account has little to say about violent or sexually charged subjects unfit for discussion in "mixed" company: would-be disciples of E. M. Hull had to work out her secrets for themselves.

"Write about what you know" was the guiding principle of many an aspirant writer. The idea is a cliché now, but in the interwar period it was a point that many people judged worth making, especially when addressing would-be writers who had not led particularly colorful lives. And, as with so many clichés, its bland obviousness obscures as much as it broadcasts. Implicit in that cliché is a general theory about writing and its relationship to other parts of life, a theory that reworked the discourse of English literary history within the context of commercial fiction.

Writers' circle members seeking publication in commercial periodicals tended to think of their work as "fiction" rather than "literature." The distinction between the two categories was established well before Q. D. Leavis pointedly used the former term to denote popular and undistinguished texts in her 1932 book *Fiction and the Reading Public.* The advice in textbooks, correspondence courses, and the like was principally directed at people aspiring to write "fiction." Literature required genius, which one either had or did not have; fiction demanded *craft,* which could be learned. "Fiction" was not created to last through the ages, or to push the limits of convention, but to entertain "ordinary" readers.[3]

In this respect, writers of what was often called the "commercial short story" shared an opinion prevalent in other quarters about the motives behind the reading of popular fiction. Cultural critics of the time remarked frequently that the majority of the population read not for self-cultivation but for "escapism." (The *Oxford English Dictionary* dates the emergence of the term "escapism" to 1933.) Both Q. D. and F. R. Leavis propounded the notion that mass-produced reading matter was a dangerous drug: it inhibited readers from connecting with genuine existence, and it spoiled them for real literature. The older Fabian Sidney Dark concurred, remarking in 1922: "Reading is regarded by a large number of persons as a mere narcotic, something calculated to make one forget. Books that are nothing but narcotics are, in the long run, as destructive of real life and real living as cocaine."[4] The terms of the critique are fundamentally romantic: true literature is faithful to reality, resisting convention and fancy, and among the threats to such a literature (and such a moral life) are the seductions of mass-produced writing.

Ironically, these severe conclusions coincide substantially with ordinary readers' explanations of why they read. Joseph McAleer, who examined working- and lower-middle-class reading habits from 1914 to 1950, found that escapism was the key motive for reading. Readers were frank about their desire for a temporary escape from their workaday lives. In the early 1950s a housewife in Tottenham, in London, told Mass-Observation: "I like love-books and murders and happy endings. What seldom happens in real life. It's nice to get away from things." Some readers even echoed the critics' analogy between escapist reading and narcotics, though understandably with more enthusiasm for intoxication. A Scottish postman told a Mass-Observer in 1944: "As the Cockney said: 'Getting drunk is the nearest way out of London,' so reading is the quickest way out of Glasgow."[5]

This lesson was repeatedly impressed upon the writers' circle members and other freelances writing for a mass readership. "Men and women do not want to read stories that reflect their own daily life," instructed the correspondence school impresario Louise Heilgers in 1920. "They want to be taken out of themselves and to transplant their minds to scenes and places over which there is still for them the glamour of romance." Writers' circles absorbed the lesson. The premise that one's fiction should serve as a diversion did not necessarily entail an assumption that the imagined reader was only basically educated. It could also reflect a sense of the situations in which one's work would be read—at home, in a canteen, while commuting. Thus Kennedy Williamson of the *Writer* encouraged prospective authors of magazine stories to think about whether their work could be read under various conditions: "Are the sentences consistently short so that the stories could be read by a straphanger, or are they complex and meant to be read in an armchair, or is there a variety in the length of the sentences?"[6]

There was an implicit but clear cultural conservatism in advising aspirants to write to entertain others rather than, say, "to express an ideal which burnt to be expressed." Sometimes the politics of the emphasis on entertainment were brought into the open. When a miner's wife wrote about coal mining for a correspondence course assignment, she received a furious response from her instructor:

> Miners are not the only men who have a hard time [during the Second World War] . . . How about the many retired folks on a tiny pension or allowance, whose previous £2 or £3 have been reduced by *half* by the income tax? . . . Instead of writing propaganda for Socialist newspapers you will do better to describe—for the housewives—what life is like in a mining village . . . Many of your readers will be people who are not in the least inclined to regard employers as slave drivers and capitalist villains of society . . . Write simply and naturally . . . Remember that your task is to *entertain*. No reader will bother after a hard day's work to read a list of somebody else's woes. Keep a strict eye on your inclination to write about the "wrongs" of mining. There are *millions* of people who will not forget that miners *did* strike while our sons and husbands were fighting the Germans . . . I advise you against writing very controversial things.

This is a vintage document of interwar conservatism (that it was written in 1944, remarked George Orwell, to whom the correspondence student forwarded it, demonstrated the "weed-like vitality of pre-war habits of mind"). It displays a virulent hostility to the organized working class. Miners are worthy Britons only when they are battling on apolitically: "So forget your grievances, and tell us something of how *you* manage in a typical mining village." At the same time, and most significantly where writing is concerned, this is very much the conservatism of Stanley Baldwin: a conservatism that denies it is political. Only proponents of reform were "political." The belief that the purpose of writing for a popular audience was to provide anodyne and "uncontroversial" entertainment harmonized with the middle-class social conventions about not "talking politics" and avoiding conflict that prevailed in many clubs and societies in the interwar period, including writers' circles.[7]

To provide an escape, popular fiction had to cater to a demand for novelty and keep up with fashion. Margaret Lees told her fellows in the Halifax Authors' Circle: "Fashions change in story writing as well as dress, and to sell stories it is essential to keep abreast of, or just in front of the times." Fashions in subject matter as well as narrative form were hard to follow, though the *Writer* and writers' circles always provided a platform for confident statements about what was in vogue at a given moment, sometimes with surprising specificity. Reporting on current editorial desires in the Thomson-Leng syndicate in 1959, Elizabeth Woan told the Newcastle Writers' Club: "The present trend seems to be for stories of working-class people, preferably shipyard workers."[8]

While popular and editorial tastes could seem capricious, experts thought they discerned a general trend toward a less extravagant escapism. The glamorous or dangerous living depicted in movies and in Glyn's books or P. C. Wren's stories of the French Foreign Legion was eminently marketable; but in other sectors of the market, including the ones that writers' groups discussed most, fantasy was tempered somewhat. Mills & Boon's romantic fiction embraced more "realistic" settings and plots, and magazine stories of "Earl and Girl" matches fell out of favor. In the 1920s a number of story papers for young women placed a greater emphasis on "ordinary" mill-town settings, and on heroines not socially dissimilar to their readers.[9]

Aspiring authors were frequently told to aim for a moderate escapism, neither wholesale fantasy nor unremitting naturalism. Beginners, Margaret Olney asserted in *Popular Writing* in 1930, often write wild, imaginative stuff; after some rejections, they swing to the other extreme and write "about the very ordinary and commonplace happenings of everyday life. Thinking that if they tell the truth and nothing but the truth, success will surely be theirs. But the same thing [rejection] happens . . . The reason is that the writer must learn the secret of imparting on paper life, as it is, but with just that touch of idealism to lift it out of the rut of the commonplace." The premise of this counsel was that "ordinary" protagonists and settings made fiction more satisfying by enabling readers to "identify with" the characters, whether directly or indirectly.[10] Though the terminology was Freudian—according to the *OED*, this sense of the expression "identify with" entered the language with the 1913 translation of *The Interpretation of Dreams*—the idea predated psychoanalysis. The idea of "escapism" entailed the belief that readers wanted to project themselves into the story, to feel that it could have happened to them.[11] Kennedy Williamson explained the "small demand for historical stories" by saying that "the present-day reader . . . finds it difficult to obtain a point of contact with these obsolete dramas and forgotten problems . . . the vast majority like to read of exciting and dramatic experiences which might conceivably—just conceivably—happen to them also . . . [M]uch of the pleasure in fiction-reading lies in self-identification with the central characters. Such self-identification is not possible if the situation is fantastically unlike anything with which the reader is familiar." Williamson advised the author of "a story for mill-girls" to put her heroine in a situation similar to her readers' lives, but added: "Admittedly, the situation in the story ought not to remain so drab and colourless as the daily life of this reader probably is. She will like her fiction 'taken out of herself'. She will like to be taken to luxurious night-clubs, and to other exotic scenes which are the antipodes of her workaday routine. Nevertheless, if she is to be taken on these voyages of the imagination, the boat must first be brought *alongside her own quay*."[12]

The validity of this argument about identification and escapism is open to question. Can it account, for instance, for the working-class boys who played at being public school chums like those in Frank Richards's Billy Bunter tales but who teased actual Eton and Harrow boys when they saw them in the street?[13] The persuasiveness of the identification argument is not my concern here, however: for the present purpose, what matters is that many teachers of writing technique believed it, and that the principle that familiarity aided identification helped license the idea that "ordinary" people could become writers.

That readers might be interested in stories without a high quotient of earls, sheiks, and fiendishly inventive ways of committing murder must have been of some relief to the provincial and suburban men and women who populated the writers' circles. Don't be discouraged if you lack strange things to write about, Wilfred Hardie counseled in the *Writer* in 1925: people like to read "even of the humblest domestic details simply because they know all about them." Hardie cited the description of the bath in Arnold Bennett's *The Great Man*. The material Bennett had at his disposal was available to all. "It is scarcely too much to say that a writer will be read widely according to his capacity to reflect the everyday experiences of his readers." Others modified this advice to make it more consonant with the writing of short, "snappy" fiction for the periodical market: E. Haworth commented in the *Writer* that aspirant fiction writers were told that they needed to change only a single element of a commonplace situation to make it exciting. Haworth's point is a variation on Margaret Olney's theme that the commonplace required a little something extra to become suitable for fiction.[14]

Writing from "first-hand knowledge" was very important. The detective novelist and former police officer Maurice Procter went so far as to break with the shibboleth that the essential mark of a writer was "a burning urge to write," telling other members of the Halifax Authors' Circle: "The first qualification for a writer . . . was not talent, or even an ability to write well, but having something to write about, knowing his subject." Writers could regard experiences as literary windfalls. A meeting of the Newcastle Writer Circle in 1944 "was held up for some little time by everyone doing their best to persuade Mr Tulip, who has personal experience of the Pacific Islands[,] that his opportunity had arrived, if he would only grasp it. Fiction written with such a background would be really saleable." By 1947 Tulip was writing a novel set in the Pacific Islands.[15]

Most amateur writers, though, had to focus on the "normal" events "which constitute the daily bread of life and are inherently dramatic and moving—to other people." Writers' circles, textbooks, and writing magazines paid considerable attention to the subject of finding "material" for fiction in one's daily life. The Louise Heilgers correspondence course promised to reveal "How to turn every hour of your life into Copy." Stories, one commentator claimed, were "everywhere about you as you go about your daily round. Plots will meet you on the bus, will come and sit by you in the train or the tube, will look at you out of the eyes of the girl or man who shares your table in the coffee shop." Women who found writing more difficult after marriage were urged to shift their focus to domestic matters: "Your character studies of office types, of people in restaurants, no longer ring true; write about your neighbours, sketches of tradespeople . . ." Observation was a faculty would-be writers were encouraged to cultivate. Some of Mass-Observation's early recruits joined in part because they felt that the work would help them sharpen the powers of observation they needed for imaginative writing. A single, thirty-three-year-old female teacher from North Devon gave this reason for becoming a Mass-Observer: "I like writing but have not a creative enough mind to find satisfactory themes of my own & this seemed to provide me with plenty of material." Asked why she joined, a twenty-two-year-old "civil servant" from Croydon replied: "Perhaps it was because I'm 'literary-minded' and thought I might get some practice in writing."[16]

In addition to scrutinizing their "daily round" and eavesdropping on conversations on public transport, some novice writers advocated going out of one's way to gather "material" for fiction. Margaret Lees, a romance novelist and serial writer, told fellow members of the Halifax Authors' Circle "how she searched for stories, by going to see people at their jobs." The commercial-traveler-cum-journalist Herbert John's routine was to write from seven in the evening until nine, then go out and talk to people. "Standing refreshment and being a good listener makes all the difference to obtaining copy," he observed. "I encouraged a post office savings bank girl to talk to me the other day, and the . . . lass laughingly obliged me with details concerning people who save and people who don't." Writing in the 1920s, John had anticipated the third of Cecil Hunt's "Ten Commandments for Writers," which were widely disseminated among writers' groups in the late 1940s and 1950s: "Live more and write less." Hunt, by this time one of the deans of the literary advice industry, elaborated: "Try everything once . . . Get into contact with people in other walks of life. Get away from 'respectable' people."[17]

In this vein, several freelances claimed in the *Writer* to have gone slumming or taken more arduous day jobs to get in closer contact with "real" life and the "vital material" it yielded. A less severe way for members of writers' circles to get new material was to invite nonwriters to speak about their line of work. Lawyers and police officers were especially welcome; the Southampton and Leeds circles were even taken on tours of police stations. There was "rather a heated argument" in the Newcastle Writers' Club in 1949 when certain members discovered that a forthcoming speaker would be a prison chaplain. What the secretary deemed "worth remembering" from the chaplain's talk was "useful information" concerning criminal motives, prison, and rehabilitation: "material" that could be used in stories about crime.[18]

Getting material in this way contravened the principle that one should write about matters of which one had first-hand knowledge. Amateur writers typically allowed some leeway for research. They were firm believers in the value of maintaining files of newspaper clippings as well as commonplace books as sources of material. The minority who courted markets of unreconstructed escapism appeared to feel no more obligation to get their material first-hand than their editors did to publish naturalistic stories. Consequently, westerns could be written from Luton and "Wild Western, Gangster, [and] Science [fiction] stories" from Newcastle. Norman A. Lazenby, the Newcastle Writers' Club's specialist in that trio of genres, advised those interested in writing for the American pulp market or—with the freeing up of paper supply at the beginning of the 1950s—for a reinvigorated British market for non-Penguin paperbacks, that they could compensate for their ignorance of crime, the Wild West, or Los Angeles with a month of intensive reading on their chosen subject. In such fiction, Lazenby told his writers' circle, "*Background* must be authentic or at least sound so."[19]

Reading could yield plots as well as background, of course.

Writers were encouraged to poach plot lines from existing stories, especially the safely uncopyrighted Bible and fairy tales.[20] If one took an existing plot and mechanically changed some key details, the result would be a new story rather than a near-copy of the original. Kennedy Williamson suggested in his book on magazine stories that a good way of "finding new plots during a period when the creative faculty is in the doldrums" was to "select a well-known short story and invert some important particular of it. In most cases a new plot will ultimately emerge." The trick should only be tried with well-known stories, so that the new work would seem allusive rather than plagiarized. One of Williamson's examples was a story by A. Macalpine Blair, published in the *Royal Magazine,* which took as its starting point Stacy Aumonier's "Miss Bracegirdle Does Her Duty," a "classic" frequently recommended to amateurs for study. In the original, the "exceedingly spinsterish" sister of an English dean is staying by herself in a French hotel, and through a string of mishaps ends up spending the night in the room of a man she discovers to be dead and who is later revealed as a notorious murderer. Blair reworked the plot by switching the sexes of the characters, turning Miss Bracegirdle into a clergyman. "Clearly," Williamson commented, "up to this point the new story is keeping fairly parallel to the original, but the author . . . now devise[s] a delicious departure from it by making the lady [in whose room the clergyman is caught] prove in the morning to be the clergyman's own wife": a religious convention is taking place, and she has arrived unexpectedly early to meet him. Though obviously derivative, Blair's work was a story in its own right: the variations made with significant details made possible a new type of scenario.[21]

Williamson tended to suggest mechanical techniques as crutches for the imagination rather than as self-sufficient formulas. Margaret Hope, who was probably taught by him when she took a writing course run by the London County Council, felt that her practice as a writer changed when her tutor suggested a story about the return of a dead soldier. This, she wrote, was an *idea,* "not a mechanical 'plot.'" She thenceforth tried to begin with ideas, rather than devising plots by taking a news paragraph and imagining how things would have turned out had one condition been different, by writing a story out of someone else's sentence, by borrowing another plot and altering it, or by taking three words at random from a dictionary and trying to weave a plot out of them. These were all useful methods, Hope said; but when she wrote this way, "I could not feel a craftsman's pride in stories evolved on these lines. My stories were being fabricated, not created."[22]

Attempts at systematizing ways of thinking about plots were often accompanied by the sort of "mechanical" practices that Hope found unfulfilling. Invention is not imagination, John Rolf opined in the *Writer* in 1940: it is more about logic than about anything else; writers develop plots through a process of "cross-examination" of their material or premises. G. J. Matson recommended that writers look at a situation in a news article and fire "What if" questions at different parts of it. This would furnish "the IDEA. Follow the questions logically and a plot will soon develop." In practice, though, "invention" was never entirely a matter of logic. There is still some room for musing amid the interstices of cross-examination in this account of the plotting process by Cecil Hunt, who was far from a believer in free inspiration: "You will witness a moving little incident on a bus and your trained mind will say: 'But suppose he *hadn't* done that, or he had said *this* . . . ' The story begins to form in your mind." Even as Ray Dorien of the Croydon Writers' Circle emphasized logic, an attenuated version of what Keats called "negative capability" haunted her advice: "If you are logical, and think your way through a problem, letting your characters work out their own solution in a way which is personal to them, then your end, comic, tragic, or happy, is there."[23]

Even works that set out grand general formulas for devising stories had such limits. The most popular "formula" book in writers' circles seems to have been Francis Vivian's *Story-Weaving*. For Vivian, who was later the (honorary) president of the Nottingham Writers' Club, "Struggle, conflict, or contest *is* the story, so that we can define a short story as *the history of a fictitious conflict*." In the mid-1920s a member of the Halifax circle lamented that Aristotle's unities had been displaced as the master theory of narrative by a modern critical vocabulary of "struggle, suspense and climax." Writers' circle records suggest that this critical lexicon, with conflict (or struggle) as its master term, enjoyed wide currency. According to *Story-Weaving*, the conflict that structured a short story had six mandatory elements: "a problem, an obstacle to [the solution of] the problem, a complication or complications (depending on the length of the story), a predicament, a crisis, [and] a climax." (A denouement was optional.) The all-important "conflict" arises from the protagonist's struggle to resolve the "problem," which becomes compounded (in the "complication") through his or her initial effort to remove the "obstacle" to the problem's solution.[24]

Vivian claimed that "all students . . . even if using different terms, agree that the formula for a short story should contain these ingredients." This claim is overblown, but Vivian's grammar of fiction was consonant with those of other coaches of aspirant writers. Martin Walter's "plot formula," which users were supposed to carry around on a card, presented three stages within a story: a situation of conflict, an aborted solution of the conflict, and a genuine solution. Like Vivian's, Walter's ultimate predicament or crisis arises out of the complicating effects of the protagonist's initial attempt to solve the problem. Gerard Bell echoed these precepts at the Newcastle Writers' Club in 1954.[25]

Though these formulas were well advertised, and rehearsed in the pages of writing magazines and writers' circles, they were not quite the engine of fictional standardization that Q. D. Leavis feared.[26] There were two brakes on the influence of plot formulas on the practice of freelance writing (as distinct from the subset of freelance stories that were published). The first relates to plot and the second to character.

Where plot was concerned, the limitation of formulas was that they failed to reveal how to end a story satisfactorily. Walter instructed writers: "Choose that solution which is the most logical and the least obvious, this preferably to extricate completely the main character." Vivian blithely said of the resolution stage: "The way in which it is done is merely a matter of invention, and here the possibilities are many." Vivian's failure to elaborate lessened the usefulness of his book, because a good ending was regarded as the capstone of an entertaining, diverting plot. Anticlimax was to be avoided at all costs. Aspirant writers, especially those attempting romantic stories for women, were firmly warned to avoid unhappy endings. Yet to be satisfying a story required an unexpected ending. Everyone knows a love story will end happily, wrote C. Clifford Howard, the director and possibly the entire staff of a Birmingham correspondence school for writers: "but by good craftsmanship you, as the author, have to make readers think: 'I don't know, though?—Perhaps Sir Herbert will . . . leaving George . . . and, therefore . . .? I wonder if that's it?' And the reader reads on all the time more certain that HIS idea is correct. The climax comes; those very few lines when you are at the top of your dramatic rhythm. The reader DOES NOT KNOW WHAT WILL HAPPEN and then, in a few lines you put him at rest and, with a darn good ending, you finish."[27]

An unusual setting or "problem" gave a story some editorially appreciated novelty, but the surprise ending was the philosopher's stone of the magazine story. "The surprise ending," an anonymous contributor declared in the *Writer* in 1921, "is so much in demand now that it has come even by successful authors to be looked upon more or less as a trick of the trade."[28] Thus, as well as peddling the familiar, the popular short story also dealt in structured unpredictability. Twists had to be plausible; they were most satisfying when readers could feel in retrospect that they should have seen them coming. Stories with twists mimicked the patterning of jokes. In humorous stories, the twist was, in effect, a punch line. In dramatic stories, the ending was not funny, but the story was structured around the twist, with the foundations laid earlier in the story, in a manner analogous to a joke's.

The desirability of a twist at the end of a story was so impressed upon aspirant writers that they regularly asked whether, as they planned their stories, they should come up with an outline of the whole plot, or start with a climax and work backward from there.[29] Advisors cited a number of writers as exemplars, including Poe, Rudyard Kipling, W. W. Jacobs, Stacy Aumonier, and W. Somerset Maugham. The most persistently recommended authors, however, and the models for stories with twists at the end, were those avatars of the commercial short story, Guy de Maupassant and O. Henry. In the latter's most famous work, "The Gifts of the Magi," a husband sells his precious watch to buy combs for his wife's hair as a Christmas gift; at the same time she sells her hair to a wigmaker to buy a chain for his watch. In Maupassant's "The Necklace" a vain petite bourgeoise loses a rich friend's necklace she has borrowed to wear to a ball, and paying for a replacement wears her down into poverty and coarseness. At the end of the story she finds out that the original necklace was made of paste.

The records of writers' circles make it clear that they frequently referred to the work of Maupassant and O. Henry to illustrate points of technique.[30] Some aspirants' stories were firmly in the O. Henry mold, as in this plot that a publisher's reader judged to be "of a kind that is used in popular fiction": "A middle-aged lady becomes engaged by correspondence with a lonely solider, and dreads their meeting for he thinks her beautiful, but happily when they do meet he has been blinded." Maupassant's supporters seem to have been more enthusiastic about him as an author they might enjoy reading: though O. Henry had plenty of admirers, he seems to have been more a model to learn from than an author whose works one would take to a desert island. In any case, it was more feasible for the apprentice to draw usable lessons from O. Henry than Maupassant. As Kennedy Williamson observed of "The Gifts of the Magi," "the plot is quite artificial—as formal as a parterre." Williamson was not dismissing the artificiality of the story, but discussing it as the paradigm of the genre of "the symmetrical story."[31] A symmetrical conceit in the O. Henry mode could be produced by linear thinking, the "logic" that John Rolf and G. J. Matson spoke of. By contrast, the type of thinking that produced the twist in "The Necklace" did not lend itself to systematization.

The second factor inhibiting a general conquest of amateur fiction by formulas such as Vivian's and Walter's was that they went too far in elevating plot at the expense of character. Vivian held back from a decisive statement about the matter, but Michael Fallon, another exponent of "conflict" as the master term of fiction, frankly said that the peculiarities of characters were of secondary importance to the structural oppositions of the plot. Characters mattered chiefly in terms of how their traits functioned as causal factors in the plot. This belief is evident in Vivian's enthusiasm for Georges Polti's morphology of plot, *The*

Thirty-Six Dramatic Situations. For instance, in the plot-type "The Innocent Despoiled by Those Who Should Protect," the character traits that really matter are the ones that make the protagonist a despoilable innocent. Debates about the relative importance of plot and character filled many a writers' circle evening without appreciable practical consequences, but few circle members would have been willing to see character as epiphenomenal. They searched assiduously for interesting people to turn into characters, and they talked at length about revealing character through dialogue. For them, the verisimilitude and "life" of a tale's characters were essential aspects of a good story.[32]

For a time, stories that concentrated on character to the detriment of action were fashionable, or less unfashionable. When a woman wrote to the *Writer* in 1930 asking whether anyone could suggest a periodical that would accept "short stories dealing in psychological revelations, somewhat after the style of Katherine Mansfield," her letter went unanswered. Such stories would have been too avant-garde for the *Writer*'s understanding of the market. During and after the Second World War, however, stories that took as their model Mansfield or Chekhov—or the Maupassant who dealt in "slices of life" rather than the Maupassant of "The Necklace"—became commercially viable. Approving the contents of a wartime anthology, the publisher Philip Unwin told one of the volume's editors: "The actual writing is good, it has vitality, sincerity, and is usually done with meticulous care, but they very seldom contain 'a real story.' They are nearly all sketches . . . I should be interested to discuss the phenomenon with you some time, as obviously you are far better read in short stories by young writers than I am, but it does seem to me that most of them lack the meaty plots which one always found in the short stories of the great masters of this art thirty or forty years ago." The editor replied quoting a recent article by L. A. G. Strong: "Periodicals such as New Writing, Modern Reading, and others have an audience that must stagger the editors of the so-called popular type of short story magazine."[33]

The relaxation of the requirement of thumping plots and surprise endings made itself felt in the work of writers' circle members. In 1952 a regular guest of the Newcastle Writers' Club read out a story that had "no plot . . . [W]e were much impressed. Lacking plot, it had atmosphere. There was no surprise ending, yet the tale was complete." The author took "as models for his writing Charles Dickens and Guy de Maupassant"—the latter in his vignette mode, no doubt. The fiction in *Circles' Choice,* a 1948 anthology of work from writers' circles' competitions edited by Edith A. Parkinson of the Nottingham Writers' Club, includes both a story with a forced twist (complete with a single-sentence final paragraph ending in an exclamation mark) and a less tightly plotted piece. A young couple ride bicycles beside a new suburban development outside an industrial town. Then the war comes; the man serves in Italy, and is reported missing right at the end of the war. The woman takes the money saved for their wedding and goes looking for him in Italy. She eventually finds him: he has lost both legs, and had asked the locals to let him stay, so that she would never find him. Reunited, they both feel some inner peace. If not wholly without precedent, the story is still quite different from ones with a dramatic twist.[34]

How thoroughgoing this change was in published stories is not something that can be established in a book that focuses on writers rather than the periodical press. Commentators made contradictory assessments of the situation. In 1951 the short story writer Norah Hoult declared in the *Writer* that "the temporary fashionable appeal of the Tchechovian story has passed." When a Maupassant fan was reading a plotless story to aspirant writers in Newcastle a year later, it hardly seems likely that (as Hoult claimed) the genre's appeal had waned because it had been overused by "the highbrow magazines of the pre-war literary coteries." Hoult may have been right that "most very short stories, such as appear in the national dailies and include detective fiction, follow of necessity the O. Henry pattern," but that pattern was not quite the unquestioned verity it had once been among those writing fiction for magazines and newspapers. The somewhat confused state of postwar attitudes to plots and twists is indicated by the remarks of Elizabeth Woan to the Newcastle Writers' Club in 1953: "Mrs Woan's biggest trouble is the end of the tale. A twist ending is not always necessary. Ursula Bloom once advised her to work backwards . . . There was a vogue for plotless stories a few years ago." By 1954 the editor of the upmarket *Lady* was trying to have it all. She declared herself interested in stories of twelve to fifteen hundred words, "rather evoking an atmosphere or a mood than containing a plot, and for preference (but how difficult it is to find!) with a sardonic twist at the end."[35]

Attempting a type of short story with some filiation to Mansfield and Chekhov was the furthest many writers' circle members and other freelance fiction writers moved from late Victorian and Edwardian narrative traditions. The minutes of circle meetings and the articles and letters in the *Writer, Popular Writing,* and other journals exhibit a hostility to modernist poetry and a vaguer aversion to "highbrow" fiction. If aspirant writers in the interwar period had voted on which contemporary literary figure they most admired, the poll would in all likelihood have been topped by Arnold Bennett. His work was only occasionally recommended as a model, presumably in part because freelances were more likely to be writing short fiction than lengthy novels. Bennett was, however, frequently discussed at writers' circle meetings, and his *Journals* were recommended as a companion for would-be authors. One member of the British Amateur Literary Association lived in a house named after Bennett's 1910 novel *Clayhanger*.[36]

If amateur writers sided with Mr. Bennett rather than Mrs. Woolf, they also distinguished themselves from "the fiction of the Victorian era." They believed that an authorial persona should not intrude into the text to pass judgments on characters or address the reader directly. In the interests of creating the "illusion of reality" deemed essential to escapism, it was important not to remind readers that they were, in fact, reading. This was not a mode of writing that came naturally: novices often wrote fiction that did not obscure the circumstances of its own production. Thus a publisher's reader complained of a novel manuscript that had "all the more obvious faults of inexperienced writing . . . there are lapses into a clumsy 'literaryese'—i.e. 'we' (meaning the author), 'this narrative,' . . ."[37] In order to conceal the mediating role of the printed page, writers were encouraged to convey information and "atmosphere" indirectly, to shun indulgent "descriptive" passages, and to depict character through dialogue rather than prose portraiture: "DON'T TELL: SHOW." It was an orthodoxy that a hallmark of good writing was "self-effacement." A good style was a simple style.[38]

The book most persistently recommended as a model of style was the Bible. Like the advertising agents who borrowed rhetorical armaments from the Bible, an exponent of "standardizing art" for profit declared: "If you want an . . . instance of the real value of simplicity, you have only to turn to the Testaments, Old and New. Which moves you most—the Old Testament that glows like a flower, that throbs like a drum, that is hot with the sunshine of glowing words—or the new, with its simple fearless undecorative narrative of the most tragic and beautiful story in the world." The editor of "a Leading Literary Journal" named the Bible as the most important stylistic model in a list he provided for readers of

Popular Writing for its "simpleness and directness . . . The creation of the world is described in under seven hundred and fifty words. How many would it have taken you?" A rare vocal dissenter from this orthodoxy was Robert Hugill of the Newcastle Writers' Club. "Don't read the Bible as a model of style," he told fellow members. Yet his rationale was not very different from that of those recommending scripture: "Pretend you are writing a letter to a friend, be simple & lucid."[39]

In lectures and published advice about writing, simplicity was regularly paired with "sincerity." A simple style was sincere because it left no room for pretension or condescension on the author's part. George G. Magnus, a literary agent and advisor harried by allegations of fraud from some of his clients, declared in *How to Write Saleable Fiction:* "Your work should bear the stamp of sincerity. You cannot treat yourself and your reader too seriously. Flippant novels are seldom found amongst the 'best-sellers.'" Sincerity was an indispensable animating force in all good—and materially successful—writing. This principle lay at the heart of the belief that people should write about what they knew, and that if they wrote about things they did not have direct experience of, the writing would be lifeless or awkward. Cecil Hunt concluded a chapter of his *Living by the Pen* with the opinion that "the prime qualifications of a novelist will, I think, always be: the ability to tell a story, the power of characterization—and sincerity. Personality and the texture of the mind are important. Literary style will never compensate for their absence."[40]

As Norman A. Lazenby's comments on research for pulp westerns indicate, not every genre demanded sincerity. Yet the power and reach of the idea are indicated by its presence even in an unblushing invitation to hack work. Philip Harrison, editor of the *Writer* in the late 1920s, called the injunction to write sincerely the most clichéd advice to the novice, but he still devoted a chapter of his *Free-Lance Fallacies* to it. Harrison's answer to the question "What Is Sincerity?" was that this all-important quality simply amounted to believing in what one was writing. Even writers concerned with sales to the exclusion of nearly everything else needed to make themselves interested in the material and the genre. Anyone "can induce in himself an interest in his own creative work. It is merely a question of fixing a particular ideal—admittedly a rather low one—firmly in one's mind and writing up to that standard . . . Sincerity, then, in this particular connection, while it cannot be simulated, can unquestionably be cultivated."[41]

Though the writers discussed here usually did not think they were contributing to "English literature," their approach to writing, especially their stress on sincerity, drew on the discourse of English literary history prevalent in the late nineteenth and early twentieth centuries, the formative periods in the lives of many writers' circle members (and other freelances, taking the autobiographical articles in the *Writer* as a guide). The main currents of this discourse are often most apparent in discussions of poetry, though their principles applied to prose as well. Discussing "Poetry and National Character" in his 1915 Leslie Stephen Lecture, Professor W. Macneile Dixon of the University of Glasgow declared: "The best school for poetry as for everything else is the school of personal experience. We may say with truth that the fortune of our literature was made by attendance on this school, we may praise our writers for their originality and variety, but there are other qualities for which we cannot praise them . . . restraint, lucidity, finish, shapeliness." These qualities, and a "native genius for individuality and sincerity," loomed large in the late nineteenth century's profusion of primers in "English literature" and its series on "men of letters." These traits were literary cognates of the purported English values of freedom and "character." And, as the historian Stefan Collini remarks, these literary qualities were routinely contrasted with "the linked characteristics of formal artificiality and moral doubtfulness in French literature."[42]

A pillar of this interpretation of English literature was Francis Turner Palgrave's *Golden Treasury,* which has been called "the most influential anthology in English literary history." In the *Golden Treasury,* the values of "simplicity of narrative," love of nature, and "reverence for human Passion and Character" reigned supreme. Unsurprisingly, Palgrave found these qualities most in evidence in the poets from whose writings these values in part derived, including Wordsworth, Keats, Shelley, and Scott. The eighteenth-century section of the anthology was correspondingly brief, and because Palgrave found the work of the metaphysical poets "often deformed by verbal fancies and conceits of thought," little of it was included. The influence of values such as Palgrave's is evident in a lecture that the Reverend T. M. Phillips delivered at the Manchester Literary Club in 1911. When Alexander Pope came of age as a poet, Phillips argued, "an intellectual poetry, uninfluenced by feeling . . . banished the great passions of which Shakespeare and Milton had sung." The eighteenth century was an "age of cold understanding," incompatible with "the growth of the nobler poetry of passion, imagination, and true appreciation of life and nature." From Cowper onward, culminating with the Romantics, nature and ultimately passion returned to English poetry.[43]

This opposition between passionate life and cold artifice was an endorsement of romantic ideas, a system of values that sets Chapman's Homer above Pope's. A pivotal figure here is the Reverend Stopford A. Brooke, the devoted Wordsworthian who recruited subscribers for the 1890 purchase of Dove Cottage as a permanent memorial to the poet. The influence of Wordsworth as a literary theorist is manifest in Brooke's primer *English Literature* (1880), which was highly praised and had sold nearly half a million copies by 1916. In Brooke's view the poets of the seventeenth and early eighteenth centuries other than Milton "set aside natural feeling, and wrote according to frigid rules of art. Their style lost life and fire; and losing these, lost art, which has its roots in emotion, and gained artifice, which has its roots in intellectual analysis." Adding to them a jab at intellectualism, Brooke's assertion reprised arguments from the prose additions to *Lyrical Ballads,* where Wordsworth asserted that the earliest poets "generally wrote from passion excited by real events; they wrote naturally, and as men; feeling powerfully as they did, their language was daring, and figurative," but that such precedents allowed later poets to mimic the formal devices of the greats "mechanical[ly]," "without being animated by the same passion."[44]

The counsel amateur writers read, heard, and perpetuated themselves was governed by the redactions of romantic values in literary judgments such as Brooke's. As we have seen, for all but the most mercenary freelances, a genuine knowledge of and concern for one's "material" was held to be a prerequisite of effective writing, and a quality that the market would reward. Imaginative fancy or indirect knowledge was rarely enough. And the textual fruits of this genuine engagement with one's material had to be expressed in clear and simple prose—the "the language really used by men," we might say with Wordsworth—unadorned by forcedly "literary" descriptive indulgences. The two imperatives were related. "It is only through close observation [that] you can avoid clichés," insisted Margaret Lees. Kennedy Williamson put the case in terms close to Wordsworth's: "It is because inexpert writers describe characters wholly out of their imagination that they drop into stock phrases, clots of words that other people have formed and which have become musty and lifeless. Surely we should find fewer heroines with hair 'the colour of ripe corn' if authors went more often to life instead of to memories of other writers for their delineations." One of Allen and Unwin's readers applied the same reasoning to an unsolicited manuscript: "The book strikes me—as many novels do—as founded on a fair acquaintance with nineteenth-century fiction rather than a sincere observation of life."[45]

Diligent observation of reality would generate more vivid images because form was secondary to content and "life." This was especially so in the case of poetry, where the idea of poetry as the product of sublime thoughts or a noble soul made it possible to think of a poem as existing in some way even before it had taken verbal form. Plot and character were the "life" of popular fiction, according to the author questionnaires and fan letters that Q. D. Leavis read, and to commentators happier about the state of popular taste, such as Roger Dataller in *The Plain Man and the Novel.* The idea that form was distinguishable from content and subsidiary to it had been assumed in Brooke's primer: "The history of English literature is the story of what English men and women thought and felt, and then wrote down in good prose or beautiful poetry in the English language."[46]

Metaphors of "embodiment" and characterizations of style and expression as vehicles for content abound in the remarks of twentieth-century aspirants and their advisors. The correspondence instructor Kenneth MacNichol used both metaphors: "The 'technique of fiction writing' serves . . . as a vehicle for the author who has a story to tell . . . It provides a body for the soul of the story, that being the part of the story which the author's own life must add to the unenlivened form." Given this way of thinking about form and content, it is not surprising that Cecil Hunt should reach for a biblical quotation to underscore his point that personality was important and that "literary style" would not compensate for its absence: "'The letter killeth, but the spirit giveth life.'"[47]

This was a popular theory of literature that militated against an approval of modernism. The opposition between the soul of content and the body of form informed another dichotomy: ranged against sincere writing was writing that made a fetish of its style, writing that (so the argument went) emphasized the intellect at the expense of the emotions. This distinction reprised Brooke's opposition between art/emotion and artifice/intellect, but adapted it to the defense of popular writing. Thus people who wrote for profit attacked the avant-garde in terms of an opposition between bestsellers/emotion and "highbrows"/intellect. Q. D. Leavis found this opposition an entrenched way of thinking among "bestselling" novelists. She quoted Gilbert Frankau and Warwick Deeping to this effect, and then quoted two anonymous responses to a questionnaire she had sent to commercially successful novelists. Wrote one: "Even if many of them [bestsellers] are not works of art, they are on the whole (except the very bad ones) closer to the fundamentals of life and of romance than much of the cleverer stuff that springs mainly from the brain and so fails to reach the *heart*." The other responded: "Technique is not one of the living qualities and the novel is primarily concerned with *life*. The core quality of the born novelist is *human*, not literary."[48]

The idea that writing needed sincerity to be commercially viable may also have defused any perceived tensions between commerce and writing: selling would not necessarily be selling out. Yet, as I argued in Chapter 2, there were few tensions to defuse, and strict amateurism had a very limited appeal as the basis for writers' organizations by the interwar period. When used in the way Q. D. Leavis's informants used it, the language of sincerity could sound like little more than a defensive ploy. It certainly had its uses in this way. Francis Vivian started out aspiring to write "literature." Hard times during the Slump drove him to try writing as a job. He took a correspondence course and by his own account lowered his standards.[49] It is easy to read self-justification in his defense of the intrinsic value of "craft" and "technique," however "cheap" the genre to which they are applied. Yet the extent to which rank-and-file members of writers' circles concerned themselves with sincerity in their relation to their material and their prose suggests that this vernacular literary theory was a genuinely meaningful way of thinking about writing and its relation to other aspects of life.

While many people in writers' circles were averse to modernism, they were accepting of "modernity." "Modern" developments such as the emergence of a mass market and increased female participation in associational life and cultural production were central to writing as an organized pursuit. Romantic ideas about sincerity and representation could be accommodated to the market because they were so completely detached from their original opposition to literary mechanization, and because the market was not perceived as incompatible with authenticity in British culture—or at least in the parts of it beyond the writ of the Leavises and T. S. Eliot. Commercial writing could therefore provide a berth for the creative self. If the oppositions underpinning aspirant writers' uses of literature did not generate anxieties, in retrospect they seem fraught with irony: when would-be writers and their guides talked about canonical literature, they subscribed to a poetics that emphasized content and the personal to the extent of almost denying the aesthetic; and when they talked about their own writing, they elevated "heart" over mere "technique," even though writers' circles and the literary advice business owed their initial appeal to the idea that, by penetrating the mysteries of technique, an ordinary person could become a writer.

Chapter 4

In My Own Language about My Own People

In 1940 George Orwell published a celebrated essay about the conservatism of juvenile fiction and its potential for stunting the political consciousness of working-class readers. The following year, Frank Thompson of the Hull Literary Club followed Orwell to railway bookstalls and newsagents, the bookshops of the working class, this time to report on women's magazines. Thompson saw the more downmarket story papers for women as peddling escapism to "girls working in factories and living in overcrowded working-class homes" and their older married cohorts. "Dream stuff—what *may* be going to happen to you, and after it hasn't and you've made shift with what's at hand, what *might* have happened to you. This, and the pictures, and the radio, will help you through to the end of your days without thinking too much about realities. These drugs will do until someone manufactures Huxley's 'soma': then it will be all dreams." So far so familiar. Yet Thompson went on to make a point we would not expect from Kennedy Williamson or the others who explained "escapism" to would-be writers: "England has been literate these fifty years; most of the girl readers of these papers ten years ago were writing bright little essays on 'My Holiday,' doing arts and crafts, and being the promising bright-eyed younger generation. There is a nasty flaw somewhere, but it is no part of this article to point in its direction."[1]

With this chapter, my focus shifts from the world of the writers' circles to that of working-class writers. The source material of this chapter is drawn mostly though not exclusively from the 1930s, a significant decade in the history of working-class authorship. There may not necessarily have been unprecedented numbers of workers writing: we cannot know for sure because we cannot account for every stray poem "written out on old school sheets, old school books, exercise books."[2] What made the 1930s distinctive was a heightened level of attention from literary patrons and publishers. In this chapter I concentrate on working-class authors themselves: examining how working-class life hindered or enabled their literary efforts and probing their motivations and the meanings that writing held for them. In the next chapter I place these authors more firmly in the context of the 1930s, exploring how the literary politics of that decade valorized working-class voices and created channels through which plebeian authors might be published.

Most of the people discussed in this chapter and the next were manual workers. In concentrating on them rather than on, say, shop workers, I am not suggesting that manual workers constituted the real or essential working class, or that they were a culture unto themselves. As I noted in Chapter 2, there was a degree of shared culture that could, as Jon Lawrence writes, "bind manual and non-manual workers in urban, industrial Britain." But the writing careers of lower-grade clerical or retail workers were not so different from those of the people discussed in the two preceding chapters. Indeed, writers such as Margaret Thomson Davis and Molly Weir, whom we met in Chapter 2, wrote entertaining pieces for newspapers, or got involved in writers' circle activities, while their employment and domestic situations remained unmistakably working class. In becoming writers, manual workers faced challenges different from those faced by other people, even other members of the working class like Davis and Weir. My concern with these distinctive challenges also leads me to limit my focus to people who were *still* manual workers (or unemployed manual workers), rather than simply of working-class origin. Workers' children who went to university play only a small part in these pages, since the cultural predicament of the scholarship boy and girl is a well-known story, and because, as people at the time, both working-class and middle-class, pointed out, the act of writing felt very different after a university education.[3]

In contrast to the participants in writers' circles and amateur journalism, nearly all the people in this story are men. Efforts to uncover working-class women writers in the first half of the twentieth century have turned up very few. And not all of these were juggling literary ambitions with the quotidian demands of working-class life at the time they became writers. Ellen Wilkinson was a Member of Parliament by the time she published her novel *Clash*. The painstaking bibliography of working-class autobiographies compiled by John Burnett, David Vincent, and David Mayall includes only a handful of female writers from the period. Weir and Davis are among them; so is Ethel Mannin, the daughter of a letter-sorter whose road to writing led, like Weir's, through a commercial college and secretarial work. For the female *manual* workers listed in Burnett, Vincent, and Mayall's bibliography, there is scant information about how they became writers. The evocative autobiography of the Bermondsey factory worker Kathleen Woodward stops tantalizingly short of her literary career. But Woodward did become a writer, and so did Ethel Carnie (Holdsworth), who wrote poetry while also working in a cotton mill in Great Harwood near Blackburn in the first decade of the century. "From a child I found myself expressing my thoughts in rhythmic forms, and deriving great pleasure from so doing." She had been supported in her writing by a member of the local literary society, as nineteenth-century northern workingman poets had been. He encouraged her to publish a book of poems, and she did so in 1907. Robert Blatchford, the editor of the *Clarion*, read Carnie's *Rhymes from the Factory* and recruited her to work for the *Clarion* and the *Woman Worker*. She left after less than a year, but she continued to contribute short stories to the *Clarion* and other periodicals while selling ribbons and laces in the Blackburn market. Between 1913 and 1931 she published eleven novels, most of them centered on working women. The circumstances in which she wrote them remain obscure, as do the details of her short-lived job at Bebel House in London "encouraging working women to express themselves in writing."[4]

In her 1939 survey *Working-Class Wives*, Marjory Spring Rice declared it "little short of a miracle" that some working-class women found "time and mental energy to belong to such organisations as the Women's Co-operative Guild, the Salvation Army, or a branch of their political party." She added that the active members of those organizations very seldom came from the poorest families, whose women "*have no time* to spare" for considerations not immediately relevant. Many of the women Claire Langhamer interviewed for her book on leisure from 1920 to 1960 "expressed the view that that once married they no longer needed, deserved or even wanted leisure for themselves; most observed that in adult life the choices of other family members took precedence over their own use of time."[5] Perhaps different expectations about what men and women might do, rather than an evidential black hole, account for the minute numbers of working-class women known to have been writers at this time.

If identifiably working-class people were scarce in writers' circles and among the contributors to writing magazines, at least some workers tried their hand at writing for "pin money," or bought the products of the literary advice industry. The correspondence pupil whose piece about mining provoked the furious criticism quoted in Chapter 3 was a miner's wife who had paid eleven pounds to take the course. The playwright Alan Bennett reports that his father, a Leeds butcher, had as a young man had "some literary ambitions" that found outlets in "going in for competitions in magazines such as *Tit-Bits* and even sending in little paragraphs and being paid." Such payments could make for welcome windfalls. When Sid Chaplin was paid £5 for his first publication, a poem in *New Writing*, he and his wife took the bus from their County Durham pit village to Darlington and bought half a dinner set for his parents' silver wedding anniversary. It cost £4.10, and the rest went on "bus fares & [a] cup of tea." At other times, authors' fees could help tide workers over lean periods.[6]

Only for a very few did the profitability of writing amount to more. In 1938, just before the Left Book Club published his autobiography *These Poor Hands*, the miner B. L. Coombes asked the editor of *New Writing*, John Lehmann, if he thought it possible to earn fifty pounds a year by writing a book and several stories. Coombes wanted to buy a house in Resolven, Glamorgan, through a building society. After he had spent twenty pounds that he had earned from writing to make a flower and vegetable garden out of the derelict yard of the house he was renting, the landlord had doubled his rent on the grounds that the property was now much more valuable. Fifty pounds was the amount Coombes reckoned he needed to support himself, his wife, and his son and keep up with the mortgage payments, on top of his earnings from the mine, which were up to three pounds a week when work was plentiful. Lehmann replied that it all depended on how well *These Poor Hands* did. "If it has even a moderate success (and in my opinion it should be more than that) you will certainly have no difficulty in earning the sum you suggest for at least three or four years. More than that I would not like to say, because the market is changeable, and one year a really good author can earn several hundreds of pounds and another year only two or three guineas."[7]

Coombes's book *was* a success: as a Left Book Club choice, it would have been sent to more than 250,000 people, and it had good reviews. On the strength of *These Poor Hands,* Coombes carved out a career as a writer and commentator on mining issues. A dramatically critical article he wrote in 1940 for *Picture Post,* the most socially important magazine of the time, brought in the biggest mailbag *Picture Post* had ever received. In the early 1940s he was broadcasting frequently—mostly nonfiction pieces about mining and miners' lives—and also submitting short stories to the BBC. He had letterhead stationery made up after the fashion of other established freelances: "B. L. Coombes, Miner-Author, Over 1,000,000 words published. Stories, Articles, Radio Talks etc." He nevertheless remained a miner, though he worked fewer hours than before. He stayed in mining partly for financial reasons and also because he believed that staying in touch with mining life was good for his writing.[8]

Very few working-class writers were able to give up manual work and write full time. The Fifeshire miner Joe Corrie managed to support himself and his family by writing plays for Scottish community drama groups. Leslie Halward and James Hanley both wrote full time and lived simply in the country—villages in North Wales in Hanley's case, Malvern in Worcestershire in Halward's. Even with such frugality, their circumstances were precarious. Hanley often had to sell off his own manuscripts or letters from famous writers, and Halward sometimes had to ask for publishing fees in advance because his financial situation was "bloody awful." And these men were "successes." One of the working men whom Jack Common corralled into writing about their lives for the book *Seven Shifts* sent Common a fragment accompanied by a "little note . . . that told of hard struggle on the distant front": "I've done three pages, and I've got nowt more to say. It cost two pints of mild and bitter, 1s. 1d.; one small Players, 6d. Total 1s. 7d. How much will 8,000 words work out at?"[9]

If beer and cigarettes were not essential writing accessories, coal or gas for heat was. A number of accounts of scholarship boys and girls from working-class homes note the difficulty of doing homework in peace: students often had to work in the same room as everyone else, with the interruptions of conversation and the wireless, because heating an additional room for one person was prohibitively extravagant. For adults, similarly, the noise of a communal room and the demands of children could make it difficult to concentrate on writing. Some workers managed. Fred Kitchen, a Yorkshire agricultural laborer, wrote his autobiography surrounded by his family, ignoring the wireless and the conversation of his wife and daughters, then staying up to write after the others had gone to bed. Others had wives who made personal sacrifices. Rene Chaplin, Sid Chaplin's wife, recalled in an interview that he would write at the kitchen table:

> *[Interviewer:]* Did you sometimes get frustrated with . . . he obviously had a very strong will to write and fitting it in-between working . . . did you sometimes feel that you were pushed out at all?
>
> *[Rene Chaplin:]* No, no, no, because I knew that that was the most important thing in his life was to write.
>
> *[Interviewer:]* So from your point of view it was encouraging him and being there for the . . .
>
> *[Rene Chaplin:]* And reading each day what he'd written.[10]

The difficulties of writing at home reached what one hopes was their nadir in the case of George Garrett, a Liverpool seaman and dock worker. Garrett was supposed to be one of the men who chronicled their working lives in Common's *Seven Shifts*. He warned Common, though: "I have a hell of a job trying to do a bit of writing where I am now. This address is on the second floor of a corporation tenement." He told Lehmann: "The whole bunch of us are crowded in together. There is no separation. All that these tenements are . . . is one room sub-divided, like a hen-coop. It is impossible to have privacy or peace." Garrett's neighbors had eight noisy children; Garrett and his wife had five children of their own, one of them a baby. "I must either terrify them into silence or wait until they go to bed," Garrett wrote. "This is generally near midnight. By that time I am too physically exhausted to do much writing. There is the problem too of extra light and coal."[11]

Garrett's frustration with his children, and with his wife, who disapproved of his spending time writing, was all the greater because he was largely confined to their tenement. As a young man he had spent time with the Industrial Workers of the World in the United States, and he helped to organize the National Unemployed Workers' Movement hunger march to London in 1922. His political activities ensured that he was blacklisted on many ships leaving Liverpool in the 1920s, and apparently on the docks as well. Because his politics had made him a local public figure, workers and unemployed people made demands on him that limited his ability to retreat to that common refuge of autodidacts and the unemployed alike, the public library. "I cant go to the Public Library to write without my being pulled about dole, relieve, maternity benefits etc"; "chaps . . . come to use me as a father-confessor and general-life guide."[12]

Garrett might have agreed with Cyril Connolly's notorious claim "There is no more sombre enemy of good art than the pram in the hall." He pulled out of *Seven Shifts* after getting three thousand words down on paper: "I . . . turned my back for a moment, and the baby just tore it in pieces." But he continued to work feverishly on a book about the experience of unemployment, for which he had an unsatisfactory contract with the publisher Lawrence & Wishart (of which more in the next chapter). Eventually he had a breakdown. "I could feel my mind going. When a man tightens his fingers around his baby's throat, he has reached a pretty dangerous condition." He spent four weeks in hospital, "half-lunatic." "Perhaps later on," he said, "I can collect my scattered mind a bit to write again, but under the present conditions it is impossible. I dare not risk it." In fact this was the end of his writing career.[13]

In *A Room of One's Own* Virginia Woolf quoted the reminiscence of Jane Austen's nephew, who noted that Austen "had no separate study to repair to" and must have had to do most of her work "in the general sitting-room, subject to all kinds of casual interruptions." Some of the power of Woolf's rhetoric stems from the fact that her book's central figure, the private room with a lock on the door, works both as a general metaphor for independence and as the most practical embodiment of it. The conditions that militated against manual workers' becoming writers were obviously different from those faced by Jane Austen, but for those workers, too, a private physical space was the most powerful metaphor, or instance—or, better, an instance with metaphorical resonances—of the mental space they needed. Garrett's letters to Lehmann and Common stress his desire for peace and privacy to concentrate on his writing, for a room with a lock on the door rather than the general sitting-room or hen-coop. If he could "rent a room" outside Liverpool, he wrote to Lehmann, "I would have a sense of freedom that would be almost impossible in the homes of any of my friends."[14]

Occasionally working-class writers borrowed Woolf's own terms. Sometimes they did so sardonically or sarcastically, as in Willy

Goldman's choice of "A Room of One's Own" as a chapter title in his autobiography, though not for a chapter about his writing. On other occasions they quoted her or closely paraphrased her without deliberate irony and without apparent awkwardness at applying arguments about middle-class women to working-class men. Garrett lectured Lehmann, who was acting as an intermediary between him and his insufficiently understanding publishers: "Now Lehmann, in your own circle, when you sit down to write, it is understood immediately that you are WORKING . . . You will probably have a room of your own to write in, not a crowded place where each member of the family is treading on the other's heels." One of the things Coombes looked forward to about owning a house rather than renting was that "I would have a quiet room to myself for writing then, and it would be heated and lighted so that I could do more work." Even renting in Resolven had been an advance: "I have now a room of my own to write in, after being crowded in a mining street for many years, and being forced to type in the bedroom at all sorts of odd times."[15]

If working life precluded time and space to write, the forced leisure of unemployment could, perversely, provide an opportunity. For Garrett, involuntary time without paid work meant confinement to the home, with the frenzy of his sons compounded by the persistent intrusions of canvassers, coalmen, and rag and bone men. Leslie Halward, in contrast, successfully used seven months' unemployment to practice his writing, and Hanley is said to have begun writing after two years' unemployment. Joe Corrie started writing in earnest during the Scottish coal-mine lockout following the General Strike in 1926.[16]

Yet the demands of manual work and long hours, the expense of heating, and the lack of space were not always insuperable. Some workers managed to carve out the time and summon the energy to write at length. The very isolation of such writers makes it impossible to know how numerous they were or what kind of lives they lived. Given this dearth of information it is worth dwelling for a moment on the unusually well documented case of Jack Overhill, who wrote an epistolary autobiography for Leslie Halward in 1950–1951. Overhill was born in 1903, in Romsey Town in Cambridge, an area proudly known, for its politics in the 1920s, as Little Russia. His father, a journeyman shoemaker who worked in the bespoke shops of Cambridge, was often out of work when the students went down for the Long Vacation. Overhill's father had grown up in a slum, one of thirteen children, and was a tyrant and an alcoholic. "My father couldn't read or write. But I could. He was political-minded. Every week from the age of seven I read [the reformist newspaper] *Reynolds* to him from the first to the last page." Overhill's father made him run errands and repair shoes. The Education Committee summoned the father and told him he was interfering with his son's education; when Jack reached fourteen, his father withdrew him from school, even though he had won a scholarship to secondary school. After several years as a college kitchen hand, Jack submitted and went to work for his father. A later stint as a bookmaker's clerk put paid to his hopes of moving into a better job via the bookkeeping, shorthand, English, and commercial arithmetic he studied at night school in his later teens. Even though he was a nonsmoking, nonbetting teetotaler, interested only in writing and learning ("just then it was French, Economic Geography, Economic History, Morse and a few other subjects"), no respectable employer would hire someone who had worked for a bookie. For the rest of his life, Overhill alternated between bookmaking and shoe repair.[17]

Overhill thus took on a role that many others did as well: the clever, artistic boy or girl plucked from school at fourteen because of family poverty and at least some parental jealousy.[18] Overhill was an obsessive reader from early childhood. He was one of the many for whom, as Jonathan Rose has shown, reading boys' magazines was not the barrier to intellectual and political development that Orwell thought it to be. "There wasn't a boy's paper or comic on the market that I didn't read every week . . . I could still [he was nearing fifty] name every boy in the remove at Greyfriars; probably in the school; St. Jim's as well." Overhill had a compulsion for writing as well as reading. Writing letters to newspapers became such an addiction that he forced himself to give it up in the mid-1930s to free up time. From 1931 he kept an exhaustive, typed diary. He wrote short stories from the age of thirteen. And from the 1930s he wrote novels at a prodigious rate.[19]

Most working-class authors wrote short stories or poems, at least at first: holding a novel together in one's head would have been extraordinarily difficult, given the manifold claims on their attention and their energy. Overhill both is and is not an exception to this generalization, because while he wrote novels, he scarcely planned them. When he began to write his first, two days before Christmas 1932, "All I did was sit down and turn on the tap. No idea even what I was going to say when I sat down at the typewriter." He wrote every day for a hundred days, and ended up with a manuscript of 140,000 words. He went on in this fashion, writing with staggering fluency or prolixity. By 1951 he had written, though not published, eleven novels; they regularly reached or exceeded 140,000 words. During the Second World War he would repair a hundred pairs of shoes a week and write at least one novel a year. At the same time he was taking examinations as an extramural student of the University of London; he would get up at five and study in an unheated room, repair shoes during the day, and write late into the night.[20]

The majority of his corpus was based on working-class life as he had known it. "All my life," he told Halward in 1950, "I've been chasing shadows in thinking it was my job to try to better the lot of my class. I'd have been better set to work writing nice romances for sentimental people instead of social reform tracts of anything up to two hundred thousand words." "Queen Street," written in 1938, charted the doings of two hundred characters in a single street over thirty years—and more than 200,000 words. Like many of his novels, "Queen Street" had much to say about sex, marriage, and illegitimate children in working-class culture. One of the reasons Harrap gave for rejecting the book was that "the author seems obsessed with sex." Overhill's concern with working-class families led him in the 1940s to attempt to write a working-class "family saga" (in this ambition he was not alone: Willy Goldman dreamed of writing one, Fred Urquhart drafted one, and James Hanley published one, his *Furys* quintet). "Thinking over this idea . . . I suddenly thought that perhaps I couldn't do better than to write it from my own viewpoint. After all, . . . I belonged to the working class . . . All I'd got to do was tell my tale; it would record and reflect the life of the working class." Overhill agreed when his mentor, the novelist Neil Bell, described him as "what medieval people called a 'chronicler' . . . 'Proletarian commentator' would be more apt today."[21]

Bell was the only writer with whom the adult Overhill was in touch, until Halward wrote to him appreciatively about his 1947 novel *The Snob*.[22] In his late teens Overhill had been involved with amateur journalism, contributing short stories "to a lot of amateur magazines in different parts of the country." He seems to have left that movement behind as an adult. When, in 1938, he read Bell's book *Mixed Pickles*, which contained a prefatory offer to help any struggling writer, Overhill became one of the fifty or so would-be writers who sent their work to Bell. After an initial, apparently insulting letter about one of Overhill's manuscripts,

"Romantic Youth," Bell wrote positively about another and sent it on to his agents. They were less impressed, but Bell continued to help Overhill, putting him in touch with prospective publishers and remonstrating with firms that rejected his manuscripts. In his letters Overhill constantly refers to Bell and quotes his opinions as if he were an oracle, combining independence and deference in a manner not unusual among autodidacts. Apart from Bell's criticism and support, Overhill was on his own, and in his first fifteen years as a novelist his only published book was self-published—at a cost of eighty-six pounds, his life savings.[23]

Overhill thus worked almost in solitude, sustained by his drive to write: when his wife comforted him after a particularly crushing rejection, she urged him "to give up writing. I told her I couldn't, it would be the end of the world. And so it would." Despite his political concerns, Overhill had no contact with the 1930s campaigns to recruit working-class authors, and he kept "chronicling" working-class lives, especially his own, well after the left moment of the 1930s had passed. Publishers were still rejecting him in the 1950s and 1960s. "I've read this man's story before, in a much longer & less bowdlerised form," runs a 1959 reader's report for Allen and Unwin. "He has reduced it to a mere 20,000 words & omitted anything which might give the BBC and its listeners offence." Overhill seems to have modified his work in response to earlier rejections. "The result is a less readable book &, because of its brevity, a less publishable one. The longer version was better & more practical, but it wasn't all that important. Not to be taken very seriously."[24]

Though his working life was very different from those of most writers' circle members, Overhill's career as a writer had some similarities with those of middle-class aspirants: he was involved in amateur journalism, for instance, and the local newspaper played an important part in his intellectual life. Local newspapers had long been outlets for working-class writers too. Ethel Carnie Holdsworth was first published in the poetry column of the *Blackburn Mail.* Overhill's contributions were in the form of letters to the editor—adult education students tended to be zealous writers of such letters—but other working-class authors had poetry and descriptive prose published in newspapers. Fred Dean, textile worker and autodidact in the Halifax Authors' Circle, sent poetry to the local paper, on one occasion submitting a poem entitled "Garden Thoughts" with alternate endings, one "Religious" and one "Secular."[25]

Unlike Overhill, Dean had his writers' circle colleagues to ask for advice, and other worker-writers also had less solitary struggles than Overhill did.[26] Lehmann's correspondence shows that quite a few working-class authors were in touch with other aspirants, whose work they would pass on to him. Jack Common, who built up networks in London and Newcastle with workers and with "men of letters" such as John Middleton Murry, proved able to locate and marshal a number of worker-writers.[27] Working-class writers with contacts in publishing and literary circles, like Common or Hanley, could be instrumental in helping newer writers into print. We can see this in the ripples spreading out from the "Birmingham group." From 1935 onward, Leslie Halward, John Hampson, Walter Allen, Peter Chamberlain, and Ivan Roe met regularly in a pub off Corporation Street in Birmingham. This was not a group of working-class novices—Peter Chamberlain was a scion of Birmingham's first family, and the group began meeting after its members had had stories published in leading journals. Hampson had also had a novel published by Virginia and Leonard Woolf's Hogarth Press. The Birmingham group did, however, reach out to other working-class writers. Hampson was impressed by a piece Walter Brierley wrote for a series of "Memoirs of the Unemployed" in the *Listener* in 1933:

Hampson made contact, and he and Allen read drafts of Brierley's novel, *Means Test Man*. Through friends of friends of Hampson's, the book found its way to Methuen, which published it. Brierley was "in turn patron to the largely working-class 'Codnor Group' back in Derbyshire, struggling, however ineffectively, to become writers or poets."[28]

Some institutions that might be expected to have served as surrogate writers' groups, the Women's Co-operative Guild and adult education organizations, seldom did so. The best-known instance of working-class women's writing in the interwar period, the Women's Co-operative Guild collection of autobiographical letters edited by Margaret Llewelyn Davies and entitled *Life as We Have Known It* (1931), was an isolated publication rather than part of a concerted working-class writing project. The guild's annual reports at the time make no reference to the book or any comparable project involving women's writing. *Life as We Have Known It* appears to have been a personal project of Llewelyn Davies, the guild's former president. The Hogarth Press, which published it, treated Llewelyn Davies as the sole copyright holder, which indicates strongly that she had accumulated these letters over time rather than inviting guildswomen to submit testimonies to her specifically for this book.[29]

In the October 1932 issue of the Workers' Educational Association (WEA) paper, the *Highway,* the seasoned adult education tutor Ifor Evans raised the question "When Will the Worker Produce His Own Literature?" Evans challenged the industrial worker to "produce out of the material of his own life a new drama, or a new fiction, or a new tradition of poetry." Aware that he was asking a great deal, Evans suggested that adult education classes might be able to support working-class writing, "by manuscript magazines," presumably on the model of amateur journalism's pass-rounds and do-it-yourself magazines. The responses published by the *Highway* concentrated on the massive structural obstacles to working-class writing—time, space, energy, money—rather than on the modest steps tutors might take to foster it. Quoting Evans and one of his critics at length in their survey of "the consumer's view of adult education," two leading figures in the field added no suggestions as to how adult education institutions could help.[30] "Proletarian literature" raised problems worth debating, but no practical ones that contemporary adult education seriously hoped to address.

Moreover, as a matter of policy, adult education was chiefly concerned with getting students to master existing works of scholarship and art, rather than produce their own.[31] This was certainly the case for one important adult education body with an extensive archive, the Oxford Extra-Mural Delegacy, which, in conjunction with the WEA, provided tutorial classes in Staffordshire, Lincolnshire, and East Sussex as well as the city of Oxford. In the late 1940s, the earliest period for which the Oxford delegacy has reports on individual tutorial classes, literature tutors occasionally noted that students had been moved to poetry by their studies; but although the tutor read their compositions, imaginative writing was not part of the mission of literature tutorials.[32] The Oxford delegacy's literature syllabi from the late 1920s through the 1930s give no sign of encouraging creative work, with one exception. Robert Woolridge's first-year literature class at Hanley in North Staffordshire in 1938–1939 manifested many of the concerns of the literary left of the time. The topics addressed included "The Marxist view of literature. What is the relationship of social environment to literature? How much does economic background tell us about great literature? . . . Is there really such a thing as 'proletarian' literature? Is [Walter Greenwood's novel] 'Love on the Dole' more proletarian than 'Pilgrim's Progress'?" Woolridge added: "Original work in composition and criticism will be welcome in addition to formal essay work. It is hoped from time to time to give various informal tests in original criticism and also literary 'projects' to individuals and small groups."[33]

Other agencies of adult education, such as the Plebs League and the affiliated Labour Colleges, do not appear to have done any more to mobilize workers as writers. The league's journal, *The Plebs,* exhibited a rather intermittent and grudging interest in literature during the interwar period. The Labour Colleges were not interested in literature or the arts, and insofar as they taught writing, it was grammar and expository prose for communicating with fellow workers and for taking on employers, politicians, and officials. (Harold Heslop's union-funded scholarship to the Central Labour College did, however, give him time to write his first novel.) An exception to the general lack of interest in imaginative writing in workers' education originated among Popular Front intellectuals. At the Marx Memorial Library and Workers' School in the late 1930s, Douglas Garman and Alick West taught a course on Marxism and literature, and they were probably the organizers of a promised "study circle" at the library to "to provide exercise in the kind of writing which workers need in their activities in their organizations, and also in self-expression generally."[34]

While adult education did not extend to writing workshops in the way writers' circles did, it was nevertheless of considerable indirect importance in the intellectual lives of worker-writers. Adult education was one of the pillars of the autodidact tradition, and several of the worker-writer discoveries of the 1930s came from that tradition. Fred Kitchen began submitting work to magazines at the suggestion of his WEA tutor. Sid Chaplin attended literature classes at the WEA and was deeply involved, before and well after he had become established as a writer, with the Spennymoor

Settlement, which organized drama productions and other activities. He was a Wesleyan lay preacher and met his future wife at a Wesley Guild meeting at which a group of men and women from various chapels in the area would meet and talk on Sunday evenings. He was also a trade union secretary and worked with miners committed to political change and self-improvement. Among his papers is a notebook "Given By Alex. Wylie to His Apprentice, Sid. Chaplin 1937," a volume of meticulously handwritten essays on trade unions, the Taff Vale and Osborne Judgments, and the leveling down of the skilled worker—the fruits of a hard-won education.[35]

For Coombes, too, self-education went with political involvement and community cultural activities. With Coombes and Chaplin, the culture of mining villages provided a seedbed for their writing but not an audience for it—that came via *New Writing* and other periodicals and publishers. Joe Corrie's writing, by contrast, was mostly disseminated through working-class institutions and political magazines. He first became known as a writer in the late 1920s when his "long series of sketches of Scottish working class life" appeared in *Forward,* the Glasgow Independent Labour Party weekly. *Forward* issued Corrie's collection of poems, *The Image o' God,* as a booklet. It sold 10,000 copies, an enormous number for a book of poetry. Corrie's play about the 1926 General Strike, *In Time o' Strife,* was performed by a semiprofessional company, the Fife Miner Players, which toured it round music halls in Scotland and the North of England for two years. Its run, an acquaintance of Corrie's claimed much later, "was only stopped by the arrival of the talkies." By the time it finished, Corrie had a substantial reputation in Scotland, and he was "turning out one-act plays for the ever-growing amateur drama movement," which eventually provided a sufficient income to support him, his wife, and their daughter.[36]

The peculiar strength of educational and cultural activities in coalmining districts in Wales, England, and Scotland is well known, but other working-class communities also had resources for mitigating a sense of intellectual isolation. In his autobiography Willy Goldman described his passage from East End "tough" to membership of a "small minority" who "behave unconventionally. They may read books surreptitiously, or adopt some other 'intellectual' pursuit." Such people "are also the lonely," seeking company and stimulation from one another. The deepest influence on Goldman was the local artist Ephraim Wise. After Wise's death Goldman worked hard at his writing (in his room of his own). He joined the library, where he met a man named Daniel, whom he had known to be "an evening classes boy," the kind toughs did not mix with. The two became friends and accomplices.[37] Working-class writers usually sensed that their artistic activities made them different from others in their communities; Goldman found himself part of a "small minority" on the margins of East End life. Yet he, like other working-class authors, felt able, and even obliged, to represent his community in writing.

Not many people on the left echoed Montagu Slater when he remarked in 1935 that "to describe things as they are is a revolutionary act in itself."[38] Slater himself did not conspicuously make the claim again. For communist authors like Lewis Jones and James Barke, the task of the political writer demanded more than describing things as they were. But other writers on the left did see at least some political value in providing a truthful picture of the working class. The idea of the transforming power of a revealed truth shaped a variety of events and movements across social classes in the interwar period. This idea encouraged people to volunteer for Mass-Observation, while the theatricality of the hunger marches involved bringing incontrovertible, breathing evidence of deprivation into the heart of prosperous towns and cities. Committing the experience of the poor and the unemployed to print was a gesture toward the same end.

We would expect such a gesture from Jack Hilton, who characterized some of his writing efforts as a "job for socialism," or Jack Overhill, who saw his writing as an attempt to "better the lot of my class." It is more surprising that Leslie Halward wrote about the psychology of unemployment and the inability of the privileged to comprehend it, when he was, as his friend Walter Allen later judged, "as unpolitical a man as I have ever met, as much likely, I think, to vote Conservative as Labour." After experimenting with derivative popular fiction for a time, Halward resolved that his vocation would be to write "in my own language about my own people."[39] The spokesman role that working-class writers adopted was not shaped exclusively by the politics of poverty and unemployment, but also by an impulse to present rounded, humane pictures of "their people." To write a story that accurately portrayed working-class life was an act of self-respect and community service. It was a point where the two meanings of the word "representation" coincide.

One of the tasks of working-class writing was to correct the stereotypes and distortions produced by authors from other classes. Halward was quite vehement in his aversion to the ways other authors wrote about "his people." He addressed the subject in a lecture entitled "Writing about the Working Class" at Fircroft Workingmen's College in Birmingham in October 1939. He deplored what was written "about my own people" by commentators who knew the working class only though "casual contact and occasional eavesdropping." Such writers "should leave the working class alone . . . if for no other reason than that working class people don't care for being examined and written about as if they were African savages."[40] (Mass-Observation's founder Tom Harrisson had called for an "anthropology of ourselves" on the grounds that more was known about the daily lives of "primitive" peoples than about the "tribes" of Britain; the idea enjoyed wide currency in the 1930s.)[41] *The Road to Wigan Pier* especially rankled. Garrett had helped Orwell do field research for that book, but he was not impressed by the finished product. "A book of that type can do a lot of damage," Garrett told Lehmann. "That it should appear as a 'Left Book' gives it an added damage." Garrett regarded his never-completed work on the experience of unemployment as a counter to Orwell's book.[42]

As well as directly rebutting middle-class "sneers" and "caricatures," plebeian authors tried to provide authentic portrayals of working-class people that would displace outsiders' accounts. Many of these texts had middle-class readers as their implied audience, and the narrative voice occasionally shifts into an explanatory mode for readers unfamiliar with the industry or trade in question. The narrator of Gordon Jeffery's "In the Welding Bay," for instance, affects the voice of a raconteur talking to an audience that shares his linguistic register ("I got silly like"; "we didn't listen muck-all to him"), but also obligingly explains technical matters to outsiders: "It was O.K. what he had told us to do. Lower the end of the electrode (they're about eighteen inches long like a knitting-needle)." Given the middle-class dominance of book and magazine publishing, it was common for a text by a working-class man to be addressed to an audience that included middle-class as well as working-class people, and for the implied reader to be defined only vaguely. "Fishmeal," Garrett's story of an emergency on a small ship, does not explain the maritime technicalities that crop up within it, but the number of these is not overwhelming. One never gets the feeling that the story was written principally for other seamen.[43]

While working-class fiction had a good deal to say about the feel of a coal-mine, the throb of factory work, or the difficulties of plastering, working-class writers were perhaps less concerned to report on the mechanics of labor than they were to capture the dramas of the life of the poor. Many works evoke the precariousness of working-class life, in depictions of mining disasters and accidents involving machinery, the vulnerability and subjection of workers and the unemployed, and the inadequacy of their coping strategies. One can certainly point to propagandist depictions of workers' solidarity, but these authors also wrote about personal conflicts within workplaces and about the divisions between the rank and file and working-class people in positions of authority, such as foremen and apprentices' masters. In Hanley's "Seven Men" and Garrett's "Fishmeal," the impending disaster of a shipwreck or a storm is shot through with the arguments and allegiances of the vessels' crews. With more optimism and warmth, Willy Goldman's "Down at Mendel's," set in an East End tailor's workshop, dramatizes the differences between Jewish workers and Gentiles, recent immigrants and second-generation East Enders, workers and union agents, even as it depicts the workers staggering toward a strike action.[44]

A different kind of qualification or ambivalence is at work in Gore Graham's "Pigeon Bill." Bill, a Yorkshire iron-molder, feels harassed by his wife and recoils from the meanness and nosiness of his neighbors. The workplace, not the neighborhood, is his community. "Bill was not conscious of it, but this comradeship of the workmates, this flowing feeling of loyalty and oneness that existed among the mass of workers herded together in the life at the works, this it was that almost alone gave him a real deep happiness; that answered a craving for beauty which exists deep in human nature."[45] Graham undercuts this ode to proletarian solidarity when he describes the consequences of Bill's late return from the masculine world of the works, the pub, and the marketplace where a communist speaker is lecturing on the politically anaesthetizing effects of leisure and family life. Bill's son is sick, and Bill's wife had pleaded with him to come home as soon as possible after work. When Bill arrives home the child is unable to speak and can scarcely open his eyes. Bill's wife has been unable to go out to get a doctor because there is no one else to mind the child. Bill now goes to find a doctor, but his decision not to try the closest one because he had been a strike-breaker during the General Strike seals the child's fate.

Working-class fiction frequently concerned itself with the tensions between men and women, work and home, and with the ways male unemployment confused the usual boundaries between home and public space and the gender relations associated with that division. Walter Greenwood's *Love on the Dole* makes this point explicitly and repeatedly, appealing to the sympathy of its intended middle-class readers for the honest workingmen whose dignity is assaulted in this way. The point is made implicitly but inescapably throughout Walter Brierley's *Means Test Man*, a novel almost as uneventful as the rainy Tuesday on the dole that is the subject of one chapter. The unemployed miner Jack Cook makes breakfast while his wife sleeps in; he also helps her with the laundry and readies their son for school, all without any sermonizing comment of the sort Greenwood's narrator provides. Jack even accompanies his wife into a sanctum of working-class women's economic responsibilities, shopping for groceries at the Co-op.[46]

Representing domestic situations implicitly emphasized that there was more to working-class life than work. Depicting the working class at play was another aspect of the concern to represent the writers' "own people" on their own terms. Pubs have an understandable prominence in this literature, not just because of their place in working-class leisure, but also because the pub is a site where work and leisure meet. One novel of the period, *Saturday Night at the Greyhound* by John Hampson of the "Birmingham group," is set entirely in a village pub in Derbyshire, and follows the doings of staff and customers over the course of an evening. Despite its setting, the novel is no ode to the people's alehouse. The Greyhound pub is run by three outsiders, newcomers to Derbyshire. Ivy Flack and her younger brother Tom grew up in Birmingham pubs and are sober professionals. Tom has what borders on an incestuous fixation on Ivy and loathes her alcoholic husband Fred. For all her exasperation at Fred's recklessness, Ivy will always trade her business sense and dignity for Fred's approval. On the Saturday night in question, Fred fritters away the pub's takings by standing drinks for the locals and gambling with them. In his vanity he imagines both that the customers like him and that he has the measure of them. Neither is true. The pub's patrons are successfully conning Fred, and they do so in a cold and hard fashion. Hampson accords them none of the warmth often associated with the plebeian trickster. The Derbyshire locals, both the customers and the two women the Flacks employ in the Greyhound, are cunning and sometimes brutal: Mrs. Tapin, one of the bar staff, catches the leaseholders' pampered dog in a noose of clothesline, strings him up, and stabs him to death. Only Fred lives the idyll of the country pub: the rest of the staff are struggling, and the calculating and hardened patrons are always "working" in some sense.[47]

Like pubs, the cinema, football, and allotments recur in the working-class fiction of the 1930s. Graham's "Pigeon Bill" is so named by his workmates because of his absorption in the classic working-class hobby of pigeon-fancying. Bill's pigeons are second only to male comradeship in satisfying that "craving for beauty which exists deep in human nature," and to help cope with his son's death he busies himself in his "pigeon-cote." The sense that keeping pigeons is not simply a hobby but an outlet for desires of beauty, freedom, something more, recurs in Sid Chaplin's story

"The Pigeon Cree." The protagonist, a Geordie named Geordie, has a shed or "cree" for his pigeons, which officialdom and—convention almost mandates it—his wife want demolished. Geordie is defeated, but he responds by selling his house, leaving his wife homeless. The pigeons, however, are not, since he uses the proceeds to buy a vacant lot beside the Council chambers, on which he builds a new house for himself and the pigeons, which use miniature trapdoors to get in and out. Amid the fairy-tale schematization of the plot, the stock characters of a tale with local color, and the humor of demotic speech ("Ah'll spank thee arse, an' hard at that"), a description of Geordie's feelings about the birds strikes a different note: "He doesn't really keep them for racing and winning prizes. This flying is still a miracle to him. When he was a kid he gazed at birds in the air with a kind of amazement. He wanted to join the big white gulls . . . He works two hundred fathoms down, but his mind is always with the winds and the wide-winged birds. He's a shifter, and goes down the mine every day at five, but before the steel cage drops like a torpedo into darkness, his eyes turns to the sky in the hope that a bird might swim into view."[48]

Chaplin's colloquialisms and dialect terms are an example of the way writing "about my own people" often called for the use of "my own language." Working-class fiction conspicuously employed dialect, slang, and technical terms from specific industries, words and phrases outside the repertoire of "standard English." Nonstandard English was handled like detail about manual work: sometimes explained for a middle-class audience, sometimes left by itself. The narrator of Greenwood's *Love on the Dole* supplies parenthetical glosses of dialect or argot for outsiders: "Leave lass a-be (alone)"; "Ah'll ne'er part wi' a brown (penny)." Greenwood wanted the novel to get its message across to middle-class readers, especially those in the South. Harold Heslop made no such concessions to sheltered readers, writing that a miner "must know when to kirve, when to knick, when to smash down the 'caunch.'" Writing in an authentically working-class fashion could entail drawing on "indigenous" forms of narration as well as local peculiarities of language and setting. Late in his career Chaplin recalled that illiteracy had been common in the pit villages of his boyhood. A culture that was not wholly literate "put a premium on good 'crack' [brisk talk or conversation] and story-telling"; "folk memory" was strong. "Listening to the crack at the corner-end, in the kitchen or out walking with the men one naturally just fell into the way of it." He noticed "the way a story shaped itself in repeated tellings, above all in favour of the economical telling phase—the best oral story-tellers never used two words where one would do . . . I can remember chasing home from the pit one night to bang out a story I called 'The Leaping Lad' . . . The story is true but as told to me sixty or seventy years after the event scarcely bore any relation at all to what actually happened. It had been 'improved' as well as whittled down to the bone."[49]

In their commitment to writing about "their" people, working-class writers implicitly accepted the idea that it was important to write about what one knew. Among writers of "saleable fiction," the importance of a genuine engagement with one's material was that this was essential for a compelling piece of fiction. For working-class writers, the importance of writing about the lives and places they knew lay in the value of honoring their communities with a truthful and artistically satisfying representation.

One writer who addressed this matter explicitly was B. L. Coombes. Coombes adopted a position similar to that of many writers' circle members on the link between authentic experience and good, living writing. He also articulated a political and moral duty to write about his "own people." Coombes did not start off this way. While he is known for his sober writing on mining life, he wrote a "romantic" novel (that is, a glamorous drama or melodrama, not a "romance novel") at the beginning of his career as an author. "I am sorry now that I did listen to the advice of some friends and try to make it very romantic because I realise romantic writing does not suit me. Industrial stories seem to be my strong point," he told Lehmann early in their correspondence. Coombes had submitted the novel to Gollancz and to Lawrence & Wishart. Gollancz's reader found the plot unconvincing and advised Coombes to "concentrate on working class novels." Lawrence & Wishart's reader agreed: "Whenever this writer deals with the working class his writing is extraordinarily alive and vivid. We think he would be well advised to concentrate on a novel that deals entirely with the working people." Coombes concluded: "I realise their remarks are just and have decided to count this work as necessary experience and to try and avoid dealing with rich gentlemen and Italian opera singers in future."[50]

Coombes took the lesson to heart. He organized his life around the conviction that continuing contact with working-class life was vital to his writing. He persisted in his dual career as a miner and writer even though it was difficult, and even though he had offers of other work, including, apparently, a public relations job with a trade union. "My trouble," he told Lehmann, "is that if I went clean out of mining I would lose the close contact that I value as a writer." To do that would be to squander his "capital" as a writer, as he put it in his rejoinder to Virginia Woolf. "Did D. H. Lawrence, a miner's son, continue to live like a miner?" Woolf had asked. Coombes retorted that Lawrence was an "unfair example": "he never became a miner. He was educated at University College, Nottingham, then became a school teacher." Had Lawrence "remained with his people," Coombes ventured, "he might have become a far greater writer."[51]

For writers' circle members, the premium on writing about

what one knew interlocked with the belief that a piece of writing owed its power to the experience crystallized therein. Consequently, form was of secondary importance, a vehicle for experience and intention. While the working-class writers of the 1930s believed, most implicitly and some avowedly, in the importance of writing from personal experience, they were not necessarily given to accepting that second principle. For Halward, style was the most important quality in a work of fiction, "what contributes most . . . to the success" of his own stories.[52] Yet while he and other working-class writers did not accept the attenuated romanticism of the writers' circles' position on the relation between authentic experience and literary merit, they accepted a different kind of popular romanticism: one in which the desire to create was mysterious and almost an affliction.

Writers' circle members did not talk about writing this way. A mood of driving practicality suffused their meetings and the pages of how-to manuals, magazines, and correspondence courses. There was good sport to be had with the specter of the novice who fancied him- or herself an artist rather than a persistent and unpretentious practitioner of a craft. Even those who talked of a burning urge to write hedged their desires, at least in public, with reasonableness by emphasizing the material success and other external validations that literary accomplishments could bring them. By contrast, even Halward, a writer whose considerable talent was, H. E. Bates wrote, "completely . . . unpretentious, and undramatic," and who "appear[ed] to keep the poet in himself under lock and key," perceived his inclination to become a writer as an epiphany: "For no reason at all that I can think of . . . I suddenly wanted to write . . . This sudden urge to express myself laid hold of me as unexpectedly as a fever. I do not think that it astonished me at the time, but it does now. Think of it. For twenty-two years I had not taken the slightest interest in literature . . . Yet there it was, this quite unreasonable desire, and there was no escaping it. It persisted, grew stronger. Something would have to be done about it."[53]

Autobiographical sources arouse even more suspicion than usual where epiphanies are concerned, but there is reason to think that Halward's *Let Me Tell You* is not wholly unreliable on this point. Like so many autobiographies of the time, it was written while the author was still in his thirties, not when he could look back across a long career. The book is not much given to playing up Halward's sensitive side. It opens with a grueling chapter on his battle with appendicitis, it pays faithful attention to his enthusiasm for boxing, and the rest of the discussion of his writing is matter-of-fact. Moreover, the course of Halward's life—a series of efforts at different trades and bouts of unemployment, little or no involvement in adult education—reinforces the claim that the decision to start writing was an abrupt and unpredictable one.[54]

Other working-class authors also saw the attraction of writing as a force over which they had little power. Hanley, early in his literary career, introduced himself to the influential publisher's reader Edward Garnett in this way: "I am a labouring man. At night I write . . . Am out working all the day on the railway—and trying to get my writing done . . . If I did not write—and live in that world of my own—I would just do what they all do down where I live. Roll up like a pig or louse and become dumb."[55] Hanley's compulsion to write is evident not just in this statement but also in his frenziedly prolific output. The same goes for Jack Overhill. Writing brought him repeated, painful disappointments, but to give it up, as he told his wife, "would be the end of the world." So he kept up his prodigious output in the face of negligible success and scant encouragement from publishers and other writers. Garrett did not use the language of affliction to describe his desire to write, but his correspondence and the way he wrote amid the pressures and claustrophobia of tenement life make it clear that his perceived need to write was visceral.

To say that Garrett, Halward, Hanley, and Overhill felt themselves overpowered by an impulse to write is not to affirm the existence of some timeless creative urge wired into "human nature." There may be such an urge, but the notion of it is also part of the body of popular ideas about creativity and art that were current in early and mid-twentieth-century Britain. Garrett believed in working-class writing as a weapon in the class struggle, and less politically active authors saw the faithful representation of their communities as a political act; but writing also meant something else in their lives, something less instrumental. For a number of them the desire to write antedated their emergence as accredited "proletarian writers." Coombes dabbled in Italian-opera-singer fiction before carving out his niche as a "miner-author"; Halward tried derivative commercial short stories for some time before settling on working-class stories as his métier. The "quite unreasonable desire" to write preceded the desire to write "in my own language about my own people."

The self-conception of plebeian authors, then, involved both representativeness and strangeness. What they saw as their rootedness in their communities enabled them to assume the role of spokesmen, even compelled them to: they acted as if their articulacy placed special community obligations on them. Their correspondence with editors as well as their public statements bespeak a sense that they, and not outsiders, were proper advocates for "their people." The same articulacy was also part of an individualized sense of being different—sometimes, a sense of being in the grip of an almost otherworldly desire to write. Animated by aesthetic as well as social and political concerns, and conscious of being artists, they were not the unmediated voices of working-class experience they were taken to be by readers and critics who casually dismissed them, and even by some of their supporters. Their relations with the publishers and Popular Front intellectuals who did so much to get working-class writers published were accordingly complicated.

Chapter 5

Class, Patronage, and Literary Tradition

Left Review, the flagship journal of the Popular Front, committed itself to the "development in England of a literature of the struggle for socialism." Much of that literature would come from what Jack Common called "the writing classes," but some of it had to come from what he called "the unprinted proletariat." From about 1934 to the outbreak of the Second World War, intellectuals on the left—most prominently those associated with *Left Review* and the Communist Party publisher Lawrence & Wishart, and the fellow traveler John Lehmann, who edited *New Writing*—sought to discover and support working-class authors. This effort always courted miscommunication and conflict—a culture clash between two groups divided, as Common's phrasing registered, by social class and (to some extent in consequence) by literary patrimony. The campaign to recruit working-class writers is a well-known episode in British history. My account of it draws on editorial correspondence, as well as on published sources, to argue that Lehmann was the most successful supporter of working-class writing at the time. H. Gustav Klaus has pointed out that few of the 1930s working-class writers were "discovered" by Lehmann: but a debut in no way ensured an ongoing career.[1] It was getting working-class men to *continue* writing that was so difficult. That was where *Left Review* and Lawrence & Wishart proved lacking, and it was Lehmann's great strength.

Efforts to find working-class authors were not confined to the left. Other editors and publishers were also keen to publish working-class "voices." Some did so for liberal or somewhat apolitical aesthetic reasons, others out of a perception that authentic stories of unemployment and poverty would be of public interest at a time when the idea of a division of Britain into the "two nations" of rich and poor seemed dismayingly relevant again. Just as it would be misleading to attribute the worker-writer boom of the 1930s solely to the Popular Front, it would be wrong to imply that the decisive influences on working-class writing were genres associated with the 1930s left, such as documentary. Many working-class authors' short stories were embedded in a literary tradition also appropriated, in different ways, by the writers of "magazine stories" in the writers' circles and correspondence schools.

In the first third of the twentieth century the British left showed little interest in literature. What concern it did show came mostly from the margins, from figures such as John Middleton Murry. In the mid-1930s Murry, the editor of the *Adelphi*, swung from "active, if eccentric socialis[m]" to fervent pacifism. Both before and after this shift, he promoted the interests of working-class writers, displaying a commitment probably related to his complicated association with D. H. Lawrence. Murry also gave Jack Common an editorial job on the *Adelphi*, which enabled Common to act as a patron to other working-class writers. Common passed Jack Hilton's novel to Murry to try to place it with Jonathan Cape. Hilton was initially wary ("Is he a square shooter?"), but he came to consider Murry "a good honest fellow." Cape accepted Hilton's novel *Champion* and subsequent books, for one of which Murry wrote an introduction.[2]

By the mid-1930s such interest in worker-writers was widespread on the left. The advent of the Popular Front dramatically recast the relationship between politics and the arts. If its impact on the Communist Party of Great Britain (CPGB) can be exaggerated, the Popular Front was nevertheless a remarkable episode in British intellectual life. Many Popular Front literary figures—not just well-known poets like Stephen Spender and C. Day Lewis—were young men with public school and Oxbridge backgrounds. The left-wing circles into which they now moved had little tradition of middle-class involvement. The membership of the CPGB was "overwhelmingly working class" throughout the interwar period, with few of the bourgeois intellectuals who played prominent roles in socialist parties in continental Europe. When bourgeois and working-class intellectuals engaged with each other in the left-wing literary movement, most of them were in unfamiliar territory.[3]

Left Review was the centerpiece of that literary movement, a forum for communists, fellow travelers, and a diverse assortment of other antifascists. Officially the organ of the British Section of the Writers' International, in practice *Left Review* became an organization in its own right (and the British Section little more than a name). At first the journal was run by an editorial board of Tom Wintringham, Montagu Slater, Amabel Williams-Ellis, and later Alick West. From the beginning of 1936 there was a single editor, first Edgell Rickword and then Randall Swingler. Rickword grew up in a Tory household in Colchester; he was educated privately and then went up to Oxford. For several years in the 1920s he edited the subsequently influential *Calendar of Modern Letters,* whose featured attacks on inflated reputations—"Scrutinies"—were an influence on the longer-lived Cambridge journal *Scrutiny.* Rickword joined the Communist Party in 1934 and remained in it until 1956, but he was quietly resistant to party discipline. Swingler, Rickword's choice as his successor at *Left Re-*

view, was the son of a dean, godson of an Archbishop of Canterbury, and the head of his house at Winchester, and gained a blue at Oxford as a runner. Like Rickword he was a poet, and like Rickword he joined the party in 1934, whereupon he threw himself into left-wing cultural organizations, including Unity Theatre, the Workers' Musical Association, and the Left Book Club. His life sounds a little like a Cyril Connolly parody of an upper-class 1930s leftist's profile, until one learns that he donated most of his inherited wealth to the party on joining.[4]

When Valentine Ackland sifted through poetry submissions to *Left Review* early in the journal's life, she was depressed to find that most originated in Oxford, Cambridge, Chelsea, and Bloomsbury, their authors "time-servers, toadies . . . desperately imitating Auden and Day Lewis." At first, the number of working-class contributors was to be boosted by a series of competitions. The competitions were organized by Amabel Williams-Ellis, a member of the Independent Labour Party and a child of the Strachey dynasty (she was Lytton Strachey's second cousin and the sister of the de facto communist John Strachey). Readers were invited to contribute descriptions of "*an hour or a shift at work*." However, encouraging working-class writers was not a stated goal, and when she reported the results of this competition, Williams-Ellis focused on the information it had yielded about work experiences—"fresh material" for contemporary novelists. Subsequent competitions were not only descriptive exercises, and some topics that could have been dealt with by reportage became occasions for short stories. Williams-Ellis printed many of the best entries and offered comments and stylistic advice. The chief discovery of the competitions was Kenneth Bradshaw, whose stories would appear regularly in *Left Review* after his debut in a competition.[5]

The competitions were Williams-Ellis's pet project. Other

members of the editorial board disliked the literary advice she gave, and once editorial duties were concentrated in the hands of the more discriminating Rickword, the number of competitions was cut back, and fewer highly commended entries made it into print. Under Swingler, competitions were abandoned altogether. As well as their perceived aesthetic failings, submissions to the competitions did not necessarily contribute to the kind of socialist literature Swingler had in mind. Too many of the stories submitted by "worker-writers," he complained in January 1938, were dominated by "the constant weight of anxiety and poverty and frustration and exploitation that bears upon the lives of the poor." Swingler did not deny the significance of these hardships, but he argued that a concentration on individual suffering was defeatist because it took the individual as its central term. The individual was never really isolated, he wrote; writers needed to envision "man" as implicated in society.[6]

Aside from questions of policy, it is possible that *Left Review*'s editors were not particularly competent or diligent at building up a cadre of working-class writers. Whether Rickword deserves to be judged in this way is unclear, though at least one working-class contributor found his extreme reserve off-putting.[7] While editing *Left Review,* Swingler mishandled the case of a "promising" working-class writer, Tom Burns. Lehmann tried several times to get Swingler to tell him whether *Left Review* would be using some of Burns's stories (Lehmann presumably wanted them for *New Writing* if *Left Review* did not take them). "I know that it is practically impossible for anybody in the 2, Parton Street building ever to answer a letter," Lehmann wrote in exasperation. Swingler eventually replied, saying that Burns's stories were over *Left Review*'s preferred length. He admitted that he had held on to them for too long and said that Burns had been "disgracefully treated." He added: "I find the business of editing comes hard to me, and I lapse into terrible inefficiencies."[8]

Whatever the consequences of inefficiencies at *Left Review,* the organizational pathologies of the publishing house it was connected with certainly hampered the promotion of working-class writing. The offices in 2 Parton Street housed not only *Left Review* but also Lawrence & Wishart.[9] Rickword worked for the firm and its predecessor while he edited *Left Review* without pay; Swingler also worked for Lawrence & Wishart, as did Douglas Garman, a *Left Review* contributor. In the late 1920s Garman had worked on Rickword's *Calendar of Modern Letters.* The *Calendar* had been bankrolled by Garman's brother-in-law and friend from their Cambridge days, Ernest Wishart. After the *Calendar* folded many of those who had worked on it became involved in the publishing house Wishart founded. Gradually, Rickword recalled, "everybody got more and more political," and in February 1936 Wishart Books amalgamated with the Communist Party's publisher Martin Lawrence.[10]

Martin Lawrence—a code for "Marx and Lenin," not an actual person's name—had dealt almost exclusively in political texts, but the new firm also published original fiction and was interested in issuing books by workers.[11] The Welsh communist Lewis Jones, who wrote two novels about mining life, felt tremendously indebted to Lawrence & Wishart, telling Douglas Garman: "In the circumstances that have developed since the first draft it is misleading to name myself as the author because yourself and the other comrade [evidently at Lawrence & Wishart] have at least as much responsibility as I for it . . . I want you to know how much I appreciate your efforts that made an idea into a fact, reminiscences and emotions into a book." Others had decidedly less positive experiences with the company. Authors complained that one staff member, D. J. F. Parsons, avoided them and humiliated them. The firm also had distribution problems. Its archives include royalty statements for titles in print in the first half of one year in the mid- to late thirties: not a single title had accrued royalties in excess of the advance paid to the author. Evidently Ernest Wishart's considerable capital, backed up by loans from other wealthy socialists, enabled the company to stay afloat despite making scarcely any money from the books it published.[12] Authors often complained that the firm was late in supplying them with royalty statements or had never given them any statement of their books' sales. Publishing decisions could take a long time because they apparently required the approval of all the company's directors, and they met together "about once in a blue moon."[13]

Lawrence & Wishart's dilatoriness was frustrating, and the firm dealt with its authors in a quite insensitive way. F. A. Ridley, a Marxist habitué of Charles Lahr's Progressive Bookshop nearby in Red Lion Street, told Ernest Wishart "not to waste the time of other proletarian authors as you wasted mine. Being a rich man you may not have realized the fact that for a man without 'private means' to waste several months on an entirely unremunerative work is an extremely serious matter for him. Another fact which, or so I should have thought, [would be] familiar to every 'communist.'"[14]

While the paths of Lawrence & Wishart and *Left Review* crisscrossed those of John Lehmann and *New Writing*, Lehmann's operation was quite different from that of 2 Parton Street. Lehmann had been educated at Eton and at Trinity College, Cambridge—institutions that facilitated his acquaintance with many of the feted writers of his generation. He also had strong ties to senior Bloomsbury figures: *New Writing* was launched while he was working with Virginia and Leonard Woolf at the Hogarth Press. Lehmann played a part in the administration of *Left Review* in its early days, but he was keen to run his own different but complementary magazine: "I think L.R. should undoubtedly have a party member as editor, and be advised by antifascist fellow-travellers. My show the other way round." As Lehmann saw it, *Left Review* was a monthly responsive to political developments, and his own magazine would be a literary quarterly and "a rallying ground for 'united front' authors." *Left Review*'s board agreed that the two publications could coexist, and Lehmann and the personnel of *Left Review* and Lawrence & Wishart continued to cooperate even after some contractual disputes.[15]

One of the titles Lehmann considered for the magazine was "The Bridge": it was to be a bridge between communists and fellow travelers, and between social classes. Lehmann wanted it to be a literary magazine that might actually be read by "the reading proletariat." At least some workers did read it and were inspired. "Even in this little mining village," wrote Sid Chaplin from County Durham, "'New Writing' is known and talked about." In letters sounding out possible contributors, Lehmann said he was "anxious to recruit promising worker writers." As the magazine became established, members of the reading proletariat began to approach him. Thus B. L. Coombes initiated contact after reading an early number of *New Writing,* "wonder[ing] if you would be interested in seeing some short stories by a working miner . . . for your next, or some future issues?" Once working-class contributors had formed a rapport with Lehmann, they pushed the work of friends his way. Lehmann also asked regular contributors to keep an eye open for potential working-class writers.[16]

Lehmann's relations with his working-class contributors were not always harmonious. Jim Phelan thought Lehmann was shortchanging him over the payment for a story (though he remained a contributor), and there were exchanges that laid bare the gulf between Lehmann's experiences and those of manual workers (Lehmann had to be convinced, for instance, that a temperature of 148° F in a ship's stokehold, mentioned in one of George

Garrett's stories, was not unrealistic).[17] On the whole, though, Lehmann built up good relationships with his working-class contributors through his literary advice and by handling the business of the magazine in a way that did not alienate them. Its records are not cluttered with complaints of unreturned phone calls, unanswered letters, long-pending decisions, and late or unsent payments of the kind found in the Lawrence & Wishart archive. Carbon copies were made of outgoing letters, and contributor files were maintained so that when Lehmann was out of the office other staff members could deal with inquiries. Whatever routine was established for the succession of junior assistants at the magazine must have been sufficient when combined with Lehmann's own well-documented enjoyment of control. Lehmann also made supportive gestures to the working-class writers he sponsored. He lent money without specifying a date for repayment, and he acted as a go-between or agent, passing stories and poems on to other publications (such as the Moscow-based *International Literature*) and arranging opportunities for his protégés at magazines with which he had a connection, such as *Tribune* and the *Geographical Magazine*.[18]

Lehmann's aesthetic sense made him unwilling to accept a piece simply because it was by a worker, and working-class writers, like others, received numerous letters with one or the other of his stock rejection phrases: "not quite my cup of tea" and "fails to come off." Lehmann formed strong views about his contributors' strengths and weaknesses and sought to impress his understanding onto their practice. He persistently discouraged Sid Chaplin and Walter Allen from writing poetry: "I myself feel that all your gifts point towards prose at the moment."[19] Because novice writers often wrote without any specific periodical in mind, publication in *New Writing* could require forceful editing (to make a stand-alone piece out of an autobiography in progress, for instance). Lehmann's editorial advice could become quite interventionist. After criticizing Coombes's second attempt at his second book, Lehmann added: "I do . . . believe that I could make a fairly successful surgical operation on the book if you will let me. It might take some time, and I might want you to re-write or enlarge certain passages, particularly the final stuff about the war."[20]

Coombes appears to have assented to the drastic reorganization Lehmann suggested (and in part undertook) for his second book, but not every working-class writer Lehmann knew would have.[21] Jack Hilton had a story scheduled to appear in *New Writing,* but withdrew it as soon as he found out that his novel had been accepted for publication. "I don't want his [Lehmann's] amendments & cuttings, He takes the bloody life out of a job . . . these pups of University boys with a flairy flare for LIT, in the worst form are too dictatorially important." Hilton differed from Coombes and others in that he was determined to "break through to independence of this lot of the little, 'big' men . . . these silver-spoon, progressive editors," and because he did not set much store in the aesthetic judgment of Lehmann or the Lawrence & Wishart staff. George Garrett was also wary of privileged men of letters, but unlike Hilton he took Lehmann's aesthetic judgments seriously. Garrett—and Goldman, Halward, Chaplin, Fred Urquhart, and others—would not have agreed with Hilton that "the pay-table rules insist that we prostrate ourselves before the goddess of English . . . English and real writing dont go to gether. When you are emotionalised, and pre-occupied, form goes bust. Form is mostly a matter of routinous exertion. It belongs to the second lick, and as [is?] to be done after creating. I would sooner create any time than do the workmanship."[22] The others were firm believers in "workmanship," and they most likely accepted Lehmann's advice because on reflection they agreed with it enough to be able to tolerate what it did to their text, and because it was based on an aesthetic reconcilable with their own. It certainly was not out of deference.

The degree of trust that Lehmann fostered, and the commonality of literary values between him and the working-class writers he published, made them loyal to him and to *New Writing* after they were established and able to command publication elsewhere. Halward apologized for sending a story to the populist literary magazine *John o' London's Weekly* when he was short of money. "I can't afford to let stories go cheaply if there's a chance of getting a better fee somewhere else, much as I like appearing in *New Writing*. And I *do* like appearing in *New Writing* and am most appreciative of the fact that the appearance of stories of mine in the book have done me a lot of good. I wish I didn't have to concern myself about how much I can get for the things I produce." Halward's comments suggest that Lehmann was on steady ground when he defended the magazine against Jim Phelan's complaint about relatively low fees for contributions: "What did make me go on unblushingly asking authors for more works, was the feeling that if they appeared in N.W. they got a special kind of publicity no other magazine could give them." It was a publicity that would multiply shortly after Lehmann wrote this, as *New Writing* was taken under Penguin's flipper. In its reincarnation as *Penguin New Writing* it reached a much larger audience by virtue of Penguin's distribution network, its sixpenny price, and its large wartime paper allocation. By the end of 1941 sales of *Penguin New Writing* settled at around 75,000, nearly ten times the best sales performance of *Horizon,* the other pace-setting literary magazine of the time. The extent and devotion of its readership in the armed forces repeatedly surprised Lehmann's friends.[23]

On at least one occasion Lehmann rejected a story that was highly "successful technically" because "to many readers of *New Writing* it would seem like a direct attack on the young unemployed." It was more common for him to reject a story whose politics he sympathized with but whose literary qualities did not impress him. Lehmann was not, as his biographer appears to suggest, interested in working-class writers solely as mouthpieces of exotic experience rather than as artists in their own right. He took pains to coax what he regarded as art out of their manuscripts; and as he told Tom Harrisson, "In fact I thought the quality of his [Garrett's] writing was quite unlike that of anyone else, Proletarian or not, who is known at the moment." Lehmann was unmoved by overt and blunt expressions of political views with which he sympathized. He responded positively to reportage, but he was resistant to Soviet-inspired forms and attempts at simple, popular folkishness. When Julius Lipton sent him a political poem for an anthology in 1935, he did not "think The Tower—poetically—comes off . . . I see that the more ballad-like poetry has value as 'marching song,' but I rather regret the over-simplification of issues. I mean I think you can make your stuff richer and deeper without losing clear and bold outlines." Lehmann believed that English literature needed reinvigoration, but did not think that revitalization could come about through a rejection of tradition—"tradition" in something like T. S. Eliot's sense, an ongoing productive struggle between new impulses and a literary inheritance. He was unimpressed by the sort of antipoetry written by Lipton and others associated with the magazine *Poetry and the People:*

> Harken to yonder bird singing on leafy tree!
> I harken; bu[t] the singing is drowned
> by the sound
> of the slaves dying, as they are crying to be free.[24]

In his approach to literature, Lehmann was a liberal. And for all the sincerity of his fellow-traveling, his political habits of thought were fundamentally liberal. He was uncomfortable with revolutionary change and heavily invested in the primacy of the individual conscience in aesthetic matters that shaded into political ones. He worked to elevate gifted working-class writers without lowering the standards of entry to the literary public. The idea of *New Writing* as a "bridge" between classes and subcultures was as much an Edwardian liberal dream as it was a 1930s Popular Front one; the title "The Bridge" calls to mind the "bridge party" between Indians and sahibs in E. M. Forster's meditation on liberalism and empire, *A Passage to India*. While Lehmann's efforts at *New Writing* are usually and properly read in the context of the culture of the 1930s left, they had affinities with the efforts of other editors and publishers, with different politics and aesthetic values, who played a greater part in recruiting working-class writers in the 1930s than is sometimes recognized.

A critical difference between the worker-writer campaign of the 1930s and the efflorescence of working-class writing in the 1970s is that the campaigners in the 1930s did not attack commercial publication. Or rather, they did not give the same priority to changing the system of publication as to finding the writers. In Lawrence & Wishart the CPGB itself endorsed a corporate structure whose operations differed from those of other publishing companies in little other than efficiency. The party and its literary intellectuals were also willing to countenance the replacement of *Left Review* by a mass-market leftish review owned by Penguin. (It never appeared.) In magazines as well as bookshops, the Left Book Club model—appropriating a commercial structure for left-wing content—was, if not generally endorsed, then not strenuously resisted. In the 1970s, by contrast, "worker writing" went hand in hand with "community publishing." Groups affiliated with the Federation of Worker Writers and Community

Publishers have tended to regard writing itself as an activity that should be open to everyone in a social democracy. The process is as important as the outcome, whereas for Rickword, Swingler, and even Lehmann the rationale for recruiting working-class writers resided in the nature of the texts they created. The work of proletarian writers was to do at least one of three things: contribute to a socialist culture; bring literature into firmer contact with contemporary "realities"; and renovate English literature with new material. Whichever goal one focused on (for Rickword it was the first two, for Lehmann the last two), the point lay in the text produced. Enabling workers to write was a welcome side effect, but still a side effect.

If the left's literary patrons did not often regard changes in the distribution and exchange of literature as intertwined with changes in its production, the working-class writers they sponsored saw no reason why publishing in *Left Review* or *New Writing* should prevent them from publishing in journals with different though broadly sympathetic politics such as the *Spectator* or *Time and Tide,* or in middle-of-the-road periodicals like *John o' London's Weekly* or *Lovat Dickson's Magazine. Argosy,* a periodical in which many writers' circle members aspired to appear, regularly accepted stories that had already been published in *New Writing,* no doubt assuming that the overlap in readership would not be large. While these journals did not constitute an ideological continuum, they were all, institutionally speaking, conventional forms of publication, unlike (for instance) Claud Cockburn's perpetually fugitive news-sheet *The Week.*

The chief exception to this rule was the early career of James Hanley. Hanley's first book was published by Eric Partridge, later famous as a lexicographer, who at this point was running a limited-edition imprint. Hanley's other early books—some novels, others novellas or just long short stories printed by themselves—

were issued by similar concerns, usually booksellers with radical politics or avant-garde aesthetics, or both, who dabbled in publishing. Hanley frequented their bookshops in Liverpool and London, and after he had left Liverpool and wage-work for rural Wales and a life of writing, he transacted much of his business through them. As well as publishing him, they bought him stationery and tobacco and placed bets on his behalf; they acted as agents for his literary work; and they sold his manuscripts for him when he needed cash urgently—there was a well-developed trade in the "relics" even of young, living authors, and letters as well as manuscripts were in demand.[25]

The most important bookseller-publisher Hanley was involved with was C. J. Greenwood, the scion of a manufacturing family from the border of Lancashire and the West Riding. The historians of The Bodley Head, where Greenwood later worked, say that Greenwood met Hanley while he was running a bookshop in South Kensington, but since bookshops seem to have been the agora of Hanley's life in Liverpool, it is possible that they met there, where Greenwood ran a short-lived shop with an Armenian friend ("books this side, carpets the other") in the middle of the Depression. Greenwood was carried away by Hanley's writing, invited the author to live with him, and began publishing his work in limited editions—first under Greenwood's own name, and then through Boriswood, an imprint that he and his friends Terence Bond and John Morris set up with the intention of publishing left fiction.[26]

Greenwood, Partridge, and the others published Hanley's early work in limited editions issued, as his admirer Henry Green put it, "at a revolting price & printed in a disgustingly exquisite way." The work's content ensured that it would be confined to such publishers and this sort of format. *Boy,* for instance, which appeared in 1931, subjects its young protagonist to rape by sailors and later to a venereal disease. Ethel Mannin, who was well known for her sexual emancipation, was appalled when she read the manuscript for The Bodley Head: "the whole book is nothing but buggery and brothels and filth and horror." Obscenity laws were diligently policed in interwar Britain: the banning of Radclyffe Hall's *The Well of Loneliness* was the most notorious case, but on a more quotidian level booksellers who dealt in illicit material could expect raids, and publishers were extremely cautious about obscenity and libel. Privately issuing a limited edition to subscribers was not legally publication, and thus circumvented the Obscene Publications Act of 1857, under which *The Well of Loneliness* had been prosecuted. Male homosexual writers and readers had long used limited editions for this reason, and there was a gay subculture connected by bibliophily, fine printing, and erotic literature, often weighted toward 1890s decadence.[27]

In Hanley's case, limited-edition publishing did not ward off obscenity proceedings. Several years after Boriswood issued *Boy*, a reader in Bury objected to it. (That a commercial circulating library in Bury stocked such a book sits uncomfortably with common assumptions about the geography of taste.) The local authorities charged the library owner and Boriswood with a common law obscene libel offense, which did not require formal publication. When the case came to trial in 1935, Neville Laski, the king's counsel Boriswood retained for the case, urged the firm's directors to plead guilty to mitigate the fine: "an energetic defence to a Lancashire jury would only be likely to result in imprisonment for all directors." They pleaded guilty; the firm was fined £250 and each of its three directors £50.[28]

In the long term, then, Hanley was no boon to Boriswood, but from about 1931 to 1934 his career had been suffering at their hands. He complained that the firm lacked sufficient funds to advertise books properly—evidently expecting the firm to act like a real publisher when it was able to handle inflammatory work such as his only because it was *not* a real publisher. Hanley did receive offers from the mainstream publishing house John Lane, which offered to buy out the rest of his contract with Boriswood. Despite its lack of money, Boriswood resisted: publishing with friends had understandable risks when things soured.[29] Eventually Boriswood released Hanley, and he signed with Chatto & Windus, the first of many major publishers he would work with. By this time, the mid-1930s, his work had attracted the interest and personal support of a constellation of noted writers: Henry Green, Nancy Cunard, Richard Aldington, J. C. Powys, Storm Jameson; E. M. Forster took up the case of *Boy* as he later would more successfully with *Lady Chatterley's Lover*. Yet Hanley ran his literary career erratically, as his correspondence makes clear, and the intervention of stellar figures did not solve his money worries or give his career any of the stability sought by, say, Willy Goldman or George Garrett.[30] As far as Hanley's writing was concerned, this did not matter: holed up in North Wales, he wrote prolifically. He resembled Jack Overhill in his will to write and the volume of his output; but in his case, unlike Overhill's, there were publishers hungry for his work, and willing, in the short term, to tolerate its author's ways.

Chatto & Windus was not the only major publisher taking an interest in "proletarian writing." The subject had become topical. In 1936 the *London Mercury* carried an article on the subject and published a number of responses, one of them by Leslie Halward, who argued that "proletarian" fiction could only be written from within the working class: F. C. Boden and Walter Brierley were ruled out because they had been to Nottingham University College and the viewpoints of their protagonists were irrevocably changed by this embourgeoisement of the mind. (Halward told the *Mercury*'s editor that Edgell Rickword's comments in *Left*

Review made him seem "very peeved that the discussion didn't take place in that journal.") In the *Mercury* later that year, William Plomer reported that a publisher was "offering a prize for a specimen of proletarian fiction, in the belief that England is a little backward in this department." Publishers were judging—or gambling on the chance—that the potential readership of working-class writing extended beyond the 50,000 or so working-class intellectuals, lower-middle-class alumni of grammar schools and provincial universities, and left-leaning professional men and women whom Julian Symons would later judge to have formed the base of the pyramid of the "political-artistic movement of the Thirties."[31]

The most straightforward reason publishers went after "proletarian writing" was its relative novelty. It was not uncommon in the 1930s to observe that the range of experience that British fiction had to draw on was worryingly limited. First on Cyril Connolly's list of the "defects of English novels" was "*Thinness of Material* . . . 90 per cent. of English authors come from the mandarin class, the experiences from which both sexes can draw are limited to three or four—a peaceful childhood, a public school education, a university, a few years in London or the provinces in which to get a job, a wife, a house, and some children. Material for one book, perhaps, which publishers and the need to earn one's living will drag out to three or four. A rigorous class system blankets down all attempts to enlarge these barriers. The English mandarin simply can't get at pugilists, gangsters, speakeasies, negroes."[32] Though he would not have appreciated the comparison, Connolly's position here is essentially the same as that of those writers' circle speakers who drew a straight line between personal experience and literary text.

Absent "negroes" and "gangsters," the largest domain of unexploited "material" was working-class life. Someone at Methuen appears to have been struck by this thought. Methuen's directors had done little to cultivate a strong fiction list, and in 1931 the company resorted to a competition for "Novels of English Life Today" as a means of bringing in manuscripts. By the mid-1930s Methuen was publishing Hanley and had engaged him to "collect . . . proletarian stories," presumably for an anthology that never appeared. Methuen also published Halward's book of short stories, *To Tea on Sunday,* and Brierley's novels *Sandwichman* and *Means Test Man,* though the latter, at least, was not a financial success. The company's promotional material for *Means Test Man* made it clear that fiction from "the unprinted proletariat" was of interest not just for its general novelty but also because of its topicality in the years during and after the Slump and the collapse of northern industry. *Means Test Man* was a "faithful picture of the moral and spiritual enervation which the Public Assistance system . . . forces upon sensitive people. It is almost the duty of every intelligent British man and woman to read this book . . . and to face up to the facts in it."[33]

Publishers' interest in getting working people, or working men, to give voice to "working-class" experiences and attitudes in a time of strife is of a piece with other publishing events of the decade. Though unemployment had been an epidemic since the early 1920s, it was in the 1930s that the condition of the working class was thoroughly aired among the middle-class public. The flood of social surveys such as John Boyd Orr's *Food, Health and Income,* the *Social Survey of Merseyside,* Penguins on the "distressed areas" and working-class wives, and newsreels and documentaries all drew attention to the predicament of the impoverished. So did "social-democratic" middlebrow novels such as A. J. Cronin's *The Stars Look Down* and Winifred Holtby's *South Riding.*[34] The Slump and industrial crises had prompted a series of "condition of England" and "two nations" books revealing the suffering of working-class families in the distressed areas. *The Road to Wigan Pier* is now the most famous of these, but there were other such travelogues: Jack Hilton wrote one; J. L. Hodson even called his *The Two Englands.* The paradigmatic text was *English Journey,* in which J. B. Priestley tried to make sense of an old, pastoral England, an urban, industrial England forged in the nineteenth century, and a swelling consumerist, standardized, and "democratic" England. To place *English Journey* and working-class writing within the same frame is not, of course, to make them equivalent. Novels by working-class men were not as popular as those by Priestley, Cronin, or Holtby; Walter Greenwood's *Love on the Dole* was the only one that became a bestseller. The spectacle of unemployment did not generate a large reading public hungry for working-class fiction, but it did make publishers think that such fiction was a responsible gamble.

It is this social context that distinguishes the mainstream publishers' work with plebeian authors in the 1930s from their dealings at other times. Established firms had a long, if irregular, history of accepting novels by workers. Two books that were touchstones for many authors and critics of working-class fiction had been published by mainstream publishers. D. H. Lawrence's *Sons and Lovers* had been rejected by Heinemann on snobbish grounds; Edward Garnett, the influential reader at Duckworth, knew Lawrence and offered to read the novel for his firm, which quickly accepted it. Robert Tressell's *The Ragged Trousered Philanthropists* was published by Grant Richards. Both before and after the Popular Front, people like Richards and Garnett—adventurous directors and readers whose opinions were taken very seriously—secured contracts for working-class writers. Certain publishing houses were especially open to these authors—Jonathan Cape, for instance, which published Greenwood and Jack Hilton in the 1930s, and Herbert Jenkins, which in the first two decades of the century had published Patrick MacGill, James Welsh, and Ethel Carnie Holdsworth.[35]

In Herbert Jenkins's case, politics may have played a significant part in the editorial decisions; in the others, a liberal cast of mind and a belief that aesthetic judgments warranted certain publishing risks were decisive. Richards published *The Ragged Trousered Philanthropists* despite rather than because of its politics. Garnett had been raised in a family of Victorian liberal values, and tried to act as a disinterested servant of literature. The working-class cast of *Sons and Lovers* did not deter him as it had Heinemann's reader, but Hanley's working-class credentials were not enough to make Garnett appreciate his writing, despite an appeal from Hanley himself and Henry Green's efforts to interest Garnett in Hanley's work. Editors of similar disposition published working-class authors in periodicals—C. B. Purdom, a high-minded editor in the tradition of the public moralist, gave Leslie Halward his first acceptance, in *Everyman,* a serious but not solemn alternative to *John o' London's Weekly* that gave special attention to submissions by "unknown authors." The publishing history of working-class writing was thus part of the history of mainstream British publishing as well as the history of Popular Front initiatives and institutions. And the texts working-class authors produced were more influenced by currents of British writing generally than by genres and styles associated especially with the literary left of the 1930s.[36]

Leslie Halward wanted to write "in my own language about my own people," but his people did not provide him with many literary models. While figures such as Robert Tressell might serve as role models as working-class men envisioned themselves as authors, the literary traditions within which they worked were hardly "indigenous" to the working class. Echoes of older works of literature sound through 1930s working-class fiction. "Mrs Gaskell's *Mary Barton,* Charles Kingsley's *Alton Locke,* Charles

Dickens's *Hard Times,* D. H. Lawrence's early fictions, had all anticipated . . . [1930s] novels in stirring the reader's sentiments and sentimentality on behalf of proletarians in hardship and economic struggle." Dickens's deathbed scenes and Lawrence's scenes of wounded or dead miners being carried to their graves by mates echo through mining novels of the 1930s. The idea of the proletarian community as "collective 'hero'" in Zola's *Germinal* underpins British novels by Lewis Jones, Harold Heslop, and Len Doherty. Hilton named Zola and Lawrence as two of his three "Literary idols." The third was Shakespeare. Hilton wrote a novel about Dunkirk called *Laugh at Polonius* and entitled his book of polemic and autobiography *Caliban Shrieks,* quoting and endorsing that other subaltern's unexpected use of literacy: "You taught me a language, and my profit on't is, I know how to curse." Though he exploited Shakespearean references (and played on Shakespeare's canonical status), Hilton wrote, as one would expect, more like Lawrence or Zola. When the BBC asked Coombes to do a broadcast on "the one book which has most affected my outlook in life," he chose the classic fictional representation of the thwarted artisan intellectual, Hardy's *Jude the Obscure.* Coombes's own fiction, however, has none of the lavish description, attention-seeking allusions, and editorializing that characterize Hardy's novels. The figures who shape an author's poetics are not necessarily those whom the author holds most dear. For working-class writers of the 1930s, the predominant stylistic influences were late nineteenth-century or contemporary novelists and exponents of the short story. In discussing how working-class fiction drew on other literary traditions, my focus is on short fiction, partly because most critical attention has been directed at novels, but more because the short story was, for manual workers as for others, the preeminent genre of the novice writer in the twentieth century.[37]

Since the bulk of the short fiction published in Britain was "commercial" and "escapist," a working-class man's initiation into the reading and writing of fiction could come through this channel rather than through high-minded autodidact ones. Lehmann believed that "men who have had no formal education beyond elementary school too often use the jargon of newspapers and the lurid style of cheap novelettes when they try to write." Evaluating a "proletarian story" for Allen and Unwin, a reader commented: "A few realistic passages have some merit as descriptions of sordid life, but the writer always falls again to the moronic depths of the threepenny mag." As children, Willy Goldman and a cousin produced a magazine with pencils and exercise books: "It was arranged that I would supply the 'stories'; my cousin the 'jokes'; some one else the 'articles' . . . The contents, I need scarcely mention, were seventy-five per cent filched from the current weeklies; what was 'original' was sheer gibberish." Goldman's fictional contributions "were full of sentences running in this style: "'You demon,' he shouted, and with a hoarse cry lurched forward . . ." Popular models were not automatically cast aside in politically conscious adulthood. Hilton, who relished his role as an independent left-wing gadfly, thought about taking a break from "semi-political novels . . . for a while" after finishing his novel *Champion*. In the meantime he was "going to do a real kiss-me-all-over-DARLING love novel. Expect it to be easy."[38]

While casting about for a way of following up his initial urge to write, Halward sought guidance from the literary advice industry. He bought several how-to manuals, including Michael Joseph's *How to Write a Short Story*. Recalling this purchase, Halward told an audience of writers and would-be writers: "Mr. Joseph's book, and indeed all the books on the subject which I have come across, are concerned with what is generally know[n] as the commercial short story . . . These things must necessarily be of a type." The rules and strategies Joseph laid down were for stories in which the plot was the most important element, followed by "construction" (the handling of action and suspense), dialogue and characterization, and finally style, which accounted for 5 percent of a story's value in Joseph's ledger. Those, like Halward, who wanted to write noncommercial stories had to make their own rules and assign their own values to the aspects of a work of fiction.[39]

Halward's mature stories break with the forms of "the commercial short story," but they remain indebted to a more respected tradition of short fiction from which the commercial story borrowed heavily. One of the pivotal moments in Halward's career was the day he read a Chekhov story in a tuppenny literary weekly. He devoured all the Chekhov stories he could find at the public library, and tried to imitate them. In particular he attempted to write with "ice-cold detachment . . . to write as if you'd been a witness and were quite unaffected by the affair, and not as if you were heart-broken because of what happened." His Chekhov "trance" was broken by an enthusiasm for Liam O'Flaherty, which was in turn tempered by an appreciation of H. E. Bates. Bates also captured the imagination of Fred Urquhart. Several years before Urquhart made his debut with a short story in the *Adelphi* (thanks to Jack Common) and became involved with the Left Book Club's Scottish Poets' and Writers' Group, he was submitting stories to Bates, who was one of the editors of *New Stories,* and working on a critical appreciation of Bates's writing.[40]

Bates's reputation is now colored by the Kentish Rabelaisianism of *The Darling Buds of May.* After the bucolic indulgence of Pop Larkin and the other characters in that book it comes as a surprise to learn that at the beginning of his career Bates was one of the regulars at Charles Lahr's Progressive Bookshop, and that Lahr published one of Bates's early books within a year or two of doing the same for James Hanley. In the late

1920s and the 1930s Bates was known primarily for his short fiction. He wrote within the emerging English short story tradition, which was heavily influenced by Chekhov—Bates had reacted to Chekhov much as Halward had—and associated with names such as Katherine Mansfield and A. E. Coppard.[41] This tradition was known especially for the "plotless" story that writers of popular "magazine" fiction sometimes opposed outright and sometimes circled round with a mix of attraction and suspicion. But it also took in less mechanical versions of the twist-in-the-tail effect that so occupied the minds of those freelances. This short story tradition was a crucial influence on working-class fiction, but one that has largely been ignored in critical discussion of thirties writing, in part because of the attention paid to the influence of documentary forms. Consider James Hanley's 1938 review of one of Halward's books. Where others reviewed Halward's collections under the rubric of "proletarian literature," Hanley placed Halward in the context of "the English short story." Hanley's own stories tended to be narratives that happened to be short, rather than purposefully brief pieces designed to deliver a single impression. He saw Halward's fiction as symptomatic of the weaknesses of this newer tradition: "The poverty of the short story can be laid at the feet of the disciples of Chekov and De Maupassant, not even excepting the over-rated Miss Mansfield, and all that their crusade can show for its pains is the stifling of the very substance that could give a new meaning and direction to the English short story."[42]

As well as in lightly plotted works, the influence of the contemporary short story is also evident in working-class authors' propensity to aim for surprise endings. Their surprises are not of the sort where the ruinously lost necklace turns out to have been a fake, but they are structurally similar and exploit their affiliation—as pastiche or as parody—with the *moralitas* at the end of a fairy tale. Coombes's "The Flame" tells of a miner who discovers a pocket of gas that will kill him if it explodes, describing his state of mind as he prepares for death with heroic humility. Suddenly the gas and the danger dissipate. Then comes the punch line: peril averted, the miner resumes work as usual. Several of Jim Phelan's stories also use surprise effects at the end. "The Slip" revolves around a wake in an Irish slum for an emaciated seven-year-old girl. There is an ongoing conversation with a reporter about how every story needs a hero. The dead girl's family has received a funeral insurance payment of thirteen pounds. They use the money for food and tobacco, and smuggle the body into a small country churchyard where they bury it for free. The hero of this story, the reporter declares in the last line, is the thirteen pounds. The story disconcertingly takes the stock notion of the folksy resourcefulness and cheekiness of the poor and embeds it in a situation of misery and squalor. Pressing forward to a punch line for which the groundwork has been laid from the beginning heightens the grotesqueness and compounds the ambivalence of the story.[43]

Fred Urquhart's stories regularly end with surprises, sometimes with a grimness that goes nowhere near as far as "The Slip," more often with wry celebration of working-class character (and "characters") in the manner of another of Phelan's stories, "Amongst Those Present," or Coombes's "The Flame."[44] The ending of Urquhart's "Sweat" is positively slapstick despite its darker purpose. Jeanie, who works in a clothing factory, is mortified by the smell of her sweat. She feels like the girl with BO in the ads in American magazines. She is, as Janet Montefiore has pointed out, a figure akin to the slum girl Orwell sees from a train in *The Road to Wigan Pier,* an instance of "the trope whereby a woman's physical degradation represents working-class oppression." On payday Jeanie spends a shilling's overtime pay on a bottle of scent, Flowers of Passion. She puts it on before seeing her boyfriend. Later, in the park, she lets him "paw" her, deciding that the fear of being an old spinster working in the factory outweighs that of losing her respectability. The boyfriend suddenly sniffs in disgust. Her face falls. "'Why the hell d'you put on all that cheap scent, Jeanie?' Harry said." The story ends there.[45]

"Sweat" was published in *Fact,* the print headquarters of the documentary movement in Britain. It appeared in number four, "Writing in Revolt: Theory and Practice." The theoretical pieces included Storm Jameson's much-cited essay "Documents." The first of the issue's examples of documentary practice is from an official report on the explosion in the Gresford colliery, which took the lives of more than two hundred miners. The excerpt consists of a colliery worker's narrative of what happened, with occasional questions by the investigators. This stenographic record is very different from the three texts by working-class writers included in this number of *Fact.* After Urquhart's piece comes a Halward story in which an unemployed man on the road takes shelter in a ruined cottage with a rich and attractive young woman. She is well-meaning but uncomprehending, thinking at first that he is hiking for recreation, and he becomes increasingly but privately enraged by their conversation. In a different way from Urquhart's "Sweat," a female character and the suggestion of sex, conspicuous by its absence in this situation, are used to articulate the injuries of class; the lesson is compounded when the woman hands the man a pound note, which he crumples up but keeps. The other working-class piece is a story by Hanley about a charwoman, treated heartlessly and stingily by the shipping company for which she works, going home to her unemployed husband and ungrateful children on Christmas Eve. In their different ways the three stories represent situations and experiences outside the mainstream of the subject matter of British writing. Yet however much their material may have approached that of *The Road to*

Wigan Pier or Mass-Observation's *The Pub and the People*, there could be no doubting that these were narratives, not reportage.[46]

Documentary and reportage, of course, were kinds of writing characteristic of outsiders, middle-class ethnographers investigating working-class communities. Yet documentary was part of the literary culture of the 1930s generally, and documentary sensibilities interlocked with the increase in published working-class writing: plebeian authors were encouraged to "document" working-class experience, without the taint of middle-class observers' prejudices. In short fiction, documentary aesthetics often made their presence felt through the advice and demands of editors. One reason for the editorial premium on straightforward descriptive writing was the desire for authentic accounts of working-class life and the related constraints of some of the slots workers were offered in publications—descriptions of an hour at work for a *Left Review* competition, accounts of their lives for *Seven Shifts*. Perhaps another reason was an editorial belief that a good way to nurture undeveloped talent was to encourage authors to describe things clearly and precisely. Lehmann, as we have seen, found the language of the pulp novelette to be the default mode of many novice working-class writers.

Yet these editorial preferences were conducive to vignette-style short stories as well as to fiction inflected by reportage. Lehmann, in correspondence with worker-writers, frequently used the term "sketch," a generic label also used by commercial writers and editors. Jameson warned middle-class writers of the dangerous ease of sliding from proper, unsentimental (and not terribly well defined) documentary to "'slices of life' in the manner of the Naturalists of the 'eighties." And "descriptive writing" did not always mean clinical reportage. The editor of *Seven* told Chaplin: "I am genuinely impressed by your prose. It is far and away the best descriptive writing I have seen in compiling the spring number of

Seven. But I don't think it should try to be a story . . . I would very much like to use some of 'Swimming' . . . if you will give me permission to throw away the drama and stick to the descriptive." The published version describes boys going swimming after a day's work in the mines; the sensuousness of the swim and the lyrical description of the industrial and natural landscape recall Hardy and Lawrence.[47]

The intersections of the forms of "the English short story" with efforts to capture working-class life and speech may be illustrated by Halward's celebrated story "Arch Anderson."[48] Halward recounts the courting of Arch and Lil, and the life they make after she becomes pregnant. They marry and live happily with their daughter. One Saturday, rain drives Arch from his gardening in their allotment and into a pub. Some men he knows press him to drink with them, teasing him about being under his wife's thumb. Eventually the teasing leads to false aspersions that Lil is having an affair with the milkman and that Arch's excessive attention to the allotment has blinded him to the affair. Arch wrestles with the suspicion, but in his drunken state he succumbs to it when he sees the milkman's cart outside their house. He bashes the milkman, and life deteriorates. Arch gets a month's hard labor; when he finds a new job, a theft at work leads to whispers that he has been in jail, and he is sacked. In every subsequent job he is the first to be let go when work is scarce, and he is unemployed more often than not.

Working-class "voices" dominate the text. Sometimes they do so in the form of extensive, spare dialogue. One full page consists of dialogue supplemented by only three narrative stage directions: "he said," "A long silence," and "Another silence." Working-class speech patterns are also worked into the text through free-indirect style—characters' "voices" are incorporated into the narration without clear demarcations of direct or reported speech. "He didn't know why, but he felt tired to-night. A bit of shut-eye wouldn't come amiss. It wouldn't that." The syntax of the narrative voice is as clipped as the words of the characters—as Walter Allen observed, there is only one relative clause in the whole story.[49] When Arch becomes smitten with Lil, however, the story switches briefly to the repetitive, accumulative patterning of a children's tale or a joke:

> He fell asleep eventually, still thinking about her.
>
> He thought about her almost as soon as he opened his eyes in the morning.
>
> He thought about her from time to time during the day.
>
> He thought about her as he sat having his tea.
>
> And the more he thought about her the more he fancied her. And the more he fancied her, the more certain he became that, somehow or other, he'd got to have her.

Only in the final paragraph of the story is the reader directly told anything about Lil's feelings: "Lil grew very pale and thin. She never reproached him for anything, for it seemed to her that, somehow or other, she was to blame." That closing sentence is a sudden break with the convention, endorsed by writers' circle guides and by many successful writers, that a short story should have a single narrative point of view, in this case that of Arch. In breaking with this one convention of the short story, it yields another device the genre prized: a wry surprise at the end. This surprise gives a poignant glimpse of another character's thoughts and indirectly points out their absence from the narrative's field of vision for most of the story. "Arch Anderson" thus combines artifice and the impression of artlessness. The "authentic" working-class diction of the narration is achieved through the free-indirect style current in fiction since Flaubert: Halward did not, and could not, write entirely "in my own language."

The British short story tradition was more of an influence on the working-class authors of the 1930s than high modernism was, but modernism was not off-limits to these authors.[50] Perhaps the most ambitious of their engagements with modernism was *Major Operation,* a 1936 novel by the Scottish dockworker, engineer, and communist James Barke. Valentine Cunningham has used a passage from this novel to argue against the common practice of seeing the politically committed literature of the 1930s as divorced from the modernist experimentation of the 1920s. Barke's polyphonic description of a demonstration in a Glasgow street conjures with canonical names from a European "tradition" and scrambles them so that, for instance, Kubla Khan becomes a horse running in a race that afternoon; the workers are estranged from tradition "except in some wry or queered or wrenched version." Barke also borrows directly, to the point of quotation, from James Joyce's *Ulysses,* dividing up sections of the novel with mock newspaper headlines, mentioning "Mrs Bloom," and repeating a pun from the book followed by the comment "good lad Joyce." Barke was a committed communist, and his novels adhere to the changing party line so diligently that the political strategies advocated in *The Land of the Leal* (1939) are not compatible with those counseled in the earlier novel. Despite party condemnation of Joyce, most stridently by Karl Radek at the Moscow Writers' Congress in 1934, Barke incorporated modernist innovations—and modernist imperatives—into his fiction.[51]

Sid Chaplin combined an interest in modernism with more traditional tastes. He tried to master classical verse forms. His notebooks include definitions of anapests and Spenserian stanzas, notes on Petrarchan versus Shakespearean sonnets. Chaplin frequently marked up drafts of his own poems to show how they scanned. Some of these unpublished poems are conventionally rhymed and have strong, regular meters. Yet he also read more daring work, and even liked Louis Aragon's surrealist poetry. Shortly after his efforts to write sonnets, Chaplin moved on to less traditionally disciplined forms. A friend judged one of his poems "too consciously Day Lewis." Another poem from the same period was a miner's prayer in dialect ("When intae darkness Ah descend / Strength with courage wilt Thou blend?"). He continued to write prose that did not decisively break with convention, and that drew on the narrative styles of northeast working-class culture. Chaplin's interest in contemporary British and European writing was a stimulus that coexisted with, and did not seriously unsettle, his interest in more traditional and local forms.[52]

Other writers on the left disagreed with Alec Brown when he declared: "LITERARY ENGLISH FROM CAXTON TO US IS AN ARTIFICIAL JARGON OF THE RULING CLASS: WRITTEN ENGLISH BEGINS WITH US."[53] Nor did working-class authors attempt to create a wholly new literature. Some of them took an interest in modernism, and the residues of "literary English" and "English literature" were always already embedded in any "proletarian" fiction. In their paths to publication, too, the working-class authors of the 1930s were not just creations of the Popular Front, but a current of the general stream of British literature. Established firms as well as left-wing publishers and editors played a significant part in bringing workers' manuscripts to light, and the fellow traveler who acted most like an established liberal editor—John Lehmann—was the most important Popular Front patron of worker-writers.

Many of the problems faced by these working-class men were different from those of writers' circle members, and the dearth of female working-class authors points up a glaring difference between the literary possibilities open to manual workers and those available to the middle class. Yet plebeian authors and middle-class aspirants did not occupy altogether separate worlds. For both, romanticism and the genre of the short story were crucial to the kinds of writers they were. But they reworked these traditions in contrasting ways. Circle members cleaved more to the strongly plotted "magazine story" pioneered in the late nineteenth century; worker-writers were more influenced by the ways H. E. Bates had developed some of the same inheritance. And where middle-class aspirants tended to cast themselves as entertainers and exponents of a craft, subscribing to a romanticism in which sincere experiences or perceptions were funneled into texts, working-class men, encouraged by the Promethean tenor of the autodidact tradition, could be readier to think of themselves as romantic artists.

Chapter 6

People's Writing and the People's War

The working-class writer as a duck was one of James Hanley's more peculiar metaphors. Writing in 1953, Hanley was recalling the 1930s interest in "proletarian writing." Working-class ducks gathered on the deck of a ship; when the ship reached strange waters, the ducks flew off. Literature needed worker-writers for a time, and then the Second World War displaced the political questions of the prewar decade.[1] However oddly, Hanley was expressing the already conventional view that the engagement between Popular Front intellectuals and working-class writers did not outlast the 1930s. To some extent this is true. Even before the Nazi-Soviet pact, some of the fellow-traveling literati had begun to part ways with more committed leftists. Nevertheless, *New Writing* continued to seek out worker-writers, new journals still gave space to working-class authors, and some of those authors blended into the literary and drinking circles of wartime London.

The most important extension—and transformation—of the popular writing initiatives of the 1930s was *Seven: A Magazine of People's Writing*. It was a tremendously popular journal, most of whose contributors were nonprofessional writers. In both its contributors and its subject matter, *Seven* had a better claim to the designation "people's writing" than any other periodical or organization of its time. It pulled in aspiring writers of different social classes, and its regular feature in which people wrote about their jobs drew on the self-documenting tradition of Mass-Observation as well as *New Writing, Left Review,* and *Fact.* Yet *Seven,* which ran from 1941 to 1947,[2] was more than just a conclusion to a story of Popular Front literary endeavor that is usually assumed to have ended with the outbreak of war. It was also the most substantial intersection of the two main currents of popular writing in the first half of the twentieth century: the tradition of working-class writing and the aspirant writers' movement represented by writers' circles. Workers and middle-class aspirants alike contributed to *Seven;* the magazine's mission merged a left-wing celebration of working people with a valorization of the ordinary that had often had a conservative (and Conservative) character in 1930s Britain; and its representation of ordinary lives owed as much to the popular press as it did to left-wing documentary. *Seven* blended Popular Front literary campaigns with the writers' circles' egalitarian precept that ordinary people were creative enough to write. Where *Left Review* and *New Writing* had sought out working-class writers in the interests of creating a socialist literature or one faithful to the realities of the time, *Seven*'s editors made a point of saying that everyone should be free to write.

Seven's politics were left-wing, but it did not follow the Communist Party's line, or indeed any firm political program: rather, it was a forum for articulations of the broad populism associated with the idea of the Second World War as "the people's war." Yet there were limits to the politicization of writing in *Seven* and even in a more overtly political writers' organization, the Front Line Generation. These limits, I will suggest, are evidence not of a weakness of popular politicization during the Second World War, but of the way fiction and poetry were perceived by many people who were just beginning to write. Even politically conscious people could tacitly assume that imaginative writing and political expression did not mix.

During the war, working-class authors associated with the 1930s mingled with other young writers, both socially and in the pages of new little magazines. Fred Urquhart had lived in Edinburgh in the late 1930s, where he organized the Left Book Club's Scottish Poets' and Writers' Group. He was a conscientious objector assigned to agricultural work, but he was often in London on leave, and was "a part of the Soho circuit." Willy Goldman also became part of this milieu of literary activity, prodigious drinking, seedy living, and splendidly bad behavior by such figures as J. Meary Tambimuttu, Dylan Thomas, and Julian Maclaren-Ross. Urquhart and Maclaren-Ross, both writers of comic fiction with some social and political barbs, became friends and drinking companions. Although Urquhart kept writing "sketches of proletarian life"—the wartime ones chronicled "randy soldiers and laundry or munition girls . . . public-house bars and cinemas and cheap lodgings"—he was assimilating to London literary life. By the end of the war he had fitted in sufficiently to become the literary editor of *Tribune,* a paper whose mission was to pull the Labour Party leftward.[3]

At *Tribune* Urquhart took over from John Atkins, whose *New Saxon Pamphlets* published some of the writers in the armed and auxiliary forces whose names recur in other wartime publications. This chain of connections and contacts is an example of the way the war brought promising writers in the forces into contact with working-class writers, junior members of the literary establishment such as Lehmann and Cyril Connolly, and younger people making their debuts as editors of publications such as *English Story, Modern Reading, Bugle Blast,* and *Writing Today.* Their editors—Woodrow Wyatt, Reginald Moore, Jack Aistrop, and, less effectually, Denys Val Baker—were at once interested in discovering new writers and compelled to find them, because they were not sufficiently established to be able to fill their pages with the work of well-known authors. Wyatt, Moore, and Aistrop were, to varying degrees, on the left, while Baker was an "individualist" with ties to "neo-romantic" anarchists and pacifists like Derek Stanford and the future sex guru Alex Comfort. Their magazines did not profess a political orientation, but they published a fair amount of work by left-wing and working-class writers. Their magazines occupied some of the ground broken by *New Writing*, and drew on the same pool of contributors.

The beginning of the war was not an auspicious time to start a periodical. More than 900 magazines and newspapers suspended publication. Paper was rationed from 1940 until 1949. Under the Control of Paper order of February 1940, publishers were allowed paper in quantities up to 60 percent of their paper consumption between August 1938 and August 1939. Because Norway was Britain's principal supplier of wood and pulp, after the German invasion of Norway this allowance was cut, initially to 30 percent. By 1943 publishers were entitled to only 6.5 percent of the quantity of paper they had used in 1938–39. It also became illegal to start a new periodical, though the enterprising devised means of circumventing the ban. One way was to take over an existing publication and transform it, while maintaining nominal continuity. Another strategy was to launch what Denys Val Baker called the "book-magazine"—treating each issue of the magazine as a free-standing book or booklet. An official at the Ministry of Information told Miron Grandea that it would be illegal for him to continue publishing *Adam* as a magazine, but that he could bring out successive volumes entitled *Eve, Cain,* and so on.[4]

One of the most substantial and durable "book-magazines" was *English Story,* the creation of Woodrow Wyatt. The Oxford-educated scion of an illustrious, "declining" family, Wyatt served in the army during the war and rose to the rank of major, though he was not involved in combat. He joined the Labour Party in 1945 and became MP for Aston in the general election of that year. Like many others, Wyatt had been excited by Edward J. O'Brien's annual anthologies of the best short stories published in Britain. One of Wyatt's own stories, first published in an Oxford undergraduate magazine, was reprinted in O'Brien's 1940 volume. Detecting a need for an outlet for previously unpublished short stories, Wyatt talked to O'Brien about starting a magazine for this purpose. After the ban on new periodicals was imposed, "the only alternative was to seek a publisher who would be willing to publish new short stories in book form." For someone so young (he was born in 1918), Wyatt had a remarkable facility for getting established figures to take him seriously, and he persuaded F. T. Smith of Collins to accept his proposal. The first issue appeared in 1941, edited by Wyatt and his wife Susan. *English Story* was supposed to be an outlet for "the 'non-commercial' story . . . one without an immediately popular appeal, which does not conform to the stereotyped pattern demanded by most magazine editors."[5]

English Story had Leslie Halward on its advisory committee and published a number of other working-class authors, including Sid Chaplin and Gordon Jeffery, the Portsmouth shipwright and trade unionist whose "In the Welding Bay" I mentioned in Chapter 4.[6] Without committing itself politically, *English Story* was picking up some of the constituency of *New Writing*. So were *Modern Reading*, which Reginald Moore founded in 1941, and *Bugle Blast*, a series of anthologies of imaginative writing from the services, principally by novice writers, which Moore co-edited with Jack Aistrop.

The channeling of working-class writers into these new periodicals was not the only mutation of Popular Front practices during the war. New literary magazines attempted to take up some of the burden of the late *Left Review*. Early in 1944 John Singer published the first number of his book-magazine *Million: New Left*

Writing, which carried poetry, fiction, and articles, and which promised play scripts and "reportage" in the future. *Million* was based in Glasgow, and among its contributors were Scottish writers and cultural gadflies such as Maurice Lindsay and Hugh McDiarmid; so was Joe Corrie. One of Sid Chaplin's submissions was rejected, but Singer asked to see more. In his programmatic essay in the first issue, "Literature and War," Singer praised "the better stories and reportage contained in collections like 'Modern Reading' and 'New Writing,'" to some degree aligning *Million* with them.[7]

Seven had started off quite differently from these left and leftish little magazines. Initially, *Seven* was dominated by poets of the "Apocalyptic" school such as G. S. Fraser and Henry Treece, and by prose writers such as Lawrence Durrell and David Gascoyne. Some time after the spring of 1940, Philip O'Connor, who had been a contributor, bought out the original editors. Because paper rationing regulations obliged him to maintain nominal continuity with the magazine's previous incarnation, O'Connor's *Seven* retained what was now an even less meaningful title. But he added the subtitle "Magazine of Popular Writing." *Seven* would now feature "non-professional writers and artists . . . Documentary Stories . . . Poems . . . Children's Writings . . . Photographs." O'Connor had grown up in France with his mother, who attempted to shore up her precarious fortune with a variety of schemes; in his teens they moved to Soho. O'Connor refused to stay at school past the age of sixteen, and lived as a tramp, a practice he would resume every so often. As well as tramping, in the late 1930s he wrote poetry and lived for a while with Charles Madge and Kathleen Raine. In his autobiography O'Connor mentions that he had some dealings with *Poetry and the People* and briefly sold the communist *Daily Worker.* "I employed the term 'dialectical materialism' frequently without knowing what I meant, and understood, indeed, little of communist theory: and my intellectual and petit-bourgeois snobbery kept me clear of working-class affiliations." The new *Seven* was just the sort of magazine one would expect from someone with ties to the surrealist poet and Mass-Observation founder Charles Madge and ambivalent relations with *Poetry and the People*.[8]

O'Connor's co-editor was the Communist Party worker Gordon Cruickshank, an elusive figure in the historiographies of British communism and literary culture. In one of the rare mentions of the new *Seven* in a scholarly work, Andy Croft says that Cruickshank was "installed . . . as editor" by Randall Swingler when the latter bought *Seven* from O'Connor shortly before the end of 1941. But Cruickshank was co-editing the magazine while O'Connor was still the owner, before Swingler bought it for a mere twenty-five pounds. Swingler had wanted to get *Seven*'s paper ration for Fore Publications, a publishing operation that he and his brother Humphrey had founded. Edgell Rickword and Jack Lindsay were involved too. The firm's main line of work was publishing 64-page pamphlets: some polemics, some fiction, and some pro-communist children's books. Swingler thought better of his plans for *Seven* and allowed it to continue, since under Cruickshank the magazine was returning a profit. When Cruickshank left to work for the party full time, he was succeeded by Sydney D. Tremayne, under whose editorship *Seven* prospered further, subsidizing Fore Publications' other operations.[9]

Tremayne, the longest-serving editor of the magazine, was a poet and had been a subeditor on the *Daily Mirror*. He was an auxiliary fireman during the war, like other writers such as Stephen Spender and Henry Green. Tremayne edited *Seven* in peculiar circumstances. In his unpublished autobiography he makes no mention of Swingler, perhaps indicating that Swingler had been called up into the armed services before Tremayne took over from

Cruickshank. Instead Tremayne refers to "Jack Lindsay's Fore Publications." Mike Flanagan, a fellow subeditor at the *Mirror* and a communist, had been told by Charlie Castro, the circulation manager of the *Daily Worker,* that *Seven* needed an editor. "I did not know who Fore Publications were," Tremayne wrote. "They did not know who I was. I never spoke to Jack Lindsay until many years afterwards, and that was briefly, at a reading of poetry. It was a strangely remote collaboration."[10]

Tremayne's political remoteness from the Communist Party worried Vernon Beste, the secretary of Unity Theatre and a member of the party's Cultural Groups Committee. While Fore Publications was never owned by the party, Beste and others treated it as if it were. Beste was also on the editorial board of the left-wing arts magazine *Our Time* and tried to discipline what he saw as aestheticist excesses there, such as its publication of poems by Dylan Thomas. When Tremayne refused to submit to an editorial board, Croft writes, he was replaced in 1944 by John St. John, a party member with no experience of publishing.[11] The later numbers of *Seven* are undated, but it is clear that Tremayne was editing the magazine until late in 1944. In Tremayne's last year, St. John was present as an assistant editor, presumably to keep him in check. After Tremayne left, there was one issue edited by Swingler and St. John, and then *Seven* was sold to Dryden Periodicals. It folded soon after.[12]

In its heyday, *Seven* had a very large readership. Sid Chaplin recalled: "*Seven* was exceptional. They got up to about 100,000 at their peak, and the stories were never much more than a thousand words each . . . And they were all from ordinary folk." Doubtless, as Tremayne believed, "the wartime famine of printed matter contributed to its success." Blackouts in British cities and the unavoidable idleness of long stretches of service life boosted reading activity during the war, and available books sold without exception. Cyril Connolly quipped in 1942 that public demand for reading matter was so desperate that he could have sold issues of *Horizon* filled with prewar railway timetables. The possible artificiality of *Seven*'s popularity, however, does not make the number of readers it reached insignificant. If it is true that the 100,000 circulation of *Penguin New Writing* at its peak made it the highest-selling "'high-brow' journal in the history of publishing," it seems fair to say that *Seven* rivaled it as the most popular left-wing literary magazine. In contrast, *Left Review* sold approximately 5,000 copies a month, and *Our Time* reached 18,000. In *Seven*'s pages, aspects of *Left Review* came into contact with forms developed in the commercial press and some of the ambitions of aspirant writers.[13]

"READERS, YOU ARE OUR WRITERS," declared O'Connor and Cruickshank in the first issue of the revamped *Seven*. After finishing the magazine, readers were urged to write or draw something for it. "This volume is entirely the work of people, like yourselves, who earn their living at jobs other than writing or drawing, and of youngsters. Get your youngsters to contribute . . . Writing is not the special preserve of a select few. You can write too. You can draw too. We think that all who can see, can write; all who can speak, can write; all who can think, can write." Making several leaps of logic, O'Connor and Cruickshank went on: "THIS MAGAZINE COULD NOT BE PUBLISHED IN GERMANY! Therefore, support it as a blow against what Fascism stands for. Get your relatives, workfriends and acquaintances around it, reading it and writing it; it is your Magazine, your Forum, make it part of your life."[14]

Elsewhere in that issue O'Connor mused on "people's writing" in a manner that emphasized its revitalizing powers for literature rather than its social and political value. When people wrote about "what's most important in their lives—their jobs," as they did in *Seven,* O'Connor argued, they produced more truthful and satisfying work than experienced writers did. "I think you'll agree that they're less skilful in evading the point than the Regulars, and in fact you get an idea both of what they're like and what the job's like, an unusual quality in modern writing which we can call popular in two senses." Implicitly lending support to "the idea that one can over-learn to write," O'Connor remarked: "It seems strange that one should teach oneself or get taught to write about life in that strange and remote way called 'journalism,' a way of writing that has spread into most fiction too." Without commenting on its commercialism, O'Connor was questioning the validity of the apparatus of correspondence schools and advice books on "journalism" (in the capacious contemporary meaning of the word) as a way into writing. "We think that children and people not used to writing make a livelier job of it than the professionals. They use the first words they think of, which are the best, arrange them in a way as exciting as the subject, skilfully evocative, because people are natural artists (and 'artists' are unnatural people)."[15]

In the following number O'Connor and Cruickshank issued a clarification of sorts, denying that they had criticized "the profession of writing." That profession was necessary, "but we also consider that all writing must be expressive of the people . . . Much professional writing today has lost contact with the people and is simply the expression of some talented, or untalented, individual mainly preoccupied with personal satisfaction and very little occupied with social problems." Although there is no mention of "Bloomsbury" or "ivory towers," it is clear that the kind of writing against which "popular writing" is being defined here is the work of privileged mandarins rather than clerical workers and housewives taking courses with the London School of Journalism. "The material in *Seven,* we think, indicates the true source of literature and destroys any suggestion that literature is the sacred territory of a few or that writers are in any way essentially *different* from other people." In rejecting fidelity to the craft, or the trade secrets, of "professional" writing in favor of a primitivist or instinctive writing, O'Connor was drawing on the same romantic tradition that the clients of the literary advice business used to different and opposing ends.[16] In a way, his romanticism was closer to that of the writers' circles than to that of Leslie Halward or James Hanley, because he denied the aura of writing and literature and insisted that the animating force of literature issued from its subject matter or author: good writing was "expressive of the people" and revealing of the subject matter—usually labor. But where writers' circle members conceived of life as a bazaar of potential material for fiction, O'Connor gestured to something like a moral obligation to yoke writing to "the people" and "social problems."

Not all the material O'Connor and Cruickshank selected for *Seven* was uncrafted testimony. Some of it would have counted as "proletarian writing" in *New Writing* and *Left Review.* James Littlejohn, for instance, contributed a short story about a working-class couple making their way ruefully to court, apparently in Glasgow. During an argument about the feasibility of getting new wallpaper for the kitchen of their tenement flat, Jock had been swearing angrily, and Mary had appealed to the police. In the month between the dispute and his trial for breaching the peace, they do not speak to each other. On the way to court, Jock hands Mary thirty shillings for new wallpaper—he has been going without cigarettes, beer, and billiards to save the money. At the trial, the cause of the argument is not explained any further than Jock saying that the existing wallpaper was there when they got married. He is found guilty and fined thirty shillings. Mary hands over the wallpaper money, and they go home. "Oc, Mary, we'll away to the pictures the night," Jock says, bringing the story to a close. The use of dialect, both in direct speech and within the narration ("The policeman . . . now lived in a braw council house in a decent scheme"), the noting of differences between tenement-dwellers and better-off members of the working class, and the choice of domestic conflict as a way of getting at plebeian life all mark Littlejohn's story as a typical piece of 1930s-style working-class fiction. And the two exchanges of the thirty shillings have the symmetry and irony of an O. Henry story like "The Gifts of the Magi," in which the wife sells her hair to buy a band for the husband's watch, and the husband sells his watch to buy combs for the wife's hair. Littlejohn's story resembles both *New Writing* material and the tightly organized short stories published in evening newspapers and in magazines like the *Strand*.[17]

Under Tremayne, *Seven* continued to publish fiction with plebeian settings and concerns. Some of the working-class writers first published in the 1930s appeared in Tremayne's *Seven*—Jim Phelan, Fred Kitchen, Fred Urquhart and, repeatedly, Sid Chaplin, who, as we have seen, recalled the magazine fondly. Recurrent devices and themes of 1930s working-class writing also color *Seven* stories by new writers, as in Gordon Allen North's "Holiday," which is about a laborer's family gearing up to go on vacation—an exercise in gentle humor that revolves around the family's matriarch. W. Glynne Jones, who had worked for years in a Llanelly steel foundry, contributed a story set in a factory that is making bombs. Following the lead of the communist "Red" Dave, the workers have set up a committee to handle the allocation of piecework, taking it out of the foremen's control. The day's piecework having been assigned, the workers relate and refute inflated rumors of calamitous air raids, listen to an old man's tirade against the Germans, and strike up a lewd song about Hitler and Mussolini, as the very different members of the workforce join together to contribute to the war effort. The wartime message is clear, but in its sympathetic description of the workers and their differences, the story echoes Willy Goldman's work. And showing how political questions can play out in activities specific to an industry was a characteristic 1930s move.[18]

Two stories by David Alexander evoked the fragility of miners' lives in the manner of earlier miner-authors. In "Accident," an injured miner waits for the doctor and worries about what will become of his pregnant wife if he is incapacitated. He recovers, and the anticlimactic story is a study in muted, "ordinary" emotions. Alexander's other *Seven* story was prefaced by this announcement: "*The author is a miner. Here he describes his most memorable adventure underground—and its extraordinary outcome. There is no fiction here.*" There is an emergency in which Alexander, or the narrator, manages to save his companions. The story closes with his receiving a bonus of two pounds and yelling to the others: "Figure it out . . . Eight of us are worth two quid to the company. That makes us mugs out at five bob a time."[19]

The central trope of *Seven* was not the proletarian, however, but the "ordinary" person. Teachers, a tuberculosis officer, and even a clergyman rubbed shoulders with plumbers and newsvendors in the magazine's pages. The working-class stories in *Seven* sometimes presented their characters as heroic figures, though they did not necessarily glamorize work in the way O'Connor and Cruickshank's editorial statements came close to doing. The depictions of white-collar work were anything but glamorizing. The narrator of Monica Mooney's poem "The Typist" declared:

> I am one of millions
> Who tap all day the thoughts of other men,
> Who are paid to hang on a peg
> Their individualism at nine A.M.[20]

While *Seven* carried fiction and poetry, much of the magazine, especially under O'Connor and Cruickshank, consisted of testimony about their work by people unaccustomed to writing. These pieces carried forward the 1930s tradition of what might be called "autodocumentary," the description, on request, of an aspect of a person's life, usually work, in *Left Review* or *New Writing*, or in Jack Common's *Seven Shifts*. Although the pieces in *Seven* read less like Mass-Observers' pointillist reports and diaries than like responses to the question "Tell us about yourself," they also had close affinities with the autodocumentary that Mass-Observation required of its volunteers or "panellists." There was a nod to the affiliation between *Seven* and Mass-Observation in the magazine's inclusion of James Stephens's account of his work as one of Mass-Observation's paid observers, visiting public libraries and tube shelters and asking people what they thought of profiteers and how they would describe Churchill in one word.[21]

Seven was a product of interwar mass culture as well as documentary. In the 1930s the very popular Scottish women's magazine the *People's Friend* ran accounts of a day in the life of this or that occupation—a doctor's receptionist, a seaside confectioner. Local newspapers did so too, judging by the *Newcastle Weekly Chronicle*.[22] Some of these "human interest" stories were in the first person, purporting to be by the receptionist or dressmaker herself, but the use of the first person was a generic device, and the items were written by freelances—including members of the Newcastle Writer Circle, in the case of the *Newcastle Weekly Chronicle*. From the 1920s onward, first-person stories claiming to be "true confessions" became widespread in the popular press, inspired by the success of the American magazine *True Story*, launched by Bernarr Macfadden in 1919. The editor of *My Story Weekly: Love Romances Told by the Girls Themselves* promised a guinea for "the best true story sent in each week." "Everyone has a story to tell. YOU are sure to have had an experience that would be a help to other girls . . . Will YOU tell it to ME? . . . All I want you to do is to write up any incident in your life which you think would be interesting." But the contributors clearly knew how to shape a story to the generic demands of a mass-market editor. The "confession" was a genre that appeared regularly in market information in writers' handbooks. As a member of the Newcastle Writers' Club later put it, "'True Confessions' need not be true. They are fiction in the 1st person." The memoirs of the freelance Herbert John reveal that at least sometimes freelances wrote the true-life stories of actors and other celebrities. This could go beyond mere ghostwriting: the writer would approach a celebrity, ask her to think of anything unusual that had happened to her, and then work the anecdote into a narrative. If the celebrity approved the story, it would be was published under the name of (and with a picture of) the "personality" rather than the actual writer.[23]

What made papers like *My Story Weekly* significant was their promotion of the idea of true stories by ordinary people. *Seven,* too, based its appeal and distinctiveness on the idea that its contents were authentic testimony by ordinary people. If the claim was not true in *Seven*'s case, the contributions were often comparatively unformed rather than worked into the formulaic shape of other "true confessions." *Seven* was a British equivalent of Mike Gold's *New Masses* in the United States, which, as Michael Denning has argued, was "not, as it has often been portrayed, simply an unlikely Russian transplant," but also an adaptation of the formula of Macfadden's *True Story.* Both Macfadden and Gold held that "'every man and woman has lived at least one big story which has that ring of truth for which authors of fictions strive with might and main' . . . Gold's vision of the *New Masses* can be seen as a radical mutation of *True Story,* an attempt to build a new culture out of the stories and confessions of manual workers."[24]

Under O'Connor and Cruickshank, then, *Seven* was a combination of commercial story paper, left review, and amateur writers' magazine. Tremayne was less permissive in his editorial practice than his predecessors. The unstructured job descriptions of their *Seven* gave way to depictions of work that had some of the journalistic shaping of newspaper human-interest articles, or stories "from other people's lives," rather than outright accounts of a particular trade. Deluged with material ("I believe that in those years I must have seen every rejected manuscript in the British Isles . . . I would call at the office with a suitcase and take manuscripts and proofs away to sort them out"), Tremayne would reject submissions, and even request rewrites from authors who already had a record of publication. He also published some relatively unconventional prose that would have been out of place in the O'Connor-Cruickshank *Seven*. Roland Gant's "Poor Peter," for instance, combines stream of consciousness and free-indirect style, and adopts the points of view of a succession of different characters as it portrays a possibly erotic friendship between two mentally retarded farm laborers.[25]

Tremayne did keep up his predecessors' policy of publishing work by amateur writers. Throughout his tenure as editor, Tremayne appealed for the magazine's readers to become its writers. One of his early statements used terms familiar from O'Connor's pronouncements: "It is our policy to encourage our readers to be our writers. For that reason we do not fill the magazine with specially commissioned articles. Most of our space is kept at your disposal. Your story really has a fair chance of getting into print . . . We want you to write about the things in which you yourself are interested. We are interested most of all in you." Tremayne put forward two not entirely compatible claims. On the one hand, he wanted "true stories"—real experiences of work, everyday life, and adventure. It was the story, the evidence of life, that mattered: "Even if you feel you cannot write very well, but have an interesting story to tell, send us the facts and we will tell the story." At the same time, he emphasized the value of writing itself, portraying *Seven* as an agent of the democratizing of writing: "It is surprising how many people who never believed they could write have found that they could, after all. You don't have to be 'literary.' Just be natural. The chatty style of a letter is often the ideal form . . . This is a magazine of people's writing in which everyone, amateur or experienced writer, has an equal chance to be printed."[26]

It is appropriate that Tremayne's recommendation of "the chatty style of a letter" should coincide with advice given in a writers' circle, since *Seven* catered to the sort of amateur author who joined circles and read guidebooks as well as to working-class people, would-be artists, or others with some desire to write but no inclination or ability to become part of the commercially oriented aspirants' movement. The pages of *Seven* frequently turn up attempts at popular genres characteristic of writers' circle members and those "amateur journalists" who sought commercial publication—genres such as the story of madness or the supernatural, common in the *Strand* and elsewhere, that recalls Conan Doyle, Poe, or Maupassant. There were also stories of marital friction, that indispensable source of popular humor. As for rhetorical or narrative strategy, both fiction and articles made use of surprise endings. An aircraft rigger putting rivets into fighters and bombers finished his account of his work with the confession: "To tell the truth, I have never been up in a plane!"[27]

Seven also bore more explicit signs of being a forum for amateurs. The London School of Journalism advertised its writing courses in *Seven*'s pages. So did the Regent Institute, which touted a booklet that explained why writing was "The Ideal Hobby in War-time." Several pieces in the magazine took writing or writing aspirations as their theme. The need for "material" discussed so persistently by aspiring writers formed the basis of a humorous story by H. L. V. Fletcher. Mr. Ashby, a lodger, is working away on his manuscript, while his Glaswegian landlady disrupts his labors with reminiscences about her life at sea with her late husband: being caught by her husband in Manila with "one of those darkish chaps," giving birth in Tokyo alone while her husband was at sea, getting caught in a typhoon, surviving a shipwreck during the First World War. Mr. Ashby says "Quite" at appropriate moments, but is thoroughly bored. "I wish I could have told our . . . [story] in a book," the landlady says, to which Mr. Ashby responds, "You should have been an authoress, Mrs. Colley." "Oh dear, no," she replies. "I wasn't clever or anything like that. Not classy, you know." After finally getting rid of her, Mr. Ashby writes a letter: "*My Dear Bruce* (he wrote), *I think my 'Algebra Up To Matriculation Standard' should be ready for the press in about a month's time. The publishers are sure it will sell marvellously . . . I have found comfortable lodgings, but unfortunately the landlady here is a shocking bore.*" The story is entitled "Not His Line": it satirizes Mr. Ashby as stiff and out of touch with boisterous "life," scarcely noticing a rich source of material that many writers would have seen as a valuable acquisition.[28]

When Tremayne said that most of *Seven*'s space was at readers' disposal, that stories about what interested readers themselves had a fair chance of getting into print, he expressed an egalitarianism reminiscent of the avowal of writers' circles and correspondence schools that anyone could become a writer. But Tremayne combined that egalitarianism with a more aggressive populism, one that disregarded the market and the conventions it prescribed for magazine stories. *Seven* valued prose about ordinary experiences not because it would help readers "identify with" them, but as part of a wartime valorization of ordinariness. *Seven* was a site where writing by "ordinary" people took up 1930s ideas about ordinariness and transformed them into a mythology of soldiers' and civilians' participation in a "people's war." Alison Light has argued that one aspect of the "reaction against loss and the ideological rupture which is marked by the Great War" was "an increased attachment to the idea of private life" and homely routine. One corpus of texts Light uses to illustrate this exaltation of the quotidian is Jan Struther's vignettes of Chelsea bourgeois life in *Mrs. Miniver,* but this structure of feeling is perhaps more closely aligned with the suburbs, whose population swelled in the interwar period. This cultural idiom "could 'feminise' the idea of the nation as a whole, giving us a private and retiring people, pipe-smoking 'little men' with their quietly competent partners, a nation of gardeners and housewives."[29]

This idiom, so in tune with the conservatism of Prime Minister Stanley Baldwin, was not the only one current between the wars, even among the suburban middle class. While, as we saw in Chapter 3, a greater homeliness came to mark "escapist" periodical fiction and Mills and Boon romances, bestsellers like E. M. Hull's *The Sheik* were not about gardening and crossword puzzles, and the cinema of course stood for the glamorous rather than the quotidian. And, as Ross McKibbin has argued in his discussion of the popularity of A. J. Cronin's novel *The Citadel,* the domestic idiom did not resonate so much with the newer, public and technical "modern-minded" middle class. Nevertheless, the rhetoric of ordinariness and littleness could also be used to articulate arguments that were not essentially conservative. A Brixton man who worked as an engineer in an electrode factory and volunteered for Mass-Observation—and as such was an archetype of the modern-minded, public-spirited lower middle class—believed Mass-Observation was "a pacifist organisation. By showing that the little man likes his pipe and his mantelpiece and his book and his sunday dinner you are doing positive work for peace. Isn't it better to say to a child 'do this' than to say 'what are you doing? then don't'? By the same token it is better to show that the little man likes his home rather than blare that he doesn't want war."[30]

After 1940 the idiom of littleness and domestic ordinariness became incorporated into the popular mythology of the war. The Baldwinian sense of history "not as the doings of the great and the good, but as that which was made by the little, ordinary people at home, 'muddling through,'" was central to the idea of a "people's war." ("The butcher, the baker and the plumber continue to make immortal history," wrote a man in the forces about the invasion of Normandy.) "Well before the bombing began," Light notes, "a patriotism of private life was being felt and expressed." Maintaining some form of civilian household and ordinary life during the blitz became emblematic of the home-front struggle, and the understated, good-humored "little man" became a key trope of wartime masculine identity. While Light interprets this reconfiguration of masculine and national identities as (among other things) a feminization of them, Sonya O. Rose points out that some of the defining characteristics of wartime Britishness, such as emotional reticence, remained "quintessentially masculine," and that the "well-publicized stoicism of British women in World War II . . . highlighted the manly vigour of the British nation as a whole." The masculinity of its soldiers, firefighters, and the like, Rose suggests, was that of the "temperate hero," a composite of an older military heroism and the homely "little man" of the interwar period.[31]

John Lehmann, who read a huge number of unpublished manuscripts during the war, was struck by "the almost total absence of the heroic note" in writing by soldiers and sailors. Tremayne asked *Seven* readers for true-life "adventure" stories. Of the few he published, most were low-key. The first was the story of a merchant seaman's trip from Marseille to London while on a long leave early in the war. The previous crew had been smugglers and the ship had been sabotaged in several ways, so the voyage was fraught with mishaps. This was indeed an adventure story, but hardly in the action-packed league of Captain W. E. Johns's popular Biggles tales. Only one of the readers' adventures Tremayne printed involved combat—an artless and rather gleeful story about shooting down an Italian plane in the Mediterranean. The majority of the stories and poetry in *Seven* were less dramatic: indeed, the boredom of much wartime service was a persistent theme. Contributors described the routine of life in the services or in their jobs, implicitly or explicitly asserting the worth of their contribution to the war effort; they joked and emphasized the importance of small pleasures in making the war bearable; and they wrote about the social and political lessons they drew from their war experience, and their hopes for reconstruction.[32]

Some authors in "reserved" occupations took pains to show that their jobs were not "cushy." Others not in the services reported how war had changed their peacetime jobs. A drycleaner explained how his clientele had changed from rich people needing frocks and tennis trousers cleaned to "our fellow townsman": the Purchase Tax made it "a wiser plan to have last year's discarded garments renovated by our tailor and cleaned and pressed by us . . . Bombed people come to us with the remnants of clothes or soft furnishings they have salvaged . . . We have got out of our pre-war rut." As the war went on *Seven* published more pieces about the new jobs that the war foisted upon people. The range of jobs described implicitly underscored the variety of ways Britons contributed to the war effort. A woman described her work in the Women's Timber Corps, measuring trees before logging parties arrived. Others recounted night shifts monitoring teleprinters for the Ministry of Information and handling meteorological information for the Royal Air Force. The representational and rhetorical work of these pieces is akin to that of the films produced by John Grierson's Documentary Film Unit, such as *Coalface, Night Mail,* and *Drifters:* recording and promoting the value of important work that might not otherwise be noticed by those whom it benefited.[33]

A recurrent theme of these accounts in *Seven* was the way very dissimilar people could come together in war work. W. Glynne Jones's story about bomb-makers, discussed earlier, conveyed this sort of message, and the point was compounded in accounts of people from different regions and classes being combined in new situations. In Robert Fane's sketch of a night on a minesweeper, some crew members are fishermen; the narrator and others are "former office and factory workers, shop assistants and the like." Some are from London, some from Yorkshire, and some from County Durham. There are differences between them, but not friction. Fane was not the only *Seven* contributor to remark on the variety of regional accents he encountered in his wartime occupation.[34]

The illustration Wilfrid Barber supplied to accompany his piece about serving in the Auxiliary Fire Service provided a delicious image of a British workforce coming together harmoniously. It was a photograph of a tea break, with an AFS man pouring tea into sixteen cups. Several pieces in *Seven* included attentive descriptions of tea as a furnishing of wartime life, and the importance of other small comforts was remarked on as well. How these "tremendous trifles" could help people cope was an established wartime script. The idea surfaces in *Journey's End,* R. C. Sherriff's enormously popular 1928 play about the trenches in the First World War. The quality and supply of the food is a recurrent talking point, and the character of Trotter, a cheerful working-class type in a play where public school old boys have the big roles, is especially concerned with food. "I mean—after all—war's bad enough with pepper—[*noisy sip*]—but war without pepper—it's—it's bloody awful!" Bodily comforts were furnishings of peacetime lives, with some kinship, perhaps, to the "little" homely things that Britain meant to many of the respondents to two Mass-Observation surveys in 1941. The singer Vera Lynn, whose performances and persona became enmeshed in popular memories of the war, wrote in her autobiography that she had seen herself as "reminding the boys what they were *really* fighting for, the precious personal things rather than the ideologies and theories."[35]

Humor seems to have been another crutch. "By far the greater part of what you send me is humorous," Tremayne remarked in an editorial letter to the magazine's would-be contributors. He added: "When a world order falls to pieces, nothing can quench your sense of fun. You intend to go on living and you know there will always be laughter. Here is victory." Apart from its wartime functions as a consolation and a gesture of defiance, the importance of humor was firmly embedded in twentieth-century British culture. A sense of humor was supposed to be one of the characteristics that made the British so different from the Germans, though it was not a trait that loomed large in accounts of the national character before the First World War. The exaltation of a sense of humor as a British—or rather, English—characteristic may have been part of the interwar cultural shift that Light has identified. It was in the interwar period, McKibbin has argued, that humor became more important than before as an emollient and a defensive strategy in middle-class social life.[36]

Scarcely any of the humor in *Seven* was set in a fictional realm untouched by the war, but some of it could have been published in peacetime with only a little tweaking. Other humorous writing by people in the forces, published in *Seven* and elsewhere, drew heavily on the comic folklore of service life. Sergeant majors were dependable sources of comic material, and many pieces turned on the absurdities of military life and red tape. *Seven* contributors also skewered bureaucracy and pomposity in civilian Britain. Joan Smith's "Monday Morning" attacked humbug in education. The narrator is a teacher maddened by her school's morning prayer-and-sermon session, an exercise in "vague generalisations, distortions and plain untruths . . . *How much we have done for India—How incapable they would be of governing themselves—How efficient the Germans, yet how far to be preferred our pleasant, haphazard way of empire building, which always gets there in the end.*" After "Prayers," she finds the classroom a relief: whatever subject is under discussion, fragments of current events break into the children's questions. One pupil asks why there are no collective farms in Britain. The "direct, naive honesty of the child" helps pierce ideology. The narrator notes that one girl says that women should look after children rather than work, echoing what must be her mother's sentiments; a few minutes later the same girl says she doesn't want brats. In the latter comment "her own fourteen years," not her mother's prejudices, "assert themselves."[37]

Positive references to collective farms and socialist movements were scattered throughout *Seven*. Tremayne printed snippets of information on life in the Soviet Union ("Where 'phone calls are free"), and a story and a memoir saluted the Russian revolutionaries of the civil war period and the antifascist forces in Spain. One item, a blend of a sketch and an opinion piece by Ralph Finn, an East Ender who had won a scholarship to Oxford, called for reconstruction of bombed-out neighborhoods financed by redistribution. The vermin-infested tenement where the narrator grew up has been destroyed in a bombing raid. Finn describes the building's horrors and exhorts a government Pied Piper to come and "finish the job which the Huns began . . . Raise a new and a cleaner and a fresher and a better city on the ruins of the old . . .

Take an acre from Lord Dunabunk—he will not miss it; a few square miles from Lord Dolittle—he does not deserve to hold them." As well as programmatic statements like this, there were stories and poems voicing vaguer sentiments about finding a "better way" to run things after the war. In one story, a guard muses through a quiet night shift about how he was not taught things that mattered when he was at school, thinking that the left wing was nothing other than a football position. He looks forward to a time "after a bit, when we get running things properly," and "the only guns you will ever see will be in museums." One of several poems that alluded to William Blake spoke of the challenge of "revealing Jerusalem over the soldier's new grave."[38]

In *Seven,* more common than plans for the future were stories and poems celebrating a social attitude thought to be characteristic of those serving in the war: a merry aversion to privilege. This attitude was often located in masculine settings, but not exclusively so. A woman who before the war had been responsible for the food in a serviced apartment block in Piccadilly recounted the fussiness of her clients, and wondered how they were coping with austerity and shortages. "Remedied of their food fads, they are probably splendid Britons," she quipped. Middle-class characters, or, more precisely, people enjoying recognizably middle-class lifestyles, usually appear only as objects of satire in Tremayne's *Seven.* Tricksters and those who one-up the privileged and pompous are depicted warmly in story after story, and a "boss's man" who joins the masons instead of the union and becomes a "demonstrator"—someone who gets paid more to do a job quicker, setting an example and depriving other workers of an excuse for slowness—is hoist by his own petard. The forces are a place of camaraderie, even when the duties are boring or unpleasant, and the authorities are not always authoritarian. In Bob Elliott's "Pay-off," the crew of a corvette that survives a convoy's disastrous passage across a stormy Atlantic find that the ship is to be repaired and they will be sent back to barracks. They do not want to leave, and complain about the admirals' decision. As the crewmen finally leave, their excellent young captain looks at the flagstaff and sees that they have stolen the ensign. "He swore and went below, but as he turned there was a covert smile on his lips." The feeling that Alison Light has observed, that history was made by ordinary people, not by the Great and the Good or the "few" to whom Churchill referred in his famous speech about the Battle of Britain, underpinned a sense that any future Jerusalem was theirs to build or inherit.[39]

Seven did not follow a clear political line, but it was firmly on the left. Nothing right-wing found its way into the magazine's pages, though several left-wing utopias did. The Soviet Union was a subject of favorable comment by contributors and by Tremayne, and the magazine's contents were generally sympathetic to the working class and hostile to privilege, whether it took the form of pompous burghers, pampered food-faddists, or exploitative mine-owners. Common to many of the stories and articles in *Seven* was a notion of "the people" that was sometimes implicitly identified with the working class, but which could extend to anyone contributing to the war effort. Work and sacrifice were the lot of ordinary people, and their many different kinds of labor gave them a stake in the Britain of the future. After 1940 the interwar idiom of ordinariness and homeliness was transformed into a populist mythology of the heroism of ordinary people, and of ordinary life as something precious to fight for.

Steven Fielding, Peter Thompson, and Nick Tiratsoo have stressed the imprecision of this kind of populism. They have argued that the majority of the population was not especially interested in a thoroughgoing reorganization of British economic and social life after the war—that radicalism, or even a sustained interest in politics, was largely the preserve of "the public-spirited middle class and the 'earnest minority' of the working class." This argument is open to debate on many points, but it cannot be effectively tested by the evidence of "people's writing" such as that in *Seven,* since published writing is necessarily the work of a minority. We can, however, ask how well the argument explains the contents of *Seven.*[40]

A good many of the political aspirations articulated in *Seven* were indeed nebulous. Some of the magazine's identifiably working-class contributors might reasonably be described as part of an "earnest minority." [41] And if Joan Smith herself was a left-wing teacher, she fits a profile common in the membership of Mass-Observation and the Left Book Club: a public-spirited and publicly employed member of the middle or lower middle class. The class origins of most *Seven* contributors cannot easily be inferred from their writing. Significantly, though, most of them were not particularly "earnest." The progressivist voices in *Seven* do not usually speak with the accents of "decent" working-class autodidacts or of the middle- and lower-middle-class people whom Orwell loved to stereotype as fruit-juice-drinkers and sandal-wearers. Even if, as Fielding, Thompson, and Tiratsoo claim, the majority of the population was politically apathetic, there was more outside the mainstream than an earnest margin.

And yet, one might retort, *Seven* was not so very political for a communist-owned magazine open to unpolished submissions in a time of much political discussion. This response is a legitimate one, and one that opens up the subject of the popular meanings and functions of writing at the time. The limits of the politics in contributions to *Seven* testify not to the extent of wartime politicization, but to the way popular conceptions of imaginative writing resisted politics. The magazine's "Pawn's Parliament" section was a forum for debate on aspects of postwar reconstruction: it displays more of a sense of politics than the magazine's fiction and poetry. For many people it made sense to think that the domains of literary expression and political expression were separate. In the writers' circles and in the pages of textbooks, writing and politics did not mix: the middle-class taboo about overt talk of politics applied to writing too. Working-class authors may have been less likely to accept this segregation than people for whom the acquisition and exercise of literacy were less difficult: for workers, reading "literature" and writing could be alien pursuits, the property of another class that they made part of their own lives only with considerable struggle. One of the paradoxes of the autodidact tradition was that its deference to the canon was combined with an impulse to reclaim great authors from the political bowdlerization that canonization involved—celebrating Shakespeare as the creator of Caliban rather than of Prospero, restoring Milton's republicanism to view. Yet even working-class men scarred by unemployment or active in trade unions could assume a separation between imaginative writing and politics when they began to write. Leslie Halward tried his hand at commercial short stories, then went through a phase of imitating Chekhov, writing about doctors and army officers; B. L. Coombes wrote about rich gentlemen and opera singers before bringing his writing closer to his political activities. In short, there are signs that it often took conscious effort to deal with political matters in fiction or poetry.

A good illustration of this contention is the Front Line Generation, a "social-literary" movement devoted to maintaining the camaraderie of writers in the armed forces and striving for a new social order. In practice, the Front Line Generation was primarily a novice writers' movement, the common denominators of whose membership were some degree of military experience and a desire to recast British society after the war. The movement entertained a catholic range of opinions about how Britain should be reconstructed: the *Seven* contributor Roland Gant, a communist, was a member; the chief organizer, Peter Ratazzi, had enthusiasms and hatreds that had fascist overtones. Ratazzi celebrated local crafts and cultures and savagely attacked conspiratorial literary and financial "cliques" and bureaucrats; there were rumors that he had been a member of the Hitler Youth in his native Netherlands before coming to Britain just before or soon after the outbreak of war.

Ratazzi saw action and was wounded serving in the British Liberation Army, but before the western front opened he busied himself organizing anthologies, book-magazines, and writers' groups. He did most of this "in the field," corresponding with contributors from one of the army's innumerable corrugated-iron Nissen huts and financing these enterprises from his army pay, according to one of his deputies. Ratazzi is a mysterious figure, all but undocumented outside his own magazines, but he clearly had an ability to spark others' enthusiasm, and—to be less charitable—to encourage the illusion that his projects were more durable and substantial than they were. During the war he edited *Writing Today* with Denys Val Baker; *Khaki and Blue,* a book-magazine of poems and stories from the forces; and the *Little A.T.S. Anthology,* its somewhat trivializing title compounded by the subtitle "The First Girl Writers in Battledress." (The Auxiliary Territorial Service was the women's branch of the army.) *Writers of To-morrow* and *New Generation* followed. Ratazzi's chief assistant was Corporal P. L. H. Smith, an army dispatch rider from Sheffield and a writer of humorous short stories. Howard Sergeant, who edited a magazine for refugees from the conservative Poetry Society, also assumed some of the responsibilities of leading the Front Line Generation.[42]

The Front Line Generation was perceived as a political as well as literary organization by those on the outside as well as its members. A representative of the Forces Writer Circle, with which the Front Line Generation had falsely claimed affiliation, declared that the Forces Writer Circle "was founded, and will be maintained, essentially for WRITERS. We want no truck with stunt politicians or spell-binders." This was almost certainly a reference to the Front Line Generation. If anyone counted as a "stunt politician," it was Ratazzi: at one point he decided to remedy his group's lack of press coverage by setting an alarm clock to go off in a locked suitcase during a concert at the Albert Hall. He is said to have told reporters afterward: "It was all very alarming, but then it is later than we think." The Forces Writer Circle's Ralph B. Durdey, also probably alluding to the Front Line Generation, deplored a "tendency in the post-war rise of several political movements to cast out attractive nets to draw in aspiring writers to their fold. The object being, it would appear, to work on the social conscience of these writers, many of them fresh from the Forces, and persuade them to turn their talent into the propaganda machines of the potential movement concerned."[43]

Despite Durdey's worries, the writing of Front Line Generation members was not particularly propagandist. The organization's leaders spelled out their agenda in a succession of editorial manifestos and ten Wilsonian "points," and while these cry out to be quoted—Ratazzi had a flair for Bloomsbury-baiting—the fiction and poetry written by members are more important in this context.[44] Most of the stories in the Front Line Generation magazines dealt with situations whose "political" aspects were not pursued very far by their authors, as in Kathleen Binns's story of a wife's conflict with the mother-in-law who lives with her, or Megan McCamley's story of a Welsh boy plucked from school to follow his father and brother into coalmining, in spite of talents that have led to the publication of a poem of his in the school magazine. Like *Seven,* the Ratazzi magazines printed poems that expressed in very general terms hopes or resolutions about a future that would not repeat the failures and tragedies of the war and the interwar period. One speaks of "the fatal legacy left us / By politicians and profiteers and careless parents," but the expression of hope for the future retreats from even this low level of political specificity into a description of

> real peace, where people will sing
> Songs of a happy people that shall rise
> Out of our struggle and our suffering.[45]

Whether this "real peace" is a communist peace, a Methodist peace, or a peace based on the welfare state that Sir William Beveridge proposed in 1942 is not a question that the poem can answer: it has a political ecumenism far removed from the more committed sorts of poetry of the 1930s.

The fiction in the Front Line Generation publications also reiterated many of the themes of *Seven.* The boredom endemic to military life is evoked. There are humorous stories, including one about a grizzled sergeant major and one poking fun at members of the Home Guard in a rural area. Others lampoon red tape and inefficiency in the army and the ATS. Where *Seven* carried several stories about couples struggling to get married or see each other under trying wartime conditions, the Front Line Generation magazines included stories of distinctively wartime romances. The most "political" story in these magazines is P. L. H. Smith's tale of an ex-socialist regaining his political fire. Moving in the opposite direction from those who shifted to the left during the war, Robert has been "washed up with politics . . . since he donned khaki." When the story opens he is being wined and dined at an expensive London restaurant by the Greshams, the wealthy industrialist family of his girlfriend Julie. Robert is appalled when their waiter is sacked in front of them following a complaint by Mr. Gresham: "In theory he had known that employment, the livelihood of families, could depend on a whim. On the soap-box he had said so. But he had never seen it happen like this in reality, swiftly." Robert thinks back to a party his first employer gave for "his unorganised black-coats" (male clerical workers were usually called "blackcoated" workers in Britain) at the time of the hunger marches. On that occasion Robert had shouted that the marchers were in town, and left the party. Now he walks out on the Greshams. Robert does not lash out at Julie the way John Osborne's Jimmy Porter does at his wife in *Look back in Anger*, but there is an analogous use of the girlfriend's family as a representative of the class enemy. The story ends with Robert's hitching a ride on a truck into an unspecified future.[46]

The fact that even a "social-literary movement" of people to whom politics really mattered did not consistently produce very politicized writing suggests strongly that the default popular attitude was to regard writing and politics as separate domains. The war prompted many people to take up poetry and fiction, but not for the sake of political expression. Writing, as we shall see, had other uses.

Chapter 7

The Logic of Our Times

"Where are the war poets?" It was a persistent question: speculating on the war's effects on poetry became a regular activity for literary journalists. Early in the war the *Times Literary Supplement* sent letters to selected authors inviting them to submit poems about the war, and when only a few obliged, the paper attacked British poets for dereliction of duty. Resenting this attempt at impressment into literary military service, C. Day Lewis wrote a short poem entitled "Where Are the War Poets?" The war, he claimed, was a struggle unsuited to a poetry that could be carved in marble:

> It is the logic of our times,
> No subject for immortal verse,
> That we who lived by honest dreams
> Defend the bad against the worse.[1]

Yet poetry and prose of non-immortal kinds—the kinds of writing that men and women in the armed and auxiliary services did in diaries, scrapbooks, and barracks newspapers—had a good deal to do with the logic of wartime. The long lulls between periods of action for many service people, especially men in the army, during much of Britain's war prompted some to try their hand at writing as a way of occupying themselves, and the permutations of the military's postings put would-be writers in each other's company. Writing was also part of the logic of the times in that self-expression, particularly in poetry, seemed a natural or apposite response to the trauma and dislocation of war, for reasons that have to do with the precedent of the trench poets of the First World War and with the romantic tradition's association of writing with deeply felt experience.

In a sense, this amateur writing had its own "logic." It was not always a reflection, and never a perfectly clear one, of popular concerns or other aspects of British culture. It was, for instance, starkly different from contemporary popular fiction and nonfiction. In *Horizon* in December 1941, Tom Harrisson reported the results of "two years of midnight reading" of "literally every book which has anything to do with the war, reportage, fiction or fantasy . . . Ninety-five per cent of it is stuff I would never have read, or even imagined could be written." To judge from these books, most of them published before the Soviet Union became Britain's ally, "Britain is fighting this war to protect the world against Auden and Picasso, the Jews, and any form of collectivism." Intellectuals, Jews, and communists were recurrent scapegoats. The heroes of the novels and nonfiction books with titles like *Heroes All, Carry on London, England's Hour, Our Finest Hour, Their Finest Hour,* tended to fall into three categories. The first was the "simple working man, usually the Cockney, and in nine cases out of ten either a char lady or a taxi driver . . . untainted by Communism." The second species was RAF heroes, and the third, "crippled heroes of pure British (generally aristocratic or near-Etonian) extraction."[2]

In their representation of danger and suffering, the items service people wrote for forces anthologies and newspapers presented a much more painful war—indeed a more martial one—than *Seven* did. Yet they were much closer to the prevailing ideal of "temperate heroism" so evident in *Seven* than they were to the books Harrisson was talking about. Members of the armed and auxiliary services wrote about bombing, combat, evacuation, dislocation, fear, injury, death, and grief: but these things often did not loom as large in their writing as they did in their lives. In fact some of the forces' literary output had very little to say about the war, as would-be freelances took advantage of wartime opportunities to hone their craft as writers of light "magazine stories." Those who did write about the war seemed to consider poetry an especially appropriate form for expressing serious feelings; prose was often written for the entertainment of the author or the readers or both, and thus struck different notes from weightier poetry.

"I started to write, partly out of boredom and partly about boredom itself." Michell Raper's remark about his National Service in Haifa in 1947–1948 could be applied to many in the forces during the Second World War. The monotony of service life, and the wearying grind of seemingly pointless regimentation, are recurrent subjects of forces writing. This was especially the case for those in the army and the women's Auxiliary Territorial Service. While the navy and the RAF were "always fighting," a large proportion of the army was stationed in camps within Britain itself between Dunkirk and D-Day. In personnel numbers, the army and the ATS dwarfed the navy and the RAF and their women's branches, the Women's Royal Naval Service and the Women's Auxiliary Air Force. In March 1944, for instance, there were 2,680,000 men in the army, 768,000 in the Royal Navy, and 1,000,000 in the RAF. As memoirs and fiction of this time suggest, and as archival materials confirm, the prolonged wait for an invasion or the opening of a western front left members of the services with swathes of time to kill or fill.[3]

For some, empty time prompted transformative introspection about their lives and the role of creative activities in them. The editors of a magazine produced by the inmates of the Changi prisoner-of-war camp in Singapore argued that prisoners of war were "compelled to disown" the "robot behaviour" of mass society. "Opportunities which may not recur in the life time of most of us present themselves: the gaining of exact knowledge be it a language or a Shakespeare play, or the ingenuity of insects; the creation of a garden and perhaps of an inner life which shall be a fortress against despair in days to come. Through such achievements we rediscover the medieval craftsmens delight in fashioning something peculiarly bone of his bone and flesh of his flesh. The creative life was becoming a luxury; with us here and now it is a deliverance from hell." For others, the changes in outlook made possible by the war were less dramatic. Jack Aistrop, who came from a background in advertising, had a hectic time in the army within Britain until he was posted to Belgium in 1944, but his literary activities during the war led to a resolution: "When this war is over, I shall turn from feature journalism to more worth-while pursuits. Never again will I ghost for the famous or infamous."[4]

How much scope life in the forces afforded for reading, writing, and other intellectual or creative activity varied widely.[5] When Tom Harrisson asked what the average forces unit library was like, Bonamy Dobrée at the War Office replied that he could not provide any specifics: they varied so much and the War Office had so little information. Some army units provided books for the "other ranks" out of regimental funds. County libraries passed books, chiefly worn copies of "lighter fiction," on to army units stationed in Britain. Sailors' charities and the Seafarers' Education Service furnished ships in the Royal and Merchant Navies with small libraries and distributed books from civilians to ships and isolated naval bases. Some foreign camps with British prisoners passed a remarkable number of books on to their inmates.[6] Steven Fielding, Peter Thompson, and Nick Tiratsoo cite a soldier's complaint that his unit library consisted of "out of date copies of *The Field, Punch* and *The Lady,* together with superannuated dumps of Edwardian bestsellers," but even if this was a typical unit library, it does not necessarily mean that the literary horizons of most service personnel contracted during the war. In one army unit within Britain, the scarcity of books meant that as well as devouring James Hadley Chase's gruesome novel *No Orchids for Miss Blandish* ("probably the widest read book in the British Army") almost all the men who typically read only out of boredom also tackled Robert Tressell's *The Ragged Trousered Philanthropists* and an exposé of Glasgow's slums. Moreover, since the soldier who complained about his unit library was writing in the Workers' Educational Association journal the *Highway,* he was probably less inclined than many amateur writers to see Edwardian bestsellers as intellectually substantial and a potential source of literary stimulus.[7]

Such an amateur was G. T. Harris, whose wartime diaries provide a rich portrait of a writing career very different from those of the well-regarded authors who made their names during the war, such as Alun Lewis and Julian Maclaren-Ross. Harris was in the RAF and worked in camps in Britain as a driver and in an office. He was working in some sales capacity immediately after the war, and appears to have come from a straitened lower-middle-class background. He was vehemently opposed to Sir William Beveridge's welfare state plan, the Labour Party, and the left-leaning magazine *Picture Post,* and was deferential to officers and NCOs. With apparent pride he recorded in his diary as he neared the end of S. P. B. Mais's *All the Days of My Life:* "A corporal assures me that my taste in Literature is definately the trick."[8] The literary tastes that the corporal commended link Harris to the writers' circles' public. Besides Mais, he read John Galsworthy and the popular right-wing commentator Philip Gibbs. He read a life of Edgar Wallace, and found Arnold Bennett's biography absorbing.

Harris was a determined writer who clearly used his diary as practice for writing novels. "About seven thirty I go to supper. The moon shines from a star studded sky, the folds in the ground appear as deep mysterious shadows in its cold light. The hangars surmounted by balls of red twinkling light are silhouetted sharply against a blue black sky[.] squares of subdued light denote the barrack rooms." Another evening: "The rain teems down and the countryside is shrouded in a grey night." Such strenuous descriptiveness could take its toll. Harris wrote one day while in transit: "It can get wearisome describing the early summer beauty. There is little to compare between Devonshire, Somerset, Gloucestershire and Worcestershire, the counties through which our route lies."[9]

Prose like this, I think, is what textbook authors had in mind when they warned novices against indulgently descriptive writing. It seems to have been a mode that suggested itself to would-be authors seeking literary effect. The young Jack Common included similar descriptive passages in his short stories.[10] Yet Harris, although his prose seems self-taught, did avail himself of at least one of the products of the literary advice industry—the agentless writer's bible, the *Writers' and Artists' Year Book*. From this work Harris got the names and addresses of prospective publishers. Despite its bulk, the *Year Book* was not exhaustive, and it did not include information on Penguin. If it had, Harris might not have sent his novel "Grey Dawn" (the title recalls James Lansdale Hodson's noted war novel of 1929, *Grey Dawn—Red Night*) to the firm early in 1940. He reported not long afterward: "Novel has been returned. Penguins were the publishers to whom I sent it. They enclose a nice letter to say that they were unable to make an offer as they do not publish original fiction, only reprints." Harris had waited anxiously for news from Penguin. "I steel myself to receive the rejected manuscript . . . Surprising how much courage it takes to face the bad penny. We authors have tender feelings. It very near breaks my heart when my brain children come back with a mere slip of paper attached." Every other publisher he submitted novels to rejected him as well. The day Penguin returned "Grey Dawn," he sent it to Allen and Unwin (one hopes he did not address the envelope the way he recorded the name in his diary: "Allen, George and Unwins"), who promptly rejected it, then to Nicolson and Watson ("Ivor Nicholas & Watson"), and after their rejection, to Secker and Warburg, who rejected it within eleven days and sent it to his old camp. Harris doubted he would see the manuscript again. "Most novels of mine come to a sticky end. Once I had a row with my landlady and burnt three manuscripts to save carrying them around. In all they consisted of about four hundred thousand words of prolisaic [*sic*] matter. Except for a few misgivings regarding one of them I was glad to get rid of these off spring."[11]

Harris's compositional habits also diverged from what a seasoned writers' circle member would have regarded as the right way to proceed. Like Jack Overhill, Harris did not plan his novels but simply started writing. Harris believed he had "a gift of improvisation." "I am beginning to see the first stages of the plot quite clear, though what will happen later is hidden in a fog as far as I am concerned." He wrote as if the novel had a mind of its own: "My novel sweeps onward to its conclusion"; "now I think I shall bring it to a conclusion which will have to be tragic for the hero must die. It is a grim business murdering your characters but it has to be done." Within three weeks of finishing this novel, he "ponder[ed] on whether I should commence a fresh novel." The following day he did start a new one.[12]

Harris saw his novels both as following bestsellers' conventions and as "unorthodox." The novel tentatively called "Vanity" was receiving a

> treatment . . . similar to that which P. C. Wren gave to Beau Geste, without of course that authors wild improbabilities. The first part is

> strictly orthodox; that is in the first person. In the second part the narrative is handed to a character who explains some of the story. The third parts and onwards are being narrated in the first person as much as I dislike the letter "I." "I" for instance have become an illegitimate child in the story. I am wondering that with the unorthodox treatment and unusual theme as to whether I shall ever get it published. Even established authors find difficulty in getting books published, and I am an unknown scribbler with unusual scribblings.

Harris evidently retained his interest in multiple narrative viewpoints or foci: in 1955 he unsuccessfully submitted to Allen and Unwin the story of a cursed pair of shoes whose successive wearers all die violently in the period of the Napoleonic wars.[13]

After he had been in the RAF for a while, Harris began using it as the setting of his novels. "In the quiet of the reading room I evolve an idea: I will write an imaginary diary of an air gunner. Perhaps I can get some publisher to accept it as the real thing." Several days later he confided: "I feel a little guilty as I write the fake diary of an air gunner on an operational station. Still I can publish it as a novel instead of the real thing." The comment reveals him to be not quite at ease with the notion of fiction. Harris also wrote a novel about Bomber Command and began another set in Fighter Command. He temporarily abandoned this in favor of writing his memoirs of the previous two years, but returned to fiction in January 1942, starting "a novel which I shall, for the time being, call [']Strike Crew' . . . The stage is set, this camp will do, and the imagination furnishes a set of suitable characters." It is noteworthy that the politically conservative Harris wrote about pilots in the heroic register that other amateur writers in the forces tended to eschew.[14]

Harris more than once referred to the magnitude of the tasks facing him and his fellow crewmen and complained about disturbances, but his RAF work and accommodation afforded him conditions under which he could work on his novels. His diary entry for 19 September 1941 neatly captures this combination of dissatisfaction and opportunity: "I sit in the office writing my quota of the novel, a task that is frequently interrupted by the phone bell ringing." Similarly, on 12 April 1940 he noted:

> In the evening I write 800 words of the novel . . . The conditions under which I write are none too good. My writing desk is composed of an old wooden locker and my seat is my bed. I begin writing at 17.15. At 17.55 I break off to go to the Naffi [canteen or recreation center] to listen to the news. While I wrote a bedlam of conversation was taking place among the lads. At 18.15 I return from the Naffi and resume writing. Still a bedlam of conversation [about which nations had fought in the battle of Dogger Bank] . . . I break off writing to argue, but my quotations from [the] official history are ridiculed. I retire from the argument and resume writing. At 19.10 hours I proceed to the cookhouse . . . Returning at 19.30 hours I write till 20.00 hours and pack it in.

At other times he wrote in the barracks reading room, though sometimes the wireless was on there. He did not "rely on inspiration to write," but wrote "to a timetable." Late in the spring of 1940, however, as the Germans advanced into France and Belgium and the evacuation from Dunkirk approached, he understandably found that "present events are so gigantic that I cannot concentrate. It is a strain as it is to compile this diary."[15]

He showed his work to two others in the camp. One, named Woodley, read most of one novel and was "fully convinced that it will sell well if I find a publisher. I, myself am not so joyful." The name of Harris's other advisor has been expunged from the diaries deposited in the Imperial War Museum. Working on the novel in October-November 1941, Harris expected to be finished soon unless this reader passed “adverse criticism.” “I complete the novel but feel dissatisfied with the end and feel curiously restless. But I shall wait ———’s decision before altering it.” And, not long afterward: “——— has done a good job with his corrections and criticisms. Faults which I would not have spotted are pointed out; he corrects my grammar and makes suggestions but does not overdo things.” Harris’s deference to his mentor was apparently partly due to his being an officer. “I see ——— and he upbraids me for passing unflattering remarks about intelligence officers in the novel. ——— of course is with the intelligence branch.” On another occasion: “I have a chat with ——— tonight and although he has only read just over half of the novel, he has formed an opinion that the thing will never pass the censor. He considers that I am bebunking and stripping the service of its glamour.”[16]

Harris had seen himself as an author before the war, and he was still writing novels in the 1950s, though none of them made it into print. But the war was an important episode in his writing career. It gave him opportunities for feedback, and it provided time to write. He managed to secure the mental space to write despite the interruptions endemic to the base (and despite his RAF obligations). Others managed in similar ways. Eric Joysmith, a commercial artist in peacetime and a petty officer in the navy who published in *Bugle Blast* and *Modern Reading,* got “his stories written in spare moments off watch in his bunk.”[17]

Not every service writer was this accepting. Alun Lewis, who had been a teacher in Wales with a fierce commitment to his writing, found that army life made it “almost impossible to write at any length on a mixed theme: so I look on my work as sketches for a future & maturer period of writing, after all this.” Lewis would stay up past lights out, “hidden behind blackouts trying to write better & better, feeling for the truth, & not being able to sleep when I do go to bed." The office of his rifle company had no typewriter: he wrote poems by hand and sent them home for his wife to type. What he saw as the anti-intellectualism of the army weighed heavily on Lewis, whereas it did not trouble G. T. Harris. Lewis railed against "a regime which is so hostile to everything it is fighting to preserve . . . I have been trying incessantly to humanise & free the unit I am with: I've started a weekly magazine, a debating society that holds mock parliaments and peace conferences: . . . and all I have earned is suspicion, resentment, a petty charge & reduction to the ranks."[18]

In this situation it was not surprising that Lewis latched onto other people interested in writing, including Julian Maclaren-Ross, a roué whom he probably would not have befriended in civilian life. "But in the army, where the strangest friendships are struck up," Maclaren-Ross recalled, "it was natural for us to draw together and to talk of intimate ambitions." Jack Aistrop was another of Lewis's wartime friends. They met in a Royal Engineers camp in the south of England, where Lewis was in charge of brigade education and Aistrop was running a camp magazine. Lewis was excited by the prospect of the magazine and gave Aistrop a story for it. Looking at the first name of the author, Aistrop realized he had read Lewis's short story in *Penguin Parade*. "We fell into the habit of spending all our evenings together, either in his office or my own, making pot after pot of tea and talking halfway through the nights."[19]

Aistrop's magazine grew "from a Company thing to Battalion and finally to Brigade at which point I demanded printing machinery." This kind of support was usually the limit of official encouragement of forces writing, though the military authorities, conscious of the holding pattern the war imposed on many members of the forces, sponsored educational services and artistic activities. Forces education had already been treated seriously before the war, and its scope now broadened. The Army Bureau of Current Affairs, chiefly concerned with education for citizenship, organized lectures and discussions about civics, reconstruction, and international politics. However, it also offered literary appreciation classes, painting classes, instruction in crafts and decorative arts, and drama performances. Writing was apparently not among the crafts the ABCA taught, though a correspondence college for the Royal and Merchant Navies provided tuition and criticism in short story writing. For the most part, institutions to support popular writing in the forces were fashioned by service people themselves.[20]

In Cairo, for instance, poets who had known one another in peacetime congregated in cafés and hotels, produced little magazines, and held poetry readings. Cairo was unusual, in part because the War Office posted so many writers—now holding officers' commissions—to the many intelligence units in the city.[21] In other military communities the networks of writers were less glamorous, and many of their members were NCOs or "other ranks." Some of these networks were formalized as clubs, such as the New Writers' Club at the RAF camp at Kirkham in Lancashire, which was coordinated by a member of the Women's Auxiliary Air Force who was interested in short stories and had started writing a novel. There was a Forces Writer Circle, organized chiefly by Leslie Mutum, an army sergeant doing public relations work. After visiting the Reading Writers' Circle, Mutum attended writers' circles in the many British towns to which he was posted. He continued his involvement with the circles after the war, and met his future wife in the Bury St Edmonds Writer Circle. When he took over a correspondence circle of writers in the services, he renamed it the Forces Writer Circle, signaling his intention to reorganize it "on Writer Circle lines."[22]

Yet there were fundamental differences between the civilian

writers' circles and their military counterpart. The FWC was a corresponding society, not a group that met face to face. It connected isolated individuals: despite the cheery tone of much of its newsletter-magazine *Gunfire,* probably more than a few of its members found service life an alienating experience, as Alun Lewis had. As a form of association, the FWC had more in common with an "amateur journalism" organization than with a writers' circle. Its main offerings were its newsletters and *Gunfire,* its advisory service, and its circulating portfolios. These portfolios were "interchanging selections of members' writings—stories, sketches, verse and reportage, by which Forces members may criticise, and submit for criticism, Mss intended for publication." The portfolios, such as the *Service Scribe,* a "manuscript magazine," thus had much in common with the "circulators" and "pass-rounds" of amateur journalists. FWC subgroups also ran their own pass-round magazines and portfolios for criticism and feedback. The FWC had connections with some of amateur journalism's more active exponents, such as the printer Lawrence Warner and the "amateur mag" editor Olive Teugels.[23]

The FWC also cultivated contacts with "the Civvy Writer Circles," some of which invited FWC members who passed through their towns to come to their meetings. Some people who had belonged to writers' circles in peacetime joined the forces circle.[24] The clearest parallel between the Forces Writer Circle and its civilian namesakes was its concern with learning the trade secrets of writing for commercial publication. *Gunfire* carried "market information"—details of the requirements of different periodicals, publishing opportunities in this or that field—after the fashion of the *Writer* and presentations at writers' circle meetings. More than a few FWC members used the services of the literary advice industry. Catchphrases from writing textbooks appeared regularly in *Gunfire;* Kenneth MacNichol's mantra—"Read, study, *write!* Observe, record, *write!* Write and reject. Write and destroy. *Write!*"—was quoted twice, once without attribution. Advice from members of the FWC itself tended to conform to the contours of that given by commercial advisory services and the *Writer.* C. Farley, who became editor of *Gunfire* at the end of 1945, wrote: "Some tyros think they must write about the very great or the very clever or the very rich in order to create 'reader-interest.'" Farley declared this a mistake: "Leave alone subjects with which you are not really familiar. Quite humble objects are frequently the root cause of moving our deepest emotions." Another contributor prefaced his discussion of "This Writing Business" with the standard rider that if you were a "genius," you did not need to read it.[25]

Who were these people? "Nearly all the work of the F.W.C. seems to be done by a handful of privates, a few corporals and a sergeant here and there," complained "Amelia Ketchup." "How about a few more of you Commissioned blokes having a bash? . . . Come now, don't be a cad, Sir." The rank and file of the FWC does indeed seem to have been drawn from the rank and file of the services. Though the documentation for them is thinner, the same generalization may well hold for the people who contributed to barracks and camp magazines. The articles in one substantial camp magazine that deal with peacetime jobs and leisure are redolent of lower-middle-class experiences: the duties of a cub reporter and office boy; the lot of an office worker and salesman who must go on a sales tour of north-country towns, staying in "Commercial Hotels"; the pleasures of rambling and youth-hosteling. Several of the member profiles in *Gunfire* are reminiscent of Mass-Observers or members of civilian writers' circles—people from lower-middle-class occupations excited by writing and keen to make it into a career more stimulating than their pre-war jobs. A commentator in an adult education journal observed in 1947: "As a way of life . . . journalism has probably exerted on the barrack-weary an appeal equalled only by that of the farm or the small-holding."[26]

"Newspapers" and "magazines" produced within camps were the most common sorts of literary collaboration or association in the forces and prisoner-of-war camps. The Army Bureau of Current Affairs encouraged them as forums for discussing citizenship and current events, but in practice a good deal of their content was humorous prose, doggerel verse, and fiction and poetry written for purposes other than civic debate. Camp periodicals fell into two categories, "wall newspapers" and "magazines." Wall newspapers were improvised papers posted in a public place and consisting of typed columns, poems, cartoons, and other illustrations. A new issue would be put up regularly, most likely weekly. Wall newspapers were extremely ephemeral: a notice board lends itself to salvage less than does a bundle of typescripts and drawings, and the fact that a wall newspaper could be updated piecemeal means that even if one had been preserved, it might be impossible to capture a single "issue." The transience of the form means that my account here rests instead on camp magazines, discrete issues of which could be retained and stored by their editors or fans. Accidents of evidence and preservation also mean that my discussion is dominated by magazines produced in prison camps. Camp magazines were sometimes substantial, printed items, as in the case of Aistrop's brigade magazine or the *Tost Times and Advertiser*, a typescript periodical produced in a British civilian internment camp in Germany, the duplication of more than 700 copies of which was permitted by the camp's authorities. In camps with less generous commanders or guards, a magazine's "print run" would be limited to several copies, if it was typed and carbon copies made, or to a single copy, if it was handwritten. They were thus like the pass-rounds of amateur journalism and the Forces Writer Circle, though they were passed round by hand rather than by post.[27]

Putting out a camp magazine or wall newspaper was always a struggle. Paper, pens, and typewriters were usually scarce: at one POW camp in Germany, the only paper available for a pantomime script was Red Cross toilet paper. Inmates of the copper-mining camp at Eisleben produced two magazines during the war, and the immediately postwar memoir of one of the editors, a young insurance clerk from Rochester named F. W. Daniels, gives a good sense of the effort involved. *Glück Auf,* which took its name from a miners' greeting, "compris[ed] three pages of hand-printed articles and one page of cartoons." After one issue the organizers were transferred to another camp, and Daniels was asked to take over. Two others did "the printing," neatly copying out the text. "People were very loth to contribute articles; there was difficulty in obtaining the thick large-size paper when Corporal Norton had gone, and the elaborate 'write-up' made an issue more frequently than at monthly intervals out of the question." *Glück Auf* lapsed after six issues. For some reason the situation changed when a new magazine, *Snips,* was launched; perhaps Geoff Smith, the editor of *Snips,* was better at coaxing forth submissions. *Snips* was a weekly and ran to ten pages. It "contained articles on all sorts of subjects by all types of people in the camp. It was very popular, though once again the difficulty was to get people to contribute." After twenty-three issues, *Snips* ceased publication. "Now that alarms in the evening are so frequent and we are plunged into darkness without warning so often, the task of presenting you with this little weekly is becoming more and more impossible. The vast majority of the Camp, while they perhaps read 'Snips' regularly, refrain completely from making any attempt at contributing to its regular issue. Finally we are short of materials; paper, ink, pens etc. and, all things considered, have decided to 'close down' upon the publication of our Christmas number."[28]

Mobilizing writers was often a challenge. The tactic, in evidence in *Gunfire* as well as in camp magazines, of publishing hyperbolic opinion pieces to goad readers into responding, was not always successful. Not every barracks or prison camp boasted a literary and artistic community like that of Cairo or even the Kirkham camp that was home to the New Writers' Club—a state of affairs that created a niche for a corresponding society such as the Forces Writer Circle. Yet committed writers and "editors" persisted, and while producing newspapers and magazines was a minority pursuit, it was a widespread one: the papers cited in this chapter originated in Germany, Italy, Libya, Japan, Singapore, and Thailand.[29]

Three main currents dominate the texts that men and women in the services wrote for anthologies and for barracks newspapers and magazines: representations of war and its consequences; celebrations of the Britain being fought for; and fiction that re-created the "magazine stories" of civilian existence. Death understandably recurred in depictions of life at the front, in bombed cities, and in antiaircraft installations. There were many poems about contemplating death, especially as embodied and symbolized in makeshift graves or corpses on a battlefield. The subject of death was also approached through depictions of its effects on relatives and comrades. In a story by Leslie Joseph in Peter Ratazzi's *Khaki and Blue,* the narrator's discovery of the body of a German airman on a beach he is patrolling prompts him to imagine the effect on "his prosaic father and his vague mother" of a wire informing them of his death. He wonders how the German pilot's mother will receive the news. Is she "a fanatic and a Jew-baiter?" Has she been bombed? He starts thinking of the war-weary women there must be in Germany, and the German scene blurs into a London one in his mind. "And when at last they came to take the body away—perhaps he didn't love all Germans as Christ would wish, but he had regained his sense of proportion."[30]

Noel A. Jones had two poems published that depicted women learning of deaths and being reminded of the dead. In one, the narrator finds the toys of a child killed in a bombing raid; the other, "The Telegram," begins:

> "It is with deep regret . . ."
> The envelope falls, crumpled by fingers
> To a shapeless ball,
> And all her past is seen in retrospect
> And ever by her side, his footsteps fall.

Jones's poems evoke a mourning stillness. Others in the forces tried to capture feelings of frenzy and mayhem as people remembered the loss of loved ones or comrades. Jack Aistrop's "The Road" splices together a serviceman's recollections of the night his friend died while driving drunk and excerpts from the driver's interior monologue. And some writers dramatized the corrupting tendencies of war. In Alan Wykes's "The Enemies," the construction of a military camp nearby disrupts a small English town. One of the soldiers quartered there is Harry Blake, a native of the town who is now much changed by his army experience. One night Harry and his mates try to steal some beer from Harry's father Joe, the publican. Joe blows a whistle for the police; all the soldiers escape except Harry, who falls and knocks himself out. "So this is war," his father says to the constable, both of them idealized, slow-moving, Hardyesque locals.[31]

Some forces writers borrowed the devices of popular magazine fiction in their treatments of these wartime themes. A. J. Willison, in "At the Going Down of the Sun," applied several tricks of the newspaper and magazine story-cum-article. As well as using a line from a familiar and appropriate source—in this case, Lawrence Binyon's poem "For the Fallen," endlessly recited in memory of the Great War dead—to indicate a theme, Willison uses another device to lend the story general relevance. He opens, not with an event, but with a question to the reader: "Have you ever met a person who didn't believe in death? I have. It all started . . ." Willison goes on to tell of a man in the RAF who writes to his wife every night but receives no mail in return. When the men have to give the addresses of their next of kin, the faithful correspondent says he cannot: the story ends with the twist that the wife died in an air raid two years before.[32]

People in the forces also used such devices in stories with peacetime settings. "R. R." contributed an O. Henryish story to *Gunfire* in which twins go into business, quarrel, and agree not to see each other again until Christmas Eve forty years thence, on the stairs of Saint Paul's. When they meet, John, from whose viewpoint the story is told, is shabbily dressed and has been living quietly in London. Christopher has been prospecting in South Africa, traveling in America, selling shares on the Bourse in Paris. The richly dressed Christopher takes John to the Ritz-Carlton and regales him with his adventures. John is relieved when they part. The narrator then reveals the twist: Christopher is in fact poor, and slinks back to his boardinghouse; John lives in a mansion. John Garrity, a cost and ledger clerk from Brixton serving as a wireless mechanic in the RAF, won the Forces Writer Circle's 1944 competition for a plot synopsis for a short story in which a medical student murders his uncle to get his inheritance. He goes swimming with the old man and stabs him with an empty syringe, injecting air bubbles into his bloodstream. The uncle dies of heart failure, and no foul play is suspected. The story is entitled "Perfect Crime." Then comes the twist: all the uncle's money goes to his widow; his lawyer says that the uncle was planning to give the student an annuity of £5,000, but died on the morning he was to have signed the new will. This *was* a "saleable" plot: indeed, someone had already sold it. *Lilliput* had included this method of murder in a 1937 article on unusual ways of killing that ingenious thriller-writers had devised.[33]

The fiction published in commercial papers and magazines provided models (and probably the inspiration) for much of the fiction in the camp periodicals. *Snips* ran a ghost story, as well as several comical romances, not a genre usually aimed at male audiences. One of the romances, "Matrimonial Bureau," mimicked Hollywood and story-magazine motifs and scenarios. The work of someone probably not "writing what he knew," it deals with a capricious young South Carolina heiress, now living in New York, who is visiting Chicago. Bored, she goes to a matchmaking agency to see what kind of man tries to meet women that way. She meets a man there, but he turns out to be an undercover reporter, not the genuine article. They part, and her boredom with Chicago returns, but she cannot bring herself to leave the city. Finally a "psycho-analyst"—those Americans!—tells her she is in love with the reporter. They get together, and he turns out to be a South Carolina native too, keen to return and run a plantation there. The city reporter who is a plantation owner at heart is not quite E. M. Hull's sheik who turns out to be a long-lost English aristocrat, but there is a strong family resemblance—and periodical fiction editors were on good terms with this family.[34]

It is possible that the author of "Matrimonial Bureau" was a freelance writer hoping to break into the American market or the British outlets for Americanesque fiction. Many of the other stories in the camp magazines give the impression of being the work of people who had read commercially produced fiction but not taught themselves its craft with guidebooks and correspondence courses. Some of the surprise endings attempted were of the it-was-all-a-dream variety that tutors warned against. In one, entitled "Thou Shalt Not," a man desperately desires a woman, who is finally revealed to be sleep, the daughter of Morpheus.[35] The stories in the camp magazines do not consistently mute their status as fictions. An authorial voice will frequently speak *ex cathedra* or *ex machina* at the close of a story: "Well that's my story: my TRUE story"; "That is the story of Pte. Ginger Findley"; "And that is how Mr and Mrs Saunders, the tennis-champions first met each other."[36] The authors of fiction published in popular periodicals, in contrast, tended to encourage the reader to forget that a story was in fact a concatenation of words on a page, drawing attention to its narrativity only when the manner of narration—such as the speech of a picturesque raconteur—was worth bringing into the nature of the fiction itself. The untutored were more likely to gravitate to demonstrativeness, finishing their stories with narrative interventions like those in children's and fairy stories.

Camp magazines in prisoner-of-war camps served different purposes from some of the other loci of popular writing during the war. They were imitations of peacetime magazines and to some extent replacements for them. They were to entertain, cheer, and inform the population of the camp, whereas *Seven, Bugle Blast,* and *Khaki and Blue* had more to do with representing wartime life as the writers had experienced it. Camp magazines' contents mimicked the gamut of genres found in magazines—short stories, poetry, humor, informative articles, opinion pieces, cartoons, mock agony aunts, puzzles. The female-dominated *Camp Chronicle,* published in a Sumatran camp some of whose prisoners were Dutch and others British, carried recipes as well.[37]

These papers carried reviews of camp musical and dramatic productions and reports on camp sporting events, sometimes humorously—the magazine of the Kobe prisoner-of-war camp in Japan, for instance, described a footrace as if the contestants were horses. They reported on camp life and condemned theft among the prisoners. In some cases, prison camp papers responded to claims made by the enemy. An editorial in *Snips* scorned the anti-Soviet claims of a pamphlet of the British Free Corps, a Nazi organization intended to get British POWs to support the war against the Soviet Union. "There are criticisms to be levelled at Soviet Russia as against the U.S.A. and Gt. Britain: for example, the evils of Atheism on the one hand, and Capitalism on the other; but for all the short comings of the democrats they are as angels of light compared with the Nazis." (The authorities at Eisleben appear not to have read English, or to have turned a blind eye to *Snips*.) Opinion pieces and poems addressed hopes for the postwar order, or criticized the bad old days that needed to be transcended. "Politicus" in *Snips* railed against the idea that profiteering and the maintenance of "the upper classes" should be regarded as "civilization" or "progress." Airing such opinions, especially under a pseudonym, did not necessarily mean that the author agreed with them completely, given that some editors encouraged controversial arguments in the hope that they might provoke rejoinders.[38]

Prison-camp papers typically carried more material about or set in prewar Britain than stories of the war, and still fewer accounts of combat and adventure. They occasionally included articles describing peacetime jobs, though not in a concerted fashion the way *Seven* did, and they ran short stories with pre- or postwar settings. One of the few pieces of fiction revolving around war experiences features a man who gets up at four-thirty in the morning, thinking he will be late for the train to the office. His wife convinces him that he doesn't have to get up until much later. It turns out that he is an ex-POW, and camp habits reassert themselves from time to time.[39] The most substantial story of civilian life in *Snips* was the serial "Molly and I," which chronicled a marriage set in a Britain that showed no signs of the war, and whose narrator was a rather incompetent spouse, no Mr. Miniver. "Molly and I" is a chain of episodes like forgotten anniversaries, arguments, and Molly's urge to spend money on a hat from *Vogue*. Along with the worn humor of the downtrodden husband there are veins of bitterness; two of the episodes end with reconciliations that do not quite disperse the feelings raised earlier on.

A recurrent genre was the description of home towns and places in the heart. Many of the accounts of Britain in the camp magazines focused on rural areas and natural beauty. There were hymns to Devon and Dorset, and memoirs and informative articles about travel in the country.[40] A newspaper in a POW camp in Thailand after the Japanese surrender carried a prose sketch of biking from London or Croydon down to Brighton, and another about going downstream through the locks to Cookham and to Cliveden Wood. The author of the second piece remarked that the prisoners had all carried some image from Britain with them during the war years: his was a mental picture of Cliveden Wood, though he had been there only twice.[41]

Since the publication of Martin J. Wiener's *English Culture and the Decline of the Industrial Spirit* (1981), it has become routine to see pastorals like these as signs of a congenital British or English antimodernism. As Peter Mandler has shown, this point of view misses the fact that most pre-1914 ruralist criticisms of modernity were made by "impassioned and highly articulate but fairly marginal artistic groups" isolated within an "aggressively urban and materialist" Britain.[42] The texts discussed here, it is worth emphasizing, testify to the opening of the countryside to lower-middle-class ramblers and motor-coach passengers: they are not tirades or paeans by Tory landowners.[43] Pastoral writing could perform the imaginative work of fantasy rather than articulate a state of affairs that modern city-dwellers actually wanted to see come about. This, I think, is what is going on in some of the poetry and prose quotations that soldiers and prisoners copied into their diaries and commonplace books, and in the pieces they wrote for camp magazines. A poem in *Snips* about regaining paradise after the war referred to "lovely English lanes." In Kobe, R. M. M. King transcribed a passage about taking a vow to "go through the lanes of England and the little thatched villages of England."[44] The recurrence of the country lane suggests that this vein of writing owed at least as much to the iconography of wartime mass culture as to any "deep English" ruralism. It was Vera Lynn who made famous the sentiment "There'll always be an England, while there's a country lane." That song was immensely popular: two months after the declaration of war, 200,000 copies of its sheet music had been sold. Another poem in *Snips* called "Thinking of Home" dreamed of the white cliffs of Dover, over which, Lynn promised in another hit song, there would be blue birds once the war was finished.[45]

As John Baxendale points out, country lanes are not all there is to "There'll Always Be an England." England will survive as long as "England means as much to you as England means to me." The content of that meaning might be a country lane or "a cottage small," but it could also be "a busy street" or the flag. For Baxendale, the song's "subtext lies in its absence of specific content: it doesn't matter *what* England means, as long as it means *something*."[46] In the pages of the camp magazines, too, Britain meant other things besides picturesque rural Britain.[47] The descriptions of home towns included Wigan and Pontefract. A. Rickman's poem about Wigan in *Snips* acknowledged that the town had no great industry or impressive town hall; but it had a rugby team and the Leeds-Liverpool canal, and

It has its Mills and Pits as well
Fish and Chips that can't be beaten.

And I have heard that in this town
The first Tripe was ever eaten.

An inclusive editorial in *Snips* acknowledged the value of the monarchy and the church, but pointed to other "precious traditions" too: "our sense of chivalry towards womankind; our religious toleration; our staunch though semi-theatrical attitude to militarism; the Hyde Park orator; Bank Holidays; Saturday football, the universal liking for Fish and Chips." The multiple references to fish and chips bespeak a celebration of the ordinary consonant with the values of *Seven*.[48]

While the war led people who had not previously seen themselves as authors to take up writing, not everything they wrote was a "literary response" to the war in the usual sense of that phrase. Imitations of magazine stories without wartime inflections appeared not just in the camp magazines, with their primary purpose of entertaining or cheering local audiences, but also in the magazine of the forces version of the writers' circle. Yet there were also poems and stories about death and air raids, about the effects of military mobilization on British towns and on individual lives, and about peacetime Devon and Wigan that were, obliquely, war literature. Among the genres people used in their literary responses to the war, poetry occupied a privileged position.

The debate about where the war poets were has been well studied, most accessibly by Robert Hewison in *Under Siege,* and I do not intend to revisit these arguments about why the Second World War produced no Rupert Brooke or Wilfred Owen, or whether Keith Douglas, Sidney Keyes, or Alun Lewis was indeed as good a poet as any of the First World War's soldier-poets.[49] The debate may become more significant if we step back and examine the assumptions underlying it. Why *should* a war generate poetry?

It seems clear that the war did lead to an increase in "the production and consumption of poetry," as Mass-Observation put it. The organization tackled the subject of poetry and the war very early on, in late 1939 and early 1940, and then again in October 1944. When Mass-Observation contacted Foyle's bookshop in 1944, an assistant said there had been a huge demand for poetry. The managers of Better Books, Zwemmer's, and Collett's agreed. Only the manager of Truslove and Hanson was less emphatic, saying that interest in poetry was not that much greater than before. What sort of poetry were people buying? Better Books and Zwemmer's sold plenty of "the fairly modern stuff"—Eliot, Yeats, MacNeice, and Day Lewis. "You might put it that any book of poetry reviewed in the Sunday Times goes very well; that's an almost certain rule," said the manager at Better Books. Foyle's sold a good deal of Wordsworth, Tennyson, and Brooke, and the 1944 anthology *Other Men's Flowers* was in great demand. Though not a collection of war poetry, *Other Men's Flowers* had martial associations, since it was edited by Viscount Wavell, who had commanded the British army in the Middle East from 1939 to 1943. It was a bestseller, and all the bookshops Mass-Observation contacted reported that it and other anthologies sold well. Even the left-wing bookseller Collett's was selling numerous copies of *Other Men's Flowers,* along with a lot of Brooke and Owen. The manager of Zwemmer's, presumably the famously snobbish Rudolph Friedmann, gave Mass-Observation this explanation of the trend: "There's a new demand on the part of the middle and lower middle classes in general—Rupert Brooke is their usual demand. All types and all classes are reading poetry—it's mostly nostalgia and sentimentalism . . . it makes them feel cosy and comfortable—the older people read the poets of the last war, and the younger ones read the ones they read just before the war . . .

it's regression—something sentimental—something to remind them of the days when they fancy they were happy—that sort of thing."[50]

The fillip the war gave to the reading of poetry was accompanied by an increase in the writing of verse. Galloway Kyle of the proudly reactionary Poetry Society and its *Poetry Review* told Mass-Observation in 1944 that he received "poems and alleged poems" from men in the army: "We get a lot of stuff sent to us from all over the world, much of it very simple—people are stirred into attempting to express their reactions in verse." Another editor, Cyril Connolly, complained in 1941 that *Horizon* was receiving an average of 100 poems a week, 70 of which should never have been written. The previous June, Connolly had noted that *Horizon* was being "inundated with poems, not only by professional poets, or even amateur ones, but in many cases by people who have never written a poem before, and yet find it comes to them as naturally as blowing out a paper bag." From all these submissions, "we can learn one important fact. Poetry is still the natural national form of self-expression, the one to which we take most readily . . . [T]he poetry of to-day is classless and is no longer the preserve of the educated and leisured."[51]

Poetry came "naturally" to people in wartime Britain in part, no doubt, because of the association between war and poetry fostered by the trench poets of 1914–1918, who were already central to the public and private memorializing of that war. The poet John Heath-Stubbs later recalled: "If there was one poet my generation really hated—really spat when his name was mentioned—it was Rupert Brooke." For those with different tastes, the poets of the First World War were positive precedents, and even companions. Lieutenant R. M. M. King copied Brooke's poem "The Soldier" into the diary he kept in the Kobe prisoner-of-war camp. At the bottom of a drawing of the graves of comrades who had died in Greece, a private wrote, echoing that same poem: "Those little plots of land shall be forever England." Brooke's "The Great Lover" was a template for at least two men away at war, one of them a POW. In Brooke's poem, the words "These I have loved" were a cue for a catalogue of the small furnishings of normal life:

White plates and cups, clean-gleaming,
Ringed with blue lines; and feathery, faery dust;
Wet roofs, beneath the lamp-light; the strong crust
Of friendly bread.

Men in the forces wrote in their own equivalents:

Electric train, rocking madly
With toast and tea . . .
Sun over public library; gold.[52]

The "naturalness" of the recourse to poetry derived from more than scripts provided by the First World War: it was part of the complex of popular romanticism. In Chapter 3 I argued that the beliefs and strategies of would-be writers of commercial fiction were premised on a popularization of English romanticism that had been common in discussions of literature and literary history. From these romantic premises, aspirants and those who advised them concluded that writers' descriptions would be vivid if they had experienced the subject matter directly and "sincerely," and that it was the "life" of the material, of the authors' experiences, that animated a piece of writing. Style and form were of secondary importance. The principle that authors should write about what they knew was a mundane aspect of a theory of art whose more aureate form was the idea that an artist was a great soul before (in terms of chronology as well as importance) being an extraordinary manipulator of words, paint, or sound. This exalted form of popular romantic thought overlaps with its more quotidian expressions in the frequent references to the Bible as a stylistic model and in the denunciation of modernism. When traditionalists referred to modernist poetry as if it were heretical rather than merely pretentious and distasteful, they were not simply indulging in tactical hyperbole but acting on the belief that poetry was animated by the spirit.

Because great poetry issued from noble feelings, it was at least plausible that deep feelings might find an appropriate outlet in poetry, great or otherwise. This belief underpinned the production of "trench poetry" in 1914–1918, and if men in the Second World War were wary of "romanticizing" war in part because of the excesses of the first war's bards, they shared their predecessors' romantic tendency to link feeling and poetic expression. Indeed, with the British population more at ease with literacy in 1939 than it had been in 1914, the romantic impulse to write was probably even more widely diffused. When a group of enthusiasts in Cairo came up with the idea of an anthology of poetry by Britons serving in the Middle East, their rationale was that "there must be a lot of poets" in the region: "Men who have been encouraged by some inward feeling, induced by war and by battle, to express in verse the many ideas flowing through their minds." Their appeal, through newspapers and the Egyptian state broadcasting corporation, brought in more than 3,000 poems. Since 1980, veterans of the resulting anthology, *Oasis,* have collected and published more poems written during the war by men stationed in the Middle East, most of whom did not write poetry before or after the war. By 1985 they had been sent 10,000 poems (and there were many more to come). This mass of verse testifies to the reach of the belief that poetry was a suitable response to war experiences and difficult emotions.[53] Tracing the movement from feeling to poetry in detail, being able to show the concrete connection between the two, poses strong evidential challenges.

One way of gaining access to this process is by examining the collection of wartime diaries and scrapbooks held by the Imperial War Museum. The poetry in this collection is not abstracted from the everyday contexts of its production, but wedged in between letters, mementoes, and diary entries.

Writing could of course be cathartic. J. Innes, prisoner of war in Thailand, wrote in 1944: “I don’t usually write this diary at night, but to night I feel terribl[y] unsettled, not at all happy, and thoroughly homesick and thought I might ease the complaint somewhat by establishing contact with home in the only way open to me—ie by writing a few lines in the diary.” But catharsis was not the only kind of emotional work that writing could perform. Writing *poetry* could also be a way of honoring or consecrating feelings. Charles William Waide, a man from Poplar serving as a gunner in the navy, recounted in his journal having gone to a cinema in Karachi and seen a film that “brought back many memories to me, & my constant thoughts were of my wife, still patiently waiting my return. I came back, & wrote this piece of Poetry.” Waide wrote other poems about his feelings for his loved ones. After describing the beauty of a sunset and an evening at sea in loftily poetic prose, he noted in his journal that he had written, and sent home, “a piece of poetry . . . which describes my feelings at that time, at the end of every day.” The first of its three stanzas runs:

I sit upon the hatchway
At the end of every day
Just sit & watch the blazing sun go down
It is then my thoughts turn deeply
To my loved ones way back home
To you dear, & my dear old London Town.[54]

The army captain Dudley Chenery, a Barclays Bank employee from Suffolk who spent most of the war as a prisoner in a mining camp in Japan, was moved to write poetry several times by the thought of his wife in England. On one occasion he wrote in his diary: "My wife & my home! . . . How much they mean to me! . . . my love and longing for them is beyond description of the greatest of poets." Right after this entry he recorded a poem, "To Brenda, My Wife," one of several addressed to her. This one begins:

Oh! Sweetest flower, thou beauteous gift of God's creation
Ne'er were the thoughts of man so distant
For so long a time as mine.
My yearning, longing, praying God will hear
And in His mercy will protect and guard you
From evil care & use of this dread time of parting.
Dear Heart, 'twas cruel a blow for me no less than you
When our beloved life so new begun
Was interrupted much against our wills
By this thing war, so thrust upon us
That our lives and all those simple things we loved
That were, in fact, ourselves, were
Set aside until God bids these
Darkening clouds disperse.[55]

Chenery's poem is both orthodox and unconventional. Unrhymed, with varying line lengths, it breaks with some of the usual verse forms favored by amateur poets. Their mainstays were four-line stanzas with AABB, ABAB, and ABCB rhyme schemes. Roughly ballad quatrains, with the first and third lines having ten syllables (on average) and the second and fourth lines about eight, were very common. Meters tended to be heavily iambic; in *this* respect, Chenery's poem is not exceptional. In addition, his ode to his wife remained conventionally "poetic," striving after titanic literary effects: God figures prominently, and so, in subsequent lines, do the sea, the sky, and the earth ("Those pleasures found in earth and sky and sea will take the place / Of great and evil things of man's creation").

It has been observed that "when English writers are in the grip of strong emotion," they often resort to "biblical language." For Chenery and others, loftily poetic language as well as biblical language was a vehicle for strong emotion. Baxendale has pointed out that when it was successful, Churchill's rhetoric "worked off both the familiarity and the special cultural status of seventeenth-century English: Shakespeare, the Authorized Version, the Anglican prayer book, and its nineteenth-century reworking in the Protestant hymn-book and Victorian melodrama. For twentieth-century Britons, who knew they did not really live in cottages [Churchill persistently called houses "cottage homes"], this was the language of special occasions." Chenery, Waide, and other poets in the armed forces worked in a more gilded register than Churchill, but theirs too was a language of special occasions.[56]

In its subject matter, "To Brenda, My Wife" is quite conventional. Many of the poems by men in the forces and prisoners of war were about missed or lost loved ones and homesickness, and Chenery's effort to strike a high-flown note was repeated by others:

> Come back my love-one! My dear love returning
> Love stands eternal, tho' youth may be fleeting
> Come in the Summer when Skye's Hills are purple,
> Sweet with the heather the wanton bees fumble
> Pure as a Zephyr from the Sound of Sleat blowing.

As these lines by Gordon Paul Charkin indicate, the commemoration of the permanent or temporary loss of loved ones could segue into laments for places in Britain. A good number of them were pastoral, but others saluted London and other cities. Chenery, who as a Suffolk native was possibly not predisposed to romanticizing the industrial North, looked back fondly on his time in a camp in Middlesbrough: "Boro' of grime, of dust, of noise, / Would that we now could share thy joys."[57]

Recalling his involvement with *Oasis* and poems by men and women stationed in the Middle East, G. S. Fraser commented that the "special feelings" these poets expressed were "often a reaction to new, strange, and picturesque surroundings . . . home-sickness (typical feelings of the civilian soldier), but not the pessimism of the First World War poems." There was, he wrote, a sense that the war was a meaningful one, and the theme of the *Oasis* poems was "less protest against war as such than feelings of a personal kind shared by many soldiers and to some degree hopes for a better world after the war. Both the sense of loneliness and the sense of comradeship are important." Poetry evoked both the happiness and the grief of military comradeship. Mike Dougland's ballad about his war experiences, published in *The Camp* (the English-language weekly that the German authorities produced for POW camps) and transcribed by at least two of his fellow inmates at Marburg, concluded with thanks to "Aussie, Kiwi, Froggie & Greek," and declared that in his old age, it was "not only of Glories of war that I'll speak, / But of life as *we knew it,* Together."[58]

In their poetry, prisoners and soldiers seldom spoke of the glories of war, though they did depict combat. One especially lurid poem about the fall of Singapore circulated somehow among prison camps as far apart as Singapore itself and Nong Pladuk, Thailand; prisoners at both camps copied it out.[59] After a heavily onomatopoeic description of battle, the author says of the casualties:

> "They have died to save the Empire,"
> Don't for God's sake ask who for,

They were simply slain and butchered,
In a "Democratic" war.

Meanwhile, "in London's 'Clubland,'" the rich are safe with their money and brandy. "Yes my masters this is WAR," runs the final line, ambiguous but unambiguously menacing. This poem, anonymous in both the places I have seen it, makes accusations more severe than those in magazines with reformist or progressivist agendas such as *Seven,* and well beyond those in much of the poetry servicemen wrote for themselves or for *Oasis.* The "hopes for a better world" that Fraser found "to some degree" in the *Oasis* poems were often expressed even more generally there than in the "new Jerusalem" poems in *Seven,* with their open-ended optimism. Hopes of personal happiness blurred into more general visions of the postwar world. Whether, in this movement, private good symbolized more general amelioration or was enough of a substitute for it is not something we can reliably judge. The overlap between the two is evoked in Sidney Stainthorp's poetic letter to his unseen child, which begins with an apology for his absence and an expression of his longing for the day when he can help teach the child, and then proceeds:

My hope and prayer are that you never may
Give some words the meanings that we use today,
You'll think of brick walls when you hear the word mortar,
And tanks will be vessels for storing up water . . .
If this can come true I shall think it worthwhile
To have spent so much time in the land of the Nile.[60]

Plenty of war poetry was lighter and less respectable than this. Sex and the prospect of a postwar boom in it were predictably recurrent topics of doggerel.[61] Mildly profane poems lampooned army life. Humorous verse, poems for the fallen, and the occasional political poem such as the indictment of Clubland found their way into the scrapbooks where people in the forces preserved mementoes from food labels and cigarette packets to programs of camp or barracks revues. Men and women also wrote directly in others' scrapbooks and albums: poetry could function as a social gesture. It was customary to ask people to sign them and add some drawing, verse, joke, or piece of wisdom. Writing in the scrapbook of Larry Phillips in the prison camp in Rezzanello, Italy, a navy lieutenant mused on the genre itself. In the old days, he said, such an album presumably contained only signatures. "But a modern generation demands more; it wants a sketch, a slightly risqué verse, or a snappy piece of prose." He tried to contribute a different phrase or verse to every scrapbook put before him in order to "conjure up again the circumstances under which we met." For Phillips, he jotted a few possibly suggestive lines that were probably cryptic to anyone outside Rezzanello. Other prisoners contributed prose and poetry describing Rezzanello village, the prison, and their life there; still others wrote verse portraits of inmates; one rewrote the song "These Foolish Things" so as to make it about war experiences (making up new lyrics for popular songs was a common practice); one transcribed a passage from Noel Coward's *Cavalcade;* another copied out a passage from Kenneth Grahame's *The Wind in the Willows* about Toad's exaggerations, adding that the POWs would have to do something similar, given how early in the war they had been caught. A clergyman prisoner wrote a brief history of the church in Rezzanello. The contents of Phillips's scrapbook were not so very different from those of a camp magazine.[62]

Elsie Dufton, a nurse from Leeds, invited her army and navy patients to sign her autograph books and write snippets of verse in them. One wrote:

> It's easy to be happy on a Sunny Day
> But when life is sad and Weary

That's the time when Nurse Dufton
Lights up the ward and make[s] us Cheerie.

Other patients contributed less specific and perhaps less original verses. A characteristic example is this one, from a man serving in the Pioneer Corps:

True Friends Are Like Diamond
Precious And Rare.
False Friends Are Like Autumn Leave's
Found Everywhere.

Dufton's autograph books are full of this sort of material. Most of the patients, almost all of them men, clearly thought that sententious verse was the appropriate thing to write in someone's scrapbook or autograph album.[63] Their lines read like greeting-card verse.

Although this comparison may sound flippant, it is quite serious, and it points to an important context of the popular composition of poetry. An examination of the collection of Christmas, Easter, and Valentine cards in the Victoria and Albert Museum makes it clear that much of the poetry of amateur writers does indeed have strong formal affinities with greeting-card verse of the early and mid-twentieth century: iambic rhythms, four-line stanzas, AABB, ABAB, and ABCB rhyme schemes.[64] It may be that the men writing in Nurse Dufton's autograph books were consciously imitating greeting-card poetry, in the way that the magazines produced in barracks and camps were imitations of the mass-cultural products of peacetime. (Charles Waide wrote verse birthday greetings for a friend that would have fitted neatly into an ersatz birthday card, and probably did.)[65] But it is more likely that amateur poetry resembles greeting-card poetry because in homes without at least a *Golden Treasury,* say, or Sir Arthur

Quiller-Couch's *Oxford Book of English Verse,* the kind of poetry encountered most often must have been greeting-card verse and newspaper poetry such as that of "Patience Strong."

Strong's poems appeared every day in the *Daily Mirror* from 1935 to 1945, and were also issued in book and calendar form. Her first book sold more than 100,000 copies within a year: a "highbrow" poet, in contrast, was lucky to sell 800 copies a year. Her poems were typographically disguised as prose, but with punctuation marks that served as implicit line breaks: "Have you lost the art of living? Does the world seem cruel to you? . . . Try forgetting and forgiving—It may change your point of view." Strong habitually dealt in rhymed couplets, ballad stanzas, and ABCD stanzas, and her subject matter was usually, as in this case, inspiring sentiments or winsome descriptions. Her work was reproduced in at least one improvised magazine, in a civilian internment camp in Sumatra.[66]

As well as familiarizing people with certain verse forms, greeting cards and newspaper verse probably reinforced the links between poetry and meaningful utterance and significant feelings, between poetry and "special occasions." Through greeting cards, verses were sold as commodities to perform ceremonial functions in daily life, to mark events both happy and sad, and to express sentiments appropriate to a particular time of year.[67] Similarly, the poetry people wrote for themselves or for their comrades in war was used to mark and adorn occasions or situations—sometimes to add merriment, and sometimes to elevate the tone, saying something that prose, whether spoken or written, was presumed to be incapable of expressing. People who turned to writing poetry as a response to war did not combine romanticism and the products of mass culture as thoroughly as writers' circle authors of "saleable fiction" did, but even this form of expression associated with individual feeling and authenticity did not exist in a sphere completely removed from commercial culture.

Whatever its impact on the literary canon, the Second World War mobilized many British people to write. Within Britain, *Seven* combined two legacies of the 1930s—the valorization of ordinariness and the campaigns to encourage working-class writers—and produced an extraordinarily popular syncretism of two major strands of "popular writing": the commercially oriented aspirant writers' movement and the intermittently conspicuous tradition of working-class writing. Life in the forces could hinder authors, but the novelty of military experience, time to write, and exposure to new people could stir others to take up writing. Some found a niche writing to entertain or hearten their comrades, replicating some of the textual products of peacetime popular culture. Others were moved to write poetry by their war experiences, acting on a different aspect of popular romanticism.

Yet while the burst of popular writing between 1940 and 1945 was in varying ways a response to the war, the texts produced often elude correlation with wartime events or social and political attitudes. Assumptions about the nature of writing played a part in limiting the political content of these texts. *Seven* and the Front Line Generation exemplified ways of linking the energies of popular writing projects with populist politics; in their moderation, they also demonstrated the limits to the compatibility of "literature" and "politics" for many people, even those who regarded themselves as "political." Violence and suffering were not screened from popular writing to the extent that politics was, but they figured less in these wartime texts than might be expected. This was not because violence and suffering were incompatible with writing, but because not all writing was undertaken to mark or to work through weighty emotions and experiences. Some people wrote emotional poetry; other people, or the same ones at different times, wrote about less dramatic aspects of the war, or about other things altogether. Although novice writers romantically believed that writing and experience were tightly intertwined, there was often some distance between the two.

Chapter 8

Popular Writing after the War

The literary populism of wartime persisted for two or three years after 1945, then dissipated for reasons that historians are at a loss to explain satisfactorily.[1] The change affected more than the content and mood of popular writing: it also meant an end to left-wing and populist efforts to seek out working-class writers. The social contexts of working-class writing changed as well. The novelists of the 1950s who claimed to speak for the working class tended to be sons of manual workers who had moved into the "lower professions." They were thus products of the expansion of the clerical and technical middle class in the 1930s and 1940s more than they were products of 1950s "affluence." The transformation of working-class communities and livelihoods placed writing in a different relation to working-class life. Faithfully representing "my own people" in fiction became less of a social obligation. In the 1950s some writers from working-class backgrounds branched out into genres far removed from realist sketches; others wrote fiction about working-class characters that served different purposes from comparable texts of the 1930s. Some even joined writers' circles.

The writers' circles were undergoing their own transformation. After 1945 the would-be writers' movement became at once stronger and more diffuse. Writers' circles proliferated and developed new activities such as summer schools. At the same time, the "middlebrow" culture alongside which the circles and writing magazines had developed was starting to break down from within, even before the social and educational changes of the 1950s and 1960s. In the interwar period, middlebrow culture had been a bulwark against modernism and perceived pretension generally; after the war, the literary "middle ground" became more of a concourse for different kinds of writing.

Crucial to this reconfiguration of taste were changes in magazine publishing. Trends in magazine publishing inevitably had a bearing on what freelances could earn from their writing. The late 1940s and the 1950s were a time of contracting opportunities in print publication. When the Ministry of Labour published a series of handbooks on potential careers at the end of the war, "the most depressing was that on journalism." Journalism was effectively a "closed profession" for adults: you had to get in young. Nor were the prospects bright for newcomers to fiction writing. Paper rationing continued to hamper book and periodical publication. Under the strain of increased competition from broadcasting and newspapers' encroachment onto magazines' territory, along with rationing and higher taxation, generalist magazines folded even when their readerships were not falling. Pay rates for contributions to periodicals did not keep pace with increases in the average wage. Magazines offered fewer openings to creative writers, and diminishing returns on what they did accept.[2]

While print was in the doldrums, radio appeared to promise new opportunities. While the BBC resumed television service in mid-1946, it took several years for television to become part of most British people's lives, and longer for it to become a market to which aspiring authors could realistically hope to contribute. Radio, by contrast, was part of the mental furniture of people who belonged to writers' circles. Like many societies meeting "in village halls up and down the country," writers' circles would often adapt the format of the BBC's *Brains Trust,* a panel of visiting or in-house experts fielding questions from the audience. The program *Stump the Storyteller,* apparently an improvisational game, was also adapted as a writing activity by the Leeds and Manchester circles. Some writers' circle members had broadcast in the interwar period—Margaret Lees of Halifax, for instance, on the North Region's *Children's Hour*—but it was not until after the Second World War that participants in the aspirant writers' movement began to submit work to the BBC in large numbers.[3]

In part, this was a consequence of the BBC's own reorganization and expansion following the war.[4] The Light Programme, begun in July 1945, played popular music, quiz shows, comedy, serials, and magazine shows such as *Woman's Hour.* The Third Programme, launched the following year, broadcast classical music, talks, stories, and plays for discriminating tastes, though its elitism can be exaggerated. The Home Service broadcast news and entertainments deemed heavier or worthier than those on the Light Programme. The Third and Light Programmes were national; the core of Home Service programming originated in London, but regional studios could opt out of particular programs and transmit their own local productions instead. After a long hiatus in regional broadcasting, a new structure was introduced in July 1945 whereby all of the United Kingdom outside London and the Southeast was divided into six "regions." Regional studios produced programs of their own and localized variants of national shows such as *Woman's Hour* and *Children's Hour.* Within a region there could be a number of studios with distinct agendas and responsibilities. The North Region was headquartered in Manchester, but it also operated studios in Leeds and Newcastle, which broadcast programs of their own as well as the northern *Children's Hour* and programs heard by the rest of the country. Informative talks were recorded in Manchester and short stories and most plays in Leeds.[5] Programs were produced by "departments" independent of the Home Service and the Light and Third Programmes. The Drama department in London, for instance, produced Home Service plays as well as Third Programme ones. The regions maintained their own Talks and Drama departments that were parallel to though smaller than London's, and plays, talks, and short stories originating in regional studios could find a national audience in repeats on the London Home Service or Light Programme.

Broadcasting offered many of the things writers' circle members sought: a regional and possibly national outlet for locally inflected writing; a wide audience and recognition; and payment. In the early and mid-1940s the BBC paid generously in comparison with print. Later in the decade its payments were lower in absolute terms—despite increases in the cost of living—than they had been in 1944; in the 1950s pay rates remained static as wages increased. The standard rate for a new short story in 1947 was a guinea per minute.[6] In that year a new system of payment was introduced. London was allowed to pay higher rates to established authors, and some of the regions also graded authors differently. The North Region believed in principle in equal pay for equal work, but made an exception for "the amateur and purely Children's Hour authors." By the mid-1950s there were three pay grades for a short story of the standard length of fifteen minutes, or 2,100–2,300 words: fifteen guineas for "ordinary contributors"; twenty guineas for "writers with a well-established outside reputation"; and twenty-five guineas for "writers in the front rank." It took some deliberation before the long-established novelist Louis Golding was placed in the twenty-guinea class, and Denys Val Baker took ten years to get beyond the fifteen-guinea mark—so fifteen guineas was evidently as much as a novice writer could hope for.[7]

This sum worked out at a little under seven guineas per thousand words. The purchasing power of that figure was much less than it had been ten years earlier, but compared with the other available options it was not a shabby sum. One veteran literary agent who specialized in short stories remarked that the fees for broadcast stories in the 1950s "don't compare with those paid by periodicals," but this was an exaggeration. Of the magazines that revealed their standard rates in the *Writers' and Artists' Year Book*—and many of the more competitive ones did not publicize their rates—a sum of three to five guineas per thousand words was common in the early 1950s. As always, it could be said that there was room at the top—*Woman's Own,* the highest-paying women's magazine, was reported in the 1954 *Year Book* to have paid 75 guineas for a 3,000-word story. By contrast, the rather upmarket *Lady* usually offered two to three guineas per thousand words. The BBC's fifteen guineas for 2,100 words was a comparatively good payment for someone who was not a star.[8]

A sign of the writing public's interest in the opportunities broadcasting presented is the number of invitations writers' groups and magazines extended to BBC producers and editors. In the interwar period the *Writer* published the odd piece by a freelance who did broadcast work, and the *Writers' and Artists' Year Book* carried short essays on how to write for radio, but it was not until after the war that BBC staff made regular appearances at writers' circle meetings, especially in the North of England, and contributed to the *Writer.* They were thus doing what magazine and newspaper editors had long done. BBC staff would inform prospective contributors which studio or department to send their submissions to, and advise them about the peculiarities of a radio genre or an individual program. Thus Richard Kelly of the Newcastle studio told the writers' circle in that city that prospective contributors of broadcast short stories should aim for a compromise between "good literature" and ordinary conversation. Stories did not have to be in the first person, but those that were had an easier conversational flow. Talks for *Woman's Hour,* by contrast, should be written as if one were talking to a friend, the program's editor told the Halifax circle. Producers, like editors, could offer hints about the proclivities of local audiences. Speaking to the Bradford Writers' Circle, Frederick Bradnum of the North Region's Drama department told his audience that northern listeners disliked fantasy and liked family plays in northern settings and adaptations of well-known northern novels.[9]

These outreach efforts appear to have been motivated not only by the BBC's commitment to public service but also by the hope that a greater proportion of the unsolicited manuscripts the corporation received might be usable on the air. The volume of submissions was immense. In Leeds in the late 1950s, Bradnum was receiving 70 to 80 radio plays a month, of which he thought only 2 or so producible. In London, according to Gielgud, 250 to 300 plays, "the majority of them unsolicited," arrived each month. "Few of these show any dramatic promise, and it is rare for the acceptance rate to be higher than two per cent." This was apparently an exaggeration, at least for the first quarter of 1953. In that time, the Drama department in London received 855 unsolicited scripts. Of these, 230 were rejected on a single reading; a further 517 were rejected after reading, checking, and rechecking by three or four readers. Finally, 108 came to Gielgud and his second-in-command, Charles LeFeaux, and 89 were accepted: "a good figure—unexpectedly high," the BBC's director-general commented. The director-general had become involved after the author Elspeth Huxley questioned the script selection process at a meeting of the general advisory council. Huxley's questions invoked the specter of a closed shop, to the irritation of the Drama department, whose staff resented the "myth" that "there are many undiscovered writers of merit who only need an opportunity to show what they can do." The BBC's board of governors resolved that "in order to protect the Corporation against charges of a closed shop policy in drama, it might be advisable to arrange for an occasional outside check of say 10% of all unsolicited scripts submitted during a certain period." A vetting scheme of this sort was tried for two months without turning up evidence of wrongheaded selection processes, and the director of Home Sound Broadcasting moved to bring the experiment in external review to an end.[10]

Despite the crush of unsolicited plays, the Drama department had the resources to have them all read by at least one staff member. Forms of response for those whose plays were not accepted varied: a simple rejection slip for those "which show no dramatic merit of any kind"; a letter or interview providing "constructive criticism" and a copy of "leaflet in which the fundamentals of radio playwriting are outlined"; and the assignment of a staff adaptor to work with the author in making a promising play acceptable. The short story readers and editors in the Talks department in London could not provide this level of feedback. At least 50 unsolicited stories arrived each week. In 1947, B. C. Horton, the staff member to whom unsolicited stories were sent first, told the head of the department that of the 350 stories she had received since taking over the job, 60 were "sufficiently competent to be sent round to the short story Producers." Of these 60, only one was accepted for broadcasting, and it had already appeared in print. The volume of submissions caused a lot of work: "40% are competent and require reading right through. Half of the rest need more than a glance at the first page. Only a few could one fairly dispose of by only glancing at the first page." Horton asked for the appointment of an outside reader to sift through the unsolicited submissions at a rate comparable to that publishers paid for readings of unsolicited novels. Though one of her superiors agreed that "we do not depend on unsolicited short stories for more than a minute fraction of our output" and "can therefore use a very coarse mesh in screening them," he felt that "as a monopoly, we have an obligation to see that every manuscript submitted is given consideration and, in my view, consideration inside rather than outside the Corporation." At some point, however, the task of reading unsolicited stories was contracted out.[11]

Of the stories selected by the Talks department, the Light Programme transmitted the most.[12] At the end of 1946 it launched *Mid-Morning Story,* which broadcast fifteen-minute stories Monday through Friday. The program ran with some interruptions throughout the 1950s. Its anticipated audience, noted David Lloyd James of the Talks department, was "working people," including housewives—"not an audience which reads short stories except in so far as they are presented with other material in newspapers and magazines." He added that a story dealing with the impact of some outwardly trifling incident was "a sophisticated taste which depends normally on a fairly advanced appreciation of fine writing." The sort of story published in contemporary magazines of a "literary" bent was, in Lloyd James's view, "beyond the appreciation of the audience we command." Midmorning stories should therefore be "good yarns rather than . . . English Literature . . . They should be complete in themselves as the stories of nineteenth century writers are commonly complete and not like those of the twentieth century, which end in a question mark." Addressing would-be radio authors, BBC personnel underscored the desirability of "a sting or a twist in the tail of it," one staff member referring explicitly to *Mid-Morning Story.* The morning story was, therefore, a slot amenable to the sort of fiction favored by members of writers' circles and contributors to the *Writer.* However, in some qualification of Lloyd James' earlier assessment, "stories of a quiet reflective nature, often purely descriptive, slight in plot, and with little dialogue," were included in a 1952 or 1953 run of the program "on literary merit and probable appeal." These works complemented the majority of the stories, which were "light in character, written somewhat on the lines of the best of those included in London evening papers."[13]

Mid-Morning Story, or *Morning Story* was it was called from 1949, was the chief route from a regional to a national audience. Regional program directors were to send London short stories they had broadcast, and one or two days every week the morning story transmitted nationally came from the regions. This system allowed the Light Programme to draw on a larger pool of contributions and gave it one of the "comparatively few opportunities when we can legitimately give elbow room to the regions." Regionalism went only so far: "Bearing in mind the national coverage of the Light Programme," regional directors were told, "would you eschew the broader dialects." Later, "stories with more local flavour, including dialect," were given priority: the regional studios were having difficulty supplying the Light Programme with enough high-quality stories of national rather than region-specific interest. One reason was that many people in the regional studios' catchment areas appeared to "continue to send their stories direct to London, still not realising that we broadcast them from here and are interested to see them." Perhaps they did so out of ignorance, or perhaps they thought that by approaching London directly they would bypass unnecessary hurdles. Regional producers, however, were sometimes less swamped by submissions and able to give a manuscript or potential contributor more time and attention. Moreover, a regional producer could act as an advocate for a regional story or author that the London staff were initially inclined to dismiss.[14]

Jessie Gray of the Halifax Authors' Circle was one beneficiary of the attention regional producers could devote to untried contributors. Several months before she joined the circle in 1958, Gray began submitting items to BBC North Region's program *The Northcountryman.* After several of her scripts were rejected, one was accepted, and because of the quality of her voice Gray was brought to Leeds to record her own script (authors were not often selected as readers). A subsequent story was rejected on the grounds that it was not northern enough. Gray sent work to a North Region morning program, *Today in the North,* and received some feedback in her rejection letter: "The story is rather too straight forward and lacks, what a journalist might call, a twist i.e. surprise ending . . . without such a twist the humour must be very strong indeed and, amusing as it could be during the daytime, the thought of 'bloodred finger ends' spattering merrily around the cellar would certainly put me, and, I suspect, many listeners, off their bacon and tomato!"[15]

During the 1960s Gray's other acceptances, as reported to the Halifax Authors' Circle, included items in the "Country and Coast" department of the *Yorkshire Post* and the "Trends" section of the *Halifax Courier.*[16] This material was probably of a piece with some of the things she was sending to BBC North Region. Many other members of writers' circles who sent short stories to the BBC and to magazines produced broadly similar work for both media. Radio plays, of course, were a genre peculiar to the broadcast medium. Although the BBC's records make it clear that there were many aspiring radio playwrights in Britain, and though producers spoke to writers' circles about the genre, the records of those circles that have left archives report few "successes" with radio drama. It is possible that amateur theatrical societies, and not writers' circles, were the associational homes of would-be broadcast dramatists.

Radio also involved other work done by writers, tasks more or less specific to the medium. Gray's colleague in the Halifax circle, Bertha Lonsdale, carved out a career as a scriptwriter, turning children's books (lots of Biggles) into plays or serials and writing talks for young audiences on topics as different as plastics and rayon, northern legends, and Captain Cook. After a poorly paid apprenticeship with children's adaptations in the late 1930s and early 1940s, she became a reliable freelance to whom the North Region regularly sent work. In the 1950s she was usually paid just over or under a guinea per minute of a script. This was roughly what a short story writer would be paid per minute, but Lonsdale's adaptations and original scripts were longer, often forty or fifty minutes. She also wrote for regional magazine programs, doing *Know Your Region* scripts for the well-known Yorkshire broadcaster Wilfred Pickles in the late 1940s and shouldering some editorial responsibilities for *What's on in the North* in the early 1960s. For all her success behind the scenes, Lonsdale seems to have hankered after being on the air. "As usual," wrote a member of the Manchester staff, "Miss Lonsdale has been present with the recording car when the recordings have been made, but she hasn't done any of the interviewing." While the BBC liked her scripts, "Her voice wasn't up to the script and she had no microphone personality. Without a clear intelligent voice." Some Halifax Authors' Circle meetings were devoted to members' reading their work onto tape so that Lonsdale could comment on their delivery, as she evidently did with some asperity.[17]

The broadcasting experiences of these two Halifax Authors' Circle members exemplify the ways radio could serve as a new "market" for aspiring writers. In Gray's case, broadcasting was a direct alternative to the magazines and newspapers to which members of the same circle had submitted work in the interwar period. For Lonsdale, broadcasting was a more oblique alternative to publication in print. Working-class as well as middle-class authors would try their hand at it.

The postwar BBC did not explicitly set out to recruit working-class writers, but its regionalism sometimes led it in that direction, since the "distinctive" aspects of a regional culture were often associated most with its working-class population. Of Vivian Daniels, who handled short stories at the Leeds studio, Stan Barstow wrote: "*He* had discovered me in the sense that he had been the first to buy my work and had produced more of it than anyone else before my novel appeared." In 1954 Daniels sent one of Barstow's stories to London as one that might be suitable for repeating on the Light Programme. Its regional character was one of its selling points, and Daniels even had something like a generic category for the story: "North country comical about a little man who had always wanted to play the drum of the village band." While Daniels used many of Barstow's stories, his acceptances were always "passive": "He had never suggested I try my hand at a radio play, nor invited me to the studio to see one produced." Although he was outshone as a supporter of local talent by his successor at the Leeds studio, Alfred Bradley, Daniels went further, for instance, than the Edinburgh Talks producer who passed on to London a short story by Alexander Duthie, "a working man, who has done some quite effective talks for us in a tough style. This is his first attempt at a story—probably a bit elementary, but just let me know if you think the idea is worth working on or if it is too crude." North Region producers regularly submitted Sid Chaplin stories to London for broadcasting to a national audience, and rebutted verdicts like Donald Stephenson's judgment that a story about a mining accident was unnecessarily macabre, unredeemed by moral heroism, and "more than a little off-putting" "at a time when recruiting for the mines was still so urgent." Chaplin had stories in *Morning Story* and other slots in the late 1940s and early 1950s, and remained in touch with the BBC. During the 1970s he wrote television scripts for the Tyneside drama series *When the Boat Comes In*.[18]

Chaplin retained the momentum as an author that he had built up from the late 1930s: as well as continuing to have short stories published and broadcast, he started to write novels. By contrast, when Leslie Halward finished his war service as an RAF ground crewman, he had to begin his career again. Halward found that there was "no longer a market for my type of story, I'd been writing about working class people, mainly the unemployed, and MY working class people no longer existed." Magazines he had written for, including *Penguin New Writing*, ceased publication. Halward struggled to get his short stories accepted for radio: they were so short, and lacked what P. H. Newby of the Third Programme called "the narrative 'pull' that broadcasting seems to demand." Since he believed he had "a gift for dialogue," and some of his stories had been told "almost entirely in dialogue," Halward decided to try radio drama. He managed to carve out a new niche writing radio plays for the BBC Midland Region. In the mid-1950s one of his producers trained for television production and "tried to wean [Halward] over to television. I failed; he had no theatrical sense although I think a remarkable talent for the short story and the radio play." Despite this failure to change his primary genre one more time, Halward had a modestly successful career as a radio dramatist from the late 1940s through the 1960s. Though "his" unemployed working class did not exist as it had in the 1930s, which he always saw as "the period when my best work was written and published," he continued to write about working-class people, albeit in updated settings. A play from 1957, for instance, deals with a group of young musicians in the Midlands trying to make a success of their jazz group and one-up each other in the process. Halward's Birmingham working-class characters and settings were now valued by producers for their regional identity as once they had been prized by editors for their class identity.[19]

Halward was far from alone in detecting a sea change in working-class life with implications for writing about the working class. Many of the novels welcomed as illuminating the condition of workers in the 1950s were by younger men who were not employed in manual jobs. That decade was a time of much discussion about the effects of consumption, "affluence," and the educational reforms of the 1944 Butler Act on "traditional" working-class culture, and about the existence of the class system itself. An emergent academic sociology probed changes within working-class "communities," most famously in Michael Young and Peter Willmott's *Family and Kinship in East London* (1957). In this climate, a "special premium attached to those who embodied as well as analysed" the postwar social changes. Richard Hoggart, who had gone from a Hunslet slum to Leeds Grammar School and then to Leeds University, was such a person; in *The Uses of Literacy* (1957), he evoked an idealized working-class past and its contemporary enemies, chiefly a putatively new commercial culture and the "candy-floss world" it entailed.[20] Some of the novelists and dramatists who were precipitately accorded pundit status in the 1950s also had this sort of cachet, especially John Braine, whose *Room at the Top* (also 1957) is the story of an accountant of working-class origin set on climbing a ladder of jobs and a corresponding hierarchy of social contacts, cars, and female trophies. While educational reforms loomed large in discussions of social mobility, few of these novelists were young enough to have been children of the Butler Act and hardly any had gone to "red-brick" universities. Rather, the social change that many of them benefited from was the expansion of clerical work and the so-called lower professions.[21] David Mercer, David Storey, Stan Barstow, Keith Waterhouse, and John Braine came from working-class families, attended grammar schools, and moved into occupations such as draftsmanship, journalism, teaching, and librarianship.

Work as a journalist on the *Yorkshire Post* and then the *Daily Mirror* gave Waterhouse security and time to work on his novels in a way that most 1930s worker-writers, or indeed coal miners in the 1950s, could not. Braine's diaries make it clear that library work enabled him to write his first novel. His library job allowed him to write through the evening, and it gave him a measure of material comfort: as a qualified librarian he earned over £500 a year, a figure that rose as the decade went on. For almost two years in the early 1950s he had tried to live by his writing alone, but his progress reports to himself reveal that in that period the novel suffered from the time and effort expended on shorter pieces.[22] Worries about money also weighed on him: Braine still regarded himself as working class, and though he talked about worldly advancement in the calculating way his protagonist does in *Room at the Top,* he also articulated fears and hopes that echoed earlier worker-writers: "Those writers who've managed to live la vie Bohème successfully have almost always been middle-class and therefore born with the conviction that they can't really starve. I know that one can really starve."[23] All the same, he was aware that starvation was less of a threat to him now, and that, having once lived in a "hellish" room with three others, he now had what Willy Goldman, B. L. Coombes, and George Garrett had wanted. "I have a room of my own; and time. I *must* make use of it." In September 1954 he abandoned freelance bohemia and went back to the security and comfort of the library. Working on the novel in his "spare time," he made much better progress, and submitted the completed manuscript to his agent thirteen months later.[24]

Not every author of the 1950s who wrote about working-class people from personal experience fits the pattern of the professional or grammar-school boy. When he finished his National Service in 1948, Alan Sillitoe was diagnosed with tuberculosis. In the eighteen months he spent in hospital, he began to apply himself to reading and writing. (Braine did the same with his eighteen months in hospital with the same disease.) Sillitoe's abortive first novel ran to four hundred pages and was written in seventeen days—a feat that recalls Jack Overhill. Released from hospital, he spent a year in the south of France and five years in Majorca, living mostly on his RAF pension of three pounds a week. Before he wrote *Saturday Night and Sunday Morning* (1958), Sillitoe bombarded editors in Britain with his work, received many rejection slips, and had the odd success like a story broadcast on the BBC Home Service and a pamphlet of poems published by Howard Sergeant's Outposts Press.[25]

Arnold Wesker's early career combined features that would not have been out of place in the interwar period with patterns distinctive to the 1950s. Like Willy Goldman, Wesker was an autodidact who gained a great deal from his intellectual sparring partners in the East End; his parents, though not formally educated, were communists committed to intellectual development and debate. As John Hampson had in the 1920s, Wesker worked as a kitchen hand in hotels, reading widely in his garret (he had an attic room in the Norwich hotel he worked in) and unsuccessfully submitting poems and stories to the *London Magazine, Modern Reading, Outposts, Lilliput, World Review, Argosy, John o' London's,* and more. After six months in a well-paying job in a Paris restaurant, he returned to Britain in January 1957 having saved enough to pay for a new and decidedly 1950s apprenticeship: a six-month course at one of the recently and precariously established film schools, in Brixton. With the friends he made there, he frequented lectures and discussions organized by the *Universities and Left Review* collective, and visited the Streatham Hill Theatre to see *Look back in Anger.* John Osborne's play had an electrifying effect on Wesker, and it inspired him to write a play of his own, *Chicken Soup with Barley.* Wesker gave his manuscript to the documentary director Lindsay Anderson, whom he had come across through the *Universities and Left Review* group. Anderson started the play on its way to the Belgrade Theatre in Coventry.[26]

In spite of exceptions like Sillitoe and Wesker, the cohort of published "working-class writers" was dominated by men whose white-collar or professional day jobs afforded them time and space for writing, and whose education eroded some of the barriers between themselves and literary culture. And there were few efforts to encourage writing by working-class people who did not have those advantages. The Popular Front literary campaigns of the 1930s had no equivalent in the late 1940s or the 1950s. When it let the magazine *Our Time* lapse, the Communist Party had lost most of its interest in the ideas of its culturally inclined members such as Edgell Rickword, Randall Swingler, and Jack Lindsay. Centre 42, the most ambitious attempt of the late 1950s and early 1960s to involve working-class people in literature and the arts, did not make the cultivation of working-class writing part of its mission.[27] In the planning stages, Centre 42 was envisioned as an arts center and a talent depot that would integrate the arts into working-class life, using the trade union movement as a bridge between artists and the public. Centre 42 reiterated some of the claims about putting art back into the community made by figures on the left in the 1930s such as Lindsay; some of its organizers drew explicit parallels with the 1930s.[28] But Centre 42 was fundamentally different from the Popular Front enterprises in that it paid little attention to the idea of enabling working people to become authors or artists themselves.[29]

Absent a project to find and nurture plebeian voices, working-class authors achieved publication as they had at other times: via established publishers and those publishers' readers. In the 1930s some mainstream publishers had seen a topical value in accounts of working-class life. In the 1950s widely discussed nonfiction texts such as *The Uses of Literacy* and *Family and Kinship in East London* tapped into an interest in changes in working-class cultures and reached a wide audience. Novels and plays too addressed questions of social mobility and working-class culture. The earliest of the celebrated texts—*Look Back in Anger, Room at the Top*—by new male writers in the 1950s focused on young men who were socially mobile or uprooted. From about 1957, Stuart Laing has argued, the "intensification of affluence imagery . . . forced the question of the relation between older and newer lifestyles."[30]

But how important was potential topical value in getting these works published in the first place? Much less so than appears at first glance, I think. *Room at the Top* is often seen as a fable of affluence, but it was conceived in the period of austerity, when Braine himself was living a fairly straitened existence; Sillitoe's and David Storey's first novels also had long gestation periods that make it questionable to see them as finely tuned to the moment at which they were published. Looking only at publication dates, it is plausible to think that the publishers of Storey's *This Sporting Life* and Stan Barstow's *A Kind of Loving* (both 1960) were jumping on the *Saturday Night and Sunday Morning* bandwagon. But the band on the wagon was not playing very loudly when Storey and Barstow's novels were accepted for publication: as Harry Ritchie has shown, "it was only in the early sixties, with the phenomenal popular success of *Saturday Night and Sunday*

Morning in film and paperback, that Sillitoe was added retrospectively to the list of the famous young writers of the fifties."[31]

The possibility that the publication of this string of "working-class novels" was not the result of savvy publishers' seeking out novelists who had a finger on the pulse of the times is lent further substance by the way Braine's agents, David Higham and Associates, received the manuscript of that "topical" book, *Room at the Top*. An agency is not the same as a publisher, but there is a degree of convergence in the kinds of judgment the two have to make; and because pushing a manuscript requires less of a commitment of effort and money than publishing one, an agency should be more likely to give a manuscript the benefit of the doubt. David Higham's "chief reader" characterized Braine's hero Joe Lampton as "a brash but good-looking and able young accountant of working-class origin," "a highly objectionable, not to say detestable person, but it is doubtful how far the author intends the reader to think so." The reader went on:

> The writing is crude and often slapdash, with a certain amount of irritatingly false toughness . . . altogether there is rather too much raw sex, and considering this is supposed to be a story of a young man's ambition, not enough social and professional climbing. All the same, the author does show the basic ability to construct and tell a story . . . The dialogue is quite fair and the characters convincing in their crude way. I don't think the book is likely to find a publisher without considerable rewriting and cutting, if then. But it does show sufficient ability to make it worth submitting to e.g. Hutchinson.[32]

Hutchinson was known to publish some downmarket novels: David Higham's reader took *Room at the Top* to be a crude, run-of-the-mill novel manuscript. The reader noted Joe's class origins and social ambitions, but did not perceive them to be a novelty or one of the book's selling points.

It therefore seems that coincidence played a part in the near-contemporaneous appearance of a number of working-class novels in the late 1950s. This publishing moment is more like the burst of working-class novels published on the eve of the First World War (by D. H. Lawrence, Robert Tressell, and Patrick MacGill), when different publishers' judgments converged without a deliberate search for authentic fictions of plebeian life, than it is like the 1930s, when there *was* a concerted search. Postwar social change helps explain why men in the "lower professions" were heavily represented among novelists of working-class life in the 1950s; social trends are less helpful in explaining why publishers took them up when they did.

The people responsible for at least some decisions to publish "working-class authors" were publishers' readers and editors who kept an eye out for working-class talent—later approximations of Edward Garnett, John Middleton Murry, and C. B. Purdom. Some of their 1950s successors had had experience in the popular writing campaigns of the 1930s and the war years. Stan Barstow's publisher at Michael Joseph was Roland Gant, who had been a repeat contributor to *Seven* and a member of the Front Line Generation. Gant also published Keith Waterhouse's first novel. The reader to whom Gant sent Waterhouse's manuscript was Walter Allen, a working-class scholarship boy who had been one of the "Birmingham group" that included Leslie Halward. He had also written criticism for publications in the *New Writing* stable in the 1940s. Allen was "a fervent advocate of the working-class novel," and he recommended Waterhouse's novel be published. Soon afterward he got Waterhouse regular assignments reviewing fiction in the *New Statesman*.[33]

The trouble with fervent advocates of the working-class novel was that, in the 1950s as well as the 1930s, they could press authors to stick to "what they knew" rather than increase their range of subject matter in the way middle-class authors might be expected to do. When Sillitoe published *The General* (1961), a novel about an orchestra in an unspecified European country coping with an unspecified war, Allen's review in the *New Statesman* praised the author for his bravery but counseled him, as the "most exciting chronicler in fiction of contemporary working-class life," to "get back to your factory-hands and Borstal Boys."[34] Sillitoe had received similar advice at a formative stage in his career from a very different sort of patron—Robert Graves. Sillitoe met him on Majorca, where Graves had lived on and off since his vow at the end of *Goodbye to All That* not to live in England again. Graves encouraged Sillitoe's poetry writing and gave him advice about his prose as well. Graves suggested that he give up his "fantasy" stories and "write a book set in Nottingham, which is something you know about." It was the same advice Lawrence & Wishart and Gollancz's reader had given B. L. Coombes when he tried writing about gentlemen and opera singers. Like Coombes, Sillitoe took the advice, and wrote *Saturday Night and Sunday Morning*.[35] Still, Sillitoe was able to get his novel with a non-working-class setting published; Coombes was not.

Conspicuously absent from the ranks of the advocates of working-class writing in the 1950s was John Lehmann. In December 1955 Lehmann responded to criticisms that his new venture, the *London Magazine*, was publishing little working-class writing in comparison with *New Writing*. The "conception of 'working-class literature' is itself out of date in the age and country of the Welfare State," he argued. "We are very much nearer a classless society in 1955 than we were in 1935." The meritocracy was enabling working-class children to move up the "social ladder" and become authors, and the "old working-class struggle" that had been the "dynamo" in 1930s writing had given out, vitiating most of the few "working-class stories in the old sense [that] do reach the office of the *London Magazine*."[36]

Lehmann was more confident about postwar steps toward classlessness than historians have been, and the industrial conflict of the late 1960s and the 1970s showed that the "old working-class struggle" had not altogether subsided.[37] Yet he had put his finger on something important in saying that the dynamo of 1930s working-class writing had stopped. In the 1930s the imperative to represent working-class culture to the more privileged of the "two nations" had both inspired working-class authors and been foisted on them by middle-class editors and publishers. That sense of the industrial working class as a nation apart had been galvanized by the chronic insecurity of working-class livelihoods in the interwar period, an insecurity that the welfare state and affluence mitigated. Moreover, while the 1950s working class retained a high level of cultural self-sufficiency, older class identities were jolted by the breakup of working-class neighborhoods, the increase in numbers of women in the workforce, and greater spending power and consumer activity. Nostalgia such as Hoggart's for the perceived certainties of "traditional" working-class life was one literary response to this new order; for other worker-writers, the effect was to weaken the impulse to write "in my own language about my own people."

To be sure, this impulse persisted. Reading H. E. Bates's stories, which had captivated Halward and Fred Urquhart twenty years earlier, helped Stan Barstow begin developing his own voice. He decided to try to do for "the semi-urban working class that I had known all my life" what Bates had done for country people. "In one flash of insight I had discovered my real material." Yet at the same time there was a greater openness to kinds of writing not closely associated with working-class life. Sillitoe's "fantasy" work was an example of this; so was an interest in science fiction, which in the early 1950s escaped from its magazine ghetto in Britain and began to be published in book form as well. Dan Morgan, a twenty-eight-year-old secretary of a WEA branch, former market gardener and coal miner, discussed his science fiction in the *Writer* in 1954. Attempting to define the genre, Morgan quoted Louis Armstrong's response "when asked to define New Orleans jazz": "'Man, when you got to ask what it is, you'll never get to know!' . . . The same philosophical remark could be applied with equal force to Science Fiction." The juxtaposition of science fiction and traditional jazz neatly captures some of the enthusiasms of aesthetically adventurous members of the working class in the late 1940s and early 1950s.[38]

Some writers who stuck to working-class characters and settings did not see their projects in terms of keeping faith with their "own people." Resisting critical attempts to enlist his plays in arguments about members of the working class breaking into the drawing-room of West End theater, Wesker asserted: "I didn't write *Chicken Soup with Barley* simply with 'working-class types' but because I saw my characters within the compass of a personal vision." Braine regarded his regional and class background as a special literary qualification in the way 1930s worker-writers had, but his view of the work his writing did differed from theirs. Braine dismissed the idea of a movement of "angry young men," but he thought that, collectively, the younger male and provincial novelists had forced the English novel "to widen its view." The Home Counties, bourgeois blinkers of the English novel when he started writing, made for a cramped field of material, Braine thought: "Do you know a good novel about an engine-driver? Why not? It's skilled, dangerous, romantic . . . Because the average English novelist couldn't even talk to the engine driver." A truly valuable novelist would need to "see what goes on around him," to "go outside," to meet the engine-driver. "For until the engine-driver & the novelist meet there is no hope for t[he] English novel." But the problem was not just that the English novel paid insufficient heed to the working class: too few novels were set in businesses or town halls. In this respect, Braine was thinking along the lines of the senior Bradford novelist, J. B. Priestley. He told Priestley a few years after the engine-driver comment: "As [you] yourself have often said the great deficiency of the English novel is that it averts its eyes from the businessman."[39]

Braine's version of literary history was highly skewed: Priestley himself was evidence of a sturdy nonsouthern, nonbourgeois tradition in the English novel. Phyllis Bentley saw Braine, Waterhouse, and Barstow as a new departure not because they were "provincial," but because of their "affluent" outlook and the fact that all of them were men. It grieved her that "no woman appears in this group," "in such marked contrast with the 1930[s] group of Yorkshire writers," including herself, Winifred Holtby, and Lettice Cooper. Braine appreciated Bentley's defense of him in 1952 against accusations that he had patronized the West Riding in the *New Statesman,* and he knew Priestley's work, of course: so his polemical focus on literary London was not a consequence of ignorance of local traditions. Rather, it points to the wider importance he wanted his work to have. While Braine could insist that it was important for novelists to say to themselves, "I will write about the people around me. I'll show them as they live, I'll build a memorial," he saw his novel as performing quite a different service from the one the 1930s working-class authors had sought to provide. The chief beneficiary of his writing was not his "own people," at last represented fairly in print, but English literature, its social compass now widened: that is the implication of his speeches, and the preoccupation of the literary ambitions recorded in his diaries. What Braine's thinking resembles most closely is not the beliefs of the working-class authors of the 1930s and wartime but those of their middle-class patrons and well-wishers who saw an idealized working-class author as a means of reinvigorating English literature by diversifying its pool of contributors and its subject matter. Braine adhered to the romantic precept shared by such unlikely bedfellows as writers' circle members and Cyril Connolly: the idea that fresh experiences, properly handled, would make for fresh writing.[40]

Braine himself was a member of a writers' circle. After the war there was a trickle of men from working-class backgrounds into amateur writing organizations. In the 1940s and 1950s Halward spoke at the writers' summer school and accepted the honorary presidency of the Birmingham Writers' Circle and the vice-presidency of the Nottingham Writers' Club.[41] Not only did working-class authors of an earlier generation such as Halward, Coombes, Chaplin, Urquhart, and James Hanley go to writers' circle meetings or contribute to the *Writer:* younger authors from working-class backgrounds availed themselves of the support and models provided by commercial amateurdom. Several working-class men wrote to or for the *Writer,* and while working as a journalist in 1951–1952, well before his first novel was published, Keith Waterhouse supplied the magazine with tips for the freelance.[42]

Sending an article or a letter to the *Writer* did not necessarily entail social contact with people in the amateur writers' movement. When working-class men wanting to write politically conscious or defiantly "working-class" fiction joined writers' circles, tensions understandably could result. While living near Hebden Bridge in 1955, Robert Roberts, the future author of *The Classic Slum,* joined the Halifax Authors' Circle, one of the more commercially minded and "apolitical" of writers' groups. At the time, Roberts was contributing short stories to the *Manchester Guardian* and writing for radio, devising a popular series for *Children's*

Hour.[43] Soon after joining the circle, Roberts ruffled feathers by suggesting to the evening's speaker, Margaret Lees, that writing stories for certain popular publications "was only hackwork." True enough, wrote Phyllis Bentley in her diary that night, "but the limitations of ML's mind correspond with those of the women's magazine editors." During the meeting Bentley had tried to change the subject. She showed no such ambivalence about standard writers' circle opinions and practices when Roberts gave an inflammatory talk entitled "Writing Short Stories" the following year: "Alas, Robert Roberts attacked the Circle, saying we ought to talk of religion & politics, the sources of our material, rather than superficial craft points. He continued pressing this after supper, in a rude & unkind manner," supported by several other members. The remaining circle members "were furious. He interrupted me and made me look foolish . . . If his ideas were adopted, they would destroy the circle." Bentley recalled the incident in her autobiography several years later. It had always been a matter of pride, she said, that circle members were "admitted without regard to their politics, religion or financial standing"; that night, "our usual happy discussions were angrily attacked and defended, some of our most distinguished and well loved members were deeply wounded, others angered on their behalf. Eventually the new member, to our loss and perhaps his, resigned."[44]

Insofar as working-class men who became authors were shaped by writers' circles and the literary advice industry, it was through their struggles with the allure and the limits of the advice offered to aspirants. In the early 1950s, when Barstow began to discern his desire to write, he started and abandoned two correspondence courses that were "intent on teaching me to please others before I tried to please myself . . . the courses I saw never did pretend that they could teach one how to *write well*, they maintained that they could teach one to *make money by writing*." Reading H. E. Bates and deciding to write about his own class were an epiphany, "and from that moment I put aside all notions of formula writing, all preoccupation with easy money, and settled down to try to become a real writer."[45]

Braine's engagement with the culture of organized aspirants was more sustained and more complicated. He was a member of the Bradford Writers' Circle for some years, and he followed a number of the strategies he would have come across there and in the writing guidebooks he read. In an improvised ledger dating from 1950, he recorded details about some twenty short stories and articles: titles, lengths, type of work, dates begun and finished, when they were typed, and where (if anywhere) they were published. Freelances were supposed to maintain records in this fashion, and the back pages of the *Writers' and Artists' Year Book* provided a template. Braine considered writing an article on the nineteenth-century Bradford industrialist Titus Salt to coincide with the centenary of the main mill at Saltaire, and was annoyed at being beaten to the idea by three others: like other members of writers' circles, he was "always frightened" of having his ideas "pinched" or preempted. One chestnut served up to would-be writers was the idea of plagiarizing and updating timeless and uncopyrighted stories such as fairy tales. A 1950 notebook of Braine's contains an outline of a plot about a queen falling in love with someone's illegitimate son. "How to put this into modern dress? Y will not be a king—unless of Ruritania," Braine scribbled, referring to the imaginary and therefore adaptable central European country invented by Anthony Hope in *The Prisoner of Zenda* (1894) and beloved of subsequent magazine fiction. Three years later Braine borrowed *Yorkshire Legends* and *English Myths and Legends* from the Bradford Central Library, feeling that the latter book would be "especially useful, as the author's most likely dead

. . . I feel it would be extremely profitable to specialise in fairy stories—I can adapt them—modernise them if I want. I'll buy some more notebooks and note the most usable ones." This time he wanted to use the fairy tales' plots for children's stories for radio. After looking over more fairy tales, he "decided to listen to 3 Children's Hours before I write one." He wrote at least one of these stories, but appears not to have sold it to the BBC.[46]

When he gave up full-time freelancing and went back to library work, Braine declared that he was abandoning "writ[ing] for money" as a career option. He now spurned the strategies of commercially minded aspirants ("Steer clear of schools of journalism," he told budding writers). Yet he remained a believer in writers' circle principles about the relationship between writing and experience. Praying for inspiration in 1952, he reminded himself that his novel "must be about what I know." If the novel was rejected, he wrote in February 1956, it would be "because it's not true enough to my own experience."[47] What had changed was that he no longer accepted that "sincere" writing was compatible with the demands of formula. Six weeks after Eyre & Spottiswoode accepted *Room at the Top,* he reflected: "Ordinary journalism—articles, serials, women's magazine stories—all, in fact, that is written to a formula—is what I mustn't do. Whatever I write must be what only I can write . . . I know that the only success I've ever had and ever will have, has been with writing that has represented the best I could do which has given *me* to the reader—for what that's worth, of course."[48] For the writers' circle rank and file in the interwar period, conventions were fair representatives of the taste of ordinary right-thinking people: they were a kind of literary superego, and to rebel against them was an act of pretentiousness and self-importance. Braine no longer sympathized with this view. Yet he held fast to another part of the conceptual apparatus of the amateur writers' movement: the idea that readers would respond well to sincere presentations of experience.

The changes in Braine's thinking are also indicative of changes in the outlook of members of writers' groups. In the late 1940s he was active in the Bradford English Society, which had long combined sophisticated literary interests with a concern for local popular writers. He gave talks there on Rimbaud and Rilke. Braine also learned some of his prose techniques from contemporary British writers remote from the land of recycled fairy tales. He chortled to himself in his diary that "people have likened my prose to all but [the one] who, I realise, I've learned most [from], Graham Greene. God help me when they find out." Not just Greene but also his Eton classmate: "Cyril Connolly is one of the people who taught me to write—tho' he didn't know it." That a proudly provincial novelist of the 1950s should feel this way about the "mandarin" Connolly may come as a surprise if one takes the posturing of "angry young men" without the requisite grain of salt. Braine's regard for Connolly would certainly have been surprising coming from a member of the Bradford Writers' Circle in the 1930s. The concerns of the aspirant writers' movement were becoming more compatible with more "highbrow" and less "practical" literary interests, as the middlebrow culture of the interwar years was transformed.[49]

Although the postwar years were not a time of abundance for people wanting to make a living by writing, they were boom years for writers' groups. The war had forced a number of groups into abeyance or hibernation, though some met during the day because of blackouts at night. Within two years of the end of the war, there were forty writers' circles in Britain, up from twenty-seven at the beginning of 1939. By the early 1950s there were at least seventy-seven. Judging by the news they reported to the *Writer*, many of these new circles were flimsy. Others, such as the Croydon circle founded in 1945, were soon large and thriving. Bigger circles such as the Croydon club and the revived Leeds Writers' Circle adopted the "group scheme, as employed by the main London Circle." In the first and third weeks of the month, there would be a general meeting of the whole circle (to hear a speaker, for instance). In the second and fourth weeks, subgroups devoted to short stories, articles, drama, and so on would meet to go over members' manuscripts.[50]

In their formative period, the writers' circles had been represented most heavily in English industrial cities and in London's suburbs (though some of the London ones were short-lived). These areas remained centers of organized writing in the 1950s. Of the seventy-seven circles extant in 1953, nine were in suburban London, nine in Yorkshire, eleven in Lancashire and Cheshire, and ten in the Midlands. In 1939, Edinburgh, Glasgow and Dundee were the only Scottish cities with writers' circles; in 1953, only Edinburgh and Glasgow were. There had been none in Wales or Northern Ireland before the war; after it, there was one in Cardiff and one in Belfast. The most significant growth was in the west and the southwest, which together accounted for eight circles.[51]

Several contributors to the *Writer* speculated after the war that women were beginning to outnumber men in writers' circles. All eight writers whose work appeared in an Oxford Writers' Circle publication in 1957 were women, and at what may have been close to a full turnout of the Bradford Writers' Circle in 1959, there were twenty women and only two men. Membership lists are available for very few circles. A roll from the Leeds circle from around 1960 lists fourteen women and four men; if "lapsed members" are included, the totals are twenty-three women and eight men. Men and women were fairly evenly matched in the roll of the Halifax circle, however. If the proportion of women in writers' groups *did* rise after 1945, this development would have been consonant with trends in an another cultural activity—adult education classes in literature and indeed adult education generally. Before the war, literature had been "the Cinderella" of the subjects offered in the Oxford Extra-Mural Delegacy's classes in England.[52] After 1945, it became the most popular, and in many courses a majority of the students were middle- and lower-middle-class women, to the irritation of some of their tutors. Raymond Williams, for instance, complained that his literature students at Cuckfield in 1947–1948, fourteen women and one man, were too inclined to treat the class as "a socialite occasion."[53]

Writers' circles remained self-supporting institutions: they did not benefit directly from increased government support of the arts in the postwar period. With spectacular exceptions such as Coventry's Belgrade Theatre, municipal governments did not outdo themselves in supporting the arts, and none of the writers' circles that have left archives appears to have been subsidized by local government. At the national level, the wartime Council for the Encouragement of Music and the Arts and its successor the Arts Council directed their support to professional musical and dramatic companies: the idea was to extend popular exposure to music and the arts, rather than to foster popular or amateur provision of them. The Arts Council did not give grants to individual writers until 1964, but before that its Poetry Panel sought to encourage appreciation of poetry through poetry-reading tours and modest subsidies to little magazines, among other things. At several points, writers' circles made unsuccessful overtures to the Arts Council and its predecessor to request funding. Eric W. White of the Arts Council also declined a request to subsidize the magazine of the Writers' Club. He did agree to serve on a brains trust at a club meeting—but later canceled.[54]

After 1945, writers' circles interacted with one another more. Previously, a group might swap manuscripts with another circle or visit its meetings occasionally: now there were attempts to create formal ties at a national level. An intercircle literary competition was started, and there was talk of a badge for circle members and other writers to enable kindred spirits to recognize one another when visiting large towns. The most ambitious piece of cooperation was the launch of an annual "summer school." Once more, it was the product of a suggestion in the *Writer.* In a 1948 editorial on the loneliness of authors and the work writers' circles did to mitigate it, Kenneth Grenville Myer suggested that one of the larger circles hold a congress. Cecil Hunt of the London circle took up the idea, and arranged a conference that would set up an annual summer school. Forty-four delegates met in London at the Institute of Journalists, members of whose Freelance Section also belonged to the London Writer Circle. The conference resolved that a week-long summer school take place the following year. Anyone could apply, but members of writers' circles would be given priority. The location of the school was discussed at length, and eventually, after the conference, Swanwick in Derbyshire was settled on as being within reach of northern and southern circles alike. The venue was The Hayes, a sprawling conference center that could accommodate several hundred participants. Much of the work of organizing the school was done by Nancy Martin, a writer of children's books who had recently helped found the Croydon Writers' Circle. The summer school in Swanwick became an annual fixture during the 1950s, and is still running. Attendance ranged from 140 to 280, and the great majority of the attendees were women.[55]

In many respects, the summer school was a year's worth of writers' circle meetings crammed into a week—not the workshop activities, but the guest speakers, the brains trusts and discussion sessions, the socializing, and the outings and picnics. It *was* a school in that one could take short courses in writing for children, for instance, or sign up for group discussions with a book reviewer. There were also speeches by well-known authors. Those taking part in the 1950 summer school included the short story writer A. E. Coppard; the spy novelist and travel writer Bernard Newman; R. C. Sheriff, author of the very popular play about the First World War, *Journey's End;* and the children's writer and radio dramatist Geoffrey Trease. Among the celebrities at later meetings in the 1950s were Vera Brittain, L. P. Hartley, the thriller writer Hammond Innes, and Arthur C. Clarke, already a "name" in science fiction before *2001: A Space Odyssey* made him world-famous. Circles outside London could usually hope at best to recruit only one or two speakers of this caliber a year. As in writers' circles' annual programs, other players in the writing business were also engaged to speak—literary agents, representatives of magazine publishers, editors of local newspapers, and various BBC staff members, including Janet Quigley of *Woman's Hour.*[56]

The advice given at the summer schools was similar in kind to that delivered at circle meetings. And, of course, circle members could chat with the speakers and instructors. Like ordinary writers' circles, the summer school was also a source of fellowship for circle members struggling with doubt, disappointments, and solitude. As well as opportunities for talking over tea, "the social side included dancing every night, whist, organized games, and facilities for attending Divine Worship on Sunday." There were coach excursions to places near The Hayes, and theater outings. The entertainment side of the school had its limits: a suggestion in 1951 that a future school be held in a holiday camp was quickly quashed.[57]

The other significant form of intercircle cooperation was the annual conference of writers' circles begun in 1947. Delegates would gather at a hotel for a weekend to hear speeches by writers and editors of local and national publications. The mayor of the host town would usually preside over the conference dinner. Though they were supposed to be national, the conferences were dominated by circles "from Yorkshire and Lancashire, with a fair sprinkling from the Midlands"; the venues were Nottingham, New Brighton in Cheshire, Blackpool, Buxton, Bridlington, and Bradford. The Bradford conference in 1953 was apparently the last. Attempts to use the conference to create a national federation of writers' circles had already failed. Opponents of resolutions in favor of federation had argued that only a minority of the country's circles was represented at the conferences. And as Harold M. Harris, then editor of the *Writer*, pointed out, many circle members would not endorse the idea of forming a negotiating body to lobby government (over paper rationing, for instance) and editors. Lobbying could make a federation seem like a trade union, compromising the respectably apolitical nature of writers' circles.[58]

While the *Writer* played a part in organizing the conferences and, with more success, the summer schools, at the same time the magazine was moving away from its longstanding role as a hub for the writers' circle movement. After some affirmations in the late 1940s that it was "pledged to give every assistance possible to the Circles both by way of publicity for their achievements and by letting their needs be known," the magazine started giving space to letters attacking the idea of writers' circles. An anonymous man who was not a writer said that his wife was the secretary of a writers' circle, "and a more fatuous waste of time I have never seen"; after joining the circle after seeing it publicized in the *Writer,* his wife had no time to write, "unless it's a long catalogue of piffling 'successes'" by members to post in the magazine. This letter was the first of many either dismissing the usefulness of writers' circles or protesting the continued inclusion of circle news in the *Writer's* precious pages. Circle members weighed in on the value of the clubs as sources of encouragement and institutions that dispelled illusions about writing. Whether in response to the complaints or to seize an opportunity, Myer dropped the pages of circle news in September 1951. (At the time, he was involved in a dispute with the organizers of the summer school.) The circles that have left archives, including the Newcastle one, which was in touch with the *Writer's* editors and referred to its contents frequently, did not appreciably suffer from the magazine's withdrawal. By the early 1950s the writers' circle movement was established enough to do without the coordinating work of the *Writer,* which had been so important in building up a network of writers' groups in the 1920s.[59]

The articles the magazine published nevertheless continued to serve an aspirant and freelance constituency oriented toward commercial publication. Henry Kowal, the editor from June 1956, was a writing coach in the tradition of Cecil Hunt, running the British American School of Successful Writing on the side.[60] Paul Vaughan's autobiography *Exciting Times in the Accounts Department* gives a delicious glimpse of Kowal's operation. In the early 1950s, as a recent Oxford graduate working in a numbing job for a pharmaceutical company, Vaughan furtively enrolled in a correspondence course in writing. In central London one day on a work-related errand, he took the opportunity of doing "something you were not supposed to do: I called in person at the offices of the Anglo-American School of Writing Success." After walking up eight flights of stairs, Vaughan entered a "dingy room . . . up in the eaves of the building" and found the proprietor of the "school" seated at a desk by himself. Kowal appeared embarrassed. "It struck me forcibly, as it should have done already," Vaughan writes, "that if he knew the secrets of writing success, he should have been keeping them to himself and writing prize-winning stories, newspaper features, and novels."[61]

The magazine Kowal took over, however, was not as homogeneously commercial and practical as it had been in the interwar period. Its previous postwar editors—Kenneth Grenville Myer, then Harold M. Harris, and then Myer again—had allowed the contents to stray into more "highbrow" territory. Harris was a journalist who, after leaving the *Writer,* joined the London *Evening Standard,* where he built up well-regarded arts pages. Myer was a Cambridge science graduate and a freelance journalist who made a decent living writing scripts and "continuity material" for *In Town Tonight* on the BBC Home Service. In 1949 he married the sister of Reginald Moore, founder of the journal *Modern Reading,* and his connections with Moore and his circle made their mark in the pages of the *Writer.* Fred Urquhart, whose work Moore had published, contributed several articles; Moore himself wrote advisory pieces; and his wife, the novelist Elizabeth Berridge, wrote to the magazine in support of Pamela Hansford Johnson's attack in its pages on the vapidity of the fiction in women's magazines. The women's magazines drew some defenders, but other correspondents agreed with Johnson, including an anonymous staff member from one women's magazine who had often seen "sensible stories about everyday incidents set against modern backgrounds rejected out of hand by my boss because she insists that what our readers want is impossible stories . . . which she calls escapist 'literature.'" Such criticism of editorial judgment and questioning of the value of "escapism" for "ordinary" readers would have had no place in the *Writer* before the war.[62]

The same goes for references to Proust. Fred Urquhart wrote an essay for the March 1954 issue on the problem of time in fiction; it prompted a letter about Proust. Several years earlier Myer had positively reviewed books by Pound and Sartre. The broadcaster Ludovic Kennedy outlined the requirements of *First Reading,* the showcase for new literature that he hosted on the Third Programme in 1953. The earlier installments of *First Reading,* edited by John Wain, had been instrumental in establishing the careers of Kingsley Amis and Philip Larkin and in fashioning the idea of "the Movement."[63] *First Reading* had been reined in after Wain's departure, and in any case most of the new voices on the program were not aesthetic revolutionaries: but they were conspicuously "new." Suggesting that the *Writer*'s audience might try to join their company, on the famously exclusive Third Programme, jarred with the magazine's previous practice. It was not that the *Writer* was becoming more exclusive and "literary"—alongside these contributions were articles by Enid Blyton, a monument to commercial success and unpretentious dedication to the production line of children's fiction. Rather, the boundaries between the cultural products regarded as "art" and the entertaining products of a commercially oriented "craft" were no longer being monitored as stringently as they had been. This shift was under way even before the post-1944 changes in education had really begun to register in British cultural life. The transformation is thrown into relief by a new aspiring writers' association, the Society for New Authors.[64]

The society was open only to aspirants who had not made a name for themselves in print. For a subscription of a guinea a year, it offered legal advice and criticism of manuscripts, and pledged to bring members' work "before the notice of those best able to establish an author." Its magazine *SONA* was central to this objective.[65] The idea that publication in an aspirants' magazine could bring a writer to the attention of critical and editorial powerbrokers who might even republish a piece from an "amateur mag" was put forth by proponents of "amateur journalism" with more optimism than realism. In *SONA*'s case, though, the claim was warranted. The BBC swiftly broadcast a fairy tale that had appeared in the first issue of *SONA,* and the *New Statesman* reprinted one of the poems therein. Three other *SONA* contributors were said to have been "approached by leading publishers for full length works as the result of their appearance in our magazine."[66]

SONA declared its pages open to "everything from Proust to [the popular thriller writer] Peter Cheyney." "We aim to publish the poems, short stories, reportage, criticism and miscellanea of all unknown men and women whose work has something of literary or social value." By work of "social value," the editor meant that of people like Orwell: "A Max Beerbohm, a George Orwell is rare enough. Baudelaires are born once a century." The ecumenism of these pronouncements was matched by the magazine's book reviews. Like the *Writer* and lesser periodicals for aspirants, *SONA* stressed the value of reference books such as the *Writers' and Artists' Year Book* and G. J. Matson's *Writers' and Photographers' Reference Guide,* and reviewed advice books. Of David Gammon's *Breaking into Fiction, SONA*'s reviewer wrote: "In a hearty sailor-like manner he comes close to the wind of commerce . . . His advice is solely for those attempting the better paid markets and might almost be more aptly called 'Breaking into Cheap Fiction.' Not that that is meant slightingly. *SONA* strives valiantly to be representative of writing as a whole, and welcomes all who speak with knowledge, no matter how high or low their brows."[67]

The magazine also treated works of criticism as an important grounding for would-be writers. *SONA* reviewed an anthology of criticism of contemporary authors, including Hemingway, Maugham, Woolf, Auden, Waugh, Bates, O'Flaherty, and Thomas

Mann, and declared that an acquaintance with these writers—not to be gained, though, by using the anthology as a crib—was a prerequisite for "even an elementary knowledge of the contemporary literary scene." The reviewer also welcomed Walter Allen's anthology of authors' comments on the craft of writing, and the symposium *Why Do I Write?* by Graham Greene, V. S. Pritchett, and Elizabeth Bowen.[68] Thus, while *SONA* reviewed commercially minded textbooks and reference materials, and carried advertisements for correspondence schools, its implied audience also included men and women interested in "breaking into" the market for "literary" fiction. It paid little heed to the taboo separating "literature" from "fiction" that had been so important to much of the advice marketed to aspiring authors in the interwar period.

A majority of members' contributions to *SONA* were closer to the culture of the writers' circles than to literary experiment. A "lorry-driver jack of all trades who has worked in the five continents, and is now attempting to capitalise and commercialise his 36 years' experience through writing," was represented by his first short story, a gentle but unsubtle tale of Australia in which a farmer's son wanders the outback in search of different experiences before he takes over the family run. An Irish woman contributed a ghost story with dark-and-stormy-night touches set in an Irish village ("So Father Tom knelt down be the bed whilst the wild western wind moaned a sad lonesome dirge an' the seagulls wheeled, screechin' an' keenin'").[69] A Society of New Authors member who courted a more highbrow audience was Michael Hamburger. Hamburger was an Oxford graduate friendly with contemporaries John Heath-Stubbs and Philip Larkin, and moved in such circles as to be invited to Stephen and Natasha Spender's flat during the war on an evening when T. S. Eliot, E. M. Forster, Julian Huxley, and Geoffrey Faber were there.

With contacts like these the Society of New Authors may seem to have been an unnecessary crutch, but Hamburger had had some difficulties in making his name as a poet. Through Stephen Spender he had met Cyril Connolly and *Horizon*'s financial backer, Peter Watson, "but something other than the circumstance that I wasn't good enough to contribute always kept me well beyond the periphery of this circle." Hamburger's autobiography does not mention his appearance in *SONA,* let alone call it decisive, but it got a poem of his into the *New Statesman.* Several years after appearing in *SONA* he was included in a *First Reading* broadcast, and after that he emerged as a "romantic," counter-Movement poet.[70]

SONA's embrace of "everything from Proust to Peter Cheyney," and the modest incursions of modernist or "highbrow" literature into the pages of the *Writer* reflect a more general shift in the social history of literature. Literary modernism no longer seemed as alien or as unbearably pretentious as it had to many earlier readers. As modernist styles had been absorbed into the everyday in advertising and design, so the downstream results of literary modernism—such as free verse, plotless short stories, and other prose that did not conform to the contours of late nineteenth-century and Edwardian narrative realism—later became more or less accepted features of the cultural landscape. By the 1960s primary school children were writing imitations of T. S. Eliot, and not just the poems that would later inspire *Cats.* The Plowden committee on primary schooling reported that after reading some extracts from Eliot, "a girl of modest ability" came up with these lines about her home life:

The smell of fish and chips
Cooking in the kitchen.
The baby crying for its feed

And our old Dad reading the newspaper.
Slippers lying around the house,
And big sister telling us off.[71]

For an illustration of the extent to which modernist forms had generated a conventional idiom for aspiring poets, consider the Writers' Club, a thirty-person organization with two London branches (in Streatham and Barking-Dagenham) that held workshop meetings and was dedicated to finding young writers. "Retirement, 1958," an anonymous poem in its cyclostyled magazine *Preface* begins:

In the ochre room
Under electric light
New retired men review their lives:
Lived always in ochre rooms under electric light
Because the day was for work.
But now there is no more work
The day is a gap
Emptiness floods coldly like dawn on hollow streets.[72]

Lines like these belong to a different world from the regular versification and rhyme of the "Georgian" aspirants in the Quill Club in the 1920s, or the Poetry Society of the 1940s, or the consolations and idylls that members of the forces wrote during the Second World War. However, a more casual or less formulaic attitude to form and genre among novice writers in the 1950s was not only a consequence of the self-assertion of a younger generation more habituated to modernism. Another shift was under way from the late 1940s to a less embattled order of taste.

The middlebrow authors and critics of the 1920s and 1930s were combative in patrolling the borders between what "ordinary people" might be supposed to like and what the mandarins of

Bloomsbury might produce. Though some of the modernist antagonists were no longer present, attacks on what they stood for were still being made after the war—by young writers and critics such as John Wain, and by more senior figures. J. B. Priestley adlibbed some Joyceanisms in the *Sunday Times* to show what an easy game modernist prose had been. While there is a strong continuity between these remarks and earlier denunciations of modernism and defenses of middlebrow realism and the social values it was supposed to embody, the institutional basis of the interwar middlebrow was coming apart. The circulating libraries and the Book Society had both been influential shapers of middlebrow taste. Now, in the early 1950s, mass-market paperbacks other than Penguins belatedly came into their own in Britain: the lag between hardback and paperback publication shrank from six or seven years to two, and more companies moved into the paperback business. These developments fatally undermined the commercial circulating libraries and seriously weakened reprint clubs such as the Book Society. The *Strand* suspended publication at the beginning of 1950, and 1960 saw the end of *John Bull,* where Louise Heilgers, the originator of what became the *Writer,* had cut her teeth. *John Bull* has been called "the last of the 'middlebrow' magazines": it had "supplied a diet of popular feature articles and short stories neither sensational nor pretentious to a general reading public since as long ago as 1882, but its market had disappeared." Surveying the situation for the Society of Authors in 1963, Richard Findlater reported: "It is the weekly review, the family 'general' magazine and the fiction magazine which have faded away, as the old-style middle-class's spare-time occupations have changed." It was "the young aspirant . . . who feels the pinch most painfully. The demand for stories today is narrower and more specialized, for the main market is in the women's magazines." Findlater also noted that newspapers now devoted more space to magazine features, "and scarcely any space at all to the stories, essays, reviews and light, literate journalism from which the talented pre-war journalist might pick up a fairly easy living."[73]

The literary advice industry came into being together with the proliferation of magazines that began in the late 1880s, the markets those magazines provided helped sustain the aspirant writers' movement fostered by the advice business, and the literary values of the aspirants' movement were buttressed by those magazines and other agencies of middlebrow culture. One custodian of those values was *John o' London's Weekly,* which ceased publication in 1954. A miscellany chiefly concerned with writers past and present, *John o' London's* was firmly middlebrow in its outlook. Its attitude to modernism—exemplified by Robert Lynd's regular front-page articles in the 1930s—was unenthusiastic, though not stridently hostile. *John o' London's* was an important feature of the aspirant writer's landscape, as the planners of the summer school were aware when they arranged their advertising and publicity. A West Country creative writing group owed its founding in 1921 to the magazine's help, and the Newcastle Writers' Club did a group analysis of a short story published in the magazine as an educational exercise. A Derbyshire man who decided to "learn to write" armed himself with a correspondence course and subscriptions to *John o' London's, Argosy,* and the *Writer.*[74]

John o' London's was said not to have suffered any significant drop in readership before its end. Rather, changes in the market, especially "the greater concentration in popular publications," made it harder for periodicals with a substantial but not massive following to turn a profit. Robert Hewison sees the passing of *John Bull* as symptomatic of "the disappearance of the middle ground between mass and minority." This is a claim that chimes with other arguments advanced about postwar British literary life in a related but different context—the "fall of the man of letters." These arguments seem to me to approximate a tendency sometimes manifest in scholarly discussions of eighteenth-century coffee houses and other public spaces: a tendency to connect abstract cultural spaces (the public sphere, the middle ground) too tightly to the institutions with which they were most associated at a critical stage in their development. Aesthetically accessible books remained popular in 1950s and 1960s Britain, their readership buoyed by new publishing strategies, including more concerted book-of-the-film marketing campaigns. What had happened to the "middle ground" between "difficult" writing and a popular readership was that some of the institutions that had promoted the idea of a cohesive and combative middlebrow collapsed, ceding some of that median territory to editors and pundits who found it less meaningful to divide the literary topography into highbrow and middlebrow zones. Writing in 1963, Harry Hopkins noted the disappearance of "that comfortable old *John O' London's Weekly*–Robert Lynd–J. B. Priestley middle ground, relaxed and pipe-puffing, yet easily confident in its possession of cultural title-deeds. Instead, there were the curious, extraordinarily assorted crowds pushing around some *al fresco* art exhibition, where one might, according to taste and without prejudice, purchase an 'appealing' dog study or some student's latest *tachiste* essay."[75]

The paradigm of an unproblematic mixing of "highbrow" and more populist reading matter was Penguin Books, which went from strength to strength in the 1950s. The first ten Penguins, published from 1935, included André Maurois's biography of Shelley, Hemingway's *A Farewell to Arms,* detective stories by Dorothy L. Sayers and Agatha Christie, novels by Mary Webb and Compton Mackenzie, and an autobiographical volume by the popular commentator Beverley Nichols, who was maliciously described as an "infallible barometer of . . . the thoughts of the unthinking."[76] The Penguin list's combination of "serious" books and entertainments, and its ability, every so often, to make the two one and the same, only intensified after the war. With the shrinking of the delay between hardback and paperback publication of a title, Penguin could reprint popular fiction much more speedily than before. And many of the great talking-point books by academics in the 1950s, from Hoggart's *Uses of Literacy* to Young and Willmott's *Family and Kinship,* reached their large audiences after being reissued as Pelicans. Penguin Classics were launched in 1945 with the *Odyssey,* which became a surprise bestseller. And, most famously, the firm published an unexpurgated *Lady Chatterley's Lover.*[77] There was more traffic passing over the "middle ground" than there had been in the interwar period. Viewed from this angle, postwar literary culture looks very different from the way it does when discussed in terms of the reaction against modernism and experimentation characteristic of the conspicuous new male novelists of the 1950s.

Conclusion

On or about the End of the Chatterley Ban

Philip Larkin infamously wrote that sexual intercourse began in 1963, "Between the end of the *Chatterley* ban / And the Beatles' first LP."[1] Like Virginia Woolf's "On or about December 1910, human character changed," it is a comment whose only half-jesting specificity embarrasses historians' claims to identify decisive moments of cultural change. But whatever happened to sex in the early 1960s, it is clear that those years mark a turning point in the popular practice of writing. The changes in the "middle ground" in the late 1940s and 1950s were to some extent "internal" to literature and the aspirant writers' movement. In the 1960s and 1970s, the meanings of writing and the strategies of would-be authors were recast by changes in the wider culture, of which the failure to ban *Lady Chatterley's Lover* and the emergence of the Beatles are two iconic though not fully representative instances.

By the early 1960s the creative outlets open to working-class youths were very different from what they had been in the interwar period. Writing for publication faced strong competition, not just from rock music but also from the visual and plastic arts. Rock and art often went together: many bands were formed in the art colleges, "one of the few opportunities for further education open to 11-plus failures or grammar-school early leavers."[2]

These other creative activities lacked the off-putting bourgeois overtones that writing could have: there was little of the Academy in design-inflected sculpture, for instance. Indeed, the working-class associations of conspicuous early-1960s "creative types" (the Liverpudlian musician, the "Cockney photographer") could themselves glamorize plebeian roots—to the extent that a wag could win a *New Statesman* competition for neologisms in 1962 with the entry "Proletentiousness: A tendency, especially in modern literary or artistic circles, to boast of real or imagined working-class origin."[3]

The relationship between rock music and literature—poetry in particular—was of course more complicated than the one providing an alternative to the other. The performance poetry scene in Liverpool took shape amid the city's jazz and pop bohemia, and some folk and later rock musicians were frank about their poetic ambitions. These changes were related to the liberalization of poetic form in "the mainstream literary world," which was "probably largely responsible for the ease in which [poetry] is now written." Yet as some astute observers noted in the early 1980s, "Such democratisation of the form co-exists with the idea that poetry is the most privileged, the most literary of all writing activities."[4]

The education system also contributed to this "democratization" of writing. After the Second World War, creative writing became a routine part of the primary school curriculum, before other aspects of "progressivism" took firm hold. In 1967 the Plowden Report on primary education endorsed the practice, noting: "The best writing of young children springs from the most deeply felt experience."[5] It is less clear how creative writing became established in secondary curricula, which were in flux in the 1960s as "comprehensive" schools replaced grammar schools and the "secondary-modern" schools to which working-class children who had failed the eleven-plus examination for grammar-school entry had formerly been consigned.[6] The 1963 Newsom Report complained that English teaching in many secondary-modern schools was "a watered down version of what [the teachers] remember from their own grammar school experiences," which meant that creative writing was neglected. *English for the Rejected,* David Holbrook's 1964 case for teaching creative writing in the bottom streams of the secondary-moderns, makes it clear that the practice was not orthodox at the time within secondary-moderns, let alone comprehensive schools mindful of examination performance or, of course, grammar schools.[7]

Creative writing's triumph over grammar was an issue that would loom large in fears about the consequences of progressivism—in 1982 the headmaster of Westminster School declared that attention to grammatical rules "encourages . . . honesty, responsibility, property, gratitude, apology and so on," and that the dethroning of grammar in education "coincided with the acceptance of the equivalent of 'creative writing' in social behaviour."[8] It is worth pointing out that students did not necessarily see creative writing homework as a liberating activity consistent with the permissive society, but it seems reasonable to think that the teaching of creative writing made the act of writing a story or a poem a less uncommon practice than it would have been in the interwar years. However, the impact of creative writing on secondary education may not have been significant until the 1970s.

The associations of writing and literature with privilege never completely dissolved. In 1984 a tutor in the Workers' Educational Association's West Lancashire and East Cheshire District thanked Olive Rodgers, who conducted writers' workshops in prisons and schools: "I think you have helped to destroy the myth that poetry is a medium which uses solely middle class language, and whose subjects are not relevant to the lives of ordinary people. Through your readings and discussions, you have helped them to realise that both poetry and prose can use the speech of working class people, and be concerned with the life which they know. Thus you have helped them to recognise that they themselves can write, frequently producing literature which is good and valid in its own right." Other people involved in the worker-writer and community publishing movement in the 1970s repeatedly encountered condescension or incomprehension from neighbors or people in the media who assumed that writers had to be "special people."[9]

This movement was a congeries of writers' groups, booksellers, local publishers, adult education workers, and socialist and feminist activists. From 1976 it had an institutional focal point, the Federation of Worker Writers and Community Publishers. As Chris Waters has shown, a good deal of the movement's work lay in encouraging and publishing working-class autobiography.[10] The movement also included writers of fiction and poetry, and many of the groups affiliated with the federation were writers' workshops. The worker-writer movement was novel in bringing the organized workshops that had long been common among middle-class aspirants into the domain of working-class literary activity. While they shared a format with the older writers' circles, these groups were not forums for novices eager to fashion themselves into authors and climb the ladder of "success." The groups affiliated with the federation also differed from most efforts to publish working-class writers in the 1930s in that they challenged conventional publishing mechanisms in search of "a more open and democratic method of producing culture (in this case books)."[11] Exploiting the innovations in printing technology so important to the underground press in the 1960s and 1970s (and, later, desktop publishing), affiliated concerns such as Centerprise and QueenSpark published autobiographies and anthologies of fiction and poetry. More than previous popular writing ventures other than *Seven,* the worker-writer movement of 1970s and 1980s treated the ability or entitlement to write as a social-democratic good in its own right, not just a means to a more varied or more socialist literature and popular culture.

Some of the strategies of the worker-writer movement were mirrored in the contemporaneous explosion of feminist writing groups and publishers, though the kinds of experiences being committed to writing by feminists, the cultural and material obstacles to their writing, and their politics of literature were different from those of working-class men. Feminists in groups associated with the Federation of Worker Writers and Community Publishers often perceived tensions between feminism and socialism, between a politics of gender and a politics of class (or a politics of gender-and-class and a politics of class). Feminists established structures independent of the federation but not dissimilar to it in institutional terms: they formed writers' workshops and support groups, and they published anthologies and pamphlets, rejecting conventional publishing as a patriarchal as much as a capitalist system.[12]

Alongside these newer organizations with their explicit and theorized politics of writing, established writers' circles persisted, and continued to provide stimulus and fellowship. There is a poignant correspondence in the Croydon Writers' Circle's papers about the death of its member Dorothy Phillips in 1963. She had been "particularly attached" to one of the circle's subgroups, which met at a member's flat; her husband remembered that she had "said it was their meetings which encouraged her to such work as she managed to do . . . Her association with the Writers' Circle has always been a most happy one and brought her much friendship and mental stimulation." Dorothy always put her husband and children first, he said: otherwise she would have been more active in the circle.[13] It is a comment that hints at the artistic and personal value of writers' circles for women with families, a value probably greater than Phillips's husband could realize. The Croydon Writers' Circle secretary to whom he wrote was Irene Byers, who, as we saw in Chapter 2, had met with resistance from her husband when she tried to recapture the stimulation and satisfaction that writing had brought her before her marriage. She must have understood why Mrs. Phillips valued the circle.

Some circles active in the 1970s were little different from their 1950s or even interwar incarnations. The television script writer Paul Abbott has recalled his experience with a writers' circle in the 1970s. He started writing as a teenager after both his parents had abandoned the family. An English teacher encouraged him to write a short story for a competition, which he won, and this success made him realize that writing could be profitable. "Then I sloped off to this tiny little weird little place in Burnley which was above the Conservative rooms, and every third Saturday they had the writers' circle, and it was full of, you know, kind of seventy-year-old women with bangs writing romantic fiction for *People's Friend* and stuff like that, and what they taught you was . . . that you have to keep writing and have to keep editing, and eventually you get the *Writers' and Artists' Year Book,* and the whole world opens up." Even the magazine of choice, the *People's Friend,* was unchanged. (Book publication was another matter: in 1963 Barbara Pym suddenly found that publishers were no longer willing to accept her novels, which apparently now seemed too "mild" and domestic in their concerns.) The writers' circle founded at Penarth in Glamorgan in 1976 was not antediluvian like the Burnley one in Abbott's account. The contributions to its 1979 anthology are all quite gentle, but they have an openness and a variety in the literary forms they use that contrast markedly with the more regimented poetry and fiction of the interwar writers' circles. By the 1980s, groups calling themselves writers' circles, including many that had been active since the interwar period, catered to a wide range of styles and creative aspirations, and the older model of learning the ropes of the market was one among many.[14]

The protean history of creativity since the early 1960s has scarcely begun to be researched in detail: these comments are at best suggestive. It is clear, however, that the cultures of popular writing discussed in this book had already begun to unravel before the more far-reaching transformations of the 1960s. These forms of popular writing, I have argued, are significant for the ways they reveal what literature and creativity meant to people outside traditional literary elites, and for the ways they throw into relief the democratization of culture.

In the 1930s V. M. L. Scott suggested that writing by people from outside the traditional community of authors would thicken the bloodstream of the national literature. Did it? The efforts of the 1930s uncovered a number of working-class authors, most of whom otherwise would not have been published or (in some cases) would not have been spurred to keep writing. Some of them stopped writing after the 1930s; others did not find literary success in the sense of writing well-received novels, but reached a substantial public by writing for radio and later, in Sid Chaplin's case, for television. The trajectory of working-class themes from the Popular Front to mainstream popular culture was not as spectacular in Britain as it was in the United States, where, Michael Denning has argued, 1930s "ghetto pastorals" reached their apotheosis in *The Godfather,* but it was still significant. In the 1950s working-class authors achieved wide readerships bolstered by film tie-ins and media interest. A number of novels of working-class life from the 1950s and 1960s (especially Stan Barstow's *A Kind of Loving* and Barry Hines's *Kes*) had their readership buoyed for decades to come by the assignment of their books in school English courses, as texts deemed "relevant" to the lives of teenagers, especially working-class ones.[15]

John Braine was apparently the only person who went from a writers' circle apprenticeship to a national reputation as a "serious" author. Insofar as that experience shaped him as a writer, it did so negatively: Braine became the writer he became in part by struggling to divest himself of what he had learned from advice about writing for money. Some circle members were famous in fields with which historians and literary critics do not often claim familiarity. John Marsh of the Halifax Authors' Circle, for instance, carved out a very successful career as a romance novelist (writing under female pseudonyms) from the 1930s to the 1980s, cleverly adapting to changes in popular attitudes to sex and love. Many other circle members remained obscure, but contributed to magazines, local newspapers, and radio, producing some of the textual furnishings of everyday life.

Yet writing by people from outside the social groups that traditionally dominated authorship matters for reasons beyond what it did or did not contribute to the canon or popular reading. If we approach the history of popular writing chiefly to add to a pantheon of authors, or in search of ancillary matter to help contextualize major literary figures, we miss much of the cultural significance of writing as an *activity*. Part of that significance, I have suggested, lies in popular writing's role in building what D. L. LeMahieu has called "a culture for democracy." *Seven* was conceived as a democratic project, the result of a conviction that "writing is not the special preserve of a select few."[16] John Lehmann was motivated not only by Popular Front values but also by a more old-fashioned liberal inclusiveness about literary activity: he was keen to extend the franchise of artistic creation to responsible workingmen. These writing initiatives that supported working-class authors depended on particular political moments. They faltered after the Nazi-Soviet pact wrote finis to the Popular Front, and after *Seven* ceased publication following the war, they vanished.

Only the aspirants' movement based in the writers' circles and enmeshed with the magazines and other products of the advice business was a self-sustaining agency of the democratization of writing. Anyone could become an author, the promise ran, by working hard and heeding certain lessons. This was a democratic principle that validated the abilities of ordinary people—people without "genius," which would take care of itself—and could reinforce suspicion of those deemed pretentious or too "clever." Advice to literary aspirants also validated their experiences, encouraging them to write about things that had happened to them or that they had witnessed. Such "ordinary" experiences were subjects that aspiring writers would be more likely to depict convincingly, the reasoning went, and subjects their readers could readily "identify with." The thinking of would-be authors and their advisors was one node in a wide-ranging examination and revaluation of the everyday in literature and the arts. This concern is evident in phenomena as different as novels that deal with a single day, uneventful short stories, newspaper features on "a day in the life" of a particular profession, Mass-Observation's surveys, and potentially interminable broadcast serials such as *Mrs. Dale's Diary, The Archers,* and, eventually, *Coronation Street.*

The aspirant writers' movement was a form of literary democratization that was faithfully wedded to the market: the publishing business was, fundamentally, an unproblematic representative of public taste; and the lessons of writing success could be imparted for a fee. The earlier aspirants' movement, amateur journalism, declined in membership as writers' circles spread, and its commitment to the amateur principle softened to the point where its magazines offered market tips and reported members' acceptances by paying publications. The nexus between "democracy" and commercialism in British cultural life has, of course, been discussed before. J. B. Priestley observed in 1934 that the things that were the most "modern" tended to be the most democratic: the paradigm of this conjunction was the commercialized leisure of the seaside town of Blackpool. It was a point that people less accepting of "modern" Britain would have agreed with: John Betjeman's nearly contemporaneous poem inviting the destruction of Slough and its "air-conditioned bright canteens" is in some ways the other side of the same coin. Priestley's point that "modern England is rapidly Blackpooling itself" has been borne out in other areas of life. Matthew Hilton, for instance, has shown how one of Priestley's own pleasures, smoking, became "democratized" as it became commercialized, through the mass production and distribution of cigarettes.[17] Yet the knot of commercialism and democratization involved niche marketing as well as standardization: everyone might be smoking cigarettes, but individual brands could attract fanatical loyalty. The periodical market from the late nineteenth century is a clear example of this trend: girls' magazines had exclusively loyal readerships even though outsiders could not see much difference between them. In the interwar period, writers' circles and their advisers typically endorsed the middlebrow literary values that built on the Victorian and Edwardian inheritance, and that were developed and disseminated by book-trade institutions such as the Book Society and by popular newspapers and magazines. This middlebrow culture set itself against modernism and the social forms of elitism with which it was supposed to be connected, and valorized the tastes of "ordinary," commonsensical readers. After 1945 this defensive cultural democracy began to give way, haltingly and never completely, to a less definite, more pluralist order of taste and creative ambition. The phrase may be less felicitous than Priestley's, but to some extent Britain was Penguining itself.

The writers' circles exemplify how much twentieth-century Britain had accepted the presence of the market in cultural life. The history of amateur writers' engagement with commercial culture is a story of dogs that did not bark: they were not anxious about "mass culture"; they did not interpret mass culture as somehow feminine; and they did not see it in terms of American cultural imperialism. These concerns were certainly present in Britain, but they were mostly the preserve of "cultivated minds," including both the Leavises. F. R. Leavis reprised the German binary of *Zivilisation* and *Kultur* in his opposition between "mass civilization" and "minority culture"; Q. D. Leavis worried about the encroachment of Fordist methods into the production of magazine fiction. Q. D. also associated mass-market literature with the feminine—in her case, not an Emma Bovary figure, but the flapper. E. M. Hull's *The Sheik,* she remarked, "was to be seen in the hands of every typist and may be taken as embodying the typist's day-dream"; associating female office workers with commodified culture had been a habit at least since *The Waste Land.*[18] Yet while intellectuals in Britain as in other European countries criticized the pernicious standardization of literature, in the domain of aspirant writers there were few such protests, and hardly any of the gendered slurs that could accompany such arguments.[19] Commercial products had long been part of the fabric of British popular culture, working-class as well as middle-class. Consequently, the proliferation of mass-market forms of reading matter and other entertainment was not destabilizing for most readers in the way it was for intellectuals acclimatizing to democracy and (still) to universal literacy. The degree to which the country accepted the market as a mechanism of ordering cultural life also enabled British popular culture to incorporate American influences relatively smoothly.

The middle and lower middle classes from which most writers' circle members came saw so little conflict between art and commerce that their governing theory of writing combined an acceptance of the market with the ideas of the romantic tradition in which the Leavises were also implicated. Drawing on late nineteenth- and early twentieth-century histories of English literature that selectively reprocessed the ideas of Wordsworth and Keats, aspiring writers conceived of style and form as mere bodies for the soul of writing. That soul came from "life"—authentic experience and the sincere representation of it. Accepting the validity of the market—or rather, envisioning the market as a simple aggregate of ordinary readers' tastes rather than as a system—they assumed that books sold well because they communicated something of "life" that resonated with readers. Sincere writing was commercially viable; and, contrariwise, the small audience for modernist writing cast doubt on its claims to value. In this matter, as in much else, novice writers agreed with the middlebrow and best-selling opponents of modernism who insisted that "heart" and not "head" was responsible for good writing. As a theory of writing this is nearly the opposite of Ezra Pound's dictum "Great literature is simply language charged with meaning to the utmost possible degree."[20]

The romantic tradition influenced popular understandings of the nature of writing in other ways as well. The belief that poetry was a fitting or natural response to powerful feelings shaped the writing of people serving in the Second World War. Poetry could commemorate feelings or events, and it functioned as a cathartic outlet. While most 1930s working-class writers believed in writing about what they knew, not all of them relegated form to secondary importance. However, some did accept another sort of popular romanticism, viewing the urge to write as a mysterious, otherworldly force. These working-class authors saw the act of writing in very different terms from the members of writers' circles and those who contributed to aspirants' magazines.

For the writers' circle members, popular romantic ideas about experience and representation were coupled with the cultural conservatism of the interwar middle class: their literary culture legitimated creative ambitions, provided that they were in the unpretentious service of entertaining or moving other ordinary people via publication in middle-of-the-road papers or magazines. Middle-class associational life and literary culture at once created scope for writing ambitions and self-expression *and* limited them with taboos on pretentiousness and excessive self-dramatization. The cultural transformations of the 1960s undoubtedly played an important part in making welcome in writers' groups work that was more personal and less deferential to the market's prescriptions or to received ideas about "what the public wants."

But the popular literary culture that formed in the interwar years was already partially "Penguined." Tastes shifted as a result of structural changes in publishing as well as vice versa. And while popular writing was shaped by its institutional, social, and political contexts, it did not always reflect them, or even its authors' experiences. Coombes and Halward started off writing about Italian divas and Russian doctors: writing about life as they had known it, in a "working-class" manner, was something they had to learn. Sometimes—during the Second World War, for instance—the ideas and practices of novice writers were out of step with their contemporary contexts, and sometimes with the writers' own political outlooks. The discourses of writing and creativity also brought the intellectual contexts of the past into the present. The nineteenth-century romantic tradition that was so important to working-class authors and middle-class freelances was transformed by "modern" developments, but it also shaped what novice writers made of twentieth-century aesthetics and commercial culture.

Abbreviations

AAD	Archive of Art and Design, Victoria and Albert Museum, London
AUA	Allen and Unwin archive, University of Reading Library
BCA	Birmingham City Archives
BL	British Library
BLPES	British Library of Political and Economic Science, London School of Economics
Brotherton	Brotherton Library, University of Leeds
CAS	Croydon Archives Service
DRO	Derbyshire Record Office
FWCNB	*Forces Writer Circle News Bulletin*
HAC	Halifax Authors' Circle
HRC	Harry Ransom Humanities Research Center, University of Texas at Austin
IWM	Imperial War Museum, London
JLP	John Lehmann papers, Harry Ransom Humanities Research Center, University of Texas at Austin
LHM	*Louise Heilgers Magazine*
LWA	Lawrence & Wishart archive, Uncat. MSS 13, Beinecke Rare Book and Manuscript Library, Yale University, New Haven
MALS	Manchester Archives and Local Studies
min.	minutes

M-OA	Tom Harrisson Mass-Observation Archive, University of Sussex Library
NLS	National Library of Scotland, Edinburgh
NWC	Newcastle Writer Circle (later Newcastle Writers' Club)
OUA	Oxford University Archives
PRO	Public Record Office, Kew
RLUN	Robinson Library, University of Newcastle
SSB	Short Story Broadcasts, BBC
Sussex	Special Collections, University of Sussex Library, Brighton
TWAS	Tyne and Wear Archives Service, Newcastle
URL	University of Reading Library
V&A	Word and Image Department, Victoria and Albert Museum, London
WAC	BBC Written Archives Centre, Reading
WAYB	*The Writers' and Artists' Year Book*
WSS	Writers' Summer School
WYASB	West Yorkshire Archive Service, Bradford
WYASC	West Yorkshire Archive Service, Calderdale (Halifax)
WYASL	West Yorkshire Archive Service, Leeds

Notes

Introduction

1. Gillian Lindsay, *Flora Thompson: The Story of the "Lark Rise" Writer* (London, 1990), 90, 104, 119, 130; Flora Thompson papers, 3/8, HRC.

2. Virginia Woolf, "The Leaning Tower," *Folios of New Writing* 2 (autumn 1940): 23.

3. B. L. Coombes, "Below the Tower," ibid. 3 (spring 1941): 34; Coombes to John Lehmann, 17 Mar. 1937; George Garrett to Lehmann, 12 July 1938, JLP.

4. Valentine Cunningham, *British Writers of the Thirties* (Oxford, 1988), 308. On Bell see Peter Stansky and William Abrahams, *Journey to the Frontier: Two Roads to the Spanish Civil War* (1966; Stanford, 1994).

5. Richard D. Altick, "The Sociology of Authorship: The Social Origins, Education, and Occupations of 1,100 British Writers, 1800–1935," *Bulletin of the New York Public Library* 66 (June 1962): 389–404. See also Raymond Williams, *The Long Revolution* (New York, 1961), 238.

6. A. H. Halsey, "Higher Education," in Halsey, ed., *British Social Trends since 1900: A Guide to the Changing Social Structure of Britain* (Basingstoke, 1988), 270; B. R. Mitchell, *British Historical Statistics* (Cambridge, 1988), 811; Nigel Cross, *The Common Writer: Life in Nineteenth-Century Grub Street* (Cambridge, 1985), ch. 5.

7. Ken Worpole, *Dockers and Detectives: Popular Reading, Popular Writing* (London, 1983).

8. Karl Mannheim, "The Democratization of Culture" (1933), in *Essays on the Sociology of Culture,* ed. Ernest Manheim with Paul

Kecskemeti (London, 1956), 175; D. L. LeMahieu, *A Culture for Democracy: Mass Communication and the Cultivated Mind in Britain between the Wars* (Oxford, 1988), 331–333; Ross McKibbin, *Classes and Cultures: England, 1918–1951* (Oxford, 1998), 527.

9. J. B. Priestley, *English Journey* (1934; Harmondsworth, 1977), 376. McKibbin, *Classes and Cultures,* 97–98.

10. Virginia Woolf, *A Room of One's Own* (1929; London, 1945), 141–142, 125.

11. Jonathan Rose, *The Intellectual Life of the British Working Classes* (New Haven, 2001), esp. 431.

12. Compare LeMahieu, *Culture for Democracy,* 105.

13. Meredith Veldman, *Fantasy, the Bomb, and the Greening of Britain: Romantic Protest, 1945–1980* (Cambridge, 1994); Stefan Collini, *Public Moralists: Political Thought and Intellectual Life in Britain, 1850–1930* (Oxford, 1991), ch. 9.

14. Joan Shelley Rubin, *The Making of Middlebrow Culture* (Chapel Hill, 1992), 143–144.

1. Middlemen, Markets, and Literary Advice

1. James Hepburn, *The Author's Empty Purse and the Rise of the Literary Agent* (London, 1968), 1–2.

2. Peter Keating, *The Haunted Study: A Social History of the English Novel, 1875–1914* (London, 1989), 33, 48–51; Victor Bonham-Carter, *Authors by Profession* (London, 1978–1984), 1:149–150, 159; Peter D. McDonald, *British Literary Culture and Publishing Practice, 1880–1914* (Cambridge, 1997), 33.

3. Society of Authors, *Forms of Agreement: Issued by the Publishers' Association; with Comments by G. Herbert Thring* (London, [1899]); J. A. Sutherland, *Victorian Novelists and Publishers* (Chicago, 1976), 89; Bonham-Carter, *Authors by Profession,* 2:33; Society of Authors, *Report of the Committee of Management for the Year Ending December 1898* (London, n.d.), 25.

4. George Greenfield, *Scribblers for Bread: Aspects of the English*

Novel since 1945 (London, 1989), 56–57; Bonham-Carter, *Authors by Profession,* 1:150–151, 168; Hepburn, *Author's Empty Purse,* 25–27, 54.

5. Hepburn, *Author's Empty Purse,* 55, 98 (numbers of agents), 97 (Bennett); Curtis Brown, *Contacts* (London, 1935), 1–2; and, for the Society of Authors, Greenfield, *Scribblers for Bread,* 61; Bonham-Carter, *Authors by Profession,* 1:171–172.

6. Curtis Brown, "The Commercialisation of Literature," *Fortnightly Review,* Aug. 1906, quoted in Bonham-Carter, *Authors by Profession,* 1:170; Keating, *Haunted Study,* 72–87 (publicizing authorship); Arthur Waugh, *One Man's Road: Being a Picture of Life in a Passing Generation* (London, 1931), 285.

7. Keating, *Haunted Study,* 30–32; Sidney Dark, *The New Reading Public: A Lecture Delivered under the Auspices of "the Society of Bookmen"* (London, 1922), 5–6.

8. David Reed, "'Rise and Shine!': The Birth of the Glossy Magazine," *British Library Journal* 24 (autumn 1998): 259–260; David Reed, *The Popular Magazine in Britain and the United States, 1880-1960* (Toronto, 1997), 96–98; James L. W. West III, *American Authors and the Literary Marketplace since 1900* (Philadelphia, 1988), 103; Joseph McAleer, *Popular Reading and Publishing in Britain, 1914–1950* (Oxford, 1992), 46–47, 53–54 (periodical market), 54 (novelists); Billie Melman, *Women and the Popular Imagination in the Twenties: Flappers and Nymphs* (Basingstoke, 1988), ch. 7 (women's periodicals); Q. D. Leavis, *Fiction and the Reading Public* (London, 1932), 57 (Mackenzie).

9. Melman, *Women and the Popular Imagination,* 113–114; Cynthia L. White, *Women's Magazines, 1693-1968* (London, 1970), 87; Raymond Williams, *Communications,* 3d ed. (Harmondsworth, 1976), 57; McAleer, *Popular Reading and Publishing,* 164–165 (D. C. Thomson).

10. Brander Matthews, *The Philosophy of the Short-Story* (New York, 1901); Keating, *Haunted Study,* 38–45 (Matthews's reception); Valentine Cunningham, *British Writers of the Thirties* (Oxford, 1988), 308 (time and concentration).

11. Reginald Pound, *Mirror of the Century: The Strand Magazine, 1891–1950* (South Brunswick, N.J., 1966), 7 (middle classes), 57, 139–

140 (stories in the *Strand*). On O. Henry and Maupassant: Jack Adrian, intro. to Adrian, ed., *Strange Tales from The Strand* (Oxford, 1991), xx; Pound, *Mirror of the Century,* 122.

12. W. W. Jacobs, "The Interruption," and Sapper, "The Idol's Eye," both in Jack Adrian, ed., *Detective Stories from The Strand* (Oxford, 1991).

13. Louise Heilgers, "The House with the Crimson Creeper," in *Tabloid Tales* (London, [1915]), 202, 20; Heilgers, *How to Write Stories for Money* (Richmond, Surrey, [1920]), 37–84.

14. Nigel Cross, *The Common Writer: Life in Nineteenth-Century Grub Street* (Cambridge, 1985), 238 (Russell). On these manuals see Chapter 3.

15. *The Writers' and Photographers' Reference Guide: 1947 Edition* (St. Ives, [1947]), 16 (Institute of Self-Expression); John Gray, *Gin and Bitters* (London, 1938), 230–271; Cecil Hunt, *Ink in My Veins: Literary Reminiscences* (London, [1948]), 35; Cecil Hunt, *Living by the Pen: A Practical Guide to All Forms of Journalism and Fiction Writing,* rev. ed. (London, 1951), 31. See also Robert Graves and Alan Hodge, *The Long Week-End: A Social History of Britain, 1918–1939* (1940; London, 1985), 62.

16. This, for instance, was what two prolific freelance writers, John Marsh of the Halifax Authors' Circle and G. J. Matson of Cambridge, charged in 1937 and 1934 respectively. Marsh lowered the fee to 1s. 6d. for every thousand words after the first; Matson charged a flat 2s. 6d. per thousand words. *Writer,* Oct. 1937, 31; *Writers' Monthly: Written and Published by G. J. Matson,* Oct. 1934, 14.

17. *The Writer's Journal: A Monthly Magazine for the Free-Lance Writer,* July 1937, front cover; *Writer,* June 1936, iii.

18. School and College Conference on English, *Report of the Language Committee* (n.p., 1940), 14–15; Dora V. Smith, *Evaluating Instruction in Secondary School English: A Report of the Division of the New York Regents' Inquiry into the Character and Cost of Public Education in New York State* (Chicago, 1941), 16; David Shayer, *The Teaching of English in Schools, 1900–1970* (London, 1972), 12, 15, 43, 49, 81, 82–83, 86, 93–94, 120–121; Hepburn, *Author's Empty Purse,* 71n.

19. T. G. Williams, *The City Literary Institute: A Memoir* (London, 1960), 27; "Mr. Kennedy Williamson's Lectures," *Writer,* Sept. 1939, 52–53; "The Editor's Lectures," *Writer,* Dec. 1940, 277; Kennedy Williamson, *Can You Write Magazine Stories?* (London, n.d.), 5, 7.

20. *WAYB 1920,* iii; Max Pemberton to Lord Northcliffe, 22 Aug. 1919, Northcliffe papers, Add. MS 62117, BL. See also McDonald, *British Literary Culture,* 96, 196.

21. C. L. Pelman, *The Natural Way of Learning a Language* (Chicago, 1903). Ennever held the copyright on this pamphlet.

22. Pemberton to Northcliffe, 22 Aug. 1919.

23. John Ramage Jarvie, "Max-Pelmanism," *Journalist,* Nov. 1920, 104; "Storytelling," *Writer,* Jan. 1922, back cover.

24. Ross McKibbin, *Classes and Cultures: England, 1918–1951* (Oxford, 1998), 526.

25. Pemberton to Northcliffe, 22 Aug. 1919.

26. The school is still in existence, but when the present owners bought it in 1992, few records from before the early 1980s survived. Michael Winckworth, personal communication, 24 July 2001.

27. Max Pemberton, *Sixty Years Ago and After* (London, 1936), 103–131 (quotation 112); Keating, *Haunted Study,* 344. Pemberton also provided literary advice before his involvement with the London School of Journalism: Herbert John, *My Litterary Adventures* (London, 1925), 5; A.H.D., letter, *Writer,* Sept. 1923, 285.

28. Pemberton to Northcliffe, 22 Aug. 1919 (asking for money); Northcliffe to Pemberton, 12 Dec. 1919, Northcliffe papers, Add. MS 62117 (refusing to be sole patron); Pemberton to G. Herbert Thring, 13 Apr. 1923, Society of Authors archive, Add. MS 63313, BL (letterhead). On salary: Pemberton to Northcliffe, 20 Sept. 1919; Northcliffe to Pemberton, 19 Oct. 1919, Northcliffe papers, Add. MS 62117; Guy Routh, *Occupation and Pay in Great Britain, 1906–79* (London, 1980), 60.

29. Pemberton to Thring, 27 Apr. 1923, Society of Authors archive, Add. MS 63313 (copyright); Max Pemberton et al., *The Short Story Course* (London, [1922]), "Supplement to Short Story Course: How to Correct Printer's Proofs," lesson 5, "Atmosphere," and lesson 12, "On Methods of Work," 5 (bureau services); Kennedy Williamson, *The Poetry*

Course (London, n.d. [1930s]), sec. A, lesson 5, "The Market for Poetry," 2, 3, and lesson 2, "The Form of Poetry," 7 ("Invictus"); Pemberton, *Sixty Years Ago,* 117 (guest "lectures"); 5.

30. Anonymous letter, *Writer,* Nov. 1923, 36; Heilgers, *How to Write Stories,* 93 (value of feedback), 94 (bureau services); *LHM,* Jan. 1921, 56 (bureau services, advice in person); *LHM,* Sept. 1920, back cover; "Fortunes in Words," *LHM,* Sept. 1920, 1 (quotation).

31. Pemberton to Northcliffe, 22 Aug. 1919; "About Ourselves," *LHM,* Nov. 1920, 21; *LHM,* Sept. 1920, back cover (investment in training); Heilgers, *How to Write Stories,* 93; *LHM,* Jan. 1921, 56 (cost of advice).

32. "A Member of the Staff," "A Career for Women," *LHM,* Nov. 1920, 27; Heilgers, *How to Write Stories,* 89.

33. As reflected, for instance, in the names of the Society of Women Journalists and the Freelance Section of the Institute of Journalists, both of which had many members who wrote fiction. Note the surprise of the latter body's historian at this fact: Cynric Mytton-Davies, *Journalist Alone: The Story of the Freelance and the Freelance Section of the Institute of Journalists* ([London], 1968), 34, 37.

34. Philip Gibbs, *The Pageant of the Years: An Autobiography* (London, 1946), pt. 2; NWC min., 20 Sept. 1955, SX88/1/3, TWAS ("more a story than an article"); John Braine, diary, 10 Aug. 1952, Braine/D2; Braine, notebook, ca. 1954, Braine/N1, pp. 29–50; Braine, diary, 21 Oct. 1953, 23 Dec. 1953, Braine/D3, John Braine papers, Brotherton.

35. Heilgers, *How to Write Stories,* 87; Louise Heilgers, "How I Began," *LHM,* Sept. 1920, 5 (articles and short stories); "The End and the Beginning," *LHM,* Feb. 1921, 62; Heilgers, *How to Write Stories,* 21 (personal qualities); "A Member of the Staff," "A Career for Women," *LHM,* Nov. 1920, 27 (fan letter).

36. *Writer,* Jan. 1926, 2 (Tuite); Hugh Tuite, *Profits and the Pen* (London, 1927); *Who Was Who among English and European Authors, 1931–1949* (Detroit, 1978), 2:978 (Gordon Meggy of the Premier School), 2:1019 (Sydney A. Moseley of the Fleet Street School).

37. *Writer,* Jan. 1940, back cover (Knight); Kobold Knight, *A*

Guide to Fiction-Writing (London, 1936), 153–154; *Writers' and Photographers' Reference Guide: 1947,* 218; *Writer,* Dec. 1941, back cover (Walter); Martin Walter, *Plot Formula* (London, [1937]); Fallon, *Inside Information* (revenue-collecting). On Walter's formula see Chapter 3. Walter got into a minor altercation with George Orwell over the latter's comments on the formula in his "As I Please" column in *Tribune* in November 1944. See *The Collected Essays, Journalism and Letters of George Orwell,* ed. Sonia Orwell and Ian Angus (London, 1968), 3:274, 290–291.

38. McAleer, *Popular Reading and Publishing,* 48.

39. Philip Harrison, *Free-Lance Fallacies: Straight Talks to Young Writers* (London, [1927]), vii; Kennedy Williamson, "When Writers Go Cross-Eyed," *Writer,* Oct. 1929, 7; Williamson, *The Uncarven Timbers* (London, n.d. [ca. 1924]); Williamson, *The Shining Traffic* (London, n.d.). On the anti-university quality of the advice industry, see Hunt, *Living by the Pen,* 10–13; John Mellon, "Mr. Freelance, M.A.," *Writer,* Mar. 1939, 172.

40. Bernard Miall, "Eugene Windermere: H. L. Senior," 29 July 1939, AUA, AURR 7/6/9. See also Miall, "Life Everlasting: M. McDonnel Bodkin" (1925), AUA, AURR A/3.

2. A Chance to Exercise Our Talents

1. Patricia Williamson, letter, *Writer,* Oct. 1923, 21; Denis Prothero, letter, *Writer,* Nov. 1923, 45; "Editorial," *Writer,* Nov. 1923, 25.

2. Janice A. Radway, *Reading the Romance: Women, Patriarchy, and Popular Literature* (1984; Chapel Hill, 1991).

3. *Writer,* Jan. 1924, 91 (competition entries); "Writer Circles," *Writer,* Oct. 1924, 20 (Birmingham); "A New Movement," *Writer,* Apr. 1924, 145 (distinctiveness of writers' circles); Leslie Bicknell, letter, *Writer,* Feb. 1927, 118; NWC min., 25 Jan. 1936, SX88/1/1, TWAS; "The London Writer Circle," *Writer,* Apr. 1924, 152; "Writer Circles," *Writer,* Feb. 1924, 108 (kinship with the magazine); "The London Writer Circle," *Writer,* Aug. 1924, 260 (magazine staff and the circle).

4. "The London Writer Circle," *Writer,* July 1924, 236 (welcoming all); "The London Writer Circle," *Writer,* Sept. 1924, 284 (women); Max Pemberton to G. H. Thring, 13 Apr. 1923, Society of Authors Archive, Add. MS 63313, BL; "The London Writer Circle," *Writer,* June 1924, 212; "The London Writer Circle," *Writer,* Aug. 1924, 260; *Singers in the Crowd: An Anthology of Poems by Members of the Quill Club* (London, 1921) (Lowndes-Yates); Nugent Beattie, "London Writer Circle," *Writer,* Jan. 1926, 74 (Chesterton); Beattie, "Forming a Writer Circle," *Writer,* Mar. 1925, 140 (Aumonier).

5. "London Writer Circle," *Writer,* May 1926, 188; HAC min., 19 May 1932, Soc. 10/1, WYASC (size); Nugent Beattie, "Forming a Writer Circle," *Writer,* Mar. 1925, 140 (organization); HAC min., 19 May 1932, Soc. 10/1 (Marsh).

6. "Writer Circles," *Writer,* Feb. 1935, 98; "Writer Circles," *Writer,* July 1947, 166; "Writer Circles," *Writer,* Feb. 1939, 134. The circles in the February 1939 list were in Birmingham, Blackpool, Bournemouth, Cork, Derby, Dundee, Edinburgh, Glasgow, Halifax, Hawick, Huddersfield, Hull, the Isle of Man, East Kent, Leeds, Liverpool, London, Manchester, Newcastle, Newton Bewley (Billingham), Nottingham, Portsmouth, Reading, Southampton, Southend, East Sussex, and West Sussex.

7. See Paul Vaughan, *Something in Linoleum: A Thirties Education* (London, 1995).

8. See Ross McKibbin, *Classes and Cultures: England, 1918–1951* (Oxford, 1998), chs. 2–3; Tom Jeffery, "A Place in the Nation: The Lower Middle Class in England," in Rudy Koshar, ed., *Splintered Classes: Politics and the Lower Middle Classes in Interwar Europe* (New York, 1990); Richard Trainor, "Neither Metropolitan Nor Provincial: The Interwar Middle Class," in Alan Kidd and David Nicholls, eds., *The Making of the British Middle Class? Studies of Regional and Cultural Diversity since the Eighteenth Century* (Stroud, 1998).

9. Alan M. Streete, "Forming a Writer Circle," *Writer,* May 1941, 44 (Bromley); A. H. Halsey, "Higher Education," in Halsey, ed., *British Social Trends since 1900: A Guide to the Changing Social Structure of Britain* (Basingstoke, 1988), 270.

10. Compare Ross McKibbin, *The Ideologies of Class: Social Relations in Britain, 1880–1950* (Oxford, 1990), 146.

11. Bradford Writers' Circle scrapbook 1951–1965, 7D95/1, WYASB; *Writer,* July 1946, 111 (Gloucester); clipping, probably from the *Halifax Courier and Guardian,* 5 Mar. 1931, HAC minute book, Soc. 10/1, p. 369.

12. B. A. Redfern, "Our Club," *Papers of the Manchester Literary Club* 32 (1906): 425–426; *Manchester Guardian,* 29 Mar. 1927. Manchester Literary Club papers, M524/1/2/13–16, MALS.

13. Fred Dean, "My Life—Mental," n.d. [late 1930s?]; Dean to Bentley, 2 Jan. 1938, 14 Jan. 1938, 24 Feb. 1938, Phyllis Bentley papers, PB/B:101, WYASC.

14. Jon Lawrence, review of *The Intellectual Life of the British Working Classes* by Jonathan Rose, *Socialist History,* forthcoming.

15. Frank Mort, "Social and Symbolic Fathers and Sons in Postwar Britain," *Journal of British Studies* 38 (July 1999): 376.

16. Molly Weir, *Best Foot Forward* (London, 1972), 131–132, 169–170, 197, 200; Margaret Thomson Davis, *The Making of a Novelist* (London, 1982), 37, 47–49, 53, 56.

17. "Halifax Authors' Circle: List of Former and Present Members: Apl. 28th, 1926 to Mar. 31st, 1964," HAC minute book, Misc. 213/1, pp. 161–162; HAC account book (not paginated), Misc. 748/1; NWC min., 6 Nov. 1945, SX88/1/1; Marcus Collins, *Modern Love: An Intimate History of Men and Women in Twentieth-Century Britain* (London, 2003), esp. 19–23, 167. Collins's main case studies are youth clubs rather than adult associations.

18. McKibbin, *Classes and Cultures,* 88; Peter Bailey, "White Collars, Gray Lives? The Lower Middle Class Revisited," *Journal of British Studies* 38 (July 1999): 285 (gender segregation); Simon Gunn and Rachel Bell, *Middle Classes: Their Rise and Sprawl* (London, 2002), 68 (mixed associations in suburbs); McKibbin, *Classes and Cultures,* 88 (joining as a couple). The two married couples in writers' circles whom I have traced met their spouses through the circles.

19. Pat Moore, "That Insulting Diminutive," *Writer,* Dec. 1939, 16;

Writer, Sept. 1931, 288. See also Gillian Lindsay, *Flora Thompson: The Story of the "Lark Rise" Writer* (London, 1990), 90, 100, 115.

20. A.H.D., letter, *Writer,* Sept. 1923, 285.

21. Eva Hope Wallace, "How I Did It," *Writer,* June 1935, 209–210.

22. See, e.g., Janice A. Radway, *A Feeling for Books: The Book-of-the-Month Club, Literary Taste, and Middle-Class Desire* (Chapel Hill, 1997), 384n3.

23. John Usborne to John Lehmann, 9 Aug. 1941, JLP (men's feelings); A.H.D., letter, Writer, Sept. 1923, 285 (husband's ridicule); H. Anderton, letter, *Writer,* Oct. 1948, 42 (sense of entitlement); Beryl d'Héricourt, letter, *Writer,* Oct. 1929, 16 (women must choose).

24. Irene Byers, "Me and Mine . . . (The personal memories of the years between the outbreak of the war and V.J. Day 1945)," [late 1980s], pp. iv, 110, 60, 64–66, 73, Irene Byers papers, 88/10/1, IWM. This text is an edited assembly of diary entries, with some interpolations and additions.

25. Ibid., 66 (mental stimulus); Wilfrid Phillips to Irene Byers, 10 May 1963, Croydon Writers' Circle minute book, Acc. 493, CAS.

26. *1951: Festival of Britain: Haworth: May 19th to September 29th: Official Syllabus* (n.p., 1951), 4–5, in Bentley papers, PB/B:111.

27. Mary A. Dunn, "Arranging a Syllabus for a Writer Circle," *Writer,* Dec. 1935, 90 (using the *Writer*); Streete, "Forming a Writer Circle," 42–44 (using the *Writer;* cajoling people).

28. John Marsh to Hilda Gledhill, 16 Nov. 1966, HAC minute book, Misc. 213/1, p. 211 (quoting an account he had written long before 1966); Nancy Martin, "Croydon Writers' Circle: Some notes on its early history," May 1966, p. 1, Croydon Writers' Circle papers, pq 570 (806); Edgar Farrow, "Forty Years On: The Nottingham Writers' Club 1927–1967," *Scribe: Magazine of the Nottingham Writers' Club* 28 (Feb. 1967); "Circle Notes and News," *Writer,* Dec. 1947, 345.

29. HAC min., 5 July 1928 (Leeds), 19 Dec. 1935 (Huddersfield), Soc. 10/1; HAC min., 27 Jan. 1942 (Bradford), Soc. 10/2; NWC min., 10 Mar. 1936, SX88/1/1 (guidelines); NWC min., 6 Jan. 1945 and 7 Aug. 1945, SX88/1/1 (Newcastle and Scottish circles).

30. Geoffrey Trease, *Laughter at the Door: A Continued Autobiography* (London, 1974), 146–149; HAC min., 14 May 1929, Soc. 10/1 (Bentley and Hambledon).

31. For examples other than the circles whose archives I am referring to, see "Manchester Writer Circle," *Writer,* Aug. 1927, 247; Dunn, "Arranging a Syllabus," 90 (Glasgow).

32. McKibbin, *Classes and Cultures,* 96–98.

33. E.g., "Barkis," "'Midnight Oil': A Fireside Reverie," in West Country Essay Club, *Literary Adventures: 1921–1922* (n.p., [1922?]), 13–16.

34. HAC min., 17 June 1931, Soc. 10/1 (competition options). On "verbs of speech": "The B.A.P.A. Reference Library," *Midnight Oil: The Literary Magazine of the British Amateur Press Association* 1 (Mar. 1939): 2; *The Writers' and Photographers' Reference Guide: 1947 Edition* (St. Ives, [1947]), 178. See also Kenneth MacNichol, *Twelve Lectures on the Technique of Fiction Writing* (London, n.d. [based on a course given in winter 1925–1926]), 43.

35. "Leeds Writer Circle: Membership Card and Syllabus for 1948," Leeds Writers' Circle papers, Acc. 3220, WYASL.

36. NWC min., 7 Jan. 1947, SX88/1/2.

37. Dunn, "Arranging a Syllabus," 90 (Glasgow); Isobel K. C. Steele, "Competitions and Practical Nights," *Writer,* Dec. 1939, 29–30 (Newcastle).

38. Phyllis Bentley, *"O Dreams, O Destinations": An Autobiography* (London, 1962), 146; NWC min., 4 Oct. 1949, SX88/1/2 (Liverpool). In 1963 Birmingham was said to have "almost 200 dramatic societies." Harry Hopkins, *The New Look: A Social History of the Forties and Fifties in Britain* (London, 1963), 430.

39. "An 'Open Night,'" unsourced newspaper clipping, 4 June 1957, Bradford Writers' Circle scrapbook, 7D95/1; HAC min., 27 Jan. 1942, Soc. 10/2 (Bradford); HAC min., 20 Oct. 1931 and 19 Jan. 1932, Soc. 10/1; Alan Jones, "Leeds Writers' Circle: Newsletter for July 1965," Leeds Writers' Circle papers, Acc. 3220 (supply and demand).

40. Bradford English Society min. books, 1932–1940 and 1945–, 39D85/1/4–5, WYASB; Edinburgh Poetry Club min. book, 1925–

1968, Dep. 173, NLS. On writers' circles' attitudes to modernism see Chapter 3.

41. "Syllabus—1937–38," *Humberside* 6 (Oct. 1938): 136 (Hull); HAC min., 8 June 1926, Soc. 10/1 ("practical Circle"); NWC min., 7 May 1946, SX88/1/2 (politics in France). The Newcastle Writer Circle changed its name to the Newcastle Writers' Club in January 1946.

42. *The Lancashire Authors' Association for Writers and Lovers of Lancashire Literature: Instituted 1909: Constitution Sanctioned at the Annual Meeting December 11th, 1915* (n.p. [Oldham?], 1915); Christopher Fry to Charles Osborne, 14 Nov. 1974, Arts Council of Great Britain Archive, ACGB/62/152, AAD (West Country Writers' Association).

43. NWC min., 6 Nov. 1945, SX88/1/1 (Durham); E. Gaukroger, "John Hyke's Second Wife," in "The Halifax Authors' Circle Annual Magazine: No. II" (June 1928), pp. 24–25, Bentley papers, PB/B:111; HAC min., 3 Oct. 1928, Soc. 10/1 (dialect writing); NWC min., 2 Mar. 1948, SX88/1/2; Arthur Nettlefold, "The Regional Novel," *Writer,* Oct. 1947, 283–285 (national appeal of regions). The publication Gaukroger contributed to was a duplicated magazine produced for a short time by the Halifax circle.

44. Simon Gunn, *The Public Culture of the Victorian Middle Class: Ritual and Authority and the English Industrial City, 1840–1914* (Manchester, 2000), 187–197.

45. Donald Reid, *The English Provinces, c. 1760–1960: A Study in Influence* (London, 1964), 248.

46. Croydon Writers' Circle min., 12 Mar. 1956, Acc. 493; NWC min., 19 Nov. 1946, SX88/1/2; Dunn, "Arranging a Syllabus," 90 (members uninterested in commercial publication); "Daily Sonnet," clipping from unspecified newspaper, 10 Jan. 1958, Bradford Writers' Circle scrapbook, 7D95/1; "After Bradford," *Writer,* Dec. 1953, 3 (sonneteer); Streete, "Forming a Writer Circle," 44; Sylvia Conway, "Leeds Writers' Circle: Newsletter for January, 1964," Leeds Writers' Circle papers, Acc. 3220 (publicizing successes); McKibbin, *Ideologies of Class,* 162–163 (hobbies).

47. David Vincent, *Literacy and Popular Culture: England, 1750–1914* (Cambridge, 1989), 214 (19th century); Ian Jackson, *The Provin-*

cial Press and the Community (Manchester, 1971), 17, 21, 30–32 (filler), 191 (syndicates); Anthony Powell, *The Valley of Bones* (1964) in *A Dance to the Music of Time: Third Movement* (Chicago, 1995), 117.

48. Reginald M. Lester, "Free-Lancing in the Women's Markets," *Writer,* Dec. 1935, 87–88; McAleer, *Popular Reading and Publishing,* ch. 6 (Thomson-Leng); James Cameron, *Point of Departure* (1967; reprint, Stocksfield, 1978), 30–32 (Thomson-Leng's formulas); Davis, *Making of a Novelist,* 53 (cultivation of authors); NWC min., 15 Apr. 1958, SX88/1/3; Joseph McAleer, *Passion's Fortune: The Story of Mills & Boon* (Oxford, 1999), 78 (Chisholm); HAC min., 18 Oct. 1955, Misc. 213/1 (Lees).

49. NWC min., 7 Nov. 1950, 20 Feb. 1951, SX88/1/2; Norman A. Lazenby, "The New British Pulps," *Writer,* Feb. 1951, 21; Derek Maggs, "The Perils of Pulp," *Writer,* May 1954, 32–33; unsourced clipping [early 1950s], Bradford Writers' Circle scrapbook, 7D95/1 (greeting cards); NWC min., 18 May 1948, SX88/1/2 (cycling-tour guides); HAC min., 27 Nov. 1962, Misc. 213/1 (Hull telephones). On the impact of broadcasting on aspirant writers see Chapter 8.

50. In the interwar period the association changed its name from the British Amateur Literary Association to the British Association of Literary Aspirants, to the British Literary Association, and then back to the British Amateur Literary Association. I refer to it all the way through as the BALA for simplicity's sake.

51. Earnest Elmo Calkins, *Amateur Journalism* (New York, 1941); Truman J. Spencer, *The History of Amateur Journalism* (New York, 1957), esp. 145–146 (Edison).

52. R. D. Bird, "The Inception of the B.A.P.A.," *Midnight Oil* 4 (1942): 2–4; Christopher A. Hoare, "Amateur Journalism, 1925–," *Literary Amateur* 5 (Nov.–Dec. 1925) (women); Amelia E. Chapman, "Emancipation of B.A.P.A. Lady Members," *Midnight Oil* 5 (1943): 1; *Interesting Items: The Oldest British Amateur Mag.,* no. 500 (Mar. 1920); Harold G. Moore, "Hail—and Farewell," *Midnight Oil* 4 (1942): 1 (American connections).

53. Some titles were *Amateurs' Help, The Novice, Amateur Siftings, The Bee, The Comet, The Ruby, The Bugler.* "The British Amateur Press

Association," *The British Amateur: Official Organ of the British Amateur Press Association* 1 (Sept. 1910): 2–3; E. A. Dench, "Notes by the Sub-Editor," *British Amateur* 1 (Dec. 1910): 16.

54. Edgar M. Farrow, letter, *Writer,* Sept. 1931, 284 (on the Nottingham Writer's Club); HAC min., 28 Apr. 1926, 18 Sept. 1928, Soc. 10/1; E. F. Murdoch, "Circulating a Portfolio of MSS.," *Writer,* Feb. 1940, 34–36.

55. Samuel Caplan, "Official: President," *Literary Amateur* 2 (May 1923): 1 (Manchester); Clyde Dane, "Official: Editor," *Literary Amateur* 2 (July 1923): 9 (Scotland). The *Literary Amateur* continued the *British Amateur.*

56. "Notes and News," *Interesting Items,* no. 502 (May 1920); Caplan, "Official: President," 9 (charges of apathy); "Full Membership List," *Literary Amateur* 2 (May 1923): 7–8. Most of the remainder of the 220 members were supportive Americans.

57. "Editorial," *Writing News,* no. 6 (Mar. 1936): 1; "International Amateur," *Midnight Oil* 5 (Mar. 1943): 4; quotation from *Bedsitter,* no. 8 (May–June 1960). At its height, *International Amateur* ran to sixty ten- by eight-inch pages. Teugels was formerly Olive Rhodes.

58. "An Appeal—Editor Wanted," *West Country Writers' Association News Letter* (1969): 13–14 (in Arts Council of Great Britain archive, ACGB/62/152).

59. Noel James, "Our Good Name," *Literary Aspirant (Official Organ of the British Association of Literary Aspirants)* 11 (Nov.–Dec. 1931): 14; "M.S.," "Which Writers Are Professionals," *Literary Amateur* 10 (Nov.–Dec. 1930); Lilian Crawford, "Editorial," *Literary Amateur* 6 (Dec. 1926–Jan. 1927).

60. Arthur du Soir, "The Library of Humanity," *Literary Aspirant* 11 (Nov.–Dec. 1931); "'The Writer,'" *Literary Amateur* 8 (July 1923): 6; George Stanley, "Let's Write a Short Story," *Twelve Pages* 13 (Nov.–Dec. 1933): 8 (*Writer*); Nancie O'Dare, "Vice-President's Report," *Literary Aspirant* 11 (Nov.–Dec. 1931): 16; "Good Markets in Provincial Newspapers," *Literary Aspirant* 12 (Nov.–Dec. 1932 and Jan.–Feb. 1933): 5 (selling and markets); A. C. Voisin, "Vice-President's Report," *Literary Amateur* 9 (Nov.–Dec. 1929) (correspondence course); Noel

James, "Now Then, Londoners!" *Literary Aspirant* 11 (Nov.–Dec. 1931): 15; "No Regrets Column: Some Recent Successes," *Twelve Pages* 13 (Mar.–June 1934): 9; "Members in the Forces," *Midnight Oil* 2 (Mar. 1940): 1 (Lester and Stephens). On Arthur du Soir see Almon Horton, *The Hobby of Amateur Journalism: An Appreciative, Illustrated History* (Manchester, 1955), 94.

61. *WAYB 1910,* iii; *WAYB 1936,* xxii; *Singers in the Crowd* (Quill Club); "The London Writer Circle," *Writer,* June 1924, 212 (Lowndes-Yates); Enid Blyton, "Sonnet," *Singers in the Crowd,* 36; Barbara Storey, *Enid Blyton: A Biography* (1974; London, 1986), 38, 45.

62. Christopher A. Hoare, "Amateur Journalism, 1925—," *Literary Amateur* 5 (Nov.–Dec. 1925).

63. "May We Remind You . . .," *Midnight Oil* 3 (1941): 4 (submitting twice); W.A.C., "Regaining Self-Confidence," *Writer,* May 1927, 178. Compare "Pro," letter to editor, *Writer,* June 1927, 210.

64. Flora Thompson, "The Tail-less Fox" and annotations thereon, Flora Thompson papers, 3/4, HRC (correspondence course); Lindsay, *Flora Thompson,* chs. 9–10, esp. 162–164.

65. "The Peverel Literary Society Verse-Writing Course," n.d. [1925–1927], Thompson papers, 3/5; "The Peverel Society of Poets and Prose Writers" (undated prospectus), Thompson papers, 3/7.

66. Lindsay, *Flora Thompson,* 104, 119, 90, 130.

67. Thompson to Arthur Ball, 9 June 1940, 22 Dec. 1931 (reporting successes); Thompson to Anna Ball, n.d. and 3 July [1944?]; Thompson to Arthur Ball, 25 Dec. 1945 (Humble Smith and Burdett); Thompson to Anna Ball, 7 Jan. 1941; Thompson to Arthur Ball, 20 June 1943 (relationship with the Balls); Thompson to Anna Ball, 3 July [1944?] (Anna's career), all in Thompson papers, 3/8.

68. Lindsay, *Flora Thompson,* 137–138; Thompson, "Tail-less Fox," Thompson papers, 3/4.

69. Flora Thompson, "The Slowest Journey," n.d., Thompson papers, 3/4 (historical anecdotes); Thompson, "The Awakening," Thompson papers, 3/2 (Mayfair story).

70. Lindsay, *Flora Thompson,* 85.

71. Quoted in Gary Taylor, *Reinventing Shakespeare: A Cultural*

History, from the Restoration to the Present (London, 1989), 215. On Bennett see Peter D. McDonald, *British Literary Culture and Publishing Practice, 1880–1914* (Cambridge, 1997), 90–93.

72. See Philip Harrison, *Free-Lance Fallacies: Straight Talks to Young Writers* (London, [1927]), 97; Leslie Halward, "Some Writers Who Have Influenced Me," talk to Birmingham Booklovers' Society, 24 Sept. 1937, Leslie Halward Papers, MS 1293/106, BCA.

73. Yorick O'Yorke, "Happy Endings," *Popular Writing,* Aug. 1929, 17. For an exception see Harrison, *Free-Lance Fallacies,* 108–109.

74. *Writers' and Photographers' Reference Guide: 1947,* 252 (Hampshire Writer Circle); NWC min., 25 Jan. 1936, SX88/1/1; "Croydon Writers' Circle: Constitution," n.d. [1945], Croydon Writers' Circle minute book, Acc. 493 (improvement); Bentley papers, PB/B:111; Bentley, *"O Dreams, O Destinations,"* esp. 147 (local civic life).

75. *Writer,* Sept. 1931, 288.

76. Stuart Hall, "The Social Eye of Picture Post," *Working Papers in Cultural Studies* 2 (spring 1972): 71–120; Tom Jeffery, *Mass-Observation: A Short History* (Brighton, 1999); Mass-Observation Day Surveys 1937—Women, microfilm roll 3; Day Surveys 1937—Men, microfilm roll 5, M-OA. Jeffery's work was written at, and first published by, the Centre for Contemporary Cultural Studies in 1978.

77. Jeffery, *Mass-Observation;* Jonathan Rose, *The Intellectual Life of the British Working Classes* (New Haven, 2001), ch. 13; Dina M. Copelman, *London's Women Teachers: Gender, Class and Feminism, 1870–1930* (London, 1996), 167–175. For a glimpse of Liverpool's literary bohemia, see Chapter 5.

78. M. P. Thomasset to Virginia Woolf, 31 Jan. 1930, Virginia Woolf correspondence, Letters III, folder on *A Room of One's Own,* Monks House Papers, Sussex.

3. Fiction and the Writing Public

1. Bernard Miall, "Shaming the Shamrock: A. Morton Nance," 28 Jan. 1939, AUA, AURR 7/6; Reginald Merton, "*The Archangel Michael* by G. F. Beckh," 21 Apr. 1924, AURR A/4; K. Gwenda David, "*The*

Seventh Member by Richard Norman," 14 Apr. 1939, AURR 7/8; Miall, report on "The Wedge" by Maurice Lucas, 20 Dec. 1950, AURR 18/9/2, URL; Robert Atkinson to Wishart & Co., 25 Mar. 1928; Wishart & Co. to Atkinson, 20 July 1938, LWA, box 4 (utopias); Miall, "The Seer of Sussex: Charles Webon," 13 May 1939, AUA, AURR 7/6 (wish-fulfillment); Miall, "*The Hundred Doors:* E. Charles Vivian," Sept. 1920, AUA, AURR A/3; Miall, "Eugene Windermere: H. L. Senior," 29 July 1939, AURR 7/6 (the gifted).

2. Edward Crankshaw, "*For I Am He.* By Francis Fay," 15 May 1939, AUA, AURR 7/8 ("rapes & beatings"); Bernard Miall, "The Thing that Matters: Everitt Shand," 1925–1926, AURR 5/8 (violent eroticism); Miall, "Life Everlasting: M. McDonnel Bodkin," AUA, AURR A/3; Miall, "*A Preliminary Canter.* Mary May," 22 Nov. 1924, AUA, AURR A/3 (mechanical analogy); Russell Green, "No prince for Cinderella: by M. Tree," 25 Feb. 1943, AUA, AURR 11/6 (formulas).

3. Francis Vivian, *Story-Weaving: A Text-Book on the Craft of Story-Writing* (London, 1940), ch. 11; "The End and the Beginning," *LHM,* Feb. 1921, 62 (fiction/literature); Kenneth MacNichol, *Twelve Lectures on the Technique of Fiction Writing* (London, n.d. [based on a course given in winter 1925–1926]), 3–4 (genius/craft).

4. Sidney Dark, *The New Reading Public: A Lecture Delivered under the Auspices of "the Society of Bookmen"* (London, 1922), 12. See also Joseph McAleer, *Popular Reading and Publishing in Britain, 1914–1950* (Oxford, 1992), 98; Valentine Cunningham, *British Writers of the Thirties* (Oxford, 1988), 261.

5. McAleer, *Popular Reading and Publishing,* ch. 3 (postman quoted 71); *Reading in Tottenham: A Report on a Survey Carried out by Mass-Observation on Behalf of the Tottenham Borough Council* (London, [1952]), 28.

6. Louise Heilgers, *How to Write Stories for Money* (Richmond, Surrey, [1920]), 21–22; NWC min., 7 Feb. 1956, SX88/1/3, TWAS; HAC min., 21 Oct. 1952, Soc. 10/2, WYASC (absorbing the lesson); Kennedy Williamson, *Can You Write Magazine Stories?* (London, n.d.), 64–65; also A. M. Coulton, "Study Your Public," *Literary Amateur,* n.s., 15 (Mar.–Apr. 1936): 14.

7. Orwell, "As I Please" (*Tribune,* 6 Oct. 1944), in *The Collected Essays, Journalism and Letters of George Orwell,* ed. Sonia Orwell and Ian Angus (London, 1968), 3:248–251. My interpretation of interwar conservatism draws on Ross McKibbin, "Class and Conventional Wisdom: The Conservative Party and the 'Public' in Inter-War Britain," in *The Ideologies of Class: Social Relations in Britain, 1880–1950* (Oxford, 1990); and Alison Light, *Forever England: Femininity, Literature and Conservatism between the Wars* (London, 1991).

8. HAC min., 19 Sept. 1946, Soc. 10/2; HAC min., 22 Feb. 1966, Misc 213/1; "'Ideas of Humour': Address to Halifax Authors' Circle," undated clipping (late 1920s or early 1930s), probably from *Halifax Courier and Guardian,* HAC minute book, Soc. 10/1, p. 364; NWC min., 15 May 1955, SX88/1/3, TWAS (fashions); NWC min., 4 June 1959, SX88/1/3 (Woan).

9. McAleer, *Popular Reading and Publishing,* 249 (Mills & Boon); George Orwell, "Boys' Weeklies" (1940), in *Collected Essays,* 1:481 ("Earl and Girl"); Billie Melman, *Women and the Popular Imagination in the Twenties: Flappers and Nymphs* (Basingstoke, 1988), chs. 7–8 (story papers).

10. Margaret Olney, "Real Life—and Fiction," *Popular Writing,* Feb. 1930, 157. An example from a writers' circle is John Marsh's talk on "The Commercial Side of Writing": "Halifax Authors' Circle: 'The Commercial Side of Writing,'" clipping from unspecified newspaper (probably the *Halifax Courier and Guardian*), 21 Sept., year not specified, HAC minute book, p. 70, Soc. 10/1. Compare Michael Denning's argument in *Mechanic Accents: Dime Novels and Working-Class Culture in America* (London, 1987), 200.

11. Olney, "Real Life," 157; "Standardizing Art: An Article for the Man or Woman Desirous of Becoming a Best Seller," *Writer,* Mar. 1921, 7; Kennedy Williamson, *Can You Write Short Stories?* (London, n.d.), 115; MacNichol, *Twelve Lectures,* 63. See also Leavis, *Fiction and the Reading Public,* 58.

12. Williamson, *Can You Write Magazine Stories,* 78–78.

13. Jonathan Rose, *The Intellectual Life of the British Working Classes* (New Haven, 2001), 325.

14. Wilfred Hardie, "Telling People What They Know," *Writer,* Feb. 1925, 122; E. J. Pinches, letter, *Writer,* Feb. 1951, 44–45; E. Haworth, "Creating from the Commonplace," *Writer,* Nov. 1941, 212–214.

15. Heilgers, *How to Write Stories for Money,* 16, 32 (first-hand knowledge); HAC min., 21 Oct. 1952, Soc. 10/2; Cecil Hunt, *Living by the Pen: A Practical Guide to All Forms of Journalism and Fiction Writing,* rev. ed. (London, 1951), 13 (burning urge); HAC min., 15 Jan. 1952, Soc. 10/2 (Procter); NWC min., 7 Oct. 1944, SX88/1/1; NWC min., 21 Jan. 1947, SX88/1/2 (Tulip).

16. Francis Vivian, "The Same Old Story," *Writer,* Nov. 1949, 10 ("daily bread"); *Writer,* Mar. 1921, 16 (Heilgers course); "The Vital Importance of Observation," *LHM,* Dec. 1920, 34; NWC min., 4 Nov. 1952, SX88/1/2; Hunt, *Living by the Pen,* 100; D. Kennedy-Bell, "Freelancing on Holiday," *Writer,* July 1921, 85 (stories and observation); I. Hudson, "Free-lance Wives," *Writer,* Sept. 1936, 268 (married women); Heilgers, *How to Write Stories for Money,* 17; HAC min., 21 Oct. 1952, Soc. 10/2; [Michael Fallon], *Factors of Fiction* (n.p., [late 1940s?]), 6–7 (cultivating observation); Mass-Observation Day Surveys 1937—Women, microfilm roll 3, respondents 8 and 126, M-OA.

17. HAC min., 21 Oct. 1948, Soc. 10/2 (Lees); Herbert John, *My Litterary Adventures* (London, 1925), 97. Hunt, who gave this speech at the Newcastle Writers' Club in February 1951, had given essentially the same talk in Nottingham in September 1948. NWC min., 5 Oct. 1948 and 26 Feb. 1951, SX88/1/2.

18. Thea Redgraves, "Get out of the Rut," *Writer,* July 1953, 37–38; Edith Simpson, "From Blackboard to Blacking Brush," *Writer,* Dec. 1949, 15–16 ("real" life); "Notes and Circle News," *Writer,* Apr. 1949, 34; Leeds Writers' Circle min., 29 June 1970, unclassified minute book, 1970–1976, WYASL (police stations); NWC min., 19 Apr. 1949, 17 May 1949, SX88/1/2.

19. *Writer,* Feb. 1950, 20; NWC min., 7 Nov. 1950, SX88/1/2 (Luton and Newcastle); Norman A. Lazenby, "The New British Pulps," *Writer,* Mar. 1951, 21 (reading); NWC min., 7 Nov. 1950, SX88/1/2 (background).

20. NWC min., 1 May 1951, SX88/1/2; John Braine, diary, 8 Sept. 1953, Braine/D3, Brotherton.

21. Williamson, *Can You Write Magazine Stories,* 40–41.

22. Margaret Hope, "Ideas NOT Plots," *Writer,* Dec. 1947, 376–377.

23. John Rolf, "A Method of Invention," *Writer,* Dec. 1940, 259–261; [C. Clifford Howard], "Plots and Their Method of Construction," lesson from the (Birmingham) Royal Press Institute's "Short Story and General Fiction" course, [1930s], Leslie Halward papers, MS 1293/109, BCA (logic); *Writers' Monthly: Written and Published by G. J. Matson,* Oct. 1934, 5; Hunt, *Living by the Pen,* 100; Ray Dorien, "Writing a Short Story: II. Working out the Story," *Writer,* Jan. 1948, 31.

24. *Writer,* Oct. 1949, 48 (Nottingham club); Vivian, *Story-Weaving,* 11 (definition), 38–44 (story elements, 38); "Novelists' Plots: The Great Constituent in Any Story: Dr. Frank King's Address to Authors Circle," clipping, probably from *Halifax Courier and Guardian,* 16 Nov. 1926, HAC minute book, Soc. 10/1, p. 368 (Aristotle); and, for the currency of this lexicon: NWC min., 26 Feb. 1951, SX88/1/2; HAC min., 25 June 1940, Soc. 10/2; NWC min., 7 Nov. 1950, SX88/1/2; [Howard], "Plots and Their Method of Construction." See also Williamson, *Can You Write Magazine Stories,* 33. For evidence of the popularity of *Story-Weaving,* see *Writer,* June 1947, 115; "Is That So?" *Gunfire: News-Bulletin of the Forces Writer Circle* 3 (Jan. 1946): 4; "Leeds Writer Circle: Membership Card and Syllabus for 1948," Acc. 3220.

25. Vivian, *Story-Weaving,* 38; Martin Walter, *Plot Formula* (London, [1937]), 3; NWC min., 2 Nov. 1954, SX88/1/3. See also [Howard], "Plots and Their Method of Construction."

26. Leavis, *Fiction and the Reading Public,* 30.

27. Walter, *Plot Formula,* 3; Vivian, *Story-Weaving,* 42, 21; Yorick O'Yorke, "Happy Endings," *Popular Writing,* Aug. 1929, 17–18; Heilgers, *How to Write Stories for Money,* 31 (avoiding unhappy endings); Howard, "Plots and Their Method of Construction."

28. "The Surprise Element in Short Stories," *Writer,* Mar. 1921, 5–6.

29. HAC min., 21 Dec. 1932, Soc. 10/2; "A Short Story: With Notes and Comments upon the Method of Its Construction: 'He, She, and It': By Louise Heilgers," *LHM,* Dec. 1920, 39; NWC min., 17 Nov. 1953, SX88/1/3.

30. E.g., "The End and the Beginning," *LHM,* Feb. 1921, 62; Christabel Lowndes-Yates, "Short Stories of Many Nations: VI. De Maupassant and the French Short Story," *Writer,* Mar. 1925, 143; HAC min., 18 Nov. 1948, Soc. 10/2; NWC min., 1 May 1951, SX88/1/2.

31. H. C. H, "Mossy Face etc. By E. N. Jamesworth," AUA, AURR A/4 (blind soldier); Williamson, *Can You Write Short Stories,* ch. 32; quotation 197.

32. Fallon, *Factors of Fiction,* 2; Vivian, *Story-Weaving,* 39, 45–49; Georges Polti, *The Thirty-Six Dramatic Situations,* trans. Lucille Ray (1916; Boston, 1940), 81.

33. Sylvia Michelle, letter, *Writer,* July 1930, 234 (Mansfield); [Michael Fallon], "Inside Information for New Writers," in Fallon, ed., *Inside Information for New Writers* (Bristol, [1947]), 15; *The Writers' and Photographers' Reference Guide: 1947 Edition* (St. Ives, [1947]), 218 (commercial viability); Philip Unwin to Reginald Moore, 28 Aug. 1943, and Moore to Unwin, 30 Aug. 1943, AUA, AUC 172/13.

34. NWC min., 2 Dec. 1952, SX88/1/2; Ivy F. Valdes, "The Keyhole," *Circles' Choice* 1 (May 1948): 9–11; E. Windass, "'Which Passeth Understanding,'" *Circles' Choice* 1 (May 1948): 1–4.

35. Norah Hoult, "The Short Story," *Writer,* Sept. 1951, 15 (and see Williamson, *Can You Write Short Stories,* 102–103); NWC min., 17 Nov. 1953, SX88/1/3 (Woan); "What *The Lady* Wants: By Its Editor, Margaret E. Whitford," *Writer,* Aug. 1954, 10–12.

36. HAC min., 27 Jan. 1940, Soc. 10/2; H.R.M., letter, *Writer,* Aug. 1939, 56; NWC min., 16 Sept. 1958, SX88/1/3; A. H. Brazier, "Poetry and Versification," *Popular Writing,* July 1929, 8 (modernism); NWC min., 29 Oct. 1951, SX88/1/2; Douglas Newton, "Avoiding Waste of Energy," *Writer,* Apr. 1939, 5–9; "New Members," *Literary Amateur* 5 (Nov.–Dec. 1925) (Bennett).

37. Williamson, *Can You Write Short Stories,* 173; Vivian, *Story-*

Weaving, 116; MacNichol, *Twelve Lectures,* 41 (Victorians); Williamson, *Can You Write Short Stories,* 173 ("illusion of reality"); Joan Eley, "*Silvertown Sunflower.* (by Francis Morel)," 30 Apr. 1950, AUA, AURR 18/9/1 ("literaryese"). Another example is Pat Sanson, "An Air Adventure," *Snips* (Sept. 1944): 252–252, copy in F. W. Daniels papers, P. 357, IWM.

38. Williamson, *Can You Write Short Stories,* 78–79; Williamson, *Can You Write Magazine Stories,* ch. 15; HAC min., 28 Apr. 1964, Misc 213/1 (avoid description); L. A. G. Strong, "Notes on Dialogue," *Writer,* July 1947, 135 ("don't tell"); C. H. Henshaw, "The Essence of Style," *Popular Writing,* Sept. 1929, 41; Philip Harrison, *Free-Lance Fallacies: Straight Talks to Young Writers* (London, [1927]), 54; Heilgers, *How to Write Stories for Money,* 20 (self-effacement, simplicity).

39. "Standardizing Art: An Article for the Man or Woman Desirous of Becoming a Best Seller," *Writer,* Mar. 1921, 7; "The Art of Writing English: By the Editor of a Leading Literary Journal," *Popular Writing,* Feb. 1930, 159; NWC min., 18 May 1948, SX88/1/2. See also Ralph Finn, "Know the Rules before You Break Them," *Writer,* Nov. 1946, 205; Denys Thompson, *Voice of Civilisation: An Enquiry into Advertising* (London, 1943), 111–112.

40. George G. Magnus, *How to Write Saleable Fiction,* 14th ed. (London, [1925]), 9; NWC min., 5 Feb. 1946, SX88/1/2 (awkward writing); Hunt, *Living by the Pen,* 136. On Magnus's troubles see three anonymous letters, *Writer,* Oct. 1923, 24; Magnus, letter, *Writer,* Dec. 1923, 70–71.

41. Harrison, *Free-Lance Fallacies,* 62–63.

42. W. Macneile Dixon, "Poetry and National Character," in *An Apology for the Arts* (London, 1944), 33; Stefan Collini, *Public Moralists: Political Thought and Intellectual Life in England, 1850–1930* (Oxford, 1991), 357.

43. Christopher Clausen, "The Palgrave Version," *Georgia Review* 34 (summer 1980): 275, 285–286; Francis Turner Palgrave, ed., *The Golden Treasury of the Best Songs and Lyrical Poems in the English Language,* 6th ed., updated by John Press (Oxford, 1994), 644; Manchester Literary Club min., 9 Jan. 1911, M524/1/2/13, MALS.

44. Stephen Gill, *Wordsworth and the Victorians* (Oxford, 1998), 244–246; Stopford Brooke, *English Literature* (London, 1880), 161; William Wordsworth, "Appendix" to *Lyrical Ballads* (1802), in *Selected Prose,* ed. John O. Hayden (Harmondsworth, 1988), 302–303. On the sales and reception of Brooke's volume, see the editorial notes on Matthew Arnold's review of the book in *The Complete Prose Works of Matthew Arnold,* ed. R. H. Super (Ann Arbor, 1960–1977), 8:441.

45. HAC min., 21 Oct. 1952, Soc. 10/2 (Lees); Williamson, *Can You Write Short Stories,* 114; [Bernard Miall], "The Abeyance: E. W. Gun," Sept. 1924, AUA, AURR A/3.

46. [Flora Thompson], "The Peverel Literary Society Verse-Writing Course," lesson 1, "Subject and Form," 1, 7, Flora Thompson papers, 3/5, HRC (poetry and form); Leavis, *Fiction and the Reading Public,* 57–60; Roger Dataller, *The Plain Man and the Novel* (London, 1940), viii–xii. The passage from Brooke was quoted approvingly in Matthew Arnold's review in *Nineteenth Century:* Arnold, "A Guide to English Literature" (1877), in *Complete Prose Works,* 8:239–240.

47. MacNichol, *Twelve Lectures,* 4–5; Hunt, *Living by the Pen,* 136.

48. Leavis, *Fiction and the Reading Public,* 68; Rosa Maria Bracco, *Merchants of Hope: British Middlebrow Writers and the First World War, 1919–1939* (Providence, 1993), 54; Manchester Literary Club min., 25 Nov. 1929, M524/1/2/14.

49. Francis Vivian, "The First Million Words," *Writer,* Oct. 1950, 16–18.

4. In My Own Language about My Own People

1. Frank Thompson, "Place aux Dames," *Humberside* 7 (Oct. 1941): 45, 50.

2. John Lucas, "An Interview with Edgell Rickword," in Lucas, ed., *The 1930s: A Challenge to Orthodoxy* (Hassocks, 1978), 5.

3. Jon Lawrence, review of *The Intellectual Life of the British Working Classes* by Jonathan Rose, *Socialist History,* forthcoming; Lawrence, "The British Sense of Class," *Journal of Contemporary History* 35 (Apr.

2000): 310–318. For the difference university education made, see "Mr. Leslie Halward to Mr. William Nuttall," *London Mercury* 34 (May 1936): 11–12; "The Proletarian Writer: Discussion between George Orwell and Desmond Hawkins," in *The Collected Essays, Journalism and Letters of George Orwell,* ed. Sonia Orwell and Ian Angus (London, 1968), 2:39. On scholarship students see Richard Hoggart, *The Uses of Literacy: Aspects of Working-Class Life, with Special References to Publications and Entertainments* (London, 1957), 238–249; Brian Jackson and Dennis Marsden, *Education and the Working Class: Some General Themes Raised by a Study of 88 Working-Class Children in a Northern Industrial City* (1962; Harmondsworth, 1966).

4. Pamela Fox, *Class Fictions: Shame and Resistance in the British Working-Class Novel, 1890–1945* (Durham, N.C., 1994), 153 (seeking working-class women writers); John Burnett, David Vincent, and David Mayall, *The Autobiography of the Working Class: An Annotated, Critical Bibliography,* vol. 2: *1900–1945* (Brighton, 1987); Ethel Mannin, *Confessions and Impressions* (London, 1930), 54–56; Kathleen Woodward, *Jipping Street* (1928; London, 1983); Patrick Joyce, *Visions of the People: Industrial England and the Question of Class* (Cambridge, 1991), 258, 274 (19th-century workingman poets); Edmund Frow and Ruth Frow, "Ethel Carnie: Writer, Feminist and Socialist," in H. Gustav Klaus, ed., *The Rise of Socialist Fiction, 1880–1914* (Brighton, 1987). On Carnie's fiction see Fox, *Class Fictions,* 153–169.

5. Marjory Spring Rice, *Working-Class Wives: Their Health and Conditions* (Harmondsworth, 1939), 95–96; Claire Langhamer, *Women's Leisure in England, 1920–60* (Manchester, 2000), 133.

6. Leslie Halward, "Breaking the Rules," talk to the Institute of Journalists, n.d., Halward papers, MS 1293/106, BCA (buying products of advice industry); George Orwell, "As I Please" (*Tribune,* 6 Oct. 1944), in *Collected Essays,* 3:248–249; Alan Bennett, "The Treachery of Books," in *Writing Home,* rev. ed. (London, 1997), 10; "Oral History Recording with Mrs. Rene Chaplin: Recorded by Helen Arkwright, 18 May 1999," p. 8, Sid Chaplin papers, 8/8; undated note by Michael Chaplin, Sid Chaplin papers, 2/2/9, RLUN. On lean periods: Jim Phelan

to John Lehmann, 31 Dec. 1940; Halward to Lehmann, 27 Jan. 1941, 8 Feb. 1941, JLP.

7. Coombes to Lehmann, 21 Nov. 1938; Lehmann to Coombes, 2 Nov. 1938, JLP.

8. Coombes to Lehmann, 9 July 1939, JLP (Left Book Club); Coombes to Lehmann, 25 Jan. 1941, JLP (*Picture Post* mail); Stuart Hall, "The Social Eye of Picture Post," *Working Papers in Cultural Studies* 2 (spring 1972): 71–120; B. L. Coombes, BBC Talks contributor file, WA8/16/1, WAC; Coombes to Lehmann, 11 July 1943, JLP (letterhead); Coombes to Lehmann, 9 Jan. 1941, JLP (staying in mining). This last letter says that Coombes's criticism of management cost him work, but he clearly was not permanently blacklisted.

9. Jack House, broadcast talk on Joe Corrie, n.d. [1964], Joe Corrie papers, MS 26551, NLS; Hanley to Tom Jones, 1 Jan. 1934; Hanley to Mr Hurst, n.d., James Hanley papers, HRC; Leslie Halward to Lehmann, 27 Jan. 1941, 8 Feb. 1941, JLP; Jack Common, preface to Common, ed., *Seven Shifts* (1938; Wakefield, 1978), vii, ix.

10. Valentine Cunningham, *British Writers of the Thirties* (Oxford, 1988), 308; Jackson and Marsden, *Education and the Working Class,* 117; University of Oxford Delegacy for Extra-Mural Studies, *Tutorial Classes Committee Report for the Year 1953–4* (Oxford, 1954), 4 (heating and study space); George Garrett to Lehmann, 10 Feb. 1937, JLP; Michael Murphy, intro. to *The Collected George Garrett,* ed. Murphy (Nottingham, 1999), viii; G. T. Harris, diary, 5 Dec. 1943, 86/91/1, IWM; Molly Weir, *Best Foot Forward* (London, 1972), 132 (writing and heating); Fred Kitchen, "Birth of a Book," *Seven* 3 (May–June 1942): 18; Arkwright, "Oral History Recording," p. 8.

11. Garrett to Common, 4 June 1937, Common papers, packet 86 (tenement, neighbors' children); Garrett to Lehmann, 5 July 1937, JLP ("hen-coop"); Garrett to Lehmann, 10 Feb. 1937, JLP ("exhausted").

12. Murphy, intro. to *Collected George Garrett,* viii, xii-xiii, xx; Garrett to Common, 4 June 1937, Common papers, packet 86; Garrett to Lehmann, 5 July 1937, JLP.

13. Cyril Connolly, *Enemies of Promise* (1938; London, 1973), 116;

Garrett to Common, 20 July 1937, Common papers, packet 86 (baby tears up manuscript); Garrett to Lehmann, 12 July 1938, JLP (breakdown); Murphy, intro. to *Collected George Garrett,* xxi-xxii, xxviii; John Lehmann, *The Whispering Gallery: Autobiography I* (London, 1955), 259 (end of career).

14. Virginia Woolf, *A Room of One's Own* (1929; London, 1931), 100; Garrett to Lehmann, 23 Mar. 1937, JLP.

15. Willy Goldman, *East End My Cradle* (London, 1940), ch. 24; quotations from Garrett to Lehmann, 12 July 1938, Coombes to Lehmann, 21 Nov. 1938, and Coombes to Lehmann, 17 Mar. 1937, JLP.

16. Andy Croft, *Red Letter Days: British Fiction in the 1930s* (London, 1990), 99; Orwell and Hawkins, "Proletarian Writer," 41; Garrett to Lehmann, 5 July 1937, JLP; Leslie Halward, *Let Me Tell You* (London, 1938), 216; Henry Yorke ("Henry Green") to Ottoline Morrell, 25 Feb. 1933, Ottoline Morrell papers, 8/3, HRC; House, broadcast talk on Corrie [1964].

17. Overhill to Halward, 20 Aug. 1950, 18 Aug. 1950, 22 Aug. 1950, Halward papers, MS 1293/107 (all Overhill's letters to Halward are in this file; subsequent references omit the file number); Evelyn M. Unwin, "No Mother Love: by Jack Overhill," Nov. 1958, AUA, AURR 3/6/40 (removed from school).

18. Compare Goldman, *East End My Cradle,* esp. 75.

19. Jonathan Rose, *The Intellectual Life of the British Working Classes* (New Haven, 2001), 321–331; Overhill to Halward, 19 Aug. 1950, 22 Aug. 1950; Deryck Harvey, "Man of Discipline at a Typewriter: Mr. Jack Overhill, Writer, Scholar, Lecturer and Philosopher," *Cambridge News,* 22 Aug. 1966 (diary).

20. Overhill to Halward, 12 Sept. 1950; 19 Aug. 1950, 21 Mar. 1951; Harvey, "Man of Discipline" (daily routine). When the local newspaper caught up with him in 1966 he had eighteen unpublished books on his shelves.

21. Overhill to Halward, 12 Sept. 1950, 28 Sept. 1950, 25 Sept. 1951. On family sagas see Goldman, *East End My Cradle,* 277; Urquhart to Lehmann, 16 Mar. 1937, JLP.

22. Overhill to Halward, 19 June 1951. The title referred to a species of cobbler, not a snob in the social sense.

23. Overhill to Halward, 22 Aug. 1950, 12 Sept. 1950.

24. Overhill to Halward, 20 Feb. 1951 ("end of the world"); [Malcolm Barnes], "Back Street Boy (Overhill)," 17 Dec. 1959, AUA, AURR 4/7/57.

25. Frow and Frow, "Ethel Carnie," 252; Oxford University Tutorial Classes Committee, "Annual Report for the Year 1947–48: C—Reports of Full-Time Tutors on their work other than that of Tutorial Classes," May 1948, p. 1, Oxford University Department of Extension Studies papers, DES/RP/2/2/12, OUA; F. D. Greetwell [Fred Dean] to editor, *Halifax Courier and Guardian,* 16 Nov. 1937, Phyllis Bentley papers, PB/B:101, WYASC. On letters to the editor, see W. E. Williams and A. E. Heath, *Learn and Live: The Consumer's View of Adult Education* (London, 1936), 129.

26. Dean to Bentley, 2 Jan. 1938, 24 Feb. 1938, Bentley papers, PB/B:101.

27. Coombes to Lehmann, 10 Mar. 1940; Chaplin to Lehmann, 9 Apr. 1943; Goldman to Lehmann, [1936]; Jim Phelan to Lehmann, [Feb. 1939? Feb. 1937?]; Fred Urquhart to Lehmann, 7 Dec. 1940, JLP. In addition to those published in *Seven Shifts,* Common's working-class writer associates included Garrett and Fred Urquhart. Common papers, packets 45, 86.

28. Walter Allen, *As I Walked down New Grub Street: Memories of a Writing Life* (Chicago, 1981), 68–71; Halward, *Let Me Tell You,* ch. 21; Lehmann, *Whispering Gallery,* 262; Halward scrapbook, pp. 6–10, Halward papers, MS 1293/104 (Birmingham); Croft, *Red Letter Days,* 177–181 (Codnor).

29. Annual reports, 1928–1933, Women's Co-operative Guild collection, MS Coll 268, vols. 4–5, BLPES; Hogarth Press archive, MS 2750, file 62, URL. Correspondence between Llewelyn Davies and the Woolfs (Monks House Papers, University of Sussex) does not shed any light on how the book came to be assembled.

30. Williams and Heath, *Learn and Live,* 137–138. This book reproduced Evans's article (133–136).

31. The painters' group that grew out of a WEA class at Ashington near Newcastle consciously breached this policy. See William Feaver, *Pitmen Painters: The Ashington Group, 1934–1984* (London, 1988), 18.

32. Oxford University Tutorial Classes Committee, "Annual Report for the Year 1946–47: B—Tutorial Class Reports," May 1947, p. 83; "Annual Report for the Year 1947–8: B—Tutorial Class Reports," May 1948, pp. 36, 91; "Annual Report for the Year 1947–48: C—Reports of Full-Time Tutors on their work other than that of Tutorial Classes," May 1948, p. 1; "Annual Report of Organizing Secretary: Session 1949–50," n.d., p. 48, Department of Extension Studies papers, DES/RP/2/2/12.

33. Tutors' syllabi, 1928–1930, 1932–1940, Department of Extension Studies papers, DES/SB/2/1/10–11, DES/SB/2/1/14–22. Wooldridge's syllabus is in DES/SB/2/1/20.

34. Janet Batsleer, Tony Davis, Rebecca O'Rourke, and Chris Weedon, *Rewriting English: Cultural Politics of Gender and Class* (London, 1985), 48–57 (*Plebs*), 54 (Labour Colleges); J. P. M. Millar, *The Labour College Movement* (London, [1980]), 216, 249–250; Andy Croft, "Who Was Harry Heslop?" in Harold Heslop, *Out of the Old Earth,* ed. Croft and Graeme Rigby (Newcastle, 1994), 11; Heslop, *Out of the Old Earth,* 169; "Marx House Literature Classes," *Left Review* 2 (Jan. 1936): 176; see also "Marx Memorial Library & Workers' School," précis of mins. of General Council meeting, 5 July 1939, LWA, box 3; Andrew Rothstein, *A House on Clerkenwell Green,* 2nd ed. (London, 1983), 75; Alick West, *One Man in His Time: An Autobiography* (London, 1969), 166.

35. Fred Kitchen, *Brother to the Ox: The Autobiography of a Farm Labourer* (London, 1940), 244; Arkwright, "Oral History Recording," pp. 3, 4, 6, Chaplin papers, 8/8 (Chaplin); Chaplin papers, 6/2/1 (Wylie). See also Joe Corrie, "Self-Training," notebook in Corrie papers, Acc. 10839; Jack Common, "Solicitor's Diary: 1899" used as notebook, Common papers, packet 14.

36. Lehmann, *Whispering Gallery,* 260 (Coombes); Alexander Reid, "Poetry, Plays and Pacifism: A Note on the Life and Work of Joe Corrie," clipping from unspecified magazine (ca. 1957) ; W. H. Vaughan to Corrie, 9 Oct. 1937, Corrie papers, MS 26551; House, broadcast talk on Corrie, [1964].

37. Goldman, *East End My Cradle,* 216–217, 278, 280.

38. Montagu Slater, "The Purpose of a Left Review," *Left Review* 1 (June 1935): 365.

39. Hilton to Lehmann, 19 May 1937, JLP; Leslie Halward, "On the Road," *Fact,* no. 4 (July 1937): 54–58; Allen, *New Grub Street,* 69; Halward, *Let Me Tell You,* 226.

40. Leslie Halward, "Writing about the Working Class," lecture at Fircroft Workingmen's College, 8 Oct. 1939, Halward papers, MS 1293/106.

41. See, e.g., "Ourselves," *Fact,* no. 4 (July 1937): 6; Edwin Muir, "New Novels," *Listener,* 13 May 1936.

42. Garrett to Lehmann, 15 Mar. 1937, 9 Mar. 1937, JLP. See also B. L. Coombes, "Below the Tower," *Folios of New Writing* 3 (spring 1941): 31, 34; Cunningham, *British Writers,* 317; and, from a later period, [Sid Chaplin], untitled notes, [Jan.–Feb. 1960], Chaplin papers, 7/2/3.

43. Garrett to Lehmann, 15 Mar. 1937, JLP; Halward, "Writing about the Working Class," Halward papers, MS 1293/106; Gordon Jeffery, "In the Welding Bay," *Penguin New Writing* 2 (Jan. 1941): 86; George Garrett, "Fishmeal," *New Writing* 2 (autumn 1936): 72–84.

44. Cunningham, *British Writers,* 310–312 (propagandist accounts); Leslie Halward, "Boss," *New Writing* 2 (autumn 1936): 33–37; Sid Chaplin, "The Boss," in *The Leaping Lad and Other Stories* (London, 1946) (foremen and masters); James Hanley, "Seven Men," *New Writing* 5 (spring 1938): 210–232; Willy Goldman, "Down at Mendel's," *New Writing* 4 (autumn 1937): 112–127; see also Goldman, "A Start in Life," *New Writing* 2 (autumn 1936): 146–159.

45. Gore Graham, "Pigeon Bill," *New Writing* 1 (spring 1936): 149, 150.

46. Stephen Constantine, "*Love on the Dole* and Its Reception in the 1930s," *Literature and History* 8 (autumn 1982): 241–242; Walter Brierley, *Means Test Man* (London, 1935).

47. John Hampson, *Saturday Night at the Greyhound* (1931; London, 1937).

48. Sid Chaplin, "The Pigeon-Cree," in *Leaping Lad,* 119, 120, 121.

49. Walter Greenwood, *Love on the Dole* (1933; Harmondsworth, 1969), 227, 221–222; Constantine, "*Love on the Dole,*" 232–247 (reaching middle-class readers); Cunningham, *British Writers,* 316 (Heslop); Sid Chaplin, "Living and Writing," n.d., Chaplin papers, 2/1/14; Chaplin, "The Leaping Lad," in *Leaping Lad.*

50. Coombes to Lehmann, 17 Mar. 1937, JLP.

51. Lehmann to Coombes, 28 Mar. 1944, 22 Feb. 1946; Coombes to Lehmann, 9 Jan. 1941, JLP; Virginia Woolf, "The Leaning Tower," *Folios of New Writing* 2 (autumn 1940): 23; Coombes, "Below the Tower," 33, 34.

52. Halward, "Breaking the Rules."

53. H. E. Bates, "Working-Class Tales," *John o' London's Weekly,* 30 Sept. 1938; Halward, *Let Me Tell You,* 161–163.

54. See also Allen, *New Grub Street,* 69.

55. Hanley to Edward Garnett, 21 Mar. 1929, Edward Garnett papers, HRC. Hanley was living in Liverpool.

5. Class, Patronage, and Literary Tradition

1. "Socialist Competition," *Left Review* 1 (Jan. 1935): 129; Jack Common, preface to Common, ed., *Seven Shifts* (1938; Wakefield, 1978), vii; H. Gustav Klaus, "Socialist Fiction in the 1930s: Some Preliminary Observations," in John Lucas, ed., *The 1930s: A Challenge to Orthodoxy* (Hassocks, 1978), 21.

2. Janet Batsleer, Tony Davis, Rebecca O'Rourke, and Chris Weedon, *Rewriting English: Cultural Politics of Gender and Class* (London, 1985), 46 (pre-1930s left); John Carswell, *Lives and Letters: A. R. Orage, Beatrice Hastings, Katherine Mansfield, John Middleton Murry, S. S. Kotelianksy* (London, 1978), 246, 250 (Murry's politics); Jonathan

Rose, *The Intellectual Life of the British Working Classes* (New Haven, 2001), 424; Andy Croft, *Red Letter Days: British Fiction in the 1930s* (London, 1990), 179; Michael Murphy, introduction to *The Collected George Garrett,* ed. Murphy (Nottingham, 1999), xxi (Murry and working-class writers); Hilton to Common, 27 Sept. 1937, 2 Oct. 1937, Common papers, packet 65; J. Middleton Murry, intro. to Jack Hilton, *English Ways: A Walk from the Pennines to Epsom Downs in 1939* (London, 1940).

3. Andrew Thorpe, "The Membership of the Communist Party of Great Britain, 1920–1945," *Historical Journal* 43 (Sept. 2000): 786; Ross McKibbin, "Why Was There No Marxism in Great Britain?" in *The Ideologies of Class: Social Relations in Britain, 1880–1950* (Oxford, 1990), 33; Andy Croft, "Authors Take Sides: Writers and the Communist Party 1920–56," in Geoff Andrews, Nina Fishman, and Kevin Morgan, eds., *Opening the Books: Essays on the Social and Cultural History of British Communism* (London, 1995), 86.

4. Charles Hobday, *Edgell Rickword: A Poet at War* (Manchester, 1989), esp. 157–158, 160; John Gross, *The Rise and Fall of the Man of Letters: Aspects of English Literary Life since 1800* (London, 1969), 254–256 (Calendar); Andy Croft, *Comrade Heart: A Life of Randall Swingler* (Manchester, 2003), esp. 48; Cyril Connolly, "Where Engels Fears to Tread," in *The Condemned Playground: Essays: 1927–1944* (London, 1945).

5. Wendy Mulford, *This Narrow Place: Sylvia Townsend Warner and Valentine Ackland: Life, Letters and Politics, 1930–1951* (London, 1988), 71; Amabel Williams-Ellis, *All Stracheys Are Cousins: Memoirs* (London, 1983), 82, 130, 132–133 (Williams-Ellis's politics); Williams-Ellis, "Our Readers Get to Work," *Left Review* 1 (Dec. 1934): 74 (competition description); Williams-Ellis, "Report on the Competition," *Left Review* 1 (Feb. 1935): 217–220; "Left Review Competition: Strike," *Left Review* 2 (1936): 24–33 (later competition). Contrast Valentine Cunningham's judgment in *British Writers of the Thirties* (Oxford, 1988), 313.

6. "Contributors' Conference," *Left Review* 1 (June 1935): 367–368 (complaints about competitions); Hobday, *Rickword,* 169–170, 187; Randall Swingler, "Editorial," *Left Review* 3 (Jan. 1938): 702.

7. Garrett to Lehmann, 23 Mar. 1937 ("outwardly phlegmatic"); Lehmann to Garrett, 31 Mar. 1937 ("ultra-reserved manner"), JLP.

8. Lehmann to Swingler, 15 June 1939; Swingler to Lehmann, n.d., JLP.

9. Ernest Wishart held the lease on the building.

10. Allan Young and Michael Schmidt, "A Conversation with Edgell Rickword," *Poetry Nation* 1 (1973): 82.

11. Hobday, *Rickword,* 168; B. L. Coombes to Lehmann, 29 July 1937, JLP.

12. Lewis Jones to Douglas Garman, [ca. 1937], Douglas Garman papers, DG 6/4, Hallward Library, University of Nottingham; Gibson Cowan to Wishart, 27 Apr. 1937, LWA, box 3; Goldman to Lehmann, 8 Oct. 1937 and 18 Oct. 1937, JLP (Parsons); Young and Schmidt, "Conversation with Edgell Rickword," 82 (distribution); royalty statements 1937–1938, LWA, box 2; Diana Poulton to Wishart, 25 Sept. 1942, LWA, box 4 (loans by Eva Reckitt to Lawrence & Wishart in Oct. 1936, Dec. 1937, and Dec. 1938, totaling £1430).

13. Lehmann to Garrett, 31 Mar. 1937, JLP. Authors' complaints: Wishart to George Barker, 18 Aug. 1937, 31 Aug. 1937; Lawrence & Wishart to Curtis Brown Ltd, 25 Nov. 1937; Wishart to Harold Heslop, 21 Feb. 1938; Gerald Kersh to Wishart, 22 Oct. 1937, LWA, box 3. The correspondence relating to Nancy Cunard's anthology *Negro* (box 3) is a striking example of Lawrence and Wishart's organizational deficiencies.

14. F. A. Ridley to Wishart, 23 Sept. 1937, LWA, box 4; Hilton to Jack Common, 27 Sept. 1937, Common papers, packet 65; David Goodway, "Charles Lahr: Anarchist, Bookseller, Publisher," *London Magazine,* n.s., 17 (July 1977): 53. Wishart had joined the party in 1936.

15. Lehmann to Wintringham, 29 Aug. 1935 (*Left Review* and Lehmann's magazine); Lehmann to Hanley, 3 Dec. 1935; Lehmann to Wintringham, 29 Aug. 1935, 31 Aug. 1935 ("rallying ground"), 31 Aug. 1935 (*Left Review* board), JLP.

16. Lehmann to Rickword, 11 Apr. 1937 ("reading proletariat"); Chaplin to Lehmann, 30 Sept. 1941, and 7 Oct. [mid-1940s]; Goldman

to Lehmann, n.d. (workers reading *New Writing*); Lehmann to Hanley, 3 Dec. 1935; Lehmann to Harold Heslop, 10 June 1936 (sounding out contributors); Coombes to Lehmann, 21 June 1936 (offering stories), and 10 Mar. 1940; Chaplin to Lehmann, 9 Apr. 1943; Goldman to Lehmann, n.d. [1936]; Jim Phelan to Lehmann, [Feb. 1939? Feb. 1937?]; Urquhart to Lehmann, 7 Dec. 1940 (sending friends' work); Lehmann to Walter Allen, 1 Mar. 1941 (asking a contributor to look for new talent), JLP.

17. Lehmann to Phelan, 23 July 1940; Garrett to Lehmann, 16 Jan. 1936, JLP. For another example see Halward to Lehmann, 24 June 1936, JLP.

18. Lehmann to Goldman, 13 Dec. 1937; Lehmann to Garrett, 26 July 1937, Lehmann to Phelan, 4 Jan. 1941; Lehmann to Coombes, 4 Mar. [19??] and 19 Apr. 1944, JLP. And see Adrian Wright, *John Lehmann: A Pagan Adventure* (London, 1998), 171; Jeremy Treglown, *Romancing: The Life and Work of Henry Green* (New York, 2000), 119, 174.

19. Lehmann to Allen, 31 July [early 1940s], 5 Aug. [1942]; Lehmann to Chaplin, 3 Jan. 1944, 13 Sept. 1944; Lehmann to Alun Lewis, 11 Mar. 1941, JLP.

20. Lehmann to Coombes, 19 May [19??], JLP.

21. Lehmann to Coombes, 29 May [19??], JLP.

22. Hilton to Common, 3 Nov. 1937 ("University boys") and 1 Aug. 1937 ("workmanship"), Common papers, packet 65; Garrett to Lehmann, 16 Jan. 1936 and [6?] June 1936, JLP.

23. Urquhart to Lehmann, 10 Nov. 1940; John Sommerfield to Lehmann, [Nov. 1940] (commitment to *New Writing*); Halward to Lehmann, 8 Feb. 1941; Lehmann to Phelan, 23 July 1940, JLP. On the sales and popularity of *Penguin New Writing,* see Wright, *John Lehmann,* 140–141; Lehmann, "Journal: from June 25th. 1944," entry for 25 June 1944, JLP.

24. Lehmann to Halward, 27 July 1938 ("direct attack") and 21 Apr. 1936; Lehmann to Swingler, 19 Dec. 1937, JLP; Wright, *John Lehmann,* 93; Lehmann to Harrisson, 28 July 1937, JLP; Lehmann to

Lindsay, 18 Jan. 1938, JLP; Lehmann to Lipton, 27 July 1935 ("marching song"); Lipton to Lehmann, 6 Aug. 1935, JLP.

25. See Hanley's correspondence with Charles and Esther Lahr, F. J. Joiner, and a Mr. Hurst, Hanley papers, HRC; and Goodway, "Charles Lahr."

26. J. W. Lambert and Michael Ratcliffe, *The Bodley Head, 1887–1987* (London, 1987), 272–273. The importance of Potter's bookshop to Hanley's Liverpool comes through in his correspondence with Tom Jones (Hanley papers).

27. Henry Yorke ("Henry Green") to Ottoline Morrell, 25 Feb. 1933, Ottoline Morrell papers, 8/3, HRC; Lambert and Ratcliffe, *Bodley Head,* 243 (Mannin); Timothy d'Arch Smith, *R. A. Caton and the Fortune Press: A Memoir and a Handlist* (London, 1983), 17 (raids); C. D. Medley to Boriswood Ltd, 10 Apr. 1935, Hanley papers, HRC (limited editions); Diana Souhami, *The Trials of Radclyffe Hall* (London, 1998), 202. On this gay subculture, see, e.g., H. Montgomery Hyde, *Christopher Scalter Millard (Stuart Mason): Bibliographer and Antiquarian Book Dealer* (New York, 1990); Timothy d'Arch Smith, *Love in Earnest: Some Notes on the Lives and Writings of English "Uranian" Poets from 1889 to 1930* (London, 1970).

28. "Summary—Report of the Police Proceedings against the Directors and the Firm of Boriswood Limited in Regard to the Book Entitled 'Boy' Written by James Hanley," n.d., Hanley papers, HRC. See also Liam Hanley, foreword to James Hanley, *Boy* (1931; London, 1992), xiv.

29. Hanley to Lahr, 12 Jan. 1934, Hanley papers.

30. Goldman to Lehmann, 13 Oct. 1938, JLP. Both Lehmann and R. A. Scott-James of the *London Mercury* had cause for exasperation with Hanley in the late 1930s; their correspondence with him is in the HRC (JLP, Scott-James papers).

31. Klaus, "Socialist Fiction," 39–41 (major publishers); William Nuttall, "The Proletarian Reader," *London Mercury* 33 (Feb. 1936): 502–507; "The Coming of the Proletarian Literature: A Symposium Assembled by the Editor," ibid. 34 (May 1936): 10–18 (Halward's letter pp. 10–13); "Correspondence: Proletarian Literature," ibid. 34 (June

1936): 147–150; Halward to Scott-James, 27 Aug. 1936, Scott-James papers, HRC; William Plomer, "The Contemporary Novel: Its Subject-Matter," *London Mercury* 34 (Oct. 1936): 508 (see also *Sunday Times,* 4 Apr. 1938, quoted in Croft, *Red Letter Days,* 49); Julian Symons, *The Thirties: A Dream Revolved* (London, 1960), 37–38. Scott-James's values and interests may be gauged from the collection of his editorials published as *The Day before Yesterday* (London, 1947).

32. Cyril Connolly, "Defects of English Novels," in *Condemned Playground,* 101. See also V. M. L. Scott, "A Proletarian Writer," *London Mercury* 34 (May 1936): 77.

33. Lehmann to Hanley, 28 Dec. 1936, JLP (collecting stories); Maureen Duffy, *A Thousand Capricious Chances: A History of the Methuen List, 1889–1989* (London, 1989), 95–96, 107.

34. Stephen Constantine, "*Love on the Dole* and Its Reception in the 1930s," *Literature and History* 8 (autumn 1982): 232. For the idea of a social-democratic middlebrow, see John Baxendale and Chris Pawling, *Narrating the Thirties: A Decade in the Making: 1930 to the Present* (Basingstoke, 1996); Ross McKibbin, *Classes and Cultures: England, 1918–1951* (Oxford, 1998), 484–486.

35. John Worthen, *D. H. Lawrence: The Early Years, 1885–1912* (Cambridge, 1991), 419–420; Andy Croft, "Who Was Harry Heslop?" in Harold Heslop, *Out of the Old Earth,* ed. Croft and Graeme Rigby (Newcastle, 1994), 12 (Herbert Jenkins).

36. F. C. Ball, *One of the Damned: The Life and Times of Robert Tressell, Author of "The Ragged Trousered Philanthropists"* (London, 1973), 167; George Jefferson, *Edward Garnett: A Life in Literature* (London, 1982); Hanley to Garnett, 21 Mar. 1929; Henry Yorke to Garnett, 9 Sept. 1931, Edward Garnett papers, HRC; Halward, *Let Me Tell You,* 199 (Purdom); C. B. Purdom, *Life over Again* (London, 1951), 138, 143. See also Jonathan Rose, "*Everyman:* An Experiment in Culture for the Masses," *Victorian Periodicals Review* 26 (summer 1993): 79–87.

37. Cunningham, *British Writers,* 309–310, 319–322 (mining novels); Graham Holderness, "Miners and the Novel: From Bourgeois to Proletarian Fiction," in Jeremy Hawthorn, ed., *The British Working-Class*

Novel in the Twentieth Century (London, 1984), 21 (collective hero); Hilton to Lehmann, 18 June 1936, JLP (idols); Jack Hilton, *Caliban Shrieks* (London, 1935), v; Coombes to Lehmann, 3 Apr. 1944, JLP.

38. Lehmann, *Whispering Gallery,* 260 (compare McKibbin, *Classes and Cultures,* 514–515); Bernard Miall, "The Nolan Brothers: B. M. Geoghegan," 19 Jan. 1939, AUA, AURR 7/6; Willy Goldman, *East End My Cradle* (London, 1940), 66–68; Hilton to Common, 27 Dec. 1937, Common papers, packet 65. Another instance of childhood mimicry of popular genres is Sid Chaplin, "A Story-Teller's Story," *Leaping Lad,* 5; Chaplin, "Living and Writing," n.d., Chaplin papers, 2/1/14, RLUN.

39. Leslie Halward, "Breaking the Rules," talk to the Institute of Journalists, n.d., Halward papers, MS 1293/106, BCA.

40. Leslie Halward, "Some Writers Who Have Influenced Me," talk to Birmingham Booklovers' Society, 24 Sept. 1937, Halward papers, MS 1293/106; Halward, *Let Me Tell You,* 164–166; Urquhart to Common, 27 Aug. 1937, Common papers, packet 45; Bates to Urquhart, 5 Sept. 1933, 26 Oct. 1933, 5 Feb. 1934, H. E. Bates papers, HRC.

41. H. E. Bates, *The Vanished World: An Autobiography* (London, 1969), 160.

42. James Hanley, "New Novels," *New English Weekly* 14 (3 Nov. 1938): 60–61.

43. B. L. Coombes, "The Flame," *New Writing* 3 (spring 1937): 131–134; Jim Phelan, "The Slip," *Penguin New Writing* 4 (Mar. 1941): 55–61.

44. Jim Phelan, "Amongst Those Present," *Penguin New Writing* 11 (Nov. 1941): 65–73. A story ending in a grim surprise is Fred Urquhart, "The Heretic," *New Writing* 3 (spring 1937): 154–164.

45. Fred Urquhart, "Sweat," *Fact,* no. 4 (July 1937): 50–53; Janet Montefiore, *Men and Women Writers of the Thirties: The Dangerous Flood of History* (London, 1996), 99.

46. Halward, "On the Road"; James Hanley, "Episode," *Fact,* no. 4 (July 1937): 59–65. This interpretation of Halward's story leans heavily on Montefiore, *Men and Women Writers,* 100–102.

47. Storm Jameson, "Documents," *Fact,* no. 4 (July 1937): 12; Sydney D. Tremayne to Chaplin, 21 Feb. 1942, Chaplin papers, 7/2/1; Sid Chaplin, "The Swimmers," *Seven* 3 (July-Sept. 1942): 7–11.

48. Leslie Halward, "Arch Anderson," *New Writing* 4 (autumn 1937): 128–141. The story is praised in Lehmann, *Whispering Gallery,* 262; clipping of a Desmond MacCarthy review of *New Writing* 4 (autumn 1937), Halward papers, MS 1293/104.

49. Walter Allen, "An Artist of the Thirties," *Folios of New Writing* 3 (spring 1941): 150.

50. As Jonathan Rose contends: *Intellectual Life,* chs. 12, 13. Rose's focus is on working-class reading, but his argument has clear implications for working-class writing.

51. Valentine Cunningham, "The Age of Anxiety and Influence; or, Tradition and the Thirties Talents," in Keith Williams and Steven Matthews, eds., *Rewriting the Thirties: Modernism and After* (London, 1997), 12, 13; Cunningham, *British Writers,* 312 (political strategies).

52. Chaplin to Lehmann, 8 Feb. 1944, JLP (Aragon); poems in Chaplin papers, 1/3: "This was the Man," n.d. (less traditional forms); anonymous annotation on Chaplin's "Toll Up," n.d. ("Day Lewis"); "Miner's Prayer," n.d.

53. "Controversy: Writers' International (British Section)," *Left Review* 1 (Dec. 1934): 77 (Brown); "Controversy: Writers' International (British Section)," ibid. 1 (Jan. 1935): 127 and note (Montagu Slater). See also Stephen Spender, "Writers and Manifestoes," ibid. 1 (Jan. 1935): 149.

6. People's Writing and the People's War

1. James Hanley, "A Writer's Day," in *Don Quixote Drowned* (London, 1953), 75–81.

2. This is not including the magazine's earlier incarnation, for reasons that are made clear below.

3. *Left News,* Apr. 1939, 1239; Fred Urquhart to John Lehmann, 13 Jan. 1941, 16 June 1944, JLP; Derek Stanford, *Inside the Forties: Lit-*

erary Memoirs, 1937–1957 (London, 1977), 67; J. Maclaren-Ross, *Memoirs of the Forties* (London, 1965), 199; Michael Hamburger, *A Mug's Game: Intermittent Memoirs, 1924–1954* (Cheadle Hulme, 1973), 100 (Goldman); [Bernard Miall], "The Clouds Are Big with Mercy: Fred Urquhart," reader's report for Allen and Unwin, 12 Aug. [1943], AUA, AURR 11/2/14 (Urquhart's wartime writing); Secretary to Lehmann to Urquhart, 19 Sept. 1946, JLP (*Tribune* job); Paul O'Flinn, "Orwell and *Tribune*," *Literature and History* 6 (autumn 1980): 205–211.

4. Joseph McAleer, *Popular Reading and Publishing in Britain, 1914–1950* (Oxford, 1992), 60–63; Denys Val Baker, intro. to Baker, ed., *Little Reviews Anthology 1945* (London, 1945), xi, xvi; Robert Hewison, *Under Siege: Literary Life in London, 1939–45* (1977; London, 1988), 91 (Grandea).

5. Petronella Wyatt, *Father, Dear Father: Life with Woodrow Wyatt* (London, 1999), 7–8; Woodrow Wyatt, intro. to Wyatt, ed., *The Way We Lived Then—The "English Story" in the 1940s* (1989; [London], 1990), 7; Woodrow Wyatt, preface to Woodrow Wyatt and Susan Wyatt, eds., *English Story: First Series* (London, 1941), 7. For Wyatt's ability to get his seniors to take him seriously, see Lehmann to Wyatt, 29 Feb. 1940, JLP; Maclaren-Ross, *Memoirs of the Forties,* 88, 89–90.

6. On Jeffery see "Notes on Contributors," in Jack Aistrop and Reginald Moore, eds., *Bugle Blast: An Anthology from the Services: Third Series* (London, 1945), 205.

7. [John Singer], "About Million," in Singer, ed., *Million: New Left Writing: First Collection* (Glasgow, [early 1944?]), 2; Singer to Chaplin, n.d., Chaplin papers, SC 7/2/1, RLUN; John Singer, "Literature and War," in Singer, *Million,* 61.

8. Ian S. MacNiven, "Seven," in Alvin Sullivan, ed., *British Literary Magazines* (Westport, CT, 1983–1986), 4:430 (original *Seven*); *Poetry and the People,* no. 20 (1940), inside front cover (advertising the new *Seven*); Andy Croft, "The Boys around the Corner: The Story of Fore Publications," in Croft, ed., *A Weapon in the Struggle: The Cultural History of the Communist Party in Britain* (London, 1998), 161n15 (O'Connor's purchase); Philip O'Connor, *Memoirs of a Public Baby*

(1958; New York, 1989), 171–173. On O'Connor see Andrew Barrow, *Quentin and Philip: A Double Portrait* (London, 2002). The new *Seven* did not appear until March 1941.

9. Croft, "Fore Publications," 149, 146–147, 150. See also Barrow, *Quentin and Philip,* 138.

10. Sydney Tremayne, "Boys do not kiss," [1970s], pp. 133–135, Sydney Tremayne papers, MS 26695, NLS. Unbeknownst to Tremayne, Castro was a shareholder in Fore Publications: Croft, "Fore Publications," 146–147.

11. Croft, "Fore Publications," 150.

12. *Seven* thus did not long outlast the war, though not necessarily (or only) because the mood it articulated had less of a constituency than before. Tremayne's successor had served as his deputy for about a year, but had no other editorial or publishing experience, and this jolt in itself might have set the magazine on its downward course. But it was very much a wartime magazine, and even with its most successful editor at the helm, it might have foundered after 1945, as many stouter periodicals did.

13. Michael Pickering and Kevin Robins, "The Making of a Working-Class Writer: An Interview with Sid Chaplin," in Jeremy Hawthorn, ed., *The British Working-Class Novel in the Twentieth Century* (London, 1984), 145; Tremayne, "The King My Father's Death," p. 104, Tremayne papers, MS 26700 (another version of Tremayne's autobiography); McAleer, *Popular Reading and Publishing,* 60–63, 73–76 (wartime reading); [Cyril Connolly], "Comment," *Horizon* 4 (Oct. 1942): 224; J. E. Morpurgo, *Allen Lane: King Penguin: A Biography* (London, 1979), 170 (*Penguin New Writing*); Croft, "Fore Publications," 145, 151 (*Left Review* and *Our Time*).

14. [Philip O'Connor and Gordon Cruickshank], "Readers, You Are Our Writers," *Seven* 2 (Mar. 1941): 25.

15. Philip O'Connor, "People's Writing," ibid., 44.

16. [Philip O'Connor and Gordon Cruickshank], "Editorial Remarks," *Seven* 2 (July–Aug. 1941): 1 (quotation); O'Connor, "People's Writing," 44 (rejecting craft).

17. James Littlejohn, "The Accused," *Seven* 2 (July–Aug. 1941): 59–61.

18. Gordon Allen North, "Holiday," *Seven* 5 [1944 or 1945]: 17–20; W. Glynne Jones, "Another Working Day Begins," *Seven* 3 (Oct.–Dec. 1942): 10–13; Reginald Moore to Philip Unwin, 5 May 1944, AUA, AUC 200/2 (on Jones). By the time of Moore's letter, Jones was working as a reader for *Argosy,* had had stories published in *Tribune,* the *Strand,* and *Our Time,* and was due to appear in Keidrych Rhys's *Wales.*

19. David Alexander, "Accident," *Seven* 5 (Apr.–June 1944): 19–22; Alexander, "Lives, 5/- Each," *Seven* 4 (Jan.–Mar. 1944): 5–7.

20. James T. McFadden, "The Sins of the Fathers," *Seven* 3 (July–Sept. 1942): 25–27; E. C. Harris, "Family Group," *Seven* 6, no. 4 (n.d.): 51–56; Monica Mooney, "The Typist," *Seven* 3 (July–Sept. 1942): 62.

21. "Most people say 'British'; some say 'British Bulldog.'" James Stephens, "Mass Observer in Wartime," *Seven* 2 (July–Aug. 1941): 28–31, 34.

22. [Isobel K. C. Steele], "In the Doctor's Waiting Room: By His Receptionist," *People's Friend,* 11 Apr. 1936; [L. M. Ellerington], "A Seaside Confectioner's Busy Day," ibid., 3 Aug. 1936; J.E.E. [L. M. Ellerington], "Dockyard Fitter's Job: At Funnel-Top in a Nor'-Easter," *Newcastle Weekly Chronicle,* 8 July 1939; L. M. E[llerington], "A Vat-Cleaner's Own Story of His Work," ibid., 19 Aug. 1939; E. E. W[oan], "A Day in the Life of One of London's Flower Girls," ibid., 1 Apr. 1938; all in NWC clippings book, 1936–1945, SX88/5/1, TWAS.

23. Ann Fabian, "Making a Commodity of Truth: Speculations on the Career of Bernarr Macfadden," *American Literary History* 5 (spring 1993): 51–76 (*True Story*); "Big Money for Your Story," *My Story Weekly,* 22 Oct. 1927, inside back cover; NWC min., 7 Nov. 1950, SX88/1/2 ("fiction in the 1st person"); Herbert John, *My Litterary Adventures* (London, 1925), 71–73, 77–80. On "confessions," see also John Gray, *Gin and Bitters* (London, 1938), 272.

24. Michael Denning, *The Cultural Front: The Laboring of American Culture in the Twentieth Century* (London, 1996), 204 ("one big story" is quoted from Macfadden).

25. Tremayne, "The King My Father's Death," pp. 104–105;

Tremayne to Chaplin, 21 Feb. 1942, 22 Sept. 1942, 2 Dec. 1942, Chaplin papers, SC 7/2/1. Roland Gant, "Poor Peter," *Seven* 3 (July–Sept. 1942): 35–37. An example of the prose: "Hello dog, liver-white spaniel from the rectory. There is the parson's wife airing herself in the meadowy air. She looks oddly at David and Peter lying beneath the tree, at David lightly stroking the curly head lying on his shoulder. What tight lips she has now, what narrow eyes. She is off to the farm, goodbye dog, calling you."

26. Tremayne, "The King My Father's Death," p. 104; Tremayne, "Boys do not kiss," p. 133 (handwritten paragraph on verso) (publishing amateurs); editorial note at foot of "Dentico," "If you are squeamish DON'T read this," *Seven* 3 (Oct.–Dec. 1942): 54; "Send Us Your Story," *Seven* 3 (July–Sept. 1942): 30 (democratizing). A later appeal also echoed O'Connor: "Remember that you, our readers, are our writers. We want you to write about life as you experience it." *Seven* 4 (Jan.–Mar. 1943): 32–33.

27. NWC min., 18 May 1948, SX88/1/2 (style of a letter); G. L. Bett, "The Casualty," *Seven* 3 (Oct.–Dec. 1942): 55–56; Roland Mathias, "Study in Hate," ibid., 5–9; Jack Adrian, ed., *Strange Tales from The Strand* (Oxford, 1991); Osmond Leslie, "The Symptoms," *Seven* 3 (May–June 1942): 40; anon., "Dear Baccy," *Seven* 3 (July–Sept. 1942): 54 (marital friction); Cyril Hughes, "Rivets in Hitler's Coffin," *Seven* 4 (Jan.–Mar. 1943): 19 (quotation).

28. *Seven* 4 (Oct.–Dec. 1943): 3 (Regent Institute); David Boyce, "If this sounds conceited—sorry!" *Seven* 3 (July–Sept. 1942): 53–54; Don Barry, "Maskerade," *Seven* 3 (Oct.–Dec. 1942): 32–34; Leonard Digby Dawson, "The Man Whose Brain Exploded," *Seven* 3 (July–Sept. 1942): 57–59; H. L. V. Fletcher, "Not His Line," ibid., 45–46.

29. Alison Light, *Forever England: Femininity, Literature and Conservatism between the Wars* (London, 1991), 211; Jan Struther, *Mrs Miniver* (London, 1989). See also Richard Trainor, "Neither Metropolitan nor Provincial: The Interwar Middle Class," in Alan Kidd and David Nicholls, eds., *The Making of the British Middle Class? Studies of Regional and Cultural Diversity since the Eighteenth Century* (Stroud, 1998), 207.

30. Martin Francis, "The Domestication of the Male? Recent Research on Nineteenth- and Twentieth-Century British Masculinity," *Historical Journal* 45 (Sept. 2002): 643–644 (cinema and glamour); Ross McKibbin, *Classes and Cultures: England, 1918–1951* (Oxford, 1998), 484–486; J. B. Priestley, *English Journey: Being a Rambling but Truthful Account of What One Man Saw and Heard and Felt and Thought during a Journey through England during the Autumn of the Year 1933* (1934; Harmondsworth, 1977), 389; John Baxendale, "'I Had Seen a Lot of Englands': J. B. Priestley, Englishness and the People," *History Workshop Journal,* no. 51 (spring 2001): 96 (non-conservative); Mass-Observation Day Surveys, 1937—Men, microfilm roll 5, respondent no. 470, M-OA (punctuation modified slightly).

31. Light, *Forever England,* 154; Raphael Samuel, "Continuous National History," in Samuel, ed., *Patriotism: The Making and Unmaking of British Identity* (London, 1989), 1:15 (from Baldwin to "people's war"); J. B. Ashby, "Norman Notebook," in Peter Ratazzi, ed., *Khaki and Blue: Writing in Battledress: New Series* (London, n.d.), 11; Keith Williams, *British Writers and the Media, 1930–1945* (Basingstoke, 1996), 206 (life in the blitz); Sonya O. Rose, *Which People's War? National Identity and Citizenship in Britain, 1939–1945* (Oxford, 2003), 157, 152–153.

32. John Lehmann, "Barrack-room Writers" (radio script for transmission on 16 Oct. 1946), JLP; "Send Us Your Story," *Seven* 3 (July–Sept. 1942): 30; anon., "Hoodoo Hulk Dodged Home," ibid., 49–51 (Marseille to London); Will Wilkinson, "Bang!" *Seven* 3 (Oct.–Dec. 1942): 65 (Italian plane). On boredom see A. C. C., "Ack-Ack Night Guard," *Seven* 3 (July–Sept. 1942): 55–56; R. C. C., "The Middle Watch," *Seven* 3 (Oct.–Dec. 1942): 27–28; Bob Wraight, "Smoke Got in His Eyes," *Seven* 5 (Apr.–June 1944): 12–13.

33. Geofray Barnett, "I Am Reserved," *Seven* 3 (May–June 1942): 58; "The Pursuit of Lady Poodley: A 16-Year-Old Member of a Newspaper Picture Library Staff Talks about His Job," *Seven* 3 (Oct.–Dec. 1942): 37–38; M. E. Weatherley, "French Cleaner in Wartime," *Seven* 2 (July–Aug. 1941): 25–27; Mabel Stonier, "Down in the Forest," *Seven* 4

(Oct.–Dec. 1943): 29–30; Joan D. Swaby, "Pages from the Diary of a News Agency Telegraphist," ibid., 43–45; "Normal Nightshift: Behind the Scenes with a Met. Assistant, R.A.F.," *Seven* 3 (Oct.–Dec. 1942): 52–53; see also E. M. Wells, "Next, Please," *Seven* 4 (Jan.–Mar. 1944): 39–42; Ilsa, "500 Men Are My Headache," *Seven* 4 (Jan.–Mar. 1943): 45–46.

34. Robert Fane, "Sunset and Evening Star . . ." *Seven* 3 (July–Sept. 1942): 15–17; Roland Gant, "Miners for Bombs," *Seven* 3 (May–June 1942): 19–20; Ilsa, "500 Men," 45–46. An instance from another publication is Louis Katin, "At the Epicerie of St . . ." in Ratazzi, *Khaki and Blue, New Series,* 14–15. The *épicerie* is a meeting place "for all the young lads from Yorkshire, and Glasgow, and Wigan, and Birmingham, and the Old Kent Road." Note the implicit working-class geography.

35. Wilfrid Barber, "Down Bells," *Seven* 2 (July–Aug. 1941): 9–12; Fane, "Sunset and Evening Star," 17; Stanley S. Barnett, "Desert Road," *Seven* 5 (Apr.–June 1944): 9–11; "The Battery Moves: by Ex-Gunner A.A," *Seven* 3 (July–Sept. 1942): 44; Denis Clarke, "Salute to a Pig," *Seven* 4 (Oct.–Dec. 1943): 41–42; R. C. Sherriff, *Journey's End: A Play in Three Acts* (1929; New York, 1934), 40; John Baxendale, "'You and I—All of Us Ordinary People': Renegotiating 'Britishness' in Wartime," in Nick Hayes and Jeff Hill, eds., *"Millions like Us"? British Culture in the Second World War* (Liverpool, 1999), 305 (Mass-Observation); Vera Lynn, *Vocal Refrain: An Autobiography* (1975; Litton, Yorkshire, 1976), 179.

36. Sydney D. Tremayne, "You," *Seven* 3 (Oct.–Dec. 1942): 30; Rose, *Which People's War,* 154; *All England Listened: The Wartime Broadcasts of J. B. Priestley* (New York, 1967), 12 (9 June 1940) (different from Germans); McKibbin, *Classes and Cultures,* 97. See also Peter Mandler, "The Consciousness of Modernity? Liberalism and the English National Character, 1870–1914," in Martin Daunton and Bernhard Rieger, eds., *Meanings of Modernity: Britain from the Late-Victorian Era to World War II* (Oxford, 2001), esp. 132.

37. Barry, "Maskerade," 34 (similar to peacetime writing); F. G. Clark, "A Sgt.-Major Brought My Morning Tea," *Seven* 3 (Oct.–Dec.

1942): 39–41; A. Challenor Chadwick, "A Letter from Joe," *Seven* 4 (Jan.–Mar. 1943): 37–38; A. S. Parker, "Sailors Do Care," *Seven* 3 (July–Sept. 1942): 28–29; A. Challenor, "A Story from Spud and Joe," ibid., 21–23; A. Challenor, "Surprising the Enemy," *Seven* 3 (May–June 1942): 8–10 (sergeant-majors and military absurdity); Denys Val Baker, "Debated in Council," *Seven* 5, no. 3 (n.d.): 49–52 (civilian Britain); Joan Smith, "Monday Morning," *Seven* 4 (Jan.–Mar. 1943): 58.

38. "Where 'Phone Calls Are Free," *Seven* 3 (Oct.–Dec. 1942): 56; O. Devereux Price, "I Fought in Russia," *Seven* 3 (May–June 1942): 13–15; Louis Borrill, "Roman Holiday," ibid., 37–39; Ralph Finn, "Especially Bugs," *Seven* 4 (Jan.–Mar. 1943): 41–42; Ralph L. Finn, *No Tears in Aldgate* (1963; Bath, 1973); A. C. C., "Ack-Ack Night Guard" (museums); Thomas W. Hicks, ". . . or a tinkling cymbal," *Seven* 3 (Oct.–Dec. 1942): 57; John Bishop, "Sunday Morning," ibid., 58; F. C. Ball, "In London," *Seven* 2 (Mar. 1941): 64–66 (Blake).

39. K. L. Simms, "Food Faddists," *Seven* 4 (Oct.–Dec. 1943): 47–48; Frederick John Tucker, "Incense for the Mayor," *Seven* 5, no. 3 (n.d.): 11–12; James Gauld, "Penny Lesson," *Seven* 3 (Oct.–Dec. 1942): 16 (middle class); George Fraser, "How Marty Got the Jitters," *Seven* 3 (July–Sept. 1942): 19–20 (demonstrator); Bob Elliott, "Pay-off," *Seven* 4 (Jan.–Mar. 1943): 5–7.

40. Steven Fielding, Peter Thompson, and Nick Tiratsoo, *"England Arise!" The Labour Party and Popular Politics in the 1940s* (Manchester, 1995), quotation 29; James Hinton, "1945 and the Apathy School," *History Workshop Journal,* no. 43 (spring 1997): 266–273.

41. The phrase "earnest minority" is a quotation from Richard Hoggart, the most influential chronicler of that minority.

42. P. L. H. Smith, "Editorial: Farewell Khaki and Blue," in Smith, ed., *Farewell Khaki and Blue: Demobilisation Issue* (London, n.d.), 4 ("in the field"); "Contributors' Roll-Call," in Ratazzi, *Khaki and Blue, New Series,* inside back cover (Smith); "The Ten Points of Front Line Generation," in Smith, *Farewell,* 58 (Sergeant). On Ratazzi's past, see Stanford, *Inside the Forties,* 125–126; "Contributors," in Denys Val Barker and Peter Ratazzi, eds. *Writing Today* (London, 1943), 131.

43. "Special Announcement: 'Front Line Generation,'" *Gunfire* 3 (Jan. 1946): 1; [C. Farley], "Editorial," *Gunfire* 3 (Feb. 1946): 2; Stanford, *Inside the Forties,* 125 (Albert Hall); Ralph B. Durdey, "On Politics and the Writer," *Gunfire* 3 (May 1946): 5.

44. "Ten Points of Front Line Generation"; Smith, "Editorial: Farewell Khaki and Blue"; Peter Ratazzi, "Now More than Ever"; and Howard Sergeant, "A Time for Decision," all in Smith, *Farewell;* Peter Ratazzi, "Khaki and Blue," in Ratazzi, ed., *Khaki and Blue: The Younger Writers in Battledress* (Slough, [1944]).

45. Kathleen Binns, "Conflict," and Megan McCamley, "The Jay's Nest," in Peter Ratazzi, ed., *Writers of To-morrow: New Sketches by Soldiers and Workers of To-day* ([London], 1945); Douglas Gibson, "Sunday Evening," in Smith, *Farewell,* 57. See also Donald Thompson, "Out of Blood, Build (Fragment)," in Smith, *Farewell,* [2].

46. Hazel Desenne, "Monotony," in Ratazzi, *Khaki and Blue,* 145; Michael Culwick, "Don't Wake the Sergeant Major," in Smith, *Farewell,* 35–37; G. A. Squires, "The Browning Gun," in Ratazzi, *Khaki and Blue, New Series,* 33–37 (humor); Harry Blacker, "Greatcoats, One," in Ratazzi, *Khaki and Blue,* 27–30; Rosemary Sinclair, "Hot Water," in Ratazzi, *Khaki and Blue, New Series,* 15–19 (inefficiency); A. E. Claydon, "Transition," in Smith, *Farewell,* 26–28; Michal James, "Amity," in Ratazzi, *Khaki and Blue,* 8–11; Antony Verney, "The Night before the Boat," in Ratazzi, *Khaki and Blue, New Series,* 39–47 (romances); P. L. H. Smith, "Beer or Champagne," in Smith, *Farewell,* 12–17.

7. The Logic of Our Times

1. G. W. Stonier, "Current Literature: Books in General," *New Statesman and Nation,* 16 Aug. 1941; Lord David Cecil, "The Author in a Suffering World: War's Impact on Literature: Art in a World of Raids and Time-Bombs," *Times Literary Supplement,* 11 Jan. 1941; [Brian Allwood], "The Present Condition of Poetry," 2 Feb. 1940, TC 73/1/G, M-OA; Robert Hewison, *Under Siege: Literary Life in London, 1939–45* (1977; London, 1988), 108; Stephen Spender, "The Creative Imagi-

nation in the World Today," *Folios of New Writing* 2 (autumn 1940): 145; C. Day Lewis, "Where Are the War Poets?" *Penguin New Writing* 3 (Feb. 1941): 114.

2. Tom Harrisson, "War Books," *Horizon* 4 (Dec. 1941): 420–422.

3. Michell Raper, "Camp 21," BBC script, recorded 20 June 1973, Michell Raper papers, 86/25/1, IWM; Angus Calder, *The People's War: Britain, 1939–45* (London, 1969), 249; *Statistical Digest of the War: Prepared in the Central Statistical Office* (London, 1951), 9.

4. "Editorial," *The Double Eight: or, The Changi Gunner* 1, no. 4 (n.d.), T. H. Toomey papers, 97/6/1, IWM; Jack Aistrop to Lehmann, [Apr. 1941?], JLP.

5. Although some well-known authors did their war service *as* authors—H. E. Bates wrote short stories under the name "Flying Officer X" for the Air Ministry—the wartime administration did not provide such openings for novices.

6. Bonamy Dobrée to Tom Harrisson, 9 June 1942, and "Royal Navy War Libraries: Small Ships" (1942), TC 20/7/A, M-OA; Ronald Hope, "Further Education for Merchant Seafarers—I," *Further Education* 1 (Dec. 1947): 198–199. For prison camps, see P. A. Belton, diary, Belton papers, 95/17/1, IWM; D. J. Chenery, diary, Chenery papers, 85/53/1, IWM; J. Innes, diary, 5 July 1943, Innes papers, 88/62/1, IWM.

7. Steven Fielding, Peter Thompson, and Nick Tiratsoo, *"England Arise!" The Labour Party and Popular Politics in the 1940s* (Manchester, 1995), 29; anon., "Reading in the Forces," n.d., TC 20/7/A, MO-A (Chase, Tressell, Glasgow).

8. G. T. Harris, diary, 22 Apr. 1940, G. T. Harris papers, 86/91/1, IWM.

9. Ibid., 21 Feb. 1940, 11 July 1940, 4 June 1940.

10. Jack Common, "The Parson's Tale," [1920s], Common papers, packet 14, RLUN: "The old church of ____ was wrapt in the warm darkness of a September night,—a soft, mellow darkness rich with the scent of cornfields and unnumbered blossoms,—a darkness which had no

touch of chill or of fear but which was peaceful and comforting[,] which a God might breathe & be glad."

11. Harris, diary, 30 Mar. 1940, 13 Mar. 1940, 17 Feb. 1940, 13 Mar. 1940, 3 Apr. 1940, 21 Apr. 1940, 2 June 1940.

12. Ibid., 27 Mar. 1940, 12 Apr. 1940, 25 Oct. 1941, 14 Oct. 1941, 17 Nov. 1941, 18 Nov. 1941.

13. Ibid., 4 May 1940; George Unwin, reader's report on "John Setter's Shoes" by G. T. Harris, 8 July 1955, AUA, AURR 1/3/55.

14. Harris, diary, 2 July 1940, 5 July 1940, 18 Nov. 1941, 26 Nov. 1941, 21 Jan. 1942.

15. Ibid., 19 Sept. 1941, 12 Apr. 1940 (also 29 Mar. 1940), 2 July 1940, 23 Sept. 1940, 25 May 1940. Compare Bruce Bain, "An Airman's Letter," in Peter Ratazzi, ed., *Khaki and Blue: The Younger Writers in Battledress* (Slough, [1944]), 33.

16. Harris, diary, 24 Sept. 1941, 4 Oct. 1941, 30 Oct. 1941, 1 Nov. 1941, 24 Sept. 1941, 22 Nov. 1941. The critic's name is scribbled out, but the initial letter B and the shape of the name make it clear that it is not Woodley.

17. Hewison, *Under Siege,* 134; "These Are the Writers," in Reginald Moore, ed., *Modern Reading,* no. 5 (London, n.d.), 132 (Joysmith); see also Bain, "Airman's Letter," 33.

18. Alun Lewis to Lehmann, 10 Jan. 1942, 10 Mar. [19??], , 10 Jan. 1942, 2 Jan. 1941, JLP.

19. J. Maclaren-Ross, "Second Lieutenant Lewis: A Memoir," in *Memoirs of the Forties* (London, 1965), 233; Aistrop to Lehmann, [late 1946 or early 1947?]; Aistrop to Lehmann, [Apr. 1941?], JLP.

20. Aistrop to Lehmann, [late 1946 or early 1947?], JLP; T. H. Hawkins and L. J. F. Brimble, *Adult Education: The Record of the British Army* (London, 1947), 207–211; Philip Unwin to Reginald Moore, 16 Apr. 1943, AUA, AUC 172/13; Hope, "Further Education for Merchant Seafarers—I," 197–199; Ronald Hope, "Further Education for Merchant Seafarers—II," *Further Education* 1 (Jan. 1948): 222–224.

21. Victor Selwyn and "J. Ch.," preface to Victor Selwyn et al., eds.,

Return to Oasis: War Poems and Reflections from the Middle East, 1940–1946 (London, 1980), xviii.

22. "Circle Notes and News," *Gunfire* 1 (June 1944): 1; "Personalities," *Gunfire* 1 (July 1944): 6; "Introducing . . . Some New Members," ibid., 8 (Kirkham); NWC min., 4 Dec. 1943, SX88/1/1, TWAS; *Writer,* June 1949, 37–39; L. T. Mutum, "Stop Press News," *Gunfire* 3 (Apr. 1946): 11 (quotation). The Forces Writer Circle's newsletter and magazine, *Gunfire,* began in 1944 and was duplicated for most of its wartime issues; later numbers were printed. The only publicly available run seems to be the one in the Imperial War Museum.

23. "A-B-C of Circle Services," *Gunfire* 2 (Mar. 1945): 6–7; "Circle Poetry Group—An Invitation," *Gunfire* 2 (Jan.–Feb. 1945): 7; Norman Benjafield, "The Circle Drama Group," ibid., 4; *FWCNB,* no. 1 (Dec. 1943): 1; ibid., no. 4 (Mar. 1944): 1, 2. Derek Maggs was active in both the Forces Writer Circle and the British Amateur Press Association: see *Midnight Oil* 8 (spring 1946): back cover; P. L. H. Smith, "Circle Markets Bureau," *Gunfire* 1 (May 1944): 10.

24. "News in Brief," *Gunfire* 2 (Dec. 1945): 4; *FWCNB,* no. 1 (Dec. 1943): 2; ibid., no. 2 (Jan. 1944): 2; for FWC members who had belonged to writers' circles in peacetime, see "Introducing . . . Some New Members," *Gunfire* 1 (July 1944): 8; "Personalities," *Gunfire* 1 (Nov. 1944): 4; *FWCNB,* no. 4 (Mar. 1944): 1; HAC min., 19 Jan. 1948, Soc. 10/2; and, generally, HAC minute book 1926–1939, Soc. 10/1, WYASC.

25. *FWCNB,* no. 1 (Dec. 1943): 1; "Is That So?" *Gunfire* 3 (Jan. 1946): 4; *FWCNB,* no. 4 (Mar. 1944): 2; Kenneth MacNichol, *Twelve Lectures on the Technique of Fiction Writing* (London, n.d. [based on a course given in winter 1925–1926]), 22; "Commentary," *Gunfire* 1 (July 1944): 7; Harold A. Albert, "Writing Success Is a Routine," *Gunfire* 1 (Nov. 1944): 3 (quoting MacNichol); C. F[arley], "'You Need Not Be Grand,'" *Gunfire* 3 (June 1946): 9; P. D. Smith, "This Writing Business," *Gunfire* 3 (Apr. 1946): 4–5 (genius).

26. *Gunfire* 3 (Feb. 1946): 7 ("Amelia Ketchup"); *Benghazi Forum: First Tuturano Edition* 1, no. 3 (n.d.): [1], and "Our Contributors,"

Benghazi Forum 1, no. 4 (4 May 1943): [1], both in *The Benghazi Forum: Tuturano Times: Reproductions from Prisoners' of War Newspapers: Published in Benghazi Camp and Camp 85 Italy* (Cape Town, n.d.); Jim Wiffen, "A Junior Reporter," *Snips,* no. 3 (30 Apr. [1944]): 49; "Molly and I: Episode IV," *Snips,* no. 8 (4 June 1944): 98–99; D. V. Norton, "The Open Road," *Snips,* no. 7 (28 May 1944): 76, F. W. Daniels papers, P. 357, IWM; *FWCNB,* no. 4 (Mar. 1944): 2; "Some New Members," *Gunfire* 1, no. 6 (May 1944): 5; Leslie W. Wilson, "Career Building," *Further Education* 1 (Dec. 1947): 215.

27. Hawkins and Brimble, *Adult Education,* 168; "Editorial," *Tost Times and Advertiser,* no. 2 (16 June 1941): 1, Misc. 15, Item 2369, IWM. Magazines probably carried less topical material than wall newspapers. I cite these items as if they were published magazines, but I also provide classification data from the archive that holds them, the Imperial War Museum.

28. "Editorial," *Camp Chronicle,* no. 3. (5 Sept. 1942): 1, Dorothy Shelagh Brown papers, DSB 2/1–2/6, 82/24/1 (P), IWM; F. W. Daniels, "Round Trip," 1945, pp. 128–129 (toilet paper), 133–134 (Eisleben magazines), Daniels papers, PP/MCR/159, IWM; "Camp Comment," *Snips,* no. 34 (3 Dec. 1944): 365. All references to *Snips* are to copies in the Daniels papers, P. 357, IWM.

29. Untitled editorial for Mar. 1944 issue of Kobe camp magazine, R. M. M. King, diary and notebook, p. 88, King papers, 82/24/1, IWM; Hawkins and Brimble, *Adult Education,* 168; *Snips,* no. 17 (6 Aug. 1944): 175 (hyperbole).

30. Leslie Joseph, "Change of Heart," in Ratazzi, *Khaki and Blue,* 23–25; see also John Atkins, "Letters to a Son," in Jack Aistrop and Reginald Moore, eds., *Bugle Blast: An Anthology from the Services: Second Series* (London, 1944).

31. Noel A. Jones, "Raiders Passed" and "The Telegram," in Smith, *Farewell Khaki and Blue,* 13, 25; Jack Aistrop, "The Road," in Aistrop and Moore, *Bugle Blast,* 2nd ser., 93; Alan Wykes, "The Enemies," ibid., 27–35. See also Pat Aspinall, "Accidental Death," in Ratazzi, *Khaki and Blue,* 47.

32. A. J. Willison, "At the Going Down of the Sun," in Smith, *Farewell Khaki and Blue,* 48–50. Another story with a twist is John Bayliss, "The House," in Peter Ratazzi, ed., *Khaki and Blue: Writing in Battledress: New Series* (London, n.d.), 19–21.

33. "R. R.," "The Brothers," *Gunfire* 1 (Dec. 1944): 13–14; John Garrity, "Perfect Crime," *Gunfire* 1 (Aug. 1944): 5–6; "By Thriller-writers: Murder Will Out," *Good to Read: Stories out of Lilliput Magazine,* no. 1 (Aug. 1937): 90–91. For Garrity's background, see *FWCNB,* no. 4 (Mar. 1944): 2.

34. "Two Ghouls," "Rendezvous Macabre," *Snips,* no. 12 (2 July 1944): 137; "Fingers and Toes," ibid., 128–129; "The Fair Invalid," *Snips,* no. 13 (16 July 1944): 167–169; Snips, "Matrimonial Bureau," ibid., 153–154.

35. Cyril Baddock, "Thou Shalt Not," *Snips,* no. 12 (2 July 1944): 127. A similar trick is played in "Interlude," *Red Tape and Stencil Wax: The Only Unofficial Organ of Its Kind Published in Hongkong* 1 (n.d.): 7, Misc. 223, Item 3205, IWM.

36. Soothsayer, "Phantom Brother," *Snips,* no. 30 (5 Nov. 1944): 314, 317; Pat Sanson, "An Air Adventure," *Snips,* no. 24 (24 Sept. 1944): 251–252; "The Fair Invalid," *Snips,* no. 13 (16 July 1944): 167–169.

37. "Household Hints," *Camp Chronicle,* no. 3 (5 Sept. 1942): 6, Brown papers.

38. King, diary and notebook, pp. 82–83 (early 1944), King papers, 82/24/1; "A Description of the International Steeplechase: Run in Greece. 1941" (Aug. 1942), transcribed in B. F. S. Jewell, scrapbook, Misc. 46, Item 774, IWM (races); *Snips,* no. 8 (4 June 1944): 79 (USSR); Politicus, "The Price of Civilization," *Snips,* no. 7 (28 May 1944): 70.

39. E. C. Beer, "Early Riser," *Snips,* no. 25 (1 Oct. 1944): 266.

40. E. C. Beer, "Glorious Devon," *Snips,* no. 19 (20 Aug. 1944): 201; H. J. Freeborn, "Three Dorset Towns," *Snips,* no. 7 (28 May 1944): 78; R. V., "A Camp Coach Holiday," and M. H. C., "The Green Roads of England," *The Newsphere* 1, no. 2 (5 Sept. 1945): 5, Misc. Box 13, Item 281, IWM.

41. "The River," *The Newsphere* 1, no. 2 (5 Sept. 1945): 4.

42. Martin J. Wiener, *English Culture and the Decline of the Industrial Spirit, 1850–1980* (Cambridge, 1981); Peter Mandler, "Against 'Englishness': English Culture and the Limits to Rural Nostalgia, 1850–1940," *Transactions of the Royal Historical Society* 6th ser., 7 (1997): 170. See also John Baxendale, "'I Had Seen a Lot of Englands': J. B. Priestley, Englishness and the People," *History Workshop Journal,* no. 51 (spring 2001): 88–89.

43. See Mandler, "Against 'Englishness,'" 172–172. Contrast Angus Calder, *The Myth of the Blitz* (London, 1991), ch. 9.

44. Peter Mandler, "The Problem with Cultural History," *Cultural and Social History* 1 (Jan. 2004): 105–106; "Paradise Regained," *Snips,* no. 13 (16 July 1944): 152; King, diary and notebook, frontispiece, King papers, 82/24/1. Also see R. Willoughby, "A Prayer," transcribed in Belton, diary.

45. Steven Seidenberg, Maurice Sellar, and Lou Jones, *You Must Remember This: Songs at the Heart of the War* (London, 1995), 29; John Baxendale, "'You and I—All of Us Ordinary People': Renegotiating 'Britishness' in Wartime," in Nick Hayes and Jeff Hill, eds., *"Millions like Us"? British Culture in the Second World War* (Liverpool, 1999), 295; Cyril Beer, "Thinking of Home," *Snips,* no. 9 (11 June 1944): 100; "Stroller," "Country Ways," *Snips,* no. 8 (4 June 1944): 84.

46. Baxendale, "You and I," 296; Wiener, *English Culture,* 41.

47. Not just England: see A. McGregor, "Britons after All," clipping from *The Camp,* n.d., Jewell, scrapbook.

48. A. Rickman, "Hometown," *Snips,* no. 13 (16 July 1944): 146; editorial, *Snips,* no. 32 (19 Nov. 1944): 323. See also the appreciative recollection of a northern city in a short story submitted to the Changi Literary Society: Denis Pethebridge, "Three Cigarettes," n.d., Denis Pethebridge papers, IWM.

49. Hewison, *Under Siege,* 108–113 and chs. 5–6.

50. [Brian Allwood], "The Present Condition of Poetry," 2 Mar. 1940, TC 73/1/G, M-OA; [Gay S. Taylor], notes on interviews with booksellers, Oct. 1944, TC 73/1/C. On Friedmann see Derek Stanford, *Inside the Forties: Literary Memoirs, 1937–1957* (London, 1977), 66.

51. Taylor, "Popularity of Poetry: Editor: *Poetry Review*," Oct. 1944, TC 73/1/C; Michael Shelden, *Friends of Promise: Cyril Connolly and the World of Horizon* (London, 1989), 91; [Connolly], "Comment," *Horizon* 1 (June 1940): 389. On the Poetry Society see Muriel Spark, *Curriculum Vitae: Autobiography* (London, 1992), 165–184. Spark became secretary of the Poetry Society and the editor of *Poetry Review* in 1947. She was evidently appointed in the belief that, as a young woman, she could easily be manipulated by the society's grandees. As many traditionalist members found to their chagrin, this belief was not well founded.

52. Hewison, *Under Siege,* 109 (Heath-Stubbs); John Lehmann, "Barrack-room Writers" (radio script for transmission on 16 Oct. 1946), p. 2, JLP; R. M. M. King, diary, p. 23 (ca. 1944), 82/24/1; B. F. S. Jewell, "In Memory of Our Comrades Who Fell in Greece," July 1942, Jewell, scrapbook; Rupert Brooke, "1914: V. The Soldier" and "The Great Lover," in *The Poetical Works of Rupert Brooke,* ed. Geoffrey Keynes (1946; London, 1970), 23, 31; James R. Stannage, "War Prisoner," *Seven* 3, no. 3 (Oct.–Dec. 1942): 60; R. Willoughby, "A Prayer," in Belton, diary, n.d. Willoughby was a POW; Stannage may have been only a figurative "war prisoner," since he was able to get his poem to a London-based magazine.

53. Denis Saunders, Victor Selwyn, and David Burk, "In the Beginning" in Selwyn et al., *Return to Oasis,* 3 (reprint of the preface to the original *Oasis* in 1943); John Hackett, foreword to Victor Selwyn et al., eds., *More Poems of the Second World War: The Oasis Selection* (London, 1989), ix.

54. Innes, diary, 15 Feb. 1944; Charles William Waide, "All This and Basrah Too" (1942), pp. 64 (Karachi), 6–7 ("London Town"), Waide papers, 95/3/1, IWM.

55. Chenery, diary, 1 May 1942.

56. Bernard Bergonzi, *Wartime and Aftermath: English Literature and Its Background, 1939–60* (Oxford, 1993), 15 (biblical language); Baxendale, "You and I," 307.

57. Gordon Paul Charkin, "'Requiem for a Wren'—1943," in *An Anthology of War Poems: Britain at War* (Amesbury, 1993), unpaginated;

copy in Gordon Paul Charkin papers, 92/27/1, IWM; Frank Austin, "London Autumn 1940," Oct. 1942, transcribed in Belton, diary; D. J. Chenery, "Middlesboro' '41," n.d., Chenery papers, 85/53/1.

58. G. S. Fraser, "On War Poetry and *Oasis,*" in Selwyn et al., *Return to Oasis,* xxxi; H. G. Moorley, "I Remember," [1941–1942], A. L. Phillips, scrapbook, Kroger H3, Misc. 98, Item 1508, IWM; Mike Dougland, "To My Comrades in Arms," 1942, in Jewell, scrapbook, and in R. L. Bowman, scrapbook, Bowman papers, 98/5/1, IWM.

59. T. Connell, scrapbook, p. 14, Connell papers, 76/87/1, IWM; Denis Pethebridge papers (unclassified at time of consultation), IWM.

60. Sidney Stainthorp, "To an Unseen Child" (1943), in Selwyn et al., *Return to Oasis,* 193.

61. Maurice Drovin, "Idle Storks," clipping from *The Camp,* 23 Aug. 1942, Jewell, scrapbook; R. G. Haydon, "Rhymes," Haydon papers, P. 469, IWM; Anon., "Leave, Compassionate, Children, Production, for the use of" (1945), in Selwyn et al., *Return to Oasis,* 201. This last poem was one of a number "circulated hand to hand in Cairo and the Desert" (*Return to Oasis,* 198n). The papers of Major J. E. Porter, 91/16/1, IWM, include a copy of this poem, attributing it to a Major Mather.

62. R. G. Haydon, "Xmas Day in the Desert," Haydon papers, P. 469 (lampooning army life); W. Campbell, "An Autograph Album," 6 Dec. 1941, Phillips, scrapbook.

63. Other examples: "May the Garden of your days / Grow in fragrance with the years"; "But it's best of all to live your span, / And be a man." One patient transcribed part of Polonius's "To thine own self be true" speech, the pinnacle of pompous sententiousness. Elsie Dufton, autograph books, 1941–1942, Misc. 124, Item 1939, IWM.

64. Buday Archive, BC 23, Word and Image Department, Victoria and Albert Museum.

65. Charles William Waide, "Birthday Greetings to Jack Gillard," 2 Apr. 1942, Waide papers, 95/3/1.

66. Valentine Cunningham, *British Writers of the Thirties* (Oxford, 1988), 297; *With a Poem in My Pocket: The Autobiography of Patience Strong* (London, 1981), 143–151 (sales figures); Patience Strong, "Point

of View," *The Quiet Hour* (1938; London, 1944), 35; Strong, *Quiet Corner* (New York, 1937); "Keep on Hoping," *Camp Chronicle,* no. 3 (5 Sept. 1942): 3, Brown papers.

67. I have not been able to discover whether cards with general statements of amity or love, not occasion-specific, were available in Britain in the 1940s.

8. Popular Writing after the War

1. See Ross McKibbin, *Classes and Cultures: England, 1918–1951* (Oxford, 1998), 486.

2. Leslie W. Wilson, "Career Building," *Further Education* 1 (Dec. 1947): 215 ("closed profession"); George Greenfield, *Scribblers for Bread: Aspects of the English Novel since 1945* (London, 1989), 29; Reginald Pound, *Mirror of the Century: The Strand Magazine, 1891–1950* (South Brunswick, NJ, 1966), 150, 190–194; Richard Hoggart, *The Uses of Literacy: Aspects of Working-Class Life, with Special References to Publications and Entertainments* (London, 1957), 274; Thomas William Heyck, "Freelance Writers and the Changing Terrain of Intellectual Life in Britain, 1880–1980," *Albion* 34 (fall 2002): 256 (pay rates).

3. Nicola Bennett, *Speaking Volumes: A History of the Cheltenham Festival of Literature* (Stroud, 1999), 15 (brains trusts); Leeds Writers' Circle, syllabi for 1950 and 1951, Leeds Writers' Circle papers, Acc. 3220, WYASL; "Notes and Circle News," *Writer,* Apr. 1949, 34; Kenneth Grenville Myer to Janet Quigley, 9 Apr. 1951, Myer contributor file 1, WAC (*Stump the Storyteller*); *Halifax Courier and Guardian,* 14 Nov. 1934; Maureen Duffy, *A Thousand Capricious Chances: A History of the Methuen List, 1889–1989* (London, 1989), 106 (Lees).

4. This paragraph is based on Asa Briggs, *The History of Broadcasting in the United Kingdom,* vol. 4: *Sound and Vision* (Oxford, 1979), pt. 2, chs. 2–3.

5. HAC min., 15 Nov. 1955, Misc. 213/1, WYASC; NWC min., 7 June 1949, 6 Apr. 1948, SX88/1/2, TWAS.

6. According to a later document, a 15-minute short story was

2,100–2,300 words, which means that an average of 147 words could be read in a minute. James Langham to P. H. Newby, 24 May 1956, SSB, file 6, R51/978/1.

7. M. T. Candler, "Fees for Specially Written Short Stories Broadcast in Home Programmes," 4 June 1947, SSB, file 4, R51/553/6 (new system); E. H. Mills to Dorothy Ross, 25 Oct. 1946, Bertha Lonsdale Copyright file 1 (North Region); Langham to Newby, 24 May 1956 (standard length); B. H. Alexander to Talks Organiser, Third Programme, [1955 or 1956], SSB, file 6, R51/978/1 (three grades); Newby to Alexander, 3 Feb. 1956, SSB, file 6, R51/978/1, WAC (Golding); Denys Val Baker, *Adventures before Fifty* (London, 1969), 47.

8. Jean LeRoy, *Sell Them a Story: Advice on the Writing and Marketing of Short Stories* (London, 1954), 119; *WAYB 1954,* 115, 57.

9. Briggs, *Sound and Vision,* 696 (especially in the North); NWC min., 3 Feb. 1948, SX88/1/2; Val Gielgud to M. G. Farqhuarson, 2 Apr. 1953, Drama Policy, file 5B, R19/280/7, WAC (informing contributors); NWC min., 6 Apr. 1948, SX88/1/2; HAC min., 16 Mar. 1954, Misc. 213/1; "Radio Plays," unidentified clipping, [ca. 1958–1959], Bradford Writers' Circle scrapbook, 7D95/1, WYASB.

10. "Radio Plays," Bradford Writers' Circle scrapbook; Val Gielgud to Ian Jacob, 5 June 1953; Lindsay Wellington to Jacob, 23 July 1953 (89 accepted); Jacob to Wellington, 27 July 1953 ("good figure"), Drama Policy, file 5B, R19/280/7; Briggs, *Sound and Vision,* 697 (Huxley); Charles LeFeaux to Farqhuarson, 26 Jan. 1953 ("myth"); D. Singer to Director of Home Service Broadcasting, 17 June 1953 (outside check); A. H. L. Mills to LeFeaux, 1 July 1953; Wellington to Director-General, 11 Mar. 1954, Drama Policy, file 5B, R19/280/7 (end of experiment).

11. Gielgud to Farqhuarson, 2 Apr. 1953, Drama Policy, file 5B, R19/280/7; James Langham, circular letter, n.d., SSB, file 6, R51/978/1; N. G. Luker to Director of Talks, 8 Aug. 1947, SSB, file 4, R51/553/6 (less feedback); B. C. Horton to Director of Talks, 14 Oct. 1947, SSB, file 4, R51/553/6; Mercy MacKenzie to N. F. Eyers, SSB, file 5B, R51/553/8; Langham to Elizabeth Rowley, 7 Aug. 1957, SSB, file 6,

R51/978/1; N. G. Luker to Assistant Director, Talks, and Administrative and Establishment Officer (Talks), 15 Oct. 1947, SSB, file 4, R51/553/6 (obligations); Controller, Talks, to Director of the Spoken Word, 22 Apr. 1953, SSB, file 5B, R51/553/8 (contracting out).

12. For short stories on the Third and Home, see Luker to Director of Talks, 20 Sept. 1946; Hilton Brown to James Langham, 6 Sept. 1945, SSB, file 3, R51/553/5; "Stories Old and New," [1946], SSB, file 4, R51/553/6.

13. David Lloyd James to Controller, Light Programme, 11 Apr. 1949, and [Lloyd James?], "Light Programme Morning Story," [Mar.–Apr. 1949], SSB, file 5A, R51/553/7; Hilton Brown, "The Broadcast Short Story," 15 Sept. 1945, SSB, file 3, R51/553/5; NWC min., 3 Feb. 1948, SX88/1/2; NWC min., 4 Sept. 1945, SX88/1/1 (twists); Chief Assistant, Talks, to Regional Programme Heads, 1 June 1953, SSB, file 5B, R51/553/8 (1952 or 1953 run).

14. T. W. Chalmers to Regional Programme Directors, 5 Dec. 1946, SSB, file 3, R51/553/5; Newby to Regional Programming Heads, 16 Aug. 1957, SSB, file 6, R51/978/1 (regions' stories broadcast nationally); H. Rooney Pelletier to Langham, 22 Feb. 1955, SSB, file 6, R51/978/1 ("elbow room"); Chalmers to Regional Programme Directors, 5 Dec. 1946, SSB, file 3, R51/553/5; Chief Assistant, Talks, to Regional Programme Heads, 1 June 1953, SSB, file 5B, R51/553/8 (limits of regionalism); Pelletier to Controller, Light Programme, 18 Jan. 1955, SSB, file 6, R51/978/1 ("more local flavour"); Paul Humphreys to Langham, 31 Aug. 1953, SSB, file 5B, R51/553/8 (direct to London); Robert Stead to Head of General Overseas Programmes, 23 Apr. 1948, SSB, file 4, R51/553/6; Edward Wilkinson to Chief Producer, Talks, 13 Feb. 1950, SSB, file 5A, R51/553/7 (regional producers as advocates).

15. HAC min., 23 Sept. 1958, Misc. 213/1; Jessie Gray to Sir, 24 Jan. 1958, Brian Blake to Gray, 9 Nov. 1959, Blake to Gray, 22 Feb. 1960, Geoffrey B. Wheeler to Gray, 8 Nov. 1960 (quotation), Jessie Gray contributor file 1, N18/2,737/1, WAC; Chief Assistant, Talks, to Regional Programme Heads, 1 June 1953, SSB, file 5B, R51/553/8.

16. HAC min., 28 July 1964, 23 Nov. 1965, 27 Sept. 1966, 25 Feb. 1969, Misc. 213/1.

17. "Notes and Circle News," *Writer,* Apr. 1949, 35; HAC min., 26 Nov. 1963, Misc. 213/1 (magazine programs); Denness Roylance to D. L. Ross, 23 June 1953, Bertha Lonsdale Copyright file 2, WAC (present with recording car); Bob Gregson, "Producer's Comments," 25 July 1950, untitled file on Lonsdale, N18/3,262/1, WAC (voice); HAC min., 15 Nov. 1958, 28 Feb. 1967, Misc. 213/1 (reading onto tape).

18. Stan Barstow, *In My Own Good Time* (Otley, 2001), 92–93 (Daniels and Bradley); Vivian Daniels to Langham, 17 Sept. 1954, SSB, file 5c, R51/553/9; Christine Orr to Hilton Brown, [Dec. 1943], SSB, file 3, R51/553/5 (Duthie); Keith Waterhouse, *Streets Ahead: Life after City Lights* (London, 1995), 16 (Bradley); Charles Brewer to Controller, Light Programme, 21 Jan. 1949; Edward Wilkinson to Chief Producer, Talks, 13 Feb. 1950, SSB, file 5A, R51/553/7; Donald Stephenson to Head of North Regional Programmes, 20 Apr. 1948; Robert Stead to Stephenson, 23 Apr. 1948, SSB, file 4, R51/553/6 (Chaplin); Sid Chaplin Copyright file 1; Chaplin television drama writer's file, T48/152/1, WAC.

19. Leslie Halward, address to Birmingham Writers' Group, 13 Oct. [late 1960s], Leslie Halward papers, MS 1293/106, BCA ("MY working class"); Halward, Talks personal file 1, WAC (struggling); Newby to Fred Urquhart, 5 Oct. 1949, Fred Urquhart Talks personal file 1, WAC; Halward, "Radio Drama," address to Writers' Summer School, Swanwick, 22 Aug. [1957], Halward papers, MS 1293/106 ("dialogue"); Victor Menzies to William Ash, 14 Apr. 1976, Halward scriptwriter file 3, RCONT 12, WAC (television); Halward to Douglas Clevedon, 28 Oct. 1963, Halward scriptwriter file 2 (1930s); Halward, "Boom Tiddly Batch Cake" (recorded 4 Dec. 1957), Halward papers, MS1293/3.

20. Stefan Collini, "Critical Minds: Raymond Williams and Richard Hoggart," in *English Pasts: Essays in History and Culture* (Oxford, 1999), 227.

21. Harold Perkin, *The Rise of Professional Society: England since 1880* (London, 1989), 272.

22. John Braine, diary, 22 May 1952, 15 Apr. 1952, 10 Aug. 1952, Braine/D2; 8 Sept. 1953, 30 Sept. 1953, Braine/D3, John Braine papers, Brotherton.

23. Braine, diary [ca. 1954], Braine/N1, Brotherton. Compare the passage quoted in Jonathan Rose, *The Intellectual Life of the British Working Classes* (New Haven, 2001), 442.

24. Braine, diary, 10 Sept. 1953, Braine/D3; Braine, "S. Shields & Cramlington," notes for a talk, [ca. 1958], p. 30, Braine/L1, Brotherton ("spare time"). Braine used Woolf's phrase on an earlier occasion too: "What I must do is sort myself out as a writer . . . I need London and I need a room of my own." Braine, diary, 6 Apr. 1950, 1D75/21/2, WYASB.

25. Alan Sillitoe, "The Long Piece," in *Mountains and Caverns: Selected Essays* (London, 1975), 24–27, 29, 36; Harry Ritchie, *Success Stories: Literature and the Media in England, 1950–1959* (London, 1988), 185–186.

26. Ronald Goldman, ed., *Breakthrough: Autobiographical Accounts of the Education of Some Socially Disadvantaged Children* (London, 1968), 178, 187; Wesker to John Lehmann, 21 June 1954, JLP; Arnold Wesker, *As Much as I Dare: An Autobiography (1932–1959)* (London, 1994), 319, 473–484, ch. 22, 465, 494, 498–501.

27. On Centre 42 see Stuart Laing, *Representations of Working-Class Life, 1957–1964* (Basingstoke, 1986), 101, 102–108.

28. Clive Barker, report and recommendations on policy for Centre 42, 26 Aug. 1961, Wesker papers, 147/2, HRC; Arnold Wesker, "Two Snarling Heads" (1960), in *Fears of Fragmentation* (London, 1970), 29; Henry Anderson, Gerald Dillon, Stanley Pinker, Ken Turner, and Sally Anderson, "Resolution 42: A Declaration on the Visual Arts from the First Group" [1961]; Wesker and Bill Holsworth, circular letter to union officials, [probably May 1960], Wesker papers, 136/9. A parallel with the 1930s is made in "Report on Meeting Held on 28th May 1961 at 2 Soho Square, London W.1 at 11.30 A.M.," Wesker papers, 147/1.

29. Compare Robert Hewison, *Too Much: Art and Society in the Sixties, 1960–75* (London, 1986), 19.

30. Laing, *Representations,* 64.

31. Ritchie, *Success Stories,* 189.

32. M. W., "*Joe for King* by John Braine," 9 Oct. 1955, David Higham archive, 183/38, HRC; John Braine to J. B. Priestley, 19 Nov. 1962, J. B. Priestley papers, HRC.

33. Barstow, *My Own Good Time,* 83; Waterhouse, *Streets Ahead,* 92–93, 105.

34. Laing, *Representations,* 80.

35. Sillitoe, "Long Piece," 34, 35–38.

36. John Lehmann, "Foreword," *London Magazine* 2 (Dec. 1955): 11, 13; Laing, *Representations,* 59.

37. Stephen Brooke, "Gender and Working Class Identity in Britain during the 1950s," *Journal of Social History* 34 (summer 2001): 773.

38. Barstow, *My Own Good Time,* 62; Brian Aldiss, *Bury My Heart at W. H. Smith's: A Writing Life* (London, 1990), 40, 42–43, 62–63 (science fiction); Dan Morgan, "Science Fiction Is down to Earth!" *Writer,* Oct. 1954, 20–21; Peter Bailey, "Jazz at the Spirella: Coming of Age in Coventry in the 1950s," in Becky Conekin, Frank Mort, and Chris Waters, eds., *Moments of Modernity: Reconstructing Britain, 1945–1964* (London, 1999), esp. 26.

39. *New Statesman,* 28 Feb. 1959, quoted in Laing, *Representations,* 91 (Wesker); Braine, "S. Shields & Cramlington," pp. 42–44, Braine/L1; Braine, "The New English Novelists," [ca. 1961], Braine/D5; Braine, "The Novelist & the Engine Driver," notes for a talk, [ca. 1958], pp. 15–16, Braine/L2; Braine to Priestley, 28 May 1962, Priestley papers.

40. Phyllis Bentley, *"O Dreams, O Destinations": An Autobiography* (London, 1962), 267; Braine, diary, 11 Apr. 1952, Braine/D2; Braine to Bentley, 10 Aug. 1953, Phyllis Bentley papers, PB/C: 56/1, WYASC; V. M. L. Scott, "A Proletarian Writer," *London Mercury* 34 (May 1936): 77; Philip O'Connor, "People's Writing," *Seven* 2 (Mar. 1941): 44.

41. Leslie Halward, "Radio Drama," address to summer school, Swanwick, 22 Aug. [1957], Halward papers, MS 1293/106; C. R.

Plomer-Roberts, "Leslie Halward," *BWG Quarterly,* no. 129 (summer 1976), in Halward papers, MS 1293/108; Geoffrey Trease to Tony Halward, 9 June 1976, Halward papers, MS 1293/108.

42. *Writer,* Jan. 1954, 29; Morgan, "Science Fiction," 21; Keith Waterhouse, "Take My Tip," *Writer,* Dec. 1951, 7, Jan. 1952, 22, Feb. 1952, 10, Apr. 1952, 30. The tips are about using abbreviations to save time when writing, reusing self-addressed envelopes, and so on. See also Wesker, *As Much as I Dare,* 313.

43. HAC min., 21 June 1955, Misc. 213/1; Andrew Davies, personal communication, 30 May 2003; Andrew Davies, "Roberts, Robert (1905–1974)," in H. C. G. Matthew and Brian Harrison, eds., *Oxford Dictionary of National Biography* (Oxford, 2004).

44. Phyllis Bentley, diary, 18 Oct. 1955, 16 Oct. 1956, Bentley papers, PB/C: 35, 36; HAC min., 16 Oct. 1956, Misc. 213/1; Bentley, *"O Dreams,"* 264.

45. Barstow, *My Own Good Time,* 60, 62.

46. Braine, diary, 14 Sept. 1953, Braine/D3; Braine to Priestley, 19 Sept. 1962, Priestley papers; "Work 16.6.50 (Finished & Projected)," Braine/D1; HAC min., 22 Feb. 1966, Misc. 213/1; Braine, diary, 11 Feb. 1953, 1D75/21/8, WYASB ("always frightened"); Braine, diary, 18 Sept. 1953, 21 Sept. 1953, Braine/D3 (Salt); Braine, untitled story outline, [1950], 1D75/21/2, WYASB; *OED,* s.v. "Ruritania"; Billie Melman, *Women and the Popular Imagination in the Twenties: Flappers and Nymphs* (Basingstoke, 1988), 118 (Ruritania); Braine, diary, 8 Sept. 1953 (modernizing fairy stories), 5 Oct. 1953 (*Children's Hour*), Braine/D3.

47. Braine, diary [ca. 1954], Braine/N1 (writing for money); *Daily Herald,* 2 Jan. 1960 (addressing young writers); Braine, diary, 12 Apr. 1952, Braine/D2, 9 Feb. 1956, Braine/D3. Several years later, he told an audience that where "background" was concerned, "my rule has always been to write from experience." "How to Write a Novel," outline of talk, [1961?], Braine/D5.

48. Braine, diary, 16 July 1956, Braine/D3.

49. Syllabus for 1946–1947, Bradford English Society minute book,

39D85/1/5, WYASB; Braine, diary, 12 Apr. 1952, Braine/D2; Braine, "S. Shields & Cramlington," p. 19, Braine/L1 (Connolly).

50. "Writer Circles," *Writer,* Apr. 1947, 32–33; "Writer Circles," *Writer,* Feb. 1939, 134; "Directory of Writer Circles," *Writer,* Sept. 1953, 20–21; Edna Franklyn, "The Leeds Writers' Circle Annual Report, 1954," [Nov. 1954], Leeds Writers' Circle papers, Acc. 3220 ("group scheme").

51. "Directory of Writer Circles," *Writer,* Sept. 1953, 20–21.

52. F. Foley, letter, *Writer,* Nov. 1953, 42; Peggy Martyn-Clark, letter, *Writer,* Jan. 1954, 42–43; *Prose and Poetry from the Painted Room: By Members of the Oxford Writers' Circle* (Gloucester, 1957); *Telegraph and Argus* (Bradford), 10 June 1959; "Leeds Writers' Circle: List of Members," [ca. 1960], Leeds Writers' Circle papers, Acc. 3220; "Halifax Authors' Circle: List of Members: 1955/6," HAC minute book, Misc. 213/1; Lawrence Goldman, *Dons and Workers: Oxford and Adult Education since 1850* (Oxford, 1995), 258–259; University of Oxford Delegacy for Extra-Mural Studies, *Tutorial Classes Committee Report for the Year 1947–48: Tutorial Classes and Summer School* (Oxford, 1948), 4 ("Cinderella").

53. Oxford University Tutorial Classes Committee, "Annual Report for the Year 1947–8: B—Tutorial Class Reports," May 1948, p. 26, Oxford Department of Extension Studies papers, DES/RP/2/2/12, OUA. This file of literature tutorial reports for 1946–1953 includes tutors' reports on individual classes, which usually give a breakdown of the student body by sex and sometimes by occupation. It is not clear whether increasing female participation in evening classes in literature was part of a broader movement of middle-class women into artistic and cultural organizations, dramatically increasing the already significant female participation in amateur drama and opera noticeable in the interwar period. The subject suffers from the general thinness of the historical literature on the arts and cultural activity at the level of local participation and organization rather than central state patronage.

54. Janet Minihan, *The Nationalization of Culture: The Development of State Subsidies to the Arts in Great Britain* (New York, 1977),

242; Jim McGuigan, *Writers and the Arts Council* (London, 1981), 6, 117–118; Arts Council of Great Britain papers, ACGB/61/5, ACGB/61/6, AAD; Heyck, "Freelance Writers," 259 (poetry); L. A. Yaxley to Secretary of CEMA, 22 Dec. 1944, Arts Council papers, ACGB/EL3/39; Croydon Writers' Circle min., 23 May 1957, Acc. 493, CAS (overtures); Eric W. White, "The Writers' Club," 4 Aug. 1959; White to Harold J. Nash, 27 Aug. 1959, Arts Council papers, ACGB/62/42/141.

55. "Introducing . . . Circles' Choice," *Circles' Choice: The Quarterly Competitive Magazine of British Writers' Circles* 1 (May 1948): 1; "MacWilliams," letter, *Writer,* Apr. 1948, 41 (badges); Kenneth Grenville Myer, "All Join In," *Writer,* Feb. 1948, 5–6; Myer, "Writers' Conference," *Writer,* Apr. 1948, 5–6; "London Conference of Writer Circle Executives: Report on Proceedings at Institute of Journalists, London, Saturday, June 12th. 1948," Writers' Summer School minute book, 1948–1961, D5886/1/1, DRO; Hugh M. Stephens, "The Conference," *Writer,* July 1948, 11–13, 36; "Writer Circles Summer School 1951," in WSS minute book; *Writer,* July 1948, 4; NWC min., 18 Jan. 1949, 20 Sept. 1949, SX88/1/2; Constance White to Mike Brewer, 8 July 1998, WSS papers, D5886/10/12 (Martin); Nancy Martin, "Report on 1950 Writers' Summer School," 2 Sept. 1950, WSS minute book; WSS annual general meeting min., 7 July 1951 and 29 Aug. 1952, D5886/1/1; NWC min., 20 Sept. 1949, 5 Sept. 1950, 4 Sept. 1951, 2 Sept. 1952, SX88/1/2; 8 Sept. 1953, 7 Sept. 1954, 4 Sept. 1956, 3 Sept. 1957, 2 Sept. 1958, 1 Sept. 1959, SX88/1/3 (attendance).

56. NWC min., 4 Sept. 1951, 5 Sept. 1950, 2 Sept. 1952, SX88/1/2; 8 Sept. 1953, 7 Sept. 1954, 2 Sept. 1958, SX88/1/3; Croydon Writers' Circle min., 10 Feb. [1964], Acc. 493.

57. NWC min., 20 Sept. 1949, 4 Sept. 1951, 2 Sept. 1952, SX88/1/2; 7 Sept. 1954 ("social side"), 8 Sept. 1953, SX88/1/3; Croydon Writers' Circle min., 15 Jan. 1958, Acc. 493; Margaret Thomson Davis, *The Making of a Novelist* (London, 1982), 56; Victor Allan, "The Fellowship of Swanwick," *Writer,* Oct. 1949, 13–15 (fellowship); *Writer,* Aug. 1951, 42; *Writer,* Sept. 1951, 41–42 (holiday camp). For a sample

of the advice given, see the lectures from the 1949 summer school published in the *Writer,* Oct. 1949.

58. "No Federation after All: Last Year's Vote Is Reversed," *Writer,* Nov. 1949, 36; programs for conferences at Blackpool (1950), Buxton (1951), Bridlington (1952), and Bradford (1953), Bradford Writers' Circle scrapbook, 7D95/1, WYASB; NWC min., 5 Oct. 1948, 4 Oct. 1949, SX88/1/2.

59. Myer, "All Join In," 5; Myer, "Full Circle," *Writer,* Sept. 1948, 5–6 (pledging support); *Writer,* May 1951, 37 ("waste of time"), 44 (defending circles); WSS committee min., 13 Oct. 1951, D5886/1/1 (dispute with Myer).

60. The school advertised regularly on the back cover of the *Writer.*

61. Paul Vaughan, *Exciting Times in the Accounts Department* (London, 1995), 44–46.

62. Greenfield, *Scribblers for Bread,* 170 (Harris); Gale Pedrick to John McMillan, 3 Feb. 1948, Kenneth Grenville Myer Copyright file 1, WAC; Elizabeth Berridge, letter, *Writer,* Aug. 1948, 40–41; Fred Urquhart, "Why This Hoodoo on Short Stories?" ibid., 6–7; Urquhart, "The Problem of Time in Fiction," *Writer,* Mar. 1954, 6–8; Urquhart, "Don't Dance on Your Publisher's Grave," *Writer,* Dec. 1950, 4–6; letter, *Writer,* Sept. 1948, 41.

63. Kenneth Grenville Myer, "Book Reviews," *Writer,* May 1951, 38–39; Ludovic Kennedy, "Think of the 'Point'—Not the 'Plot,'" *Writer,* Dec. 1953, 6–8. On *First Reading* see Ritchie, *Success Stories,* 11–18; Kate Whitehead, *The Third Programme: A Literary History* (Oxford, 1989), 197–205.

64. The Society's institutional history is unclear. For some gleanings, see Christopher Hilliard, "A Writer's Capital: Aspiring Authors and the Uses of Creativity in Britain, 1920–1960" (Ph.D. diss., Harvard University, 2003), 383–384.

65. "Society of New Authors," *SONA: A General Interest Magazine Introducing New Names, New Talent,* no. 1 [1949]: 4; "Explanation," ibid., 5. Only members could be published in *SONA,* but membership did not guarantee publication.

66. "By New Authors," *SONA,* no. 2 (n.d.): 47; "Society of New Authors," ibid., back cover.

67. "Society of New Authors," *SONA,* no. 1 [1949]: 4; "Books for New Writers," ibid., 44–46.

68. "Books Reviewed," *SONA,* no. 2 (n.d.): 46–47.

69. "Background," *SONA,* no. 1 [1949]: 6; K. Alwyn, "Jackeroo," ibid., 11–15; Ismay McVeagh, "Night Call," ibid., 15–17.

70. Michael Hamburger, "Two Poems," ibid., 42; Michael Hamburger, *A Mug's Game: Intermittent Memoirs, 1924–1954* (Cheadle Hulme, 1973), 78–80, 88, 102; card index of items read on *First Reading,* WAC; Robert Hewison, *In Anger: British Culture in the Cold War* (New York, 1981), 100.

71. *Children and Their Primary Schools: A Report of the Central Advisory Council for Education (England),* vol. 1: *The Report* (London, 1967), para. 605. On advertising and design see D. L. LeMahieu, *A Culture for Democracy: Mass Communication and the Cultivated Mind in Britain between the Wars* (Oxford, 1988), 208–214; Michael T. Saler, *The Avant-Garde in Interwar England: Medieval Modernism and the London Underground* (New York, 1999).

72. Eric W. White, "The Writers' Club," 4 Aug. 1959, and anon., "Retirement, 1958," *Preface* 7, no. 2 (n.d.): unpaginated, in Arts Council papers, ACGB/62/42/141.

73. Priestley quoted in Ritchie, *Success Stories,* 10; Richard Findlater, *What Are Writers Worth?* (1963), rpt. in Peter Davison, Rolf Meyersohn, and Edward Shils, eds., *Literary Taste, Culture and Mass Communication* (Cambridge, 1978–1980), 10:292–297, 302–303; Stuart Laing, "The Production of Literature," in Alan Sinfield, ed., *Society and Literature 1945–1970* (London, 1983), 128 (paperbacks); Greenfield, *Scribblers for Bread,* 118, 121; Heyck, "Freelance Writers," 251; Thomas Kelly, *A History of Public Libraries in Great Britain, 1845–1965* (London, 1973), 343–344; Hewison, *Too Much,* 24 (*John Bull*); also Kennedy, "Think of the 'Point,'" 6. Richard Findlater was the nom de plume of Bruce Bain, a contributor to Peter Ratazzi's magazines during the Second World War.

74. WSS committee min., 12 Apr. 1950, 3 May 1951, 9 Feb. 1952,

12 Dec. 1953, 26 June 1954, D5886/1/1; L. Harkness, "The Club," in West Country Essay Club, *Literary Adventures: 1921–1922* (n.p., [1922?]), 1; NWC min., 18 Nov. 1947, 4 Sept. 1951, SX88/1/2; Clement Pashley, letter, *Writer,* Mar. 1952, 44–45.

75. Hoggart, *Uses of Literacy,* 274 (*John o' London's*); Hewison, *Too Much,* 24; John Gross, *The Rise and Fall of the Man of Letters: Aspects of English Literary Life since 1800* (London, 1969); Heyck, "Freelance Writers," 253–254; Harry Hopkins, *The New Look: A Social History of the Forties and Fifties in Britain* (London, 1963), 245–246.

76. Richard Williams, *The First Thousand Penguins: Penguin Main Series 1–1000: A Bibliographic Checklist with a Guide to Their Value* (Scunthorpe, 1987), 1. Quotation from Derek Verschoyle, "At the End of the Garden Path," *London Mercury* 38 (May 1938): 78–79.

77. J. E. Morpurgo, *Allen Lane: King Penguin: A Biography* (London, 1979), 215–216, 314–322; Laing, *Representations,* 40.

Conclusion. On or about the End of the Chatterley Ban

1. Philip Larkin, "Annus Mirabilis" (1967), in *Collected Poems,* ed. Anthony Thwaite (1988; New York, 1989), 167.

2. Peter Mandler, "Two Cultures—One—or Many?" in Kathleen Burk, ed., *The British Isles since 1945* (Oxford, 2003), 140–142.

3. Harry Ritchie, *Success Stories: Literature and the Media in England, 1950–1959* (London, 1988), 201.

4. Dave Morley and Ken Worpole, eds., *The Republic of Letters: Working Class Writing and Local Publishing* (London, 1982), 90.

5. *Children and Their Primary Schools: A Report of the Central Advisory Council for Education (England),* vol. 1: *The Report* (London, 1967), paras. 601–612.

6. But see David Shayer, *The Teaching of English in Schools, 1900–1970* (London, 1972), 159–166.

7. Ibid., 158 (Newsom); David Holbrook, *English for the Rejected: Training Literacy in the Lower Streams of the Secondary School* (Cambridge, 1964), 4–5.

8. Quoted in Morley and Walpole, *Republic of Letters,* v.

9. [Bob Braddock?] to Olive Rodgers, 13 Mar. 1984; Olive Rodgers, "The Federation of Worker Writers and Community Publishers: 1983/4 Report," Feb. 1984, Arts Council papers, ACGB/62/93, AAD; Morley and Walpole, *Republic of Letters,* 57, 60.

10. Chris Waters, "Autobiography, Nostalgia, and the Changing Practices of Working-Class Selfhood," George K. Behlmer and Fred M. Leventhal, eds., *Singular Continuities: Tradition, Nostalgia, and Identity in Modern British Culture* (Stanford, 2000); Carolyn Steedman, "State-sponsored Autobiography," in Becky Conekin, Frank Mort, and Chris Waters, eds., *Moments of Modernity: Reconstructing Britain, 1945–1964* (London, 1999), 49. As well as the federation's own publications (published by Comedia/Minority Press Group), see Janet Batsleer, Tony Davis, Rebecca O'Rourke, and Chris Weedon, *Rewriting English: Cultural Politics of Gender and Class* (London, 1985), 133, 168, 170. There is also a file on the federation's dealings with the Arts Council in the Arts Council papers, ACGB/62/93.

11. Morley and Walpole, *Republic of Letters,* 145–152, 64 (quotation).

12. See, e.g., Eileen Cadman, Gail Chester, and Agnes Pivot, *Rolling Our Own: Women as Printers, Publishers and Distributors* (London, 1981), ch. 4.

13. Wilfrid Phillips to Irene Byers, 10 May 1963, and Croydon Writers' Circle min., 13 Mar. 1960, Acc. 493, CAS.

14. Paul Abbott interviewed by Francine Stock on *Front Row,* BBC Radio 4, 16 May 2003; Barbara Pym, *A Very Private Eye: An Autobiography in Diaries and Letters,* ed. Hazel Holt and Hilary Pym (New York, 1984), 217–222, 230, 234, 236–238; Penarth Writers Circle, *Second Impression* (Cowbridge, 1979).

15. V. M. L. Scott, "A Proletarian Writer," *London Mercury* 34 (May 1936): 77; Michael Denning, *The Cultural Front: The Laboring of American Culture in the Twentieth Century* (London, 1996), 231; Batsleer et al., *Rewriting English,* 118–119; Shayer, *Teaching of English,* 170–179.

16. [Philip O'Connor and Gordon Cruickshank], "Readers, You Are Our Writers," *Seven* 2 (Mar. 1941): 25.

17. J. B. Priestley, *English Journey* (1934; Harmondsworth, 1977), 376; Matthew Hilton, *Smoking in British Popular Culture, 1800–2000: Perfect Pleasures* (Manchester, 2000), 126.

18. F. R. Leavis, *Mass Civilisation and Minority Culture* (Cambridge, 1930); Q. D. Leavis, *Fiction and the Reading Public* (London, 1932), 30 (Fordism), 138 (typists).

19. Compare Andreas Huyssen, "Mass Culture as Woman: Modernism's Other," in *After the Great Divide: Modernism, Mass Culture, Postmodernism* (Bloomington, 1986).

20. Ezra Pound, *A B C of Reading* (New Haven, 1934), 14.

Manuscripts and Archives Consulted

Birmingham City Archives

Halward, Leslie. Papers.

British Broadcasting Corporation Written Archives Centre, Reading

Drama Department. Drama Policy files, 1949–1964.
First Reading. Card index of contributions.
Short Story Competition file, 1948–1949.
Talks Department. Short Story Broadcasts files, 1943–1964.
Talks Department. *Woman's Hour.* Policy file, 1946–1954.
Aistrop, Jack. Contributor files.
Braine, John. Contributor files.
Brierley, Walter. Contributor files.
Chaplin, Sid. Contributor files.
Common, Jack. Contributor files.
Coombes, B. L. Contributor files.
Gray, Jessie. Contributor files.
Halward, Leslie. Contributor files.
Hanley, James. Contributor files.
Harris, Harold M. Contributor files.
Kennedy, Ludovic. Contributor files.
Lonsdale, Bertha. Contributor files.
Moore, Reginald. Contributor files.
Myer, Kenneth Granville. Contributor files.
Newby, P. H. Contributor file.
Urquhart, Fred. Contributor files.
Wain, John. Contributor files.

British Library

Society of Authors Archive.
Northcliffe Papers.

British Library of Political and Economic Science, London School of Economics

Women's Co-operative Guild Collection.

Croydon Archives Service

Croydon Writers' Circle. Minute book.
Martin, Nancy. "Croydon Writers' Circle: Some notes on its early history." Typescript, 1966.

Derbyshire Record Office, Matlock

Writers' Summer School, Swanwick. Papers.

Harry Ransom Humanities Research Center, University of Texas at Austin

Armstrong, Terence Ian Fytton. Papers.
Bates, H. E. Papers.
Coppard, A. E. Papers.
Cunard, Nancy. Papers.
David Higham [Higham, Pearn and Pollinger] Archive.
Garnett, Edward. Papers.
Golding, Louis. Papers.
Hanley, James. Papers.
Heppenstall, Rayner. Papers.
Jameson, Storm. Papers.
Lehmann, John. Papers.
Morrell, Lady Ottoline. Papers.

Osborne, John. Papers.
P.E.N. Papers.
Priestley, J. B. Papers.
Prokosch, Frederic. Papers.
Scott, Paul. Papers.
Scott-James, R. A. Papers.
Selvon, Samuel. Papers.
Stanford, Derek. Papers.
Strong, L. A. G. Papers.
Thompson, Flora. Papers.
Walpole, Hugh. Papers.
Wells, G. H. Papers.
Wesker, Arnold. Papers.

Imperial War Museum

"The Newsphere." Typescript duplicated newspaper from unspecified prisoner-of-war camp in Thailand, 1945.
"Red Tape and Stencil Wax." Typescript duplicated newsletter of the British Army Civil Affairs staff in Hong Kong, [1939–1940].
"Tost Times and Advertiser." Typescript duplicated newsletters from Tost Civilian Internment Camp, 1941.
Arct, Bohdan. Scrapbook.
Baber, Moria. "War Poems: 1945." Notebook.
Belton, P. A. MS Narrative and diary.
Bowman, R. L. Scrapbook.
Brahms, Caryl. Diary.
Brown, Dorothy Shelagh. Diary and papers.
Byers, Irene. "Me and Mine . . . (The personal memories of the years between the outbreak of the war and V.J. Day 1945)." Typescript, [late 1980s].
Chenery, D. J. Diary and papers.
Connell, T. Scrapbook.
Daniels, F. W. Papers.
Dufton, Elsie. Autograph books.

Harris, G. T. Diary.
Haydon, R. G. Papers.
Hooper, Ben C. F. Papers.
Innes, J. Diary.
Jewell, B. F. Scrapbook.
King, R. M. M. Diary and papers.
Madoc, G. C. Papers.
Pethebridge, Denis. Papers.
Phillips, A. L. Scrapbook.
Porter, J. E. Papers.
Raper, G. M[ichell] H. Papers.
Speed, Florence M. Diary.
Stalag 8B. Scrapbooks.
Stow, D. C. F. Papers.
Toomey, T. H. Papers.
Waide, C. W. Papers.

Liddell Hart Centre for Military Archives, King's College, London

Ratazzi, Peter. Letter to B. H. Liddell Hart, 1950.

Manchester Archives and Local Studies

Manchester Literary Club. Minute books.

National Library of Scotland

Corrie, Joe. Papers.
Edinburgh Poetry Club. Papers.
Finlay, Ian Hamilton. Letters to Derek Stanford.
Tremayne, Sydney. Papers.

Oxford University Archives

Department of Extension Studies. Papers.

Public Record Office, Kew

AIR 2/6562.
AIR 20/4884.
ED 12/530.
INF 1/350.

Tyne and Wear Archives Service, Newcastle-upon-Tyne

Newcastle Writer Circle. Minute books and scrapbooks.

University of Leeds, Brotherton Library

Braine, John. Diaries and notebooks.
Leeds Philosophical and Literary Society. Papers.

University of Newcastle, Robinson Library

Chaplin, Sid. Papers.
Common, Jack. Papers.

University of Nottingham, Hallward Library

Garman, Douglas. Papers.

University of Reading Library

Allen and Unwin Archive.
Glyn, Elinor. Papers.
Hampson, John. Papers.
Hogarth Press Archive.

University of Sussex Library

Monks House Papers.
Tom Harrisson Mass-Observation Archive.

Victoria and Albert Museum, Archive of Art and Design

Arts Council of Great Britain Archive.

Victoria and Albert Museum, Word and Image Department

Buday Archive.

West Yorkshire Archive Service, Bradford

Bradford English Society. Minute books.
Bradford Writers' Circle. Scrapbooks.
Braine, John. Diaries, notebooks, scrapbooks and correspondence.

West Yorkshire Archive Service, Calderdale

Bentley, Phyllis. Papers.
Halifax Antiquarian Society. Letter book and minute book.
Halifax Association for the Encouragement of the Arts. Minute book.
Halifax Authors' Circle. Minute books and papers.

West Yorkshire Archive Service, Leeds

Leeds Writers' Circle. Papers.

Yale University, Beinecke Rare Book and Manuscript Library

Lawrence & Wishart Archive.

Acknowledgments

Since this book features more than a few authors complaining of unimaginative publishers, incompetent editors, unsupportive spouses, and the loneliness of the writing life, perhaps I should say straight out that it is *not* an encrypted autobiography. Many people have helped me, and enriched my life, over the years I have been working on this book. My primary debts are to three extraordinary scholars. Susan Pedersen has been a perceptive critic and a tireless supporter, challenging my ideas and assumptions, but also pressing me toward finding an approach that was truly my own. David Blackbourn's feel for cultural history has been an inspiration, and his incisive and sympathetic criticisms have made this book much better. Peter Mandler is so generous with his time and his ideas that he is almost ubiquitous in acknowledgments pages: but at the risk of repeating what many others have said, I want to record how much I value all the ways he has brought his imagination, his learning, and his sense of the large and the small questions raised by the practice of history to bear on the way I write and think.

Many other people have helped shape this book. Fred Leventhal has been a much-appreciated source of support and advice. Patrice Higonnet has shown inordinate faith in the project and its author. In conversation and through his comments on my work, Jon Lawrence has taught me a lot about British social history. It was thanks to Stephen Greenblatt that I started to think about writing and its meanings as a problem in cultural history. D. L.

LeMahieu and Martin Francis both read early versions of the first three chapters and improved them greatly through their painstaking criticisms. Laura Lisy and Mark Baker commented on chapters at a time when both had many pressing commitments; the stimulus and warmth of their friendship are a less specific but even greater debt.

For comments on my work and the subject matter along the way, I am grateful to Zayde Antrim, David Armitage, Laura Beers, Lawrence Black, Bo-Mi Choi, Hera Cook, Donald Fleming, Ben Hett, Seth Koven, John Lowerson, Joseph McAleer, S. P. McKenzie, Ross McKibbin, Deborah Montgomerie, Eric Paras, Linda Peterson, Denise Phillips, Barry Reay, Penny Russell, Alice Staveley, Judith Surkis, Gustavo Turner, Deborah Valenze, Chris Waters, Katja Zelljadt, and Joe Zizek. Sonya O. Rose and Andrew Davies generously shared their unpublished work with me. Janet Hatch, Cory Paulsen, and Laura Johnson helped me in many ways, not least by finding me office space for a critical phase of the writing. On my research trips to Britain, Damon Salesa, Andrew Denny and Nicola Newbegin, Simon Ladd and Jane Davidson, and David Bowden and Clare Needham were the best of hosts.

This book could not have been written without the generous support of a number of institutions: the Mrs. Giles Whiting Foundation; the Krupp Foundation; and, at Harvard University, the Graduate School of Arts and Sciences, the Department of History (for travel funding from the John Clive Fund), and the Committee on General Scholarships. A fellowship at the University of Auckland enabled me to revise the manuscript. I am grateful to the university's Research Committee, and to Caroline Daley and James Belich for all the work they did to secure the fellowship for me. The book was finished at the University of Sydney, and I want to thank my colleagues in the history department for making me so welcome. Shane White and Richard Waterhouse have been academic leaders and mentors that any scholar would envy.

At Harvard University Press, Kathleen McDermott gambled on this book when it was still in its early stages, then shepherded it through the publication process with care and insight. Few authors have the privilege of having their prose improved by an editor as inspired and painstaking as Camille Smith.

The mainstays of my research have been the British Library and the Harry Elkins Widener Memorial Library at Harvard. At Widener, Barbara Burg and the interlibrary loans staff worked wonders. Much of the book is based on the collections of local and municipal archives in Britain, institutions whose staff have been invariably helpful: the Calderdale, Bradford, and Leeds branches of the West Yorkshire Archive Service; the Croydon Archives Service; Manchester Archives and Local Studies; Birmingham City Archives; the Derbyshire Record Office; and the Tyne and Wear Archives Service. I have also relied heavily on the holdings of four other archives. I would like to thank the researchers' paradise that is the Harry Ransom Humanities Research Center at the University of Texas, Austin, especially the famously hospitable Pat Fox; the BBC Written Archives Centre, especially Mike Websell and Erin O'Neill; the special collections department at the University of Sussex Library, especially Joy Eldridge and Dorothy Sheridan; and the departments of documents and printed books at the Imperial War Museum.

I am also grateful to the libraries of the universities of Leeds, Newcastle, Nottingham, and Reading; the National Library of Scotland's manuscripts department; the Bodleian Library, Oxford; the Oxford University Archives and in particular Simon Bailey; the Public Record Office; the British Library of Political and Economic Science at the London School of Economics; the Liddell Hart Centre for Military Archives at King's College London; the Beinecke Rare Book and Manuscript Library at Yale University; the Archive of Art and Design and National Theatre Museum Reading Room in the Victoria and Albert Museum's Blythe House; the Word and Image department of the Victoria and Albert Museum; and the reference staff of the Historical Manuscripts Commission.

Finally, I have some older and deeper debts to acknowledge. I would not be a historian without the gifts and sacrifices of my parents, Anne Hilliard and John Hilliard, my brother Andrew Hilliard, and my aunt Susan McClennan. I cannot thank Sarah Graham enough for all that she has done for me and done without, as we have both lived with this book, nor say here how much she means to me. The book is for her.

Index